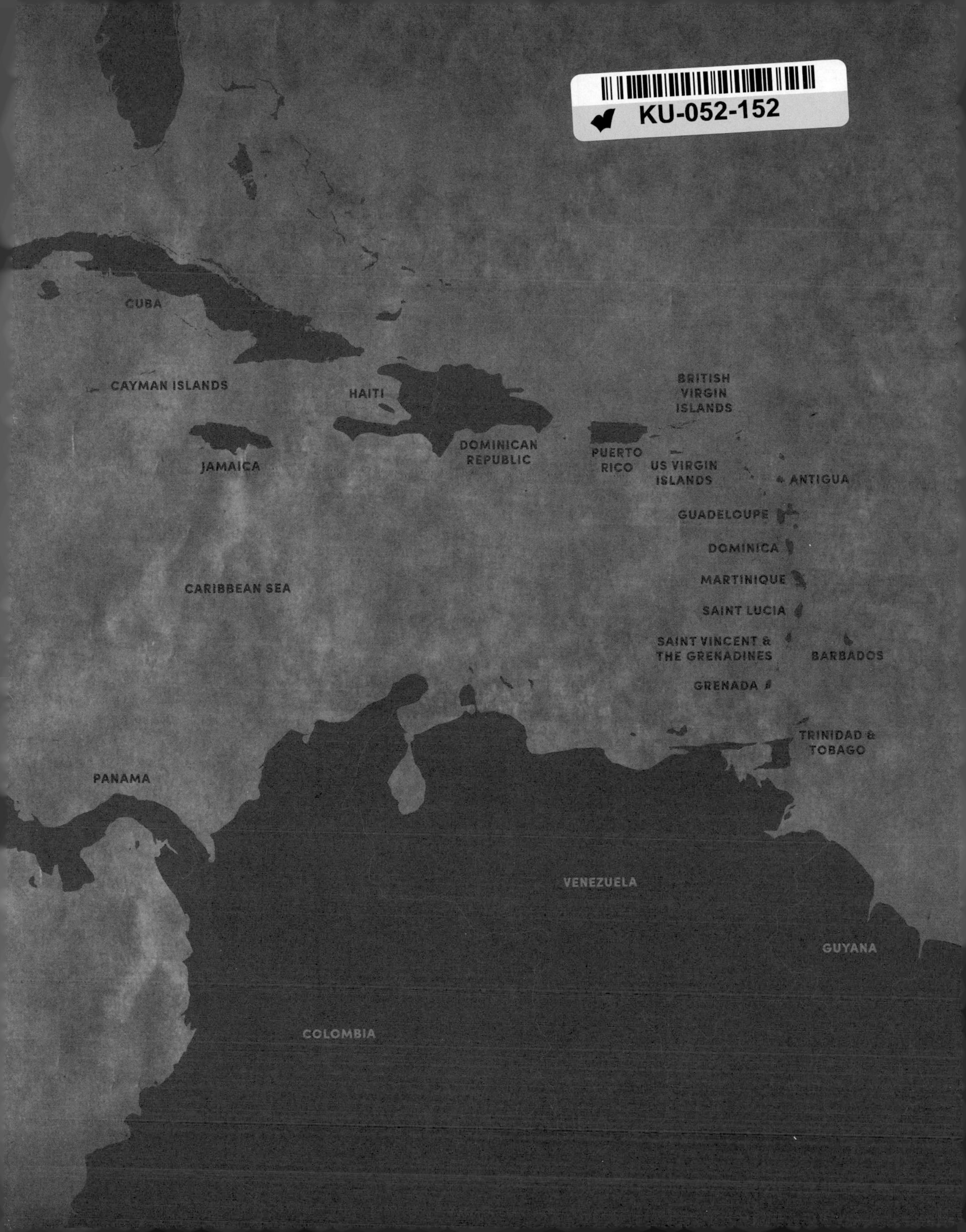
CUBA
CAYMAN ISLANDS
HAITI
JAMAICA
DOMINICAN REPUBLIC
PUERTO RICO
BRITISH VIRGIN ISLANDS
US VIRGIN ISLANDS
ANTIGUA
GUADELOUPE
DOMINICA
MARTINIQUE
SAINT LUCIA
SAINT VINCENT & THE GRENADINES
BARBADOS
GRENADA
TRINIDAD & TOBAGO
CARIBBEAN SEA
PANAMA
VENEZUELA
GUYANA
COLOMBIA

THE CURIOUS
BARTENDER'S
RUM
REVOLUTION

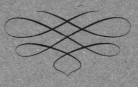

THE CURIOUS

BARTENDER'S

RUM
REVOLUTION

TRISTAN STEPHENSON

WITH PHOTOGRAPHY BY ADDIE CHINN AND TRISTAN STEPHENSON

RYLAND PETERS & SMALL

LONDON • NEW YORK

Designer Geoff Borin
Commissioning Editor Nathan Joyce
Head of Production Patricia Harrington
Picture Manager Christina Borsi
Art Director Leslie Harrington
Editorial Director Julia Charles
Publisher Cindy Richards

Prop Stylist Sarianne Plaisant
Indexer Vanessa Bird

First published in 2017 by
Ryland Peters & Small
20–21 Jockey's Fields
London WC1R 4BW
and
341 E 116th St
New York NY 10029

www.rylandpeters.com

10 9 8 7 6 5 4 3 2

ISBN: 978-1-84975-823-9

A CIP record for this book is available from the
British Library.

US Library of Congress CIP data has been applied for.

Printed in China

CONTENTS

INTRODUCTION

It was with equal parts of excitement and expectation that I embarked upon writing this book, the fifth in the series, and by far the most ambitious. Why? Because this is rum, of course, the most diverse, contentious and fascinating of all the world's drinks… not to mention the most geographically dispersed!

As such, my journey has taken me across over 20 countries and dozens of islands. I've travelled to distilleries on horseback across active volcanoes, through rivers in a 4x4 and around tiny islets by boat. The lingering taste of rum has coated my mouth as I watched the sun set over the Amazon, and as the sun rose on the Virgin Islands. Rum made me dance the salsa in Cuba, drink all night with locals in Barbados and swim in the sea at dawn in Martinique. I've bought rum for $10 a gallon and $100 a shot. I've met people who depend on rum for the livelihood of their families, and have encountered islands that depend on rum for the livelihood of their communities. Is there another drink that offers such a taste of the human world?

Of course, this was never rum's intention. Rum is a spirit that has soaked into the history books and is bound to the places that make it. When we talk about *terroir* in wine and spirits, we refer to the impact of climate and geography on the taste of a drink. Rum's *terroir* is its past, and the flavour of many of the rums we drink today are an echo of island history more than they are the intentional formation of taste and aroma compounds. Rum does not need to be aged in cask to taste old – it is a multi-sensory mouthful of an era of discovery, conquest, colonization, exploitation and trade.

But rum is more than just a quaint artefact of history's tectonic shifts. On many occasions, rum was there, making the history. Rum was the fire in the bellies of armies and navies, and the shackles that bound generations of slaves. It gave cause to revolutions: on plantations and across nations. It helped to establish global trade networks, kept the weak in bondage and turned rich men into gods.

In the 21st century, we are still living in the aftermath of the colonial era, and as rum struggles to find its place in the world, we need to remember these things more than ever. Rum is a rich tapestry of styles, and each island or national style is an intricate cultural pattern, described by tradition, technology and trade.

This means that rum style varies a lot. For better or for worse, "rum" is a loose category, vaguely strung around sugarcane and the 50-or-so countries that currently make it – bad news if you're looking for a neat summary; good news if you like being surprised and enjoy exploring new flavours.

I believe there's something for everyone in this spirit. Drunk neat, rum is a marvel. In mixed drinks, it is magical. Virtually any cocktail will willingly have its base spirit substituted for (the right) rum, but the stable of classics in this category speak for themselves: Daiquiri, Mojito, Piña Colada and Mai Tai to name but a few.

So let's go to the Caribbean and to some of the most beautiful places on earth. It won't always be pretty though as rum is far from a picture postcard. This is raw spirit –, a spirit with real character. A free spirit, you might say.

PART ONE
THE HISTORY OF RUM

HUMBLE ORIGINS

While it's likely – but by no means certain – that rum and sugarcane spirits originated in the Americas, the same cannot be said for the cane itself. Sugarcane, a fast-growing species of grass, is the base material from which all rums are made, whether it's in the form of the juice of the plant itself, the concentrated syrup made from the juice, or the molasses – the dark brown gloop that is leftover when you crystallize sugar out of the juice.

Over half of all the countries in the world grow sugarcane today, but 10,000 years ago you would have needed to travel to the island of New Guinea in the South Pacific to find any. We know that sugarcane is indigenous to the island, thanks to a unique ecosystem that exists there, of which sugarcane is a key component. Sugarcane is the sole source of food for the New Guinea cane weevil, a native species of beetle that bores into the cane stem and munches through the sweet fibrous interior. Also a resident of New Guinea is a type of tachinid fly that parasitizes the cane weevil with its larvae. The fly is dependent on the beetle for survival and the beetle is reliant on the sugarcane. For such a fruitful piece of symbiosis to have developed between the two insects, it is likely that sugarcane must have been growing on New Guinea since the last ice age.

For early indigenous communities of New Guinea, known as the Papuans, the sugarcane offered an abundance of calories in the simplest possible form of energy: sugar. Early human settlers gnawed on the rough stem of cane, before developing tools to extract the juice, either with a couple of rocks, or with a pestle and mortar. The juice of the cane offered a nice, instant hit of energy, but the high sugar content that made it so desirable was also one of its major drawbacks. When combined with the tropical environment, the juice was prone to fermenting within a matter of days. The answer was to boil the juice down into a kind of honey, or to heat it until dark brown sugar crystals formed on the sides of the pan.

Of the hundreds of heirloom varieties of cane that grow wildly in New Guinea, only the sweetest, *Saccharum officinarum*, also known as Creole cane, was selected for cultivation. It was transported west to Indonesia, the Philippines and mainland Asia, and east to Fiji, Tonga, Hawaii and Easter Island.

Sugarcane was widely cultivated in India too, which was something Persian Emperor Darius I discovered when he invaded in 510BC. When Alexander the Great arrived in India in 325BC, one of his generals was in awe of the plant that could "bring forth honey without the help of bees, from which an intoxicating drink can be made." Later, around the second century AD, the first recorded sugar mill was built in India and scholars documented how to manage a cane plantation. Sugarcane infiltrated Indian society on many levels; it was used medicinally for humans and as food for elephants, and the juice was fermented into wine known as *gaudi* or *sidhu*. It also became a symbol used in Hindu and Buddhist faiths. It's also India that we must thank for the word "sugar", which is thought to be derived from the Prakrit word *sakkara*, meaning sand or gravel.

BELOW LEFT It has been theorised that sugarcane was first domesticated as a crop in New Guinea around 6000BC.

BELOW Sugarcane is still consumed by many modern-day Papuans, and for a few it forms a key component of their diet.

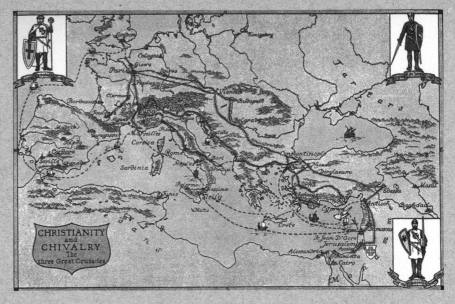

RIGHT Sugar was extremely rare in northern Europe until the 11th century, when Christian crusaders brought the sweet tasting spice back with them from the Holy Lands.

BELOW RIGHT The earliest types of commercial Indian sugar mills were effectively giant garlic presses. The extracted juice flowed out of the crucible into a receiving vessel.

CHRISTIANITY
and
CHIVALRY
The
three Great Crusades

SUGAR ARRIVES IN EUROPE

Having conquered India and infiltrated China and Japan, in around 600AD, cane was transported west, to Persia. The timing was exquisite, as the rise of the Islamic faith would soon serve as a vehicle for sugar's journey further westward to Europe.

The Arabs were a well-organised and technologically impressive bunch. The vast scale of their rapidly growing empire meant that trade between regions was fluid. Their agricultural prowess and advanced water management systems allowed plantations to flourish like never before. By the turn of the eighth century AD, the Umayyad Empire stretched from Pakistan to Portugal and all along the north of Africa. Sugarcane was grown on the banks of the River Nile, and was cultivated by the Moors on Sicily, Malta and southern Spain. The island of Cyprus became a vivid green Arab sugar garden. One Italian traveller wrote of Cyprus in the 15th century that "the abundance of the sugarcane and its magnificence are beyond words."

Arabic physicians used sugar in a variety of medicinal preparations, such as *shurba* (sherbet), which back then was sweet hot water taken as medicine; *rubb*, a preserve of fruits in sugar; and *gulab*, a rose-scented sweet tea.

Those who were committed to the Islamic faith abstained from drinking, so fermented cane juice was off the table. There is no evidence that the Arabs, or the Moors ever distilled fermented cane products either, but given that it was the Moors, who introduced distillation to Europe by way of Italy, and considering the freedom of access to sugar products that these people enjoyed, I don't think it's too much of a stretch to speculate that the experiments of an Islamic alchemist might have resulted in the world's first proto-rum.

Northern Europe would have to wait until the Crusades before they got their first real taste of sugar. Crusaders brought sugar back to England from the Holy Lands, and by 1243 the Royal Household of Edward I was getting through nearly 3,000 kg (6,600 lbs) of sugar in a single year. At that time in Europe, sugar was regarded as a spice, valued as highly as vanilla or saffron today. A 1-kg (2.2-lbs) bag of sugar would have set you back the equivalent of £100 ($125) in today's money. Reserved only for those with sufficiently deep pockets, sugar was used by the wealthy as an extravagant signifier of status, added even to savoury dishes just because, well… why not? The hunger for sweetness was not limited to the upper classes, though. The compulsion for sugar was universal, and the human brain was wired to want it.

As European powers clambered to reclaim lands from the Moors, they discovered areas dedicated to growing sugarcane. Learning the secrets of cane cultivation, they planted more wherever it would grow. But besides the most southerly islands, Europe was not particularly well suited to growing sugarcane. Winters were too cold and the rainfall was insufficient. Rhodes, Crete, Cyprus, and Malta operated plantations under Christian rule, and the cane was shipped to Venice for refinement into sugar.

The early 15th century saw Portugal conducting increasingly adventurous voyages along the west coast of Africa. In 1421 the island of Madeira was sighted by sailors passing by the west coast of Morocco. This island, which would prove to be a vital step (both physically and commercially) toward the colonial plantation system, was very well suited to sugarcane cultivation. The first shipments of sugar arrived in Bristol, England in 1456, and 50 years later, Madeira was producing 1,800 tons (2,015 US tons) of sugar a year: equivalent to around half of all the sugar consumed in Europe at that time.

Another crucial development in the story of sugar and of rum occurred at around the same time. In 1444 the first boatload of 235 slaves was shipped out of Lagos by the Portuguese. A cheap workforce would prove to be an essential component of plantation economics, and these were the first of millions of African slaves whose lives would be lost to sugar.

NEW WORLD ORDER

Christopher Columbus's historic first voyage of 1492, after securing the support of King Ferdinand and Queen Isabella of Spain, was intended to plot new trade routes with the East Indies. The Spanish had been slower at entering the spice and silk trade than the Dutch or English, owing to the protracted Reconquista of the Iberian peninsular from its Muslim occupants.

Columbus proposed a radical shortcut to the east (by heading to the west) and with it presented the opportunity to gain a competitive edge over rival European powers in the hunt for gold, silk, pepper, cloves and ginger.

On the first voyage, the trade winds propelled the navigator across the Atlantic in five weeks, first sighting land at San Salvador in the Bahamas (which Columbus was convinced was Japan), then Cuba (which he thought was China) and then Hispaniola. The island of Hispaniola – now shared between Haiti and the Dominican Republic – was of particular interest to Columbus because he believed a wealth of gold lay hidden there. He encountered the friendly indigenous Taíno people and wrote about them in his letters to King Ferdinand and Queen Isabella. Columbus received small gifts of gold and pearls from the Taíno, and even left a party of 39 men behind to establish a small colony.

Upon his return to Spain, Columbus was welcomed as a hero. He presented the Spanish monarchs with tobacco, pineapples, a turkey, and a hammock, all of which were previously unknown to European culture. On his second voyage in 1493 Columbus returned to Hispaniola, this time with a fleet of 17 ships, 1,200 men and 1,500 sugarcane shoots.

Many history books include accounts of Columbus and his son Ferdinand, who oversaw the planting of sugarcane on Hispaniola on the second voyage. Columbus's father-in-law was a sugar planter on Madeira and Columbus was no doubt aware of the crop's value in Europe. He was a man driven by greed as much as he was adventure, and in the back of his mind was a promise from the Spanish crown of a 10% share of all profits generated by newly established colonies. But according to Fernando Campoamor in his landmark 1985 book *El Hijo Alegre de la Cana de Azúcar*, the explorer was unable to conduct the cultivation experiments he intended because the delicate plants did not survive the sea crossing. What is certain is that seven years later, in 1500, Pedro di Atienza successfully transported and planted sugarcane seedlings on Hispaniola. It was probably only then that the early settlers discovered that sugarcane flourished in the tropical Caribbean climate.

Gold, on the other hand, remained elusive. So too did the promised spices and silk. These lands were not the East Indies after all, although the likes of Christopher Columbus would go to their death beds still believing it so. The absence of any immediate value is one of the reasons that the Spanish defended the

Caribbean so poorly over the 100 years that followed, instead directing their attentions to the precious metals that Central America offered. This allowed the Dutch, English and French to swoop in and pick up their share of the island booty. The Europeans realised the potential of sugarcane. Consequently, the plantation system and the sugar-refining industry, rather than the harvesting of spices and silk production, were destined to shape the economy and society of the West Indies and Brazil.

As the sea spray settled on the shores of the Caribbean region, it must have seemed a place of enormous agricultural potential to the European settlers: fertile lands, clear waters, year-round sunshine, and a trusting native populace just waiting to be put to task – there was a problem with that, however.

Within the space of a single generation the indigenous Carib, Warao and Arawak people who occupied most of

BELOW The method for making sugar in the Caribbean remained almost unchanged for over three centuries.

the Caribbean islands were almost entirely eradicated. As colonies expanded, tens of thousands melted away panning for gold in rivers, in fruitless mining operations, or on plantations, and those who resisted slavery were slaughtered by European forces (mostly Spanish) who possessed superior weaponry and a greater knowledge of how to use it. Many, it seems were executed under orders from Christopher Columbus himself. The biggest killer of all, however, was disease. Measles, mumps and smallpox plagued the indigenous populace, who lacked the antibodies and medicine to combat European viruses effectively. The Dominican Friar Bartolomé de las Casas wrote that when he arrived in Hispaniola in 1508, "there were 60,000 people living on this island, including the Indians; so that from 1494 to 1508, over three million people had perished from war, slavery and the mines." He added: "Who in future generations will believe this?"

FAST-GROWING GRASS

In the early 1500s, the Portuguese established the first sugar plantations in South America. They were in the states of Bahia and Pernambuco, on Brazil's moist eastern coastline. The grass flourished, and by 1550 there were five sugar refineries in Brazil, and the Portuguese were shipping sugarcane presses and vats over from Europe to aid the pursuit. But compared to other tropical commodities, like cotton or tobacco, sugarcane was a much tougher beast to manage. A sugar planter needed a superior understanding of agricultural practices, factory management skills, the ability to deal with agricultural diseases, a huge supply of water and enough money to bankroll the whole operation as lands were cleared and crops planted. But more than anything, a planter needed a cheap and plentiful labour force. Brazilian natives were hunted down for this purpose in expeditions called *bandeiras*. Once captured, these men and women were put to task, but as was the case in Hispaniola, they quickly succumbed to diseases. A bigger, more dependable workforce was needed, and fortunately for Portugal, they had access to one.

The West African slave trade had been held in state of near monopoly by the Portuguese since the 1440s, so the next logical step was to connect the dots between their trading outpost in Elmina (on Africa's Gold Coast) and their developing colonies in the Americas.

That "Middle Passage", as it is known, was sailed for the first time by Portuguese mariners in 1510. These sailors brought black slaves with them and recorded their presence on the ship's manifest. Thousands more slaves followed over the next 378 years.

The "first in, last out" approach was a consistent theme in the history of slavery. Cuba, Hispaniola and Puerto Rico were all early adopters of African slaves and among the most reluctant to give it up (some would argue that the Dominican Republic still hasn't – see pages 91–92) and they too required the manpower to manage their extensive sugarcane plantations. Spain's obsession with gold had spread their empire thinly across the Central American belt. With the Spanish weakened by the endeavour, the British, Dutch and French made it their business to harass both their ships and settlements persistently through the unofficial employment of, *bucaneros* and privateers (see pages 23–24). Naturally the mercantilist Spanish were none too keen for their colonies to trade with rival nations, and these embargoes stunted the growth of the Spanish sugarcane industry to the point where the crop didn't become dominant on any of their occupied islands until the 19th century.

Back to the 17th century, and sugar production in Brazil was showing no signs of abating. This was partly thanks to the Dutch West India Company, which had seized the colonial territory of Pernambuco from the Portuguese in 1630 and began rampantly planting more cane. Ten years later, the Dutch began shipping slaves from equatorial Africa, which became a critical juncture

RIGHT Despite being the largest Caribbean island, the scale of sugar production on Cuba didn't truly ramp up until the late 19th century.

BELOW RIGHT In Brazil, on the other hand, large-scale sugar production was relentless from the late 16th century onwards.

Cuba: Corte de Caña.
Cutting Sugar Cane.

in the establishment of further Dutch plantations, as well as securing sugar's position in the infamous triangular trade (see pages 20–21). In 1612, the total production of sugar in Brazil had reached 14,000 tons (15,400 US tons). But by the 1640s, Pernambuco alone had 350 refineries, exporting more than 24,000 tons (26,500 US tons) of sugar annually to Amsterdam.

Sugar was becoming difficult to ignore as a New World commodity as demand for sugar in Europe continued to rise. It was around this time that the British and French Caribbean took a greater interest in sugarcane cultivation. The British established a settlement on Barbados in 1627 and the French followed suit on Martinique in 1635. The first plantations on these islands were used to grow cotton and tobacco, or fustic wood and indigo (both used in the manufacturing of dyes). Early settlers persevered with these crops for the better part of two centuries, but in the 1640s, there was a rapid shift towards sugarcane. This came about after the Portuguese recaptured Pernambuco from the Dutch West India Company, who immediately sought to establish trading opportunities in the Caribbean.

And so it was that Dutch traders sailed north. Spilling into the Caribbean, they presented the English and French a complete commercial and logistical solution for sugarcane, along with a century's worth of combined practical know-how of how to run a plantation. The seed was planted, and once established the sugar production in the Caribbean increased at a furious rate. Barbados's sugarcane production grew

from 7,000 (7,700 US tons) to 12,000 tons (13,200 US tons) in the second half of the 17th century, while on Guadeloupe, exports grew from 2,000 tons (2,200 US tons) in 1674 to 10,000 tons (11,000 US tons) in the space of 25 years.

Over the next 100 years, sugar would become the most valuable trading commodity in the world; it became very much the oil of its day. But more than just a commodity, sugar production provided one of the original means and motivations for European expansion, colonization and control in the New World, precipitating a course of events that would forever shape the destiny of the Western Hemisphere.

RUM'S SLOW BIRTH

By the middle of the 17th century, sugar was being grown on most of the islands of the Caribbean, and it was during this period that the first British and French rums were distilled. Exactly where and when this happened is a matter that we shall debate shortly, but one thing that we can be sure of is that rum was not the first alcoholic beverage enjoyed by New World booze hounds.

Richard Ligon, an English colonist who lived in Barbados between 1647 and 1650, gives us one of the best insights about life on the island during its early English colonization. In his book *A True and Exact History of the Island of Barbados*, he wrote, "The first [drink], and that which is most used in the Island, is Mobbie, a drink made of potatoes." Mobbie was a kind of potato beer, produced using a variety of fermented red (sweet) potatoes known to the native Caribs as *mâ'bi*. It was the job of the women to boil the potatoes and mash them up, then add them to large earthenware vessels along with water, molasses and spices, such as ginger. The mixture would then naturally ferment over a period of a few days and your efforts would be rewarded with a kind of spiced potato beer.

Similar drinks to this were made from the crop cassava. Known as *ouicou* in the Carib language, in Barbados cassava wine was called *parranow* or *perino*. According to Ligon, its taste was comparable to "the finest English beer". Many Carib women wound up toothless after a lifetime's *ouicou*-making, which involved chewing on a mouthful of grated cassava, then

spitting it into a calabash (a container formed from the shell of a gourd-like fruit) filled with water and more cassava. The enzymes in the women's saliva converted the starches into fermentable sugars and airborne yeast took care of alcohol production. The acid in the raw cassava was responsible for the tooth decay.

Other wines and beers were enjoyed too, produced from the fermentation of plantain, bananas, plums, oranges, limes, wild grapes and tamarind. Pineapple wine – which even on paper sounds delicious – got a thumbs up from Ligon, with the ever-enthusiastic colonist describing it as "the Nectar which the Gods drunk". The French missionary Père Labat also remarked on the "extremely agreeable" taste of pineapple wine.

Delicious as some of these drinks may have been, there is no evidence to suggest that any of them were ever distilled into strong spirits, and there's a very good reason for that. At the turn of the 17th century, distillation in Europe was seldom practised by anyone other than physicians who were generally trying to uncover the next big medicinal cure-all or the secret to eternal life. But strong alcohol was about to enter a transitional phase that would see it graduate from the medicine cabinet to the bar room.

Distillation was introduced to Europe by the Moors in the 11th century – yes, the same people that brought sugarcane to the Europeans' attention – after which it was documented by scholars at the earliest recorded medical school in Salerno, southern Italy, before migrating north to Antwerp, Amsterdam, and other places that didn't necessarily start with an 'A'. The precursor to whisky, *aqua vitae* ("water of life"), had found its way to Ireland and Scotland by the middle of the 15th century, where it was renamed in the Gaelic language *uisge beatha*. Meanwhile, the Dutch, who were among the earliest practitioners of distillation in Europe, were experimenting with *brandewijn* ("burnt wine"): a grape-based spirit that would later be known as "brandy".

Critical to a distillation operation was the still itself, which would heat the fermented beer or wine, evaporating the alcohol (which has a lower boiling point than water) and condense it into a crystal clear

LEFT A 17th-century woodcut print depicts the "personal involvement" of manufacturing cassava wine on the Caribbean island of Hispaniola.

concentrate. In Europe, the first commercial distilleries were purpose-built to manufacture genever, whisky and brandy. In the Caribbean, they came about as supplementary operations to a sugar refinery. The oldest pot stills were generally under 450 litres (100 US gallons) in size and made from hammered copper. Brazil was ground zero for distillation in the Americas, probably receiving stills by way of Madeira, and it was most likely sugarcane that was used as the base material for their experiments. In 1533, when sugar mills were established at São Jorge dos Erasmos, Madre de Deus, and São João, the planters also installed copper alembic stills to produce *aguardiente de caña* ("fire water of cane"), which is the earliest example of the spirit that would later be known as *cachaça*. The ruins of Brazil's first *cachaça* distillery at São Jorge dos Erasmos have been excavated recently by archaeologists and designated as a historical site. In fact, the uptake of distillation in Brazil was so frenzied that, according to some historical accounts, Brazil had 192 distilleries in 1585, and that number was set to double by 1630.

For close to 100 years, Brazil remained the only place in the Americas producing cane spirits. As inconceivable as this may seem, it's a solid depiction of the extreme isolation that the earliest New World colonies experienced, and the poor exchange of knowledge that came as a result. This was the dawn of globalization, but it was also a time where journeys took weeks not hours and the dissemination of knowledge took decades.

The British and French had a fairly good excuse of course – they weren't farming sugarcane during this period – but the Spanish? The Spanish Empire were operating sizeable sugarcane plantations in Mexico,

ABOVE LEFT Unlike this large 19th-century distillery, the first Caribbean rum plants were merely addenda to sugar mills.

ABOVE RIGHT Prior to the invention of the vacuum pan, sugar was made by ladling boiling juice between successively smaller pans.

Cuba, Puerto Rico and Hispaniola, as far back as the 1550s. There's no record of distillation in any Spanish colonies until the 1640s, however, which more than anything is indicative of the Spanish Empire's isolationist approach to global domination.

The rise of Caribbean rum ultimately came as a result of that most dependable of all ocean trading people, the Dutch. Holland dominated international commerce in the 17th century – their East and West Indies Trading Corporations arguably became the world's first mega corporations. This was a nation that wasn't motivated by discovering gold, or by a desire to convert the godless natives to Christianity. The Dutch were capitalists, driven by the commercial opportunity and saleable commodities like coffee, spices and sugarcane. Sugar's exit route from Brazil came via the Dutch, who, when forced to relinquish Dutch Brazil in the 1640s (see page 15), required immediate action to keep their sugar empire running. It would be the Dutch who would later supply most of the copper stills in the Caribbean, too.

In 1644, a Dutchman by the name of Benjamin Da Costa brought sugar refining equipment to Martinique and it's possible that he brought alembic stills with him too. It's also possible that they were already there, as a manuscript from 1640 (when the colony was only five years old) states that the slaves were drinking a "strong eau de vie that they call brusle ventre [stomach burner]." Since it's unlikely that slaves would have access to imported brandy, one would have to assume that this *brusle ventre* was distilled from a locally grown source of fermentable sugar – and yes, it was probably sugarcane.

In Barbados, however, it seems that distillation might have preceded the full-scale arrival of sugarcane to the island. Sir Henry Colt, a British traveller, visited the four-year-old colony of Barbados in 1631, when there were scarcely more than a few hundred inhabitants on the island. Colt reported that the people were "devourers upp of hott [sic] waters and such good distillers thereof." Whether these spirits were made from cane or some other vegetable or fruit remains a mystery, but five years later, the Dutch émigré Pietr Blower brought distillery equipment to Barbados from Brazil. This was a crucial step in the development of rum, as it is alleged that Blower was the man who introduced the concept of distilling spirits from waste from the sugar-refining process, rather than valuable cane juice.

For centuries, sugar refineries had been converting sugarcane juice into sweet crystals, but nobody had found a good use for the molasses – the thick, dark syrup that was left behind. Up to 40% of the weight of the molasses was pure sugar, but the technical practicalities and associated costs of extracting the remaining sugar meant that it wasn't worth the effort. Like a tightly locked chest containing a wealth of sweet treasure, as long as the chest remained locked, it was worthless. For many islands, molasses was deemed too bulky and not cost-effective to ship abroad.

In some cases it was simply discarded into the ocean – enough to "make a province rich" according to one Hispaniola official in 1535 – or used as a fertilizer for the next season's sugarcane crops. Sometimes it was used as animal feed, or reboiled to make a cheaper form of sweetener known as *peneles*, which was used to make gingerbread. In most instances it contributed to the diets of slaves, whether as food itself, or as a fermented drink. The tropical climate, coupled with high levels of sugar in the molasses, meant that fermentation was inevitable – especially given that molasses was commonly left lying around for weeks at a time. The consumption of fermented molasses was not limited only to slaves, either. Colonial life was tough on everyone, and alcohol an essential distraction to the hardships of the age of discovery. In a part of the world where beer, wine and spirits were all imported at great expense, one couldn't be too discriminating over the source of the intoxicant.

One of the earliest references of colonists consuming molasses wine comes from 1596 when English chaplain Dr Layfield reported that the Spanish colonies in Puerto Rico enjoyed a drink called *guacapo*, which was, "made of Molasses (that is, the coarsest of their Sugar) and some Spices". This molasses wine was known as *guarapo* and *guarapa* to the Spanish, *garapa* to the Portuguese (in Brazil) and *grappe* to the French.

KILL DEVIL

Once sugarcane spirit becoming a regular feature in the plantations of the New World, it was only right that they were given a proper name. It should have been a simple affair, but this was booze birthed out of effluent

LEFT This map of Barbados was drawn in 1683, by which time the British had already controlled the island for over 55 years.

made by slaves – it was never going to be an easy process. Sadly, history is not so complete that all the colloquial terms and slang references to this spirit that would later be known as rum are available to us. The road to a liquor called "rum" was no easier than any of the rest of rum's turbulent passage through time. What we do know is that before rum there was "kill devil".

Why the spirit was called kill devil is not clear. Probably because it was strong – perhaps strong enough to kill a devil? – but more likely through a corruption of language of one sort or another. The French referred to the stuff as *guildive*, which is probably a compound of the old French word *guiller* (meaning "fermentation") or the Malay word *giler* ("crazy") and *diable* ("devil"). When the English heard it spoken they distorted into the suitably dangerous sounding kill devil.

Kill Devil bears no resemblance to "rum", of course. "Rum" is cited by most historians as an abbreviation of "rumbullion": a word originating from the county of Devon, England, meaning "a great tumult or uproar" and may have been used by Devonian settlers in Barbados. Rumbullion was first mentioned in 1652 by Barbados resident and wealthy sugar planter Giles Silvester, and it's the only time we see the word linked with kill devil. He was clearly not a fan of rumbullion: "the chiefe fuddling they make in the island is Rumbullion, alias Kill-Devil, and this made of suggar [sic] canes distilled, a hot, hellish, and terrible liquor."

For me, a more likely scenario than the borrowing of a faintly appropriate Devonian word, is that rumbullion came about as a fusion of different English and French words. In 16th-century England, the word "rum" was used to mean "excellent, fine or good" and was informally coupled with "booze" to form the Elizabethan slang term "rum booze", which was used colloquially to reference wine (though appearing very little in texts). John P. Hughes, a linguistics expert and the author of *The Science of Language* suggests that at the time, "rum booze" was popularly pluralized into the word "rumboes", which, in turn was singularised into "rumbo" to refer to "strong punch". Rum was simply a shortened form of "rumbo". The word rumbullion may have emerged from the amalgamation of rum and the French word *bouillon* (meaning "hot drink"), referring to a hot, strong, punch. If this is beginning to sound confusing, we're not quite done yet.

There are other competing theories about the origin of the word rumbullion, however. Some historians suggest that rumbullion derives from the large drinking glasses used by Dutch seamen known as a *roemer*. Others think that rum could also be derived from the word *aroma* or the latter part of the Latin word for sugar: *saccharum*. Some researchers have posited that the word rum heralds from the Sanskrit *roma* ("water"), an opinion shared by many 19th-century dictionaries. Other etymologists have mentioned the Romani word "rum", meaning "strong" or "potent". However the word "rum" came about, it was also the basis of "ramboozle" and "rumfustian", both popular British drinks in the mid-17th century. Neither was made with rum, however, but rather eggs, ale, wine, sugar and various spices.

The first recorded use of the word "rum" to describe a sugarcane spirit comes from 1650, and it also comes from the island of Barbados. A deed for the sale of the Three Houses Plantation in the parish of St Philip, Barbados included in its inventory "four large mastick cisterns for liquor of rum." Further confirmation that rum was here to stay (and indeed that it was on the move) comes from English traveller George Warren's 1667 book *An impartial description of Surinam upon the continent of Guiana in America*: "Rum is a spirit extracted from the juice... called Kill-Devil in New England!"

This blunt, monosyllabic word seemed a fitting sound to describe a drink of such humble origins. "Rum"

the ship's captain traded for manufactured items, such as textiles, cutlery and weapons. Leaving Europe, the ships next sailed south to Africa, where they traded for human cargo. The slaves were transported across the Atlantic Ocean to the Caribbean, where they were sold at auction and sent to work on the plantations, growing sugar and ensuring the continuation of the cycle. As the colonies of North America became better established, a second triangular trading system was developed that effectively cut Europe out of the equation. Both systems are paramount to the history of sugar and rum because an estimated two-thirds of the 1.5 million African slaves who made the voyage between 1627 and 1775 were put to work on sugarcane plantations.

Although the slave trade was abused to its fullest and most abominable extent by European powers during the 17th and 18th centuries, the African slave trade existed in Africa and the East Indies as far back as the 1100s. Operated by the kings of West Africa, tribesmen from Central and South African regions were kidnapped and sold by chiefs from Angola and the Ivory Coast, often in exchange for *akpeteshie* or *burukutu* – a type of date palm wine.

This fondness for fermented alcoholic beverages among the kings of Africa was important, as along with cloth, gunpowder and ironware, it would later be leveraged by European traders keen to exchange rum for slaves. Distilled spirits were unknown in Africa, so when these supercharged liquids called *rum*, *rhum*, *aguardiente* and *cachaça* were offered to the kings, they were keenly received. Whether it was rum or some other manufactured commodity from Europe or the colonies, this exchange of product for human cargo is cited by some historians as the birth of capitalism and the global economy.

During the six-week voyage across the ocean, on average one-third of all slaves perished en route. Those that didn't die were often malnourished, ill and/or psychologically traumatized. Traders recognized this, so they compensated for their lost human cargo by overcrowding their ships, which really only had the effect of worsening the problem. The slaves were chained into the hold so tightly that there was no

was quickly adopted by planters in the Spanish- and French-speaking colonies of the Caribbean, translating to *rhum* and *ron* respectively.

THE TRIANGULAR TRADE

Triangular trade is the name given to a trading system conducted between three specific areas. The best-known triangular trade route was the commercial platform that linked the Caribbean and American colonies with their European colonial powers and the west coast of Africa between the 16th and 19th centuries. This trading system was necessary because of the regional demand for the goods generated by the other regions in the triangle, and was propelled by the powerful trade winds that traversed the Atlantic – for an African slave it must have seemed that even the planet itself was aligned against them.

In the Caribbean, ships were loaded with sugar, rum, coffee and spices, which were sent to Europe where room to move. Men were afforded a space of 180 x 37 cm (6 x 1¼ ft), and women even less. Water and food were heavily rationed, and buckets provided the only means of disposing of human waste. The gruesome living conditions lead to outbreaks of typhoid, measles and yellow fever. In some extreme instances, 90% of a ship's hold were pronounced dead upon arrival in port. On some occasions, entire ships were lost, as slaves mounted insurrections against their captors. Some of these mutinies were successful, such as the *Clare* in 1729, and others resulted in the death of everybody on board.

The crew, which generally comprised lowlifes and criminals, really didn't have it much better. They were just as vulnerable to contracting diseases, but also bound to the backbreaking tasks that filled their days and weeks.

GREAT RUMBLINGS

Despite the availability of molasses, the earliest rums were often made from the sucrose-rich skimmings or scum that were collected during the sugar refining process. Now this stuff really was useless, and the collection and subsequent fermentation of the skimmings illustrates, more than anything, the thriftiness of the early sugarcane planters. There are reports of distilleries in both the French and British Caribbean making rum in this way through the 1640s, until molasses finally became the *de facto* base material across all Caribbean islands.

As is the case with most things in rum's history, this came about as a result of economics more than good taste. Most plantations in the mid-1600s made two types of sugar: dark muscovado; and low-quality *peneles*. This approach resulted in the maximum quantity of sugar with as little as possible waste, which, in turn, limited the quantity of rum that could be manufactured. Semi-refined white sugar sold for twice the price of muscovado, but it also generated more waste. As the demand for rum increased, planters on every island in the Caribbean turned to molasses.

The earliest account of rum-making in Barbados comes from Richard Ligon's *A True and Exact History of Barbados* (1647). Ligon offers detailed drawings of a sugar mill and still-house, which comprised two pots

and a cistern. The cistern was likely made from mastic wood (in a time when the forest of Barbados were still being cleared) and was presumably used for fermenting the sugar skimmings from the mill. The pots differ in size, suggesting a similar routine to that which is used in the production of malt whisky, where the larger of the two pots was used for the principal distillation of "low wines", and the smaller used for the second distillation of high-strength spirit. This is a surprisingly sophisticated setup for the 17th century, and far more elaborate than the stills being employed on Martinique during the same period.

Jean-Baptiste du Tertre, who toured Martinique in the 1640s, describes in his 1654 book *Histoire Générale des îles Saint-Christophe, de la Guadeloupe, de la Martinique et autres de l'Amérique* a single pot-still that he calls a *vinaigrerie*. It is connected to a worm-tub condenser and is operated by slaves, who made an "intoxicating liquor" using sugar skimmings for personal consumption.

Over the 50 years that followed rum's uneasy birth, the spirit swept across the Caribbean like a tropical typhoon. What had, at first, been a drink for slaves, was now starting to fill the punch bowls of white planters, but this wasn't all that it was filling – rum soon took its rightful place aboard ship's manifest, stored in barrels and stacked in the cargo hold of every trading ship across the region.

The steep rise in rum consumption through the Caribbean and later in Europe meant that rum needed to get its game face on. The 17th century would see rum reinvent itself time after time, evolving from skimmings-based moonshine to a fully fledged industry that would make fortunes for the planters in Barbados, Jamaica and Sainte-Domingue.

RIGHT This 1823 drawing forms part of the series "Ten Views in the Island of Antigua" and shows slaves loading barrels of sugar onto boats.

Speaking of Barbados, the esteemed distiller William Y-Worth wrote an account of a Barbadian rum recipe in 1707 in which the product was fermented "together with the remains of the former distillation". This is the first reference to the use of "dunder" (the residual liquid after distilling rum) in rum production. It's interesting that the recipe does not herald from Jamaica, where the practice would become a hallmark of the Jamaican style (see page 48).

Samuel Martin, an Irish immigrant with plantations in Antigua, operated an estate that covered 245 hectares (605 acres), of which 160 hectares (400 acres) was used for growing cane in 1756. Martin published "An Essay on Plantership" in 1786 that includes a recipe for rum comprising, "one-third scum from cane juice, one-third of water from washing the coppers, and one-third lees." This was left to ferment for 24 hours, after which molasses is added gradually to build up the yeast cell count and "yield a due proportion of rum".

With more plantation operators recording their recipes, further refinement and specialization ensued. The late 18th century is full of accounts from experienced distillers (especially in Jamaica) who were, for the first time, aware of *terroir*, the importance of pH in fermentation, consistency and more refined distillation techniques. Rum had well and truly evolved beyond the second-thought hooch to an art that required careful consideration and documentation. Why? Because it made money, of course.

OLD SUGAR HOUSE, N°138 GALLOWGATE

ABOVE Glasgow's second sugar refinery, called the Old Sugar House, was erected in 1669 by a group of Glasgow merchants to refine sugar imported from the Caribbean.

RUMMING AROUND THE BRITISH ISLES

The 18th century was a period of massive growth for the Caribbean rum industry, which saw exports to Britain, North America and parts of Northern Europe increase at an astonishing rate. In 1690, little if any rum was imported into the UK. In 1697, a measly 100 litres (26 US gallons) or one-quarter of a sherry barrel arrived on British shores. By 1750, 4.5 million litres (1.2 million US gallons) of rum arrived in British ports, and that number was set to triple over the next two decades to the point where rum accounted for 25% of all the spirits consumed in British Isles in 1780.

The sheer volume of rum available to the British drinker didn't do much to elevate the spirit's reputation, and for the time being it occupied a curious position in the eyes of the 18th-century drinker. This was a spirit that was labelled by its challengers as a drink for slaves or common men, and yet it was being manufactured by wealthy plantation owners with strong connections to the British aristocracy. As such, the upper classes, whose focus remained fixated on wine and brandy, saw rum as a quaint, yet potentially dangerous and exotic novelty. The lower classes stuck with the "bang for your buck" mantra, which, in London at least, meant gin – 45 million litres (12 million US gallons) of it in 1750 alone. That just left the middle classes, who were priced out of the brandy market and keen to avoid genever so as to disassociate themselves from the gin-guzzling masses.

But this was more than just a case of class and financial resources. Availability played a big part in the decision-making process, too, and nowhere more so than in the lesser populated extremities of the

British Isles, especially towns and cities on the western coastline, like Bristol, Liverpool and Falmouth, which developed into industrial trading hubs for Caribbean imports. The availability of rum in these towns lead to some entrepreneurial types establishing blending houses. Amazingly, there are accounts of sugar refineries and distilleries opening in Glasgow, Liverpool and London, as far back as the 1670s. Given that so little (if any) rum was imported into Britain at that time, it's quite possible that the first taste of rum for many British people was in fact British rum!

As volumes grew through the latter part of the 1700s, one thing remained fairly steady: around 85% of the rum imported was Jamaican, and most of the remaining 15% was from Barbados, who at the time exported more to the colonies in North America.

But not all the rum that flowed into Britain was destined to stay there. British rum drinkers had a preference for the higher strength Jamaican rum. Barbados rum was mostly re-exported to other European territories. Demand was especially high in Ireland, which consumed more rum than England and Wales combined in the latter part of the 18th century.

YO HO HO

It's almost impossible to talk about rum without referencing pirates, but the significance of piracy in the story of rum is hugely overplayed. Real pirates were little more than rag-tag packs of ocean-going militia, comprising wandering criminals, social outcasts, and debtors, with bills that no honest man could pay. Some pirates operated as "privateers" – a form of legally sanctioned pirating, introduced by Elizabeth I to disrupt Spanish colonial efforts. Some of the famed wrongdoings of pirates and privateers are as legendary as they sound (see Captain Morgan on pages 192–93), but many of our perceived pirate stereotypes are either dramatic embellishments of the truth or just pure fiction.

The golden age of pirating came about at the end of the 17th century, which coincided with the first sugar plantations establishing themselves in the Caribbean. Rum was in a nascent state during this time; it was in production and available locally, but not yet the widely traded international commodity that it would soon become. The merchant ships of the late 17th century were more often packed with wine, French brandy and

Dutch genever. And it's those drinks – not rum – that typically "shivered a pirate's timbers".

In fact, the association between pirates and rum was all but nonexistent until 1883, when Robert Louis Stevenson penned *Treasure Island*. Originally serialized in a children's magazine, the novel was written around 50 years after the last pirate had walked the plank. Stevenson probably had less reference material concerning rum and pirates to go on than we do today, and while the geographical connection between piracy and rum is easy to establish, it's highly unlikely that pirates were as committed to rum drinking as Stevenson would have us believe.

The word "rum" appears 57 times in *Treasure Island* ("brandy" appears just 14 times), and most famously on the opening page:

> *"Fifteen men on the dead man's chest - Yo-ho-ho, and a bottle of rum!"*

This sea shanty, like most of the rest of his book, was a product of Stevenson's imagination, and these words were never consciously spoken by a pirate, or anyone else, until *Treasure Island* appeared on book shelves. It's alleged that Stevenson found the name "Dead Man's Chest" among a list of Virgin Island names in a book by fellow novelist Charles Kingsley, possibly in reference to the Dead Chest Island off Peter Island in the British Virgin Islands. It's likely that Stevenson's "bottle of rum" is the single greatest contributor to the rum-swigging pirate cliché, but rum wasn't the only piece of pirate mythology perpetuated

RIGHT A (barely) walking cliché of what a pirate probably wasn't. Except for the fact that in this instance, he is uncharacteristically without a bottle of rum.

ROBERT LOUIS STEVENSON'S
TREASURE ISLAND

:: ARTHUR BOURCHIER ::
As "LONG JOHN SILVER"

by Stevenson. Treasure maps, gravel-throated west-country accents, and walking around with a parrot on one's shoulder are all creations of Stevenson's.

The image of the rum-guzzling pirate has proved a difficult one to shake. Stevenson's book, along with fictional characters that it has influenced, such as Captain Hook from J.M. Barrie's *Peter Pan* and more recently Jack Sparrow from the *Pirates of the Caribbean* franchise, offer a glamorous portrayal of criminality on the high seas, where morals are loose and the rum flows freely. My favourite line from *Treasure Island* that concerns rum is delivered by Long John Silver himself. While recovering from a sword fight Silver refuses medical attention, insisting that rum will suffice, "I lived on rum, I tell you. It's been meat and drink, and man and wife, to me".

A RUM RATION

In the spring of 1655, English Vice-Admiral William Penn set sail from Barbados with a fleet of 37 war ships and several thousand soldiers. His intention was to take the island of Hispaniola from the Spanish, but the attack was ill-prepared and mismanaged. Penn was reluctant to return to Barbados with his tail between his legs, however, so he opted instead to sail further west, and attempt to seize the less desirable Spanish colony of Jamaica. This time he was successful, resulting in the establishment of what would, by the early 1700s, surpass

Barbados as Britain's most valuable Caribbean territory. The capture of Jamaica on May 17 1655 also marked the start of a Royal Navy tradition that would remain in place for over one-third of a millennium: *the rum ration*.

Or so the story goes. In fact, there is no documented evidence to confirm that rum was rationed to troops in Jamaica. What we do know is that Jamaica was a tobacco island under Spanish rule, and grew only a token gesture of sugarcane to satisfy the local market. We also know that there are no accounts of rum production or rum consumption on the island prior to the arrival of the British in 1655. So it seems strange that the capture of Jamaica, of all places, served as the catalyst for the Navy rum ration, and especially so when one considers that the fleet had just sailed from Barbados – an island that was known to be producing cane spirits at that time! Even if rum was being made in Jamaica in 1655, it would only have been for local consumption, and in 1654 the population of Jamaica was just 2,500. Where then, would stocks of rum sufficient to fill the bellies of seven thousand British sailors be conjured up from?

There are solid historical references to rum rationing on ships at Port Royal, Jamaica, in the 1680s, and it's fair to assume that the practice was going on in Jamaica for some years prior to that. Given the island's dominance in both sugar and rum production in the 18th century, it would have been convenient for some historians to establish a link between the Royal Navy arriving there and rum appearing on-board their ships. But I for one

think that it's likely that rum was not new to sailors in 1655 and that it was issued to them before the capture of Jamaica as well as afterwards.

One thing's for sure though: life on a 17th-century Royal Navy ship was a living hell. Squalid living conditions, biscuit rations, strict punishment and the constant fear of death by disease or hostile encounter. Alcohol was a necessary antidote on these voyages, and the traditional maritime appetite for alcohol was never more voracious than during this period when men were spending longer at sea than ever before. Sailors were dispensed beer rations at an agreeable rate of one gallon per day, but the beer was prone to turning sour after a couple of weeks at sea and that left only slimy water as a source of refreshment. Some time in the middle of the 17th century, sailors became acquainted with rum. In those days, Royal Navy ships operated autonomously and there was no standard regulations or code of instructions (seamen and even officers wouldn't have standardized uniform for another 100 years). So the practice likely began on a micro-level then spread steadily throughout the rest of the fleet as rum became more available. Rum (and other spirits) was the natural choice of refreshment for sailors, because on long voyages it didn't go sour in the barrel – indeed, it improved!

Then there was the fact that it was strong stuff, which the sailing men no doubt approved of. We can only guess at the real strength of the spirit back then, though. Distillation techniques were mostly rather crude in the 17th century, and it wasn't until 1816 that Sikes's hydrometer was invented and the ability to measure strength (proof) accurately became a reality. The term "proof" (in its capacity as a gauge of alcoholic strength) originated in the Royal Navy, and more specifically with regard to rum. It was the task of the ship's purser (the supplies handler) to assess the quality of all incoming food and drink stocks from the port, as well as to manage their rationing among the men. Where rum was concerned, this meant testing the alcohol content to ensure that the liquid wasn't diluted by some unscrupulous trader wishing to squeeze some extra cash out of his client. The test was conducted using gunpowder, wherein the rum was mixed with a small quantity of the powder and heated with an open flame. The burning of the gunpowder was observed by the purser, who gauged the ferocity of the flame to calculate the strength of the rum. There were no percentages or degrees on his scale, however – rum was either deemed

ABOVE Edward Vernon: Royal Navy Admiral, mixologist and grogram coat advocate.

strong enough or not. The test became known as the "proof" test. Rum that burned like dry gunpowder was "proven" to be of adequate strength, and that strength happened to be 57% alcohol by volume. Rum burning hotter or brighter than gunpowder was clearly stronger, and those rums were labelled "over-proof".

The Royal Navy demanded that all rums stored on Navy ships were over-proof. Perhaps this was because a barrel of "under-proof" rum spilt its contents all over an adjacent cask of gunpowder causing the gunpowder to burn poorly and rendering a ship defenceless. Or perhaps it was just the mariners hankering for the burn of strong spirit. The Navy's policy changed in 1866 when all Navy rum was prescribed at 4.5 under-proof, which is where it stayed for the duration of the ration.

From the mid-1600s until the 1730s, rum was rationed to sailors without rules or guidelines. In fact, there are very few accounts of rum rationing at all until the 18th century, and those that do exist are rather vague. In February 1727, Captain Gascoigne of the *HMS Greyhound*, which was stationed at Port Royal, wrote to the Navy Board suggesting that a "double allowance of rum" might encourage the men under his command to work harder.

In 1731, the first documented regulations "Relating to His Majesty's Service at Sea" were published, which reveal both what a daily rum ration constituted and that the ritual had spread beyond the Caribbean, into wider Royal Navy operations. The regulations stated that a standard issue gallon of beer was equivalent to "a pint of wine or half a pint of brandy, rum or arrack". Whether rum, brandy or arrack (which would have served as a substitute for rum or brandy in the East Indies), a half pint of strong spirit a day is equivalent to ten double shots (50 ml or 2 oz) – every day.

With that much alcohol flowing through a sailor's veins, it's amazing that sailors felt the need to smuggle extra stocks of rum on-board during shore leave. One trick commonly employed by shrewd seamen in the Caribbean involved emptying coconuts of their milk and refilling them with rum before boarding the ship. Extra drams were also occasionally issued by officers as rewards for exemplary service or acts of heroism. Before going into battle, captains sometimes ordered a "tot" (a ration) for the crew to make them more "brave and willing."

BELOW Not content with inventing "grog", Admiral Vernon achieved what Hosier couldn't, capturing Portobello in 1739.

RUM, GROGGERY AND THE LASH

For many sailors, rum would become their only form of liquid intake, and was the cause of no shortage of accidents, disputes and deaths. But alcoholism was really only a single strand in a sorry tapestry of malnutrition and poor hygiene on-board Navy ships. During the 18th century diseases killed more British sailors than combat did, and the biggest killer of all was scurvy – a deficiency in vitamin C. One of the most horrendous examples of this was Vice-Admiral Hosier's siege of Portobello, which over a six-month period resulted in the death of 4,000 men from 'fever' compared to only a handful who died in battle.

This plight of the seaman was recognized by one man. Admiral Edward Vernon was adored by his men for his obvious concern for their wellbeing, and for his exceptional leadership skills in battle. Vernon petitioned for the rum ration to be reduced, but more crucially,

that it should be mixed with water, limes and sugar. His pleas were heard, and in 1740 the rum issue became gospel. The concoction was served twice daily, once between 10am and 12pm, and another between 4pm and 6pm. This new drink needed a name, and with the sailors' known ability for inventive language, it was called "grog" – named for the grogram waterproof boat cloak that was the trademark apparel of Admiral Vernon.

With fresh lime juice featuring in the diet of every sailor in the Navy from 1740 onwards, there's no telling how many lives that would have otherwise been lost to scurvy were saved by Admiral Edward Vernon's cocktail. The mixture of rum to water (and other ingredients) was set at 4:1 in favour of water, but this was prone to change depending on who was in charge. As such, the mixture seamen used for grog was named by compass points. Due North was pure rum, and due West was water alone. WNW would therefore be one-third rum and two-thirds water, and NW half and half. If a seaman had two "nor-westers," he'd had two glasses of half rum and half water.

THE BLACK TOT

In the 19th century, there was a slow change of attitude towards intoxication among active servicemen. In 1824 the tot of rum was halved in size to one-quarter of a pint (one gill) and the sailors were compensated by an increase in pay and additional rationing of meat, cocoa and tea. As early as 1850 the Admiralty's "Grog Committee" met to discuss the problems associated with over-consumption of alcohol among seamen, and shortly after they released a report which confirmed the relationship between drunkenness and discipline, recommending that the ration be abolished. Rather than abolish it the Royal Navy Commission reduced it again, this time half a gill (one-eight of a pint).

Following these reductions in quantity it seems that the Royal Navy took a greater interest in the quality of the rum. Since the inception of the tot, the Navy were prone to shop around, initially buying most of their stock from Jamaica and Barbados. But by the 19th century, their preference tended to lie with Guyana. From 1783 onwards all purchases were made through the sugar broker, ED & F Man & Co., who continued to supply the Navy right up until 1970 when the ration was abolished. In 1908 the Royal Navy

ABOVE British Royal Navy sailors grab the largest vessels they can get their hands on for their twice-daily issue of grog from the ship's rum tub.

purchased 420,000 gallons of "Demerara rum". All rum shipments were sent to the Royal Victoria Yard where they were blended in linked vats which were never entirely emptied. This brought a degree of consistency to the liquid, in much the same way as a solera system works (see page 55). James Park's *Nelson's Blood* (1983) details an account from one P. Curtis, who was a chief petty officer stationed at *HMS Terror* in Singapore shortly after World War II. He recounts an evening where no less than six chief pursers got together with various samples of blending stock and over the course of two hours of appreciating "the glow which spreads from the stomach and engenders that wonderful feeling of peace and bonhomie", they established a blend of rums that was agreed to be perfect by all present. The blend comprised: "fifty-five percent Demerara, thirty percent Trinidad, with the remainder from Natal and Mauritius."

But while Curtis and company were fine-tuning the taste and aroma of a Navy tradition three-hundred years in the making, other men, in offices, were again calling for the rum ration to be done away with. It had been over 100 years since the tot had been dropped to half a gill, during which time the Navy had fought two world wars and built aircraft carriers and nuclear submarines. Yet still, all over the world, rum was dispensed twice daily to service men and women.

On January 28 1970, the "Great Rum Debate" took place in the House of Commons. Despite impassioned speeches from the likes of MP James Wellbeloved, who argued that, "there is some evidence from people who serve at sea in Her Majesty's ships and in the Merchant Navy that a tot of rum can have a stabilising effect upon the stomach, and this is indeed a matter of considerable importance", it was decided that the rum ration had no place in the modern Navy. July 31 1970 would forever more be known as "Black Tot Day", when the last pipe of "Up Spirits" was chimed and the final ration issued at 11am – 24 times, in 24 time zones, across the globe.

By contrast with other members of the Commonwealth, the Royal Australian Navy had already discontinued the rum ration nearly 50 years earlier, in 1921. Two other Commonwealth navies retained the rum ration after the Royal Navy abandoned it, however. But less than two years after Black Tot Day, March 31 1972 became the final day of the rum ration in the Royal Canadian Navy. The New Zealand Navy displayed an impressive level of commitment to the rum ration, holding out until February 27 1990.

By means of compensation, British seamen were allowed an extra can of beer as part of their ration. The remaining rum stocks (which were mostly stored in casks) were put up for auction. They were bought by Chief Petty Officer Brian Cornford, who had served in Royal Navy submarines during World War II. Cornford had the ships drop their remaining supplies off at Gibraltar, where with the help of John Kania, a cellar master under his employment, they undertook the laborious task of decanting the barrels into 1-gallon (1.2-US gallon) earthenware flagons, which were wrapped in wicker, sealed with wax and date-stamped. The flagons were then sold on again, with many of them ending up in Gibraltar bars during the 1970s and 1980s. They are now much harder to get hold of, although I do have one in my collection which is wax stamped with the year 1956. I plan on cracking it open on July 31 2020 to mark the 50-year anniversary of Black Tot Day.

There are countless reports of rum still making an appearance during particularly cold military operations during the 1980s and 1990s. By this point it took the form of a bottle of Lamb's or Pusser's however, rather than the original wicker-covered 1-gallon demijohns. Trawling through the military internet forums these days, there is plenty of anecdotal evidence to support the notion that rum still has a place in the modern Navy. And while it may not be dispensed through the official channels it's clear that there's a lasting legacy of strong booze that's difficult to erase completely.

NEW ENGLAND RUM

Bourbon whiskey has been the spirit of the United States for the past 150 years, but long before the first farmers mashed the first corn, it was rum that filled the tavern cups.

As with the tropics, alcohol played an important role in the physical and mental conditioning of colonists, for whom it provided medicine and nourishment for both body and mind. Colonizing required its own set of skills, and re-establishing the psychological muscle memory of learned social rituals was key to the general mood of colonial society. Alcohol played its own part in this, and when coupled with the fact that colonists possessed a "deep seated distrust of water" (as Wayne Curtis puts it in his book *And a Bottle of Rum*), making one's own hooch was damn near essential.

So the colonists began brewing – beer mostly, from cereals, like rye and dark barley malts, but also from corn, apples, pumpkin and other fruits and fermentable sources. But these crops were needed for the equally important act of eating. So wines were imported too, from Portugal, Madeira and France, but this was not cheap. Not to mention that a dependence on Europe for your evening's night cap was, psychologically, a step backward rather than forward. What colonists really yearned for was the freedom and independence to work a hard day in the fields, and then drink hard, home-grown, liquor at night… (and sometimes in the day, too).

The first rum distillery was built on Staten Island, New York in 1650 (and a second in Boston in 1657), just a decade after the first Caribbean operations manifested themselves, and barely a generation after the Pilgrim Fathers established the colony of Massachusetts. Molasses arrived by boat from the Caribbean, where, at the time, there was an overwhelming surplus of the stuff, and once again it was the Dutch who provided the know-how to convert it into a strong spirit. And since rum was unlikely to have been traded by boat in any meaningful quantity until the late 1650s, it's fair to surmise that distilleries in Massachusetts and New York were inspired to make rum independently of their Caribbean cousins.

For colonies on Barbados and Martinique, early distilling was a simple means of leveraging value out of industrial waste, but in New York and Boston, no sugar mills existed, so the purchase of bulk shipments of molasses and the establishment of distilleries to process it testifies to the resourcefulness of the colonists where matters of high-strength alcohol were concerned.

In the space of a decade or so, rum was everywhere. As the population of the colonies increased, so too did the demand for rum, although this was at a far greater rate than the distilleries could keep up with. Rum was available in every tavern and tippling house, and it was drunk widely at home where it was also used in cooking – sometimes even finding its way into a recipe for "fryed bacon" – or when served once to Rev. Elijah Kellogg, "with salt fish and crackers". Rum was used as a currency – it was traded with native Americans for furs (and used as leverage once a dependency had been established), or as part payment of wages. Rum was made in and consumed in colonial towns, in scraggly half-built villages, halfway up mountains and in the remote northern ports around Newfoundland. Rum was produced domestically, but also flowed in from Barbados (which was considered to be the best rum-producing country of that time) along with regular shipments from Grenada and Antigua. Given that these spirits were no doubt shipped in barrels, the preference for imported spirit may have been down to the simple softening of the spirit by the oak cask.

Rum was the most widely consumed drink of its time. It was drunk on an abusive scale, which was likeable to London's disastrous "gin craze" of the early 1700s. By the middle of the 18th century, the average American adult was drinking a bottle-and-a-half of rum every week.

The most common way to do this was the easiest – straight-up and sometimes followed by a glass of water. Sometimes the water and rum were mixed before knocking it back, and when sweetened and spiced they formed a drink known as *mimbo*. More commonly it was mixed with molasses, where the drink was instead called *bombo*.

But cocktail etiquette was loose in those days, little was off-limits, and rum was mixed with anything that was found lying around: it was mixed with shrub vinegars in a "Switchel", mixed with hard cider in a "Samson" and combined with beaten eggs in a "Bellowstop".

But the best drink of the era was unquestionably the "Flip", which required some equipment, however. It consisted of a large earthenware bowl, to which rum, sugar (or molasses), ale and spices were added. The mixture would be stirred before – in a most dramatic turn of events – a hot "loggerhead" was stabbed into its murky depths. A loggerhead is a kind of fire poker with a ball on the end, which tended to be the first weapon men went for during drunken brawls (hence the phrase "at loggerheads"). But this wasn't all about theatre; the use of the hot loggerhead affected the drink in a number of ways: first – and most obviously – it heats it, though not to the point of it being a "hot" drink, but rather a "warm" one. The intense heat also causes the bubbles in the beer to expand, which foams up the drink, adding a bit of drama to proceedings. Finally, the heat of the loggerhead also cooks the drink, caramelizing the sugars and creating *Maillard* reactions, that contribute toasty, cooked, qualities. The caramelization also produces bitter flavours, that in turn balance the sweetness of the beer and sugar.

The Flip existed in a time before the widespread hopping of beer, and this searing process introduced some of the bitterness that hop flowers would normally provide. Combine all of the above elements together: sweetness, aromatic spice, homely cereal notes, fruitiness, gentle warmth, foamy texture and a more-ish bitterness, and you're left with one of the great drinks of all time – produced using only blacksmith's tools and the foraged scraps of an adolescent colonial society.

THE REVOLUTIONARY SPIRIT

"I know not why we should blush to confess that Molasses was an essential Ingredient in American Independence. Many great Events have proceeded from much smaller causes."

John Adams, second President of the United States

The North American molasses trade was a useful little earner for the British Caribbean planters, who charged 10p (£20 or $27 today) a gallon for the stuff. The British Empire was highly attentive to the needs of these powerful business leaders, and therefore keen to maintain a healthy trade between colonies. But the North Americans were a savvy bunch, and in the pursuit of favourable prices, they soon began trading with the entire Caribbean region and especially the French. Saint-Domingue, Martinique and Guadeloupe sold molasses at around half the price of the British product – a bargain only made possible by a surplus of product and favourable re-export tariffs set by the French government to curb the enormous quantities of sugar and molasses that was landing in French mainland ports. By 1730, the colony of Massachusetts was importing over 90 per cent of its molasses requirements from the French West Indies.

The British planters were not happy about this, and in response, the British parliament introduced the Molasses

Act in 1733. The Act imposed a tax on molasses imported from foreign colonies, such as the French or Dutch West Indies, at a rate of 6p (£12 or $20 today) per gallon. This brought the price of a gallon to around 10p (£20 or $27 today) regardless of where you bought it from. This did not sit well with New England and the other colonies. Rum was the currency of the North America trading enterprise, but more than that it was a manufactured item that was of their own making, not imported, not a hand out, but representative of the blood and sweat of the overall colonial endeavour. History teaches us that there's a fine balance to be had where matters of tax on alcohol (or products related to the production of alcohol) are concerned. If actually collected, the molasses tax would have slowed economic growth in New England and destroyed much of the rum industry in the process. In this instance the tax was poorly policed and expertly evaded. This was one of the first examples of mass civil disobedience among the colonists, and cited by some historians as the first murmuring of revolutionary uprising.

Three decades passed and an average of only £2,000 (£400,000 or $660,000 today) of tax revenue was collected each year. By the 1760s, the British were strapped for cash following the Seven Years' War (1754–63), which had doubled the national debt. In response, parliament raised taxes on many imported goods, but also passed a modified version of the Molasses Act. The ensuing Sugar Act of 1764 halved the rate of taxation on molasses, but on this occasion Britain was going to make damn sure it was paid. Policing was overseen by the British Army and a fleet of 27 mobile Royal Navy ships who were permitted to pursue smugglers on the high seas. The Act also throttled the trade in timber and other colonial goods with French colonies.

Just like the earlier Molasses Act, this new legislation was an enormous threat to the American rum industry, which by this point was making 80% of its 6 million gallons (22 million litres) of annual consumption from imported molasses. The colonists, who viewed the new Act as a great injustice, took to the streets with placards and pamphlets. In what could almost be classed as a "democratic" turn of events, the tax was reduced (in

29 Boston Boys throwing tea into the harbour

LEFT The so-called Boston Tea Party is often seen as the catalyst for the American Revolution, but the revolutionary seed was planted by sugar, molasses and rum.

1766) to just 1p (£2 or £3.50 today) a gallon. But this rollback of taxation policy represented a major paradigm shift in the relationship between colonist and crown. A growing sense of fortitude seasoned the punch bowls of New England taverns, and rum nurtured the first stirrings of dissent. Aware that they had buckled in the face of popular demand, Parliament launched a counter-offensive and imposed direct taxes on the colonies for the first time. The Stamp Act of 1765 required colonists to pay tax on every piece of printed paper they used. The Tea Act of May 1773 granted the British East India Company a monopoly on tea sales in the American colonies. The cry went out across the colonies "no taxation without representation!"

The iconic Boston Tea Party took place six months later, in December 1773 during which the Sons of Liberty destroyed a huge shipment of East India Company tea. In February 1775, Parliament declared Massachusetts to be in a state of rebellion, and in April of that year conflicts broke out, commencing with battles at Lexington and Concord. The American Revolutionary War had begun.

FINDING SUCCESS IN THE 19TH CENTURY

Up until the middle of the 19th century, the sugar business remained the dominant economic activity across all but the smallest of the Caribbean islands. But the abolition of the Atlantic slave trade by the European colonial powers between 1807 and 1818, followed by the Slavery Abolition Act of 1833, which outlawed slavery in the British Empire, demanded a rapid transition for planters from slave labour to a free labour system.

This necessitated profound changes in the running of plantations and distilleries, from recruitment to welfare and workforce management. The upshot was that making sugar was going to cost more money from now on. In addition to workforce challenges, the productivity of Caribbean sugar estates was beginning to suffer thanks to soil exhaustion, which had rendered entire sections of Barbados unsuitable for growing sugarcane by the 1820s. This had a positive impact on Demerara sugar, however, which if left unchecked threatened to flood the market and destabilize commodity prices.

ABOVE Despite the gradual decline of the sugar industry on Barbados, there were still dozens of sugar estates at the end of the 19th century, like Spring Hall in St. Lucy.

This came at a time when Europe, and especially France, was busy developing an alternate sugar source: sugar beets. By 1837, there were 542 sugar beet factories in France producing 35,000 tons (38,600 US tons) of raw sugar annually. By 1890 over half the world's sugar came from sugar beet. This increased the global availability of sugar and lowered its value at a time when plantations cost more than ever to run.

The old system was broken, the financial margins simply didn't add up, and the business plan needed a drastic re-write. Hundreds of small mills (and distilleries) across the British Caribbean closed during this period, or were consolidated into larger industrial operations. Others ceased refining activities but doggedly persevered with rum production. This set the stage for the next turn in rum's long journey as the islands attempted to commercialize their distilleries in a world that wouldn't stand still.

Fortunately, the industrial age was there to help, revolutionizing distillery technology and shaping rum flavour in the process. Rum-making methods hadn't evolved much in three centuries, and the pot still

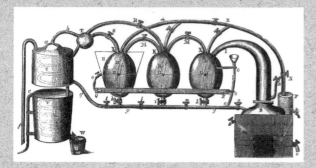

followed the same basic distillation principles that had been established in the ninth century. Rum was still produced in batches, which was time-consuming and costly, and highly prescriptive as far as the final flavour of the spirit was concerned. A continuous still was needed; a device that could process fermented beer or wine and turn it into high-strength alcohol without all the faffing about.

The first attempt at this came from an illiterate Frenchman by the name of Edouard Adam, who patented a prototype continuous still in 1804. Adam's column was a horizontal arrangement that linked together a series of what Adam called "large eggs", with pipes that would route alcohol vapour from one egg to the next. The design is highly reminiscent of the pot still and retort set ups that are still used in some rum distilleries today.

The column-shaped Pistorius still arrived in 1817. The pioneering design was adapted the following year by Dutch sugar trader Armand Savalle, which in turn became a popular design among rum distillers, especially in the French Caribbean. Later versions were developed by the French engineer Jean-Baptiste Cellier-Blumenthal, and Robert Stein, the owner of the Kilbagie distillery in Fife, Scotland.

Then, in 1830, came the revolutionary design patented by the Irishman Aeneas Coffey. The Coffey still was the first of its kind to sustain a truly continuous process of distillation. It was a work of genius for its time, as evidenced by the fact that the same basic design is used in many distilleries today.

The French and Spanish rum-makers were the earliest adopters of the continuous still, while the British stuck to their pots. This tactic proved successful (for the time being) as the trademark high-ester Jamaican style became a spirit category in its own right. Export volumes reached all-time highs and the

cash piled up, so much so that it garnered the attention of great chemists and engineers, who applied scientific principles to rum-making through research into yeast, fermentation and dunder (see pages 46–48). They sought to understand the nuances of rum production, with the aim of broadening rum styles as tastes shifted to lighter styles. By the end of the century, Jamaican distillers were producing high- and low-ester marques, and rum export values outpaced that of sugar.

The French island of Martinique (see pages 130–147) experienced a similar trajectory of growth, with exports increasing by a factor of 20 between 1850 and 1890. This unprecedented surge in uptake was largely due to the devastation of European vineyards by the *phylloxera* mite. When wine and brandy stocks dwindled, the French looked to the colonies for a source of hard liquor, and Martinique was only too happy to oblige.

The arrival of the continuous still divided the rum-producing world into two camps: those with pots and those without. Lighter styles were considered purer and therefore higher in quality, while pot-still rums developed a reputation for being smelly and rough. A style somewhere in the middle of the two was deemed to be something that most people would get along with nicely. But these heavy and light rums were limited by the equipment that was used to make them. The solution presented itself eventually and gave rise to a new faction within the rum canon: blenders.

Blending was a British invention, and one that would later become synonymous with Scotch whisky. With America's attentions shifted to whiskey production, and the Royal Navy fully invested in dramming, rum was becoming a drink with increasingly British associations.

Blenders established themselves on both sides of the Atlantic, applying a degree of credibility to the liquor where there was once none. Blending stretched volumes of good-quality stuff and covered up the not so good ones. But more than anything, it gave a guarantee of quality and authenticity.

A RUM SUPERPOWER

The arrival of the column still in Cuba set the stage for a new, lighter, cleaner style of rum that would become the hallmark of the best-selling rum brands in the world today. Cuban rum captured the imagination of the US, helped to establish rum's relevance within cocktail culture and fostered the development of some of the world's best bartenders (not to mention bars) in the early 20th century.

In an age of Martinis and Champagne, light rum was a necessary deviation for a category heavily rooted in, well, heaviness. Light rum didn't need to be tamed with aggressive flavours, or blended down. This rum was for mixing, sipping and swigging back from a highball as you mambo across the dance floor.

The continuous still came at just the right time for the Spanish islands, where distilleries began popping up in the late 18th century. Lucrative trading with the newly independent US meant that islands like Cuba quickly became the most industrially advanced in the region. In the 19th century, sugar- and rum-making were enterprises tied directly to Cuba's social and economical successes or failures. Geographically dislocated from its Spanish motherland, Cuba was also a world away in terms of its drinking habits. The rum made in Cuba became a product that could legitimately be called "Cuban" and that helped to establish the concept of identity and individuality among the Cuban people. Rum still resonates strongly on this island, because of the countless families of Spanish origin that helped to establish the Cuban identity by making and selling rum made from Cuban molasses.

By the 1860s, there were a remarkable 1,365 distilleries on Cuba, and the island exported 20.5 million litres (5.4 million US gallons) of rum each year – providing much-needed succour to soldiers during the American Civil War – and placing Cuba only behind Martinique in the rum rankings. So far as sugar was concerned, Cuba became the top producer in the world, outpacing Jamaica and all the other British colonies combined.

Cuba fought three wars against the Spanish between 1868 and 1898, culminating in a US-assisted victory and the agreement of Spain to relinquish all claim of sovereignty over the island. The Cuba libre trade-off heralded a new era of aggressive American influence that shaped the geopolitical landscape of the north Caribbean for decades to come. American sponsorship also helped to shape the sugar industry on Cuba, consolidating mills and distilleries into larger industrial operations that churned out rum at record-breaking levels. Finally, it transformed Havana into a party town that was seen by some as chic and sophisticated, and by others as an intoxicant of the soul, with its casinos, cocktail coupes, and the greatest bartenders of the age: the *cantinero*.

Cocktail culture was already well established in many American cities by this point, but had failed to penetrate the colonial Caribbean because there was little call for it. Havana was just 160 km (100 miles) from Key West in Florida, and only a few hours by plane (once commercial air travel was established) from New York or Washington. At a time when the Temperance movement was gathering pace in the US, Cuba became the "local bar" of America. When Prohibition took effect in the US in 1920, America brought cocktail culture to the Cuban party and Cuba

RIGHT Bacardí adverts in Cuba in the 1940s stated "El Que a Cuba Ha Hecho Famosa" (The one that has made Cuba famous).

BELOW Carnival time in Havana: a great opportunity to drink Cuban rum and drive fast cars in a circle.

CARNIVAL TIME, HAVANA, CUBA.

supplied all the rum. A joint advertising campaign between Bacardí and Pan Am airlines gave birth to such slogans as, "Leave the Dry Lands Behind," and "Fly to Cuba and Bathe in Bacardí rum." The tourism to the island doubled in a period of ten years, growing from 45,000 annual visitors in 1916 to 90,000 in 1926.

At that time, most of the (good) hotels in Havana were under the ownership of US companies, and the city became an intimate hotbed of various exotic vices complete with race track, sporting arenas and theme parks (it could be argued that Havana was a theme park) all serviced by the indebted Cuban populace. One of the better outcomes of this arrangement was some of the greatest rum cocktails in the world today: Mojito (see page 215), Daiquiri (see page 224), El Presidente (see page 237) and Mulata, to name a few.

These drinks, while based on formulae of older whiskey- or gin-based cocktails, were conceived and executed by the *cantineros*, who tended bar for some of the greatest names of the era. The journalist Hector Zumbado described these celebrity service industry professionals as "Diplomatic, polyglot, like skilled ambassadors. Discreet and reserved."

The bars of this era are just as legendary as the men who tended them: the famed Havana establishment Sloppy Joe's – where the *cantineros* were known to make 100 daiquiris in a single (large) shaker – diverted its attentions from food to drink during Prohibition. La Floridita became "La Cuña del Daiquiri" ("The Cradle of the Daiquiri") under the legendary Constantino Ribalaigua Vert, who captained the bar team from 1918.

The Asociacion de Cantineros de Cuba served as a bartenders' trade union that operated apprentice schemes, ran extensive training programs and even trained bartenders in English, which was essential if they were to service the parched throngs of incoming American and British vacationers.

Prohibition established the market for Cuban rum in America, and once it was repealed, the American appetite for a "cleaner" style of rum endured – evident in the rise of even more neutral vodka. The Cuban approach spread through other rum-producing regions, even influencing distilleries which had in the past been stalwarts of the pot-still approach, such as Trinidad. Cuban rum endured too, but more through its most famous progeny, Bacardí, and its legacy as the modern rum standard, than as an island of rum distillers.

WAR AND SURVIVAL

As the Cuban spirit soared, the first decade of the 20th century was a complete disaster for Martinique, which up until that point had remained the world's biggest rum producer. The catastrophic eruption of Mount Pelée, on May 8 1902 wiped out dozens of distilleries that surrounded Sainte-Pierre – touted the rum capital of the world – and export volumes from the island dropped from 18 million litres (4.8 million US gallons) in 1901 down to around half that in 1903. The decade that followed became a period of consolidation, as the surviving distilleries took the opportunity to snap up smaller plantations and increase their production capacities. These larger molasses distilleries became known as producers of *rhum industriel*

BELOW LEFT Sloppy Joe's in Havana... hold on a second, is that Noel Coward and Alec Guinness at the bar?!

BELOW RIGHT The legendary Floridita sells Daiquiris at twice the price of other Havana bars – but they're worth it.

while the older, smaller operations that tended to farm and juice their own cane, produced *rhum agricole*.

Meanwhile, the British Caribbean sugar industry was in its death throes, as competition from rival sugar beet and Central and South American producers saw commodity prices plummet. The entire industry had been flipped on its head: sugar was no longer the high-value spice that it had once been, but the spirit formerly known as "Kill Devil" was becoming a premium product! Trinidad switched to oil, Grenada to spices and Barbados to tourism; all maintained distilling operations, but for the time being, their respective rum markets contracted to local trade only.

Guyana began to mine bauxite (aluminium ore), which competed with sugar for economic dominance. However, the sugar industry survived thanks to biannual harvests, a quality product and the importation of cheap labour: over 250,000 Indians between the latter 19th and early 20th centuries. Large wholesale contracts from British blenders also kept rum distilleries working in spite of continued consolidation.

In Jamaica, the Sugar Experiment Station opened in 1905. It had the aim of perfecting the agriculture of sugarcane on the island, as well as exploring the potential for further diversity in Jamaican rum. Quality improved, and the European market maintained a healthy demand for it. In spite of this, 80 Jamaican distilleries closed in the first half of the 20th century.

World War I supercharged rum production across the region, as the French government issued rations of *rhum agricole* to an army of 1 million soldiers. Approximately 136 million litres (36 million US gallons) of rum were exported from Martinique during the war, accounting for 75% of the island's export revenue. British rum was drunk in French trenches too. When water came up to your knees it was no doubt a welcome respite from the misery of trench warfare, leading to one British soldier to remark, "Rum of course is our chief great good. The Ark of the Covenant was never borne with greater care than is bestowed upon the large stone rum-jars in their passage through this wilderness."

Despite the growth of bourbon, rum production in the US continued into the 20th century, and nowhere more so than in the former British colonies of New England and Massachusetts. Prohibition put an end to that of course, but it was not the only disaster to befall the US rum business.

ABOVE The catastrophic eruption of Mount Pelée in 1902 destroyed the town of Saint-Pierre, engulfing some of the biggest and best rum distilleries in the Caribbean at that time.

January 15 1919 was an unusually warm day in Boston, which might have been why the US Industrial Alcohol Distilling Company tank, which was filled with 16 million litres (2.3 million US gallons) of molasses, decided to buckle, spilling its contents into the streets and harbour. The flood killed 21 individuals and injured more than 150 others while damaging an estimated $1 million (£6 million or $10 million today) of property. The 1919 tragedy inundated the newpapers with conspiracies and conjecture about how the tank had failed so epically. It is even said that on a hot summer's day, there is still a lingering scent of molasses in the North End and around Commercial Street.

The rest of the Spanish-speaking Caribbean adopted Cuban techniques in an effort to exploit the growing market for Cuban rum. Rum distilleries multiplied in Puerto Rico during the early part of the century and the Dominican rum industry flourished thanks to an influx of Cuban workers in the 1880s. New distilleries popped up across Central America too, in Panama (1922) Nicaragua (1937), and Guatemala (1939) – all of them leveraging the American appetite for lighter rum.

FULL CIRCLE

By the end of the 16th century, sugarcane had crossed the Pacific and arrived back to the islands from which it originated, leaving a trail of war, taxation, trade and culture in its wake. The Americas continued to dominate the industry, right up until the end of the 19th century, but Asia would soon become the sweetest spot on earth. Of the top five sugarcane growers in the world today, four are Asian (though

even combined, they do not match the colossal production levels of Brazil – the world's top producer).

Wherever sugarcane could grow, rum was never far behind. In South Africa, rum was known simply as "cane". In Dutch Indonesia, cane was used (along with palm) to make a similar spirit to rum called *arrack*.

Sugarcane arrived in Australia in 1788, on the ships of the First Fleet. Through the colony's first 25 years, until the first coins were minted in 1813, rum was New South Wales' *de facto* form of currency. When the first permanent regiment (the New South Wales Corps) arrived in 1790, they served as both colonial enforcer and financial regulator, overseeing the importation and distribution of rum among the colonists and getting rather rich off the back of it. This led to their nicknaming as the "Rum Corps".

In 1806, Governor William Bligh arrived in New South Wales, a man already written in legend for his part in the Mutiny on the Bounty – the notorious incident in which he and 18 loyalists were set adrift by acting Lieutenant Fletcher Christian and forced to survive on rum rations as they travelled 6,500 km (3,500 nautical miles) to reach safety. Bligh's leadership qualities once again proved to be fuel enough for a revolt, when the Rum Corps staged the Rum Rebellion, deposing Governor Bligh who had attempted to destroy illegal stills and curtail the quantity of overpriced rum that filtered through the Corps' cellars. The Rum Rebellion is the first and only instance of the overthrow of the Australian government.

Australia was so far away from the Caribbean and Europe that most of the imported rum came via India or Java. Casks of Bengal rum (which was reputed to be stronger than Jamaican rum) were in the hold of nearly every ship from India, and Indian merchants grew wealthy thanks to the Sydney

trade, sending their ships "laden half with rice and half with bad spirits", according to the Australian historian Geoffrey Blainey.

The popularity of rum "down under" didn't falter, and the island's first legitimate sugar mills and rum distilleries were built in northern Queensland in the 1860s. The view was taken that white men lacked the stamina to work the plantations, so an estimated 62,000 labourers were brought to Queensland between 1863 and 1904. Virtually all of them came from the indigenous populations of New Guinea, Vanuatu, the Solomon Islands and the New Hebrides – Australia was one of the last places on earth to cultivate sugarcane, but its workforce was supplied by one of the first.

In 1869, the world's first and only mobile rum distillery was born: the *SS Walrus* was taken over by the Pioneer Floating Sugar Company and fitted out with a working sugar mill and distillery. It travelled up and down the Albert and Logan Rivers in Queensland, anchoring at wharves near the cane fields. The mill was capable of crushing 2 tons (2.2 US tons) of sugar a day and used the leftover molasses to make rum. As ingenious as a floating rum distillery sounds, it was a failure. Distilling operations ceased in 1871 and the ship was decommissioned two years later. The oldest surviving legal distillery in Australia is Beenleigh, Queensland, which was originally founded by Francis Gooding and John Davy in 1884 – a time when there were over a dozen rum distilleries in Queensland.

Distillation in the Philippines has a history dating back to the 16th century, but the nation's first rum distillery was born out of an old *aguardiente* (a strong spirit, translating as "fiery water", which is often made from sugarcane) and "tuba" (a type of palm wine) distillery in Hagonoy. In 1856, the distillery was acquired by Valentin Teus y Yrisarry and, six years later, a rectifying plant was built in Isla de Tanduay.

By the 1930s, the rum produced here was branded as "Tanduay Rhum" and its packaging was changed from the 45-litre (10-gallon) *dama juana* container to the more practically sized 750-ml (25-oz) glass bottles. Tanduay is the third highest selling rum brand in the world today.

In the Indian Ocean, the Madine Distillery Company was established on the volcanic island of Mauritius in

1926 and has survived along with a further five distilleries (Charamel, Rhumerie de Mascareignes, Gray's, Oxenham and St. Aubin) taking the island's total to six – and that doesn't include the blenders! Sugarcane was introduced to Mauritius by the Dutch via Java, and the earliest record of rum distillation takes us back to 1850 and one Pierre Charles François Harel. The island produces both molasses and cane juice rums, and exports around 600,000 litres (160,000 US gallons) a year at present.

Nearby Réunion has an even longer history of rum, with the first stills arriving in 1704. The first modern distillery was set up by Frenchman Charles Panon-Desbassayns, and by 1842 there were 12 sugar mills and six distilleries on the island.

By 1928 that number had increased to 31 distilleries, 16 of which had sugar mills attached to them. The collapse of trade with occupied France during World War II forced the closure of two of the mills and all of the distilleries save for Isautier distillery which was founded by Charles Isautier in 1845. The Isautier distillery remains in operation today, run by the sixth generation of the family. Only two others have survived, and both of them are now subsidiaries of Group Quartier Français: Savanna distillery, which was originally established in 1870, and Rivière du Mât. The latter two produce the most famous rum brand on the island: Rhum Charrette.

TIKI TIME

Caribbean tourism started in 1778 when the Bath Hotel and Spring House were built on the island of Nevis. Further resorts appeared on the Bahamas, Barbados, Cuba and Jamaica in the late 19th century – destinations that were serviced by regular steam boat charters from the US. The rise of air travel and the availability of residential air conditioning, in the early 20th century, encouraged further tourism to the region, transporting those who could afford it to paradisiacal islands that offered an imaginative alternative to monochrome America.

Those who were less well-off were no less desirous for the same experience, and this was the catalyst of an American trend towards Hawaiian music, as well as the renaissance of 19th-century "tropical" literature, such as *Moby Dick* and *Treasure Island*. Cocktail bars, like the Coconut Grove in Los Angeles's Ambassador Hotel, capitalized on the fad, installing plastic palm trees and

bringing island magic to the Hollywood set. But this was still the domain of the Martini and black-tie – a place for dancing and sipping, and largely indistinguishable from any other stylish nightclub of the era.

Then tiki came along.

With its roots in South Pacific mythology, tiki is best known for its flaming torches and wild-looking humanoid statues (or totems). For the rum lover, the cult of tiki grew to a similarly reverential status, mostly through the actions of a pair of American restaurant operators, who infused various elements of island culture into a no-frills, marketable product. For a mid-century American, tiki represented the thrill of being transported elsewhere – away from the office, the hardships of war, the anonymity of white spirits and moderation. Rum – with its associations with island life and the laid-back culture that comes with that (and of course sugar's ancient origins in Polynesia) – made it a perfect pairing for the grass-skirt revolution.

By the late 1950s, glass buoys, *exotica* music and drinks as big as your head were available in dozens of cities across the US and beyond. Two men in particular built thatched-roof empires off the back of tiki: Ernest Raymond Beaumont Gantt aka "Donn Beach" and Victor Bergeron aka "Trader Vic".

Gantt was born in Texas, but he left home young, touring the Caribbean with his grandfather for a few

BELOW Hawaii became an American territory in 1898, by which point it was a significant grower of sugarcane. It became a major tourist destination in the age of jet travel.

— MEA HOOMANAO-"A thing to remember"-

years, then, when Prohibition took effect, he became a bootlegger, smuggling contraband rum into the US from the Bahamas. In the 1930s, Gantt moved to Hollywood, and once Prohibition was repealed, he opened a bar in an old tailor's store called "Don's Beachcomber" (the name was later changed to "Don the Beachcomber's"). It was a modestly sized place, but charming to look at with its ramshackle array of artefacts that Gantt had salvaged along his travels: carved masks, flotsam, puffer fish and other marine items.

The drinks lineup started out as a modest punch-style offering, but soon extended as Gantt (which, by now was officially known as "Donn Beach") experimented with potent spices, tropical fruit juices and his own blend of rums. This was revolutionary mixology for the time, orchestrated by a man who had a deep understanding of how ingredients could be layered and paired – a philosophy that later became known as Don's "Rhum Rhapsodies". As the catalogue of popular original cocktails expanded, Donn became increasingly secretive about the recipes, just as his rivals became ever more intent on obtaining them. To that end, his bartenders constructed the cocktails using coded or numbered bottles, the contents of which were unknown to them. Rum was personally selected by Donn, usually arriving from Jamaica or Guyana.

In 1937 a one-legged man named Victor Bergeron took an interest in Don the Beachcomber's bar. Bergeron was a San Francisco native who had opened a restaurant called Hinky Drinks in Oakland in 1934. The 30-capacity venue was inspired by Vic's trips to Cuba where he had met La Floridita's legendary *cantinero* Constante. As such, it was Cuban sandwiches and daiquiris on the menu at Hinky Dinks.

Vic was even more inspired by the multi-sensory spectacle that was Don the Beachcomber's, however, to the point were he offered to go into partnership with Donn. His proposal was rebuffed, though. Then, one day, in 1937, he closed Hinky Dinks, reopening and reinventing it as Trader Vic's.

Vic reinvented himself too, assuming the persona of "Trader Vic" and all the imaginative backstory that came with it. No longer was it a childhood bout of tuberculosis that had lost him a leg – instead it was the result of shark attack. Vic regaled his patrons with numerous tall tales of "The Trader's" adventures, most of them occurring in places that Vic wouldn't actually experience for some years to come. As flimsy as most of his stories were, it didn't matter. Vic was the consummate businessman and like layers of teak veneer, Vic constructed a substantial brand, putting himself right at the centre of it.

Vic expanded his operations in the 1940s, to Seattle, then Beverly Hills, then on to the most iconic of all Trader Vic outposts: San Francisco. This four-storey operation was largely a food-led destination, curiously specializing in Cantonese cuisine. There were bars there too, of course, dispensing all manner of rum-spiked concoctions from the Dr. Funk (made with "Jamaica or Martinique" rum and pastis) to the Flamingo (made with "Puerto Rican rum, Angostura bitters, cucumber rind, and 7-Up") all served in brightly coloured vases, garnished with flowers and elaborate pieces of tropical plant matter.

By the early 1960s, there were 20 Trader Vic's across the US and around the same number of Don the Beachcomber's, too. Sadly, for Donn, he didn't own most of them. Divorce lost him the rights to the business and further expansion was overseen by his ex-wife Sunny Sund. Donn went and fought in World War II, and upon his return, settled in Oahu, Hawaii, finding some success in taking tiki culture back to where it all began.

By the 1970s tiki and cocktail culture in general were already in decline. When mixed drinks re-emerged in the 1980s, the legacy of tiki was present – in the drinks themselves, in their striking, almost ostentatious appearance and in their ludicrous names. If only the attention to ingredients displayed by Donn and Vic was there too. It was the dawn of the dark age of drinking.

THE NEW REVOLUTION

In the late 20th century, global rum sales remained largely stagnant but the sales split shifted considerably. Small distilleries across the Caribbean dropped like flies, through consolidation deals, or from being priced out of the market by favourable tariffs and tax breaks for larger operations. Rum became a bulk wholesale product. Great chunks of rum history were misplaced when these operations closed, taking with them centuries of traditional practices that are all but absent from the Caribbean today. With no clear route as to where rum had come from, the entire concept of rum became obscured. The cry went out, "what is rum?"

For many (like my parents) it was a colonial relic from a pre-industrial era; potent, pungent and consumed only by an older generation. For many others, it was Bacardi – a multinational brand that transcended the entire category. The message was incoherent and it set rum back an entire generation.

Then, finally, it seemed as though the fog was beginning to clear. In the first decade of the new millennium, rum was the fastest growing major spirit category in the world, with sales increasing by 40%

over the 10-year period. Most of the growth was seen in Asia, which is now the biggest rum-drinking market in the world. Consumption doubled there between 2000 and 2010, thanks to emerging local brands like McDowell's No. 1 Celebration, which is not only India's most popular rum, but, as of 2015, the biggest-selling rum brand in the world – shifting 17.8 million 9-litre (2.4-US gallon) cases over the year.

But what about premium rum? Whisky, Cognac, vodka and gin – all had achieved some level of premiumization in the 1990s. Now, in the new millennium, it was rum's time to shine.

New releases from old distilleries trickled in, taking a lead from whisky and Cognac. These were fancily packaged products claiming good provenance and long maturation. Spiced rums were introduced and Barbados and Trinidad experienced a revival. Then new, aged releases followed from the French-speaking islands, the Spanish-speaking islands, Latin America and beyond. Realization set in: rum was being produced across dozens of countries, in numerous styles, and now at a broad range of prices.

In Europe, Spain and Germany are the largest rum markets and Spain is by far the biggest consumer of aged rum, with the market currently dominated by Brugal and Barceló brands from the Dominican Republic. France and UK lean towards white rum, but aged rum, along with spiced offerings, is the fastest growing section of the category. Globally, the market for spiced and flavoured rums has doubled over the past 10 years, and it's these spirits that fill the glasses of the next generation of drinkers. Spiced rum now accounts for 8% of the total global rum category.

This diversity is cause for great celebration, but the absence of enforceable overarching legislation has also become one of rum's biggest challenges in the 21st century. In all the revolutionary excitement, noone remembered to strategize the correct approach to marketing "new rum". Rather, rum brands have blindly snatched at cues from Scotch and vodka categories, recycling them into an abstract of rum.

The category has rediscovered itself and yet, the question is still valid, "what is rum?" It's a spirit made from sugarcane products and sometimes aged in barrels. It is the most diverse spirit category in the world today. It's a consumer product that has shaped the geopolitical and cultural landscape of our world more than any other.

PART TWO
HOW RUM IS MADE

THE SCIENCE OF THE SUGARCANE

Sugarcane is a giant of the *Gramineane* (grass) family, certain varieties of which can grow up to 6 metres (20 ft) tall. The green leaves of the plant look like giant blades of grass, but the stem has a similar appearance to bamboo (also a member of the grass family) with a stem comprising interconnecting boney-looking joints, known as nodes. Each stem is typically 3–4 metres (10–13 ft) in height and about 5 cm (2 in) in diameter. Thanks to its size and leaf surface-area-to-mass ratio, sugarcane is a champion photosynthesizer. In the prime sugarcane-growing regions of the tropics, a single square metre (11 square feet) of sunshine can produce up to 17 kg (37 lbs) of sugarcane in a season.

And we're going to need it. It's estimated that the world will consume 174 million tons (191 US tons) of sugar in 2017 and around 80% of that sugar will be extracted from cane, the remainder coming from sugar beets. Both of these plants are unusual because they store energy in the form of sucrose instead of starch. Starch is the energy of choice for the rest of the plant kingdom because it isn't water soluble and doesn't draw water into the storage cells. In the case of sugarcane, this sucrose is dissolved into fluid in the stem of the plant. Good news for us, but bad news if you're short on water, because sugarcane needs a lot.

Shortly after the cane has flowered, it stockpiles sugar in preparation for growth in the following year, but if you cut it down at the right time, it's possible to literally raid the candy store. Thanks to centuries of continued cane cutting, the plant has retaliated by packing even more sugar into its stem, to the point where around one-fifth of its pressed juice is pure sugary goodness.

AGRICULTURE AND TERROIR

Being a grass has its advantages. One of which is that the plant does not require annually re-seeding. If cut correctly, the leftover stub will send up new stalks (called a *ratoon*) each season for up to 10 years. Successive harvests give decreasing yields however, so after 4–6 seasons it becomes necessary to replant the entire field. Mechanically harvested fields require more frequent replanting.

Cane *terroir* (a term that describes the soil, topography, and climate of environment in which the plant is grown) and cane variety is far less of a concern for rum producers that use molasses as their base material than it is for *rhum agricole* (see page 46) distillers or those that use cane juice or cane honey as their sugar source. This is because most, if not all, of the geographical and climactic influences that shape the material will be deadened during the sugar refinery process.

For those distillers that use cane juice as their base material (a practice popular in the French islands of the Caribbean) the variety of the cane, where it is grown, when it is harvested and how it is harvested are all scrutinized. The specific agriculture of the cane is often one of the major points of difference between distillers, discernible right through to the finished product. This begins with the variety of cane, where each type offers

LEFT The cane that grows near the clay- and silt-rich soils of the northern coastline of Jamaica has been highly regarded for its high yield of sugar for over 250 years.

slightly different levels of sugar concentration (referred to as *Brix* and measured in ° Brix) and preferred growing conditions. Some varieties have been specifically bred or hybridized to be more disease-resistant, to thrive in volcanic soil, at higher altitudes or in hotter, low-lying regions. Others are prized more for their flavour, such as B69-566 or "Blue Cane"– named after the colour of the yeast that naturally forms on it – which was originally bred in Barbados and now proudly features in various single-varietal release rums from Martinique and Guadeloupe.

There are other colours assigned to different cane varieties: red, green and blue. These colours do not always reflect in the appearance of the cane itself, though. Blue cane is more mauve in appearance, which the Martinican poet Patrick Chamoiseau seems to agree with when he described the "purple swathes of sugar cane [and] heady aroma of the first cane flowers."

Cane grown on higher ground, where humidity also tends to be higher, usually grows taller. This means it has a higher overall sugar content than low-grown canes, but the concentration of sugars is slightly lower. For the commercially minded rum manufacturer, higher concentrations of sugar are preferred, because this means more alcohol per ton of cane.

SUGARCANE PROCESSING

"You have to know how to cut the cane, talk to it as it falls, bundle it right away, take it to the grinders with due respect."

Patrick Chamoiseau, poet

Sugarcane is harvested during the dry season, which typically lands between January and July in the Caribbean and Latin America. Where possible, the cutting is done by machine, but it's still necessary to hand-cut the cane if the terrain is on a steep hillside, or generally impassable.

Cutting sugarcane by hand has to rank as one of the worst jobs on the planet. It's back-breaking, monotonous, hot and dangerous. I have tried my hand at it a number of times, and after only five minutes of cutting and stripping the cane with a machete, I was desperate to never cut another piece ever again.

On some plantations, where cane is cut by hand – and especially those in Latin America – the cane is first burned before it is harvested. While not an environmentally sound practice, this does make the hand-harvesting process a lot easier and reduces labour costs. The fire scorches the outside of the cane, which minimizes juice loss during cutting. It doesn't damage the main structure of the cane, but it does strip the cane of any dry pieces of fibre, and protects the dense grass from the attention of dangerous insects and snakes.

Where cane is cut by machines – usually by a sugarcane harvester, which was originally developed in the 1920s – it's usually conducted in tandem with a tractor trailer. The sugarcane harvester has a pair of conical shaped drills at the front that wind around, grabbing the cane and wrenching it from the earth. Underneath the cabin of the machine, the cane is chopped into smaller pieces in such a way that the extraction of juice is avoided and the green leaves are processed out of the mix. Less than a second has passed, and the cane pieces are now at the rear of the vehicle, where they are conveyed up, before being mercilessly tossed sideways into a trailer that's pulled along by a tractor.

Mechanical harvesting is only possible on flat or very nearly flat terrain, so the majority of the world's sugarcane is still cut by hand. Mechanical harvesting is more damaging to the cane itself compared with cut cane, and the farmer suffers greater harvest losses. It's also more ecologically damaging because it compacts soil and damages the root and stem of the remaining plant stub.

Quite recently there have been advances in smaller cane harvesters so they now look more like large lawnmowers. These machines aim to make the hand-harvesting process less gruelling in environments where large machines are impractical or unaffordable, and cause less damage to the environment.

However the cane has been cut, it's possible to encounter it being transported by any means imaginable. During the Caribbean harvesting seasons, roads and tracks are littered with dropped lengths of cane, which ideally needs pressing within 48 hours to prevent the sucrose being broken down into simpler sugars by the enzyme invertase.

Once the cane arrives at the mill, the crop is weighed and the value calculated. In some countries it is a legal requirement that a sample of cane is taken and the sugar content measured. Sweeter cane makes more alcohol, and is naturally worth more money, so this encourages farmers to cut it only when the plant has reached its peak ripeness. Once calculated, the sweetness and the weight are entered into a formula that gives a price that the farmer is paid.

In large sugar refineries and the biggest distilleries in Martinique and Guadeloupe, the cane is dumped onto large patios and pushed around by bulldozers that load it onto conveyor belts. In smaller distilleries, like River Antoine in Grenada, the canes can be bundled together and unloaded by hand.

MAKING SUGAR AND MOLASSES

Since most rums are made from molasses, which is a by-product of the sugar-refining process, it's useful to first understand how sugarcane is processed in the context of a modern sugar mill.

Once it has arrived at the mill, the sugarcane is fed into a series of conveyor belts and rolling cutters, which break and squash the cane into sequentially smaller pieces until all that's left is *bagasse* (pulp fibre) and free-running juice. The smell of these places is pungent — always sharply acidic like vinegar (indicating the constant presence of airborne yeast) — but also earthy, vegetal and of course sweet. Water is added during milling to help flush as much sucrose from the plant as possible.

Next, the heavy impurities from the raw cane juice are removed by a process of clarification, which sees a strong alkaline known as "milk of lime" (calcium hydroxide slurry) added to the juice. This neutralizes the acids, which prevents the sucrose from converting into starch. The lime slurry needs to be removed, however, so the juice is carbonated at high temperature, which converts the calcium hydroxide into calcium carbonate (limestone), which can easily be filtered out. Sulphur dioxide is added to the juice, which increases the acidity, lowering the juice from a pH of 9 to a pH of 5. It also bleaches the juice, helping to improve the flavour of the sugar and lightening the colour.

The next stage is concentration, where most of the water is evaporated from the juice, leaving behind a super-sweet syrup. This is performed in a low-pressure boiler (called a vacuum pan) which places the liquid under a partial vacuum as it is heated, lowering the boiling point, and avoiding the caramelization of the sugars in the juice.

Next comes crystallization, where the last portion of the water is evaporated under very strict controls. Seed grain (sugar granules) are fed into the vacuum pan and as the water evaporates, more crystals begin to form. This process is typically repeated three times, and each time the remaining syrup becomes darker and more viscous. After the third boil, the sugar crystals leave the vacuum pan as a thick brown snowball of sugar, at which point it is classed as muscovado sugar. This is then sent to a centrifuge for further refining into raw sugar of at least 96° Brix (the percentage of sugar by mass).

The syrup that is left in the pan is molasses, and is graded based on the number of times it has been boiled. The leftovers after the first boiling is known as "first syrup" or "light molasses". This has a relatively high sugar content and would typically be sent for further boiling, but it can be sold as "treacle" for baking. The remnants from the second boil are classed as "dark molasses" or "medium molasses" — it too can be used as a baking ingredient but one with far less purity and a good deal more colour. The remaining syrup from the third and final boil, when no more sugar can be liberated from the syrup, is "blackstrap molasses". It's not that there isn't any sugar left (blackstrap molasses from cane comprises roughly 30–40% sucrose and 20% other sugars) – it's just that it costs more money to extract the remaining sugar than the sugar itself is worth.

For the rum-maker, it's blackstrap that is of the most interest: just over half of all the rum distilleries in the Caribbean and Latin America (disregarding Haiti's 500-or-so distilleries that produce the fellow sugarcane spirit clairin) use blackstrap as their base material. But the distilleries using molasses are, on the whole, much bigger than the French island's *agricole* operations, so molasses-based rums account for over 90% of all the rum made in the Caribbean and Latin America. As black as boot polish, it's a viscous sludge that smells of liquorice (licorice) and iron and looks like congealed blood.

During cane sugar refining, no part of the cane is wasted. Once the juice is pressed, the *bagasse* is burnt. One ton of dry *bagasse* is equivalent in energy value to two barrels of fuel oil, and the heat it produces is used to create steam energy, which powers mills and pumps. Since fresh *bagasse* still contains around 50% water, it's usually dried on patios before being burned.

CANE HONEY

Cane honey is concentrated juice of the sugarcane plant. It's produced during the evaporation stage of the sugar-refining process and takes on the appearance of a thick honey-like syrup and is around 75° Brix. Cane honey intended for rum is usually made in much the same way as it is in a sugar mill (see left), only the process ends before the vacuum-pan stage, thus preventing crystallization of the sugar. When the rum-maker wishes to use the cane honey to make rum, they dilute the syrup with water, back down to around 20° Brix before fermentation.

Cane honey rums differ from those made from cane juice, because many of the volatile organic compounds that are present in the juice are lost during the evaporation process. This typically results in a fermentation with fewer congeners (substances other than alcohol produced during fermentation), which means far less of the banana and vegetal madness present in *agricole*-style rums. In truth, cane honey rums are closer in style to molasses rums, but much of this depends on how conducive the fermentation and distillation processes are to retaining the character of the base material.

With the exception of St. Nicholas Abbey (see pages 74–77) in Barbados, the distilleries that use cane honey to make their rums are all in Latin America (Guatemala, Panama and the Dominican Republic). And all of them run quite short fermentations and produce high-strength column-still distillates, so almost any trace of the cane honey flavour is lost. But even if these were pot-still rums, I think it's questionable whether – after a few years' maturation – you could pick out a cane honey rum among a selection of other molasses-based rums.

Rum producers that use cane honey tend to promote the flavour benefits, but the use of cane honey over molasses really boils down to economics. Whether it's taxes, subsidies, the price of sugar, price of molasses, or the cost of the labour force, sometimes it just makes better business sense to turn sugar cane into rum rather than sugar and molasses rum. These distilleries could of course just make cane juice spirits (in the agricole style), but cane syrup has the benefit of being a stable product. One that can be tucked away in a safe place and fermented long after the harvesting season has ended.

LEFT Base materials for rum-making are available from this roadside seller in Grenada (if you can excuse their spelling).

USING CANE JUICE IN RUM

Rums that are made from sugar cane juice rather than molasses, are most commonly referred to as *rhum agricole*. This is a French term, which translates to "agricultural rum" or "farm rum". In the past, the term *rhum agricole* usually referred to a small, self-sufficient type of producer rather than to the material that they made their rum from. Indeed, sugar cane juice rums were known as *rhum de vessou*, and cane syrup and molasses rums known as *rhum de syrup* and *rhum de melasse*.

Just as today's "craft" distilleries are keen to remind us of their relatively small operations, *rhum agricole* also spoke of boutique production and cottage industry. Larger operations, which tended to be in urban areas, and usually purchased their base material from a third party, were known as *rhum industriel* distilleries (see pages 60–61).

Rhum agricole rums begin their lives with similar mechanical processing as in sugar refineries – this isn't surprising, since many of them are a tribute to an old sugar mill. Once the cane is cut, the clock starts ticking and the race is on to mill the plant as quickly as possible to ensure maximum sugar – and therefore alcohol – yield. The cane is pressed, typically through a series of roller mills linked together by conveyor belts. In some distilleries, water is added at the time of pressing, and in the most modern examples, the quantity of water is adjusted by a computer in order to reach the optimum level of sweetness in the pressed juice. Foam and scum from the pressing, along with any debris/dirt or pieces of cane fibre, are filtered out of the juice, which is then sent for fermentation.

Cane juice rums are not to everyone's tastes. For me, there's a far stronger link to the plant and field with *rhum agricole* over those made from molasses and that's down to the fact that there are fewer stages of human intervention in the manufacturing process.". Factors like cane variety, terroir and processing technique become highly relevant in this style, which opens up additional levels of distinction between similar products. As Dave Broom puts it in *Rum* (2003): "it's somehow appropriate that the French make rum in this fashion as, in many ways, it is one step closer to wine."

FERMENTATION

Fermentation is an essential stage of the rum-making process because it is here where all the alcohol is made! Through the action of millions of yeast cells, alcohol molecules are manufactured from the sugars present in molasses or sugarcane juice/syrup. But fermentation is also a crucial stage in the development of flavour in a rum – that is, if the rum you're making is to be flavourful. There are many factors at play during fermentation, some of them easier to control than others, but the key variables here are the type of yeast that is used and the length of the fermentation.

These days, most distilleries use a distiller's yeast to ferment their molasses or cane products. This will be a specific strain of the fast-acting yeast *Saccharomyces cerevisiae* – the same species that has been used by brewers and breadmakers since ancient times. The type of yeast used will not only affect the yield of alcohol, but can also control the rate and intensity of fermentation, and ultimately the complex flavourful congeners that are created. Distiller's yeasts offer the most efficient rate of conversion, but often do so at the cost of flavour. Some distilleries use proprietary yeast strains that aim to produce specific flavours during fermentation.

Yeast can be added to the fermenting vessel in one of two ways, either by tipping 20-kg (44-lb) bags of living culture in by hand, or by pumping liquid yeast in through pipes. Some more modern distilleries use yeast propagation tanks, which provide optimal conditions for yeast cell cultures to multiply before further sugars are added. Some more traditional rum distillers don't add

LEFT Cane mills such as these are common to all *agricole* distilleries. This one is at Damoiseau distillery on Guadeloupe.

a yeast culture at all, instead allowing natural airborne yeasts to let fermentation works its magic.

If the distillery is making rum from cane juice, it's a ready-made source of sugar and ready to be fermented straight out of the cane. In the case of molasses and cane juice, these products are too dense to be fermented as they are – which is also the reason why they constitute a "shelf-stable" product (i.e. one that can be stored safely at room temperature) – so they must be diluted with water first. A distillery may also add a yeast nutrient to the molasses, which helps to promote a healthy fermentation. This typically takes the form of ammonium sulphate, which helps to boost nitrogen levels and keep the yeast active.

When a yeast is exposed to a sugary environment in the tropics, it gets to work in less than an hour. Fermentation begins with the metabolic process called glycolysis, where yeast converts one glucose (sugar) molecule into two pyruvate molecules. Pyruvate is a form of "free energy" that can be used to create other energy-providing compounds, and this is exactly the same process that takes place in the human body to convert glucose into a usable energy currency.

Pyruvate features three carbon atoms. During the fermentation of bread, it is these atoms that combine with the yeast and oxygen to make carbon dioxide (CO_2). Voilà: your bread proves. In the case of fermenting sugary liquids, such as molasses and cane juice, the liquid doesn't have access to much oxygen – a layer of CO_2 sits on top of the brew, and oxygen can't penetrate down through the liquid. This lack of oxygen means that the process is described as "anaerobic". In this instance the pyruvate can't combine all its carbon with oxygen (to create CO_2), so it instead produces molecules of ethanol, methanol and other types of alcohol.

Heat can become problematic in the hot environments in which rum distilleries traditionally locate themselves, and if the temperature of the fermentation rises above 38°C (100°F), there is a chance that the yeast cells will die in a kind of hot soup of their own making. It's for this reason that some distilleries run liquid-cooling lines through their fermenters, to cool things down a little. In non-traditional rum-producing regions, the problem is flipped on its head, and sometimes it's necessary to warm the fermentation vessels gently to promote yeast culture growth and encourage fermentation.

It is the ethanol that gives the fermented liquid its alcoholic strength, but the other alcohols produced, along

RIGHT Fermentation tanks at La Favorite on the island of Martinique. Nitrogen and phosphate are sometimes added as nutrients for yeast, and the fermentation may also be acidified to prevent bacterial contamination.

with development of aldehydes and esters, are the true designators of flavour. The variety and quantity of these compounds is dictated by a whole number of factors that are not limited to the mineral content and pH of the cane juice or the syrup/molasses and any added water; the length and temperature of fermentation and the type of yeast used are also key factors.

Longer fermentation is the most significant of these factors, as highlighted by the 30-day "flavour-makers" (i.e. the month-long process of fermentation) that take place at distilleries like Hampden Estate (see pages 126–27) in Jamaica. These rums owe much of their flavour and aroma to complex organic compounds called esters, which are generated during longer fermentations when acids in the wash/wine react with alcohols. The acids themselves are created by the secondary fermentation of alcohols, and by the action of *lactobacillus* bacteria on residual sugars. Esters are also created by the organic reduction of aldehydes that are themselves created by the oxidation of alcohol. Low-molecular-weight esters are present in many natural fruits, herbs and flowers, and it's these compounds that give us the suggestion of fruitiness or floral aroma in rum. More esters are produced in longer fermentation (at the sacrifice of alcohol content) as the alcoholic wash/wine is given an extended opportunity to oxidize and reduce.

A lighter style of rum needs only a short fermentation (typically 18–48 hours, because the product is intended to be light in flavour). Heavier rums tend to be fermented for as much as five days – we'll explore distilleries' approaches to this in *The Rum Tour* chapter.

The final strength of the fermented wash/wine will vary according to many of the factors listed above, not least of all the sugar content (Brix) of the starting wort. In general though, wash/wine strength will sit somewhere between 5 and 8%, so something like a strong beer.

MUCK & DUNDER

Some Jamaican distilleries undergo a process known as "dundering" during fermentation, which is similar to that of sour-mashing in the Bourbon industry. However, with Bourbon it's a simple case of adding leftover acidic stillage (or *vinasse*) to the ferment, whereas with dunder there's a little more to it… and it isn't pretty.

A "dunder pit" is where this magic/horror takes place. In this pit, the waste stillage is mixed with cane vinegar, fresh molasses and water, and the whole horrific mess is aerated over a period of hours. The precise cocktail of ingredients is designed to create the perfect breeding ground for bacteria, and this oozing mass of infected goo is affectionately referred to as "muck". As the bacteria multiply, they produce a range of long-chain fatty (carboxylic) acids, each of which will come in handy during fermentation when they react with alcohol to create esters. The resulting aromas are funky beyond all measure, like defiled fruit. Aficionados of the style call it "hogo", which is derived from the French term *haut gout* (good flavour), a term that also lends itself to that most infamous affliction of the gourmand – gout.

There are many historical references to "muck holes" from the early 20th century, during a time when high-ester Jamaican rums were sought-after ingredients for culinary applications such as in candy production. The muck hole operates like a bioreactor with the aim of creating nice, complex carboxylic acids. The problem is that, if left unchecked, the muck becomes overly acidic, resulting in the production of ammonia, before finally stalling. This is managed by adding the alkaline lime marl (crumbly sedimentary rock comprising limestone and

clay), which keeps the pH in check and helps create acid crystals/salts which could be drawn off as fresh stillage was added. Cane vinegar is added because it's made from acetic acid. This is good from a flavour standpoint as – being the shortest chain acid – it readily bonds with lime marl to form salt crystals. Acetic acid trades places with longer-chain acids, and allows them to partake in the creation of more interesting aroma-giving esters.

POT DISTILLATION

Pot stills are the simplest and oldest form of distillation. They work like large kettles: an alcoholic wash/wine is heated, the vapours are channelled up to the top (neck) of the still and then into the condenser where they are converted back into a liquid. Pot stills are usually made from copper, which is used because of its high thermal conductivity, malleability and catalytic properties.

Distillation in pots is quite inefficient, however, and distillation runs are often repeated in a batch process to increase alcohol strength. Logic would suggest that any alcoholic liquid that is heated should produce a vapour of 100% pure alcohol, but some water inevitably finds itself into each distillation because water vapour and steam are generated even at very low temperatures.

In a traditional pot still, the first distillation only produces a "spirit" of around 25–30% alcohol by volume (ABV). The second distillation results in a liquid of typically 65–75% ABV – sufficient in strength to be called a spirit. It's possible to distil this spirit a third time – although I know of no rums that do so – but there is little advantage in doing this, as the crudeness of the process limits the potential concentration of alcohol.

It's not just alcohol that carries through in pot distillation. As the wash/wine is heated from the bottom, the system generates upward pressure that forces alcohol and water precipitates, as well as volatile aromatic molecules (but not colour) up through the neck of the still, along the lyne arm and down into the condenser. Taller stills produce a lighter style of spirit, because they make it harder for heavier compounds to make the journey uphill. Short stills encourage the transfer of heavier compounds into the condenser, making a rum style with greater depth and lingering flavour.

Tall stills give a spirit more interaction time (and space) with copper. Copper has a purifying effect on a distilled spirit, and a greater degree of interaction removes

LEFT A beguiling if not just downright confusing, dunder chart at Hampden Estate. I hope it makes more sense to them than it does to me.

sulphurous flavours and heightens the cultivation of delicate fruit and floral aromatics. This is especially so in small stills, since there is a greater surface area of copper in relation to the volume of liquid. Of course, the effects of size vary based on how much liquid is put in the still too. The shape of the still also has a part to play, with the different forms encouraging a varying degree of reflux in the system. A short still can produce spirit that is reminiscent of a tall still by bulging out and pinching in at certain stages up the neck of the still.

Modern stills are powered by steam coils or steam jackets, but older examples can be directly fired by an oil or gas flame or by burning wood or *bagasse*. Direct firing is thought to produce a spirit heavier in character, as hot spots on the inside of the still burn the wash/wine (and especially any insoluble matter contained in it) causing complex caramelizations, Maillard reactions, charring of solid matter and the production of furfural (an oily liquid with an almond-like aroma) and sulphur compounds that may carry through into the final product.

Whatever the style of rum, it's always necessary to "cut" the freshly distilled spirit during the second distillation to remove dangerous and unpleasant smelling compounds. The first cut is known as the "heads" and contains higher alcohols and ketones, which besides being toxic also give the spirit the aroma of glue or turpentine. The heads typically represent the first 5% of a complete run, and after collection they are sometimes redistilled in the next batch to liberate any remaining ethanol. Next the main body of the spirit (known as the "heart") begins to flow from the condenser – this is effectively high-strength white rum. Finally, towards the end of the run, it's necessary to make a second cut, as the "tails" begin to come through. These comprise heavier, oily alcohols that can give a spirit a rough and unclean flavour, as well as making it cloudy in appearance. Again, some distilleries will redistill a portion of the tails too.

The exact cut of the "heart" differs according to the distiller's preference, with every subsequent litre of distillate highlighting specific characteristics generated during fermentation – from light florals, to citrus freshness, down to vibrant berries and rich, dark fruits.

RETORT IS THE ANSWER

In the world of rum, pot stills rarely operate in isolation. Most have a pair of "retorts" connected between the lyne arm and the condenser. A retort is like an additional, smaller pot that conducts a further distillation

ABOVE AND RIGHT Pot-stills – like those at Mount Gay (above) and St. Lucia Distillers (right) – are the backbone of the world's best blended rums.

of the spirit vapour, increasing the strength and removing the need to run a second "batch" distillation.

The pot is filled with alcoholic wash/wine as normal, which is heated until the vapour (of around 30% ABV) is carried over into the first retort. Here it is met by "low wines" from the previous distillation, which mix with the vapour and boil, doubling the spirit vapour strength up to roughly 60% ABV This vapour carries over into the next retort, which contains the "high wines" from the previous distillation. The spirit vapour once again increases in strength, this time up to 88% ABV, and then passes into the condenser. The liquid that flows off is then cut four ways: heads, heart (rum), high wines and low wines, where the latter two are recycled back into the retorts ready for the next distillation.

FAR LEFT A collection of steel and copper columns of different lengths and widths at the La Mauny distillery in Martinique.

LEFT The wider the column, the higher the potential throughput. The more plates the column has, the greater the purity of spirit.

COLUMN DISTILLATION

The important distinction to make between pot stills and column stills is the concept of a "batch" process. In pot distillation, the efficiency of the distillation and the character of the resulting liquid is orchestrated by duration of the distillation and the timing of the cuts – it is an artisanal process requiring both technical training and an understanding of the organoleptic properties of the spirit. A column still is different. It's a continuous process that need never end so long as there is a good supply of alcoholic liquid fed into the system, and it's for this reason that the column still is sometimes referred to as a "continuous still". But there is a common misconception that all column stills are the same, and that they all produce the same, largely neutral, industrial spirit. This is an unfair assessment, however. Generally speaking, the more columns in a continuous still setup, the purer – or to put it another way, "neutral" – the resulting spirit becomes.

Column stills seem like quite modern innovations, but they have been around since the 1830s and early versions were being developed 200 years before then. One of the first continuous stills was invented by Frenchman Edouard Adam, who attended chemistry lectures under Professor Laurent Solimani at the University of Montpellier. Amazingly, Adam was illiterate, but despite that apparently minor setback, he developed and patented the first type of column still in 1804. Unrecognizable from the stills you can see on page 49, Adam's column was a horizontal arrangement that linked together a series of "large eggs", with pipes that routed alcohol vapour from one egg to the next. The strength of the spirit increased in each subsequent egg, whilst the leftover stuff was recycled back at the start again.

The Pistorius still, which was patented in 1817, was the first still to be arranged in a column shape. Steam was pumped up from the bottom and beer from the top and distillation took place on a series of perforated "plates" arranged through the length of the column. This design worked best because it allowed for a smooth graduation of temperature change from higher at the bottom to lower at the top. Since ethyl alcohol boiled at exactly 78.3°C (172.9°F), in theory you could fraction spirit vapour off the column at a height that corresponded to that temperature and capture a very high-strength spirit, leaving most of the (undesirable) residual flavour behind.

Subsequent iterations were developed in France and Scotland, and by 1830 the final design had been settled upon, fully realized in a design patented by the Inspector General of Excise in Ireland, Aeneas Coffey. The "Coffey Still" or "Patent Still" was a truly continuous process, where fermented beer (or wine) was pumped in and high-strength alcohol drawn off. It was even quite energy-efficient for its time, using the cool pipes that fed beer into the system as condensing coils for the hot alcohol vapours exiting it – like a dog eating its own tail.

In Coffey's design, two columns are at work, with both of them separated into chambers by a series of perforated plates. Starting in the rectifying column, the wash/wine is carried down through a coiled pipe and heated as it goes. The wash/wine is then pumped up to the top of the analyzer column, where it is sprayed on to the top plate, and falls through the holes, gradually making its way to the bottom. At the bottom of the analyser, steam is pumped into the system, which rises up to meet the falling wash/wine. This has the effect of stripping the alcohol from the wash/wine, which then rises back up the analyzer; it is then pumped out (owing to the pressure) before travelling down to the base of the rectifier. Once there, it continues to evaporate upwards, with each plate acting like a single distillation run. As it nears the top, it begins to cool, because only the lightest part of the vapour can continue upwards. Once it reaches the collecting plate (which is set by the distiller) the spirit is allowed to flow out, fully concentrated and up to 95% pure alcohol.

The number of plates in the two columns dictates the final strength of the spirit: fewer plates produce a more characterful, less refined liquid. More plates, more columns, and taller columns result in a purer style of distillate, but it also means a greater degree of flexibility in the style of distillate that is produced, as different combinations of columns are connected or removed from the sequence. Most Latin American distilleries operate entirely with columns, often producing different weights of marque that can be used in a final blend.

HYBRID STILLS

Although hybrid stills seem like relatively new innovations, they have their origins in much older distilleries. Some of the first column stills on Puerto Rico and Cuba were in fact hybrids – pot stills with columns mounted on top. These days, a hybrid still usually looks like a pot still with a column connected on the side. By opening and closing the plates on the column, the distiller can select how heavy or light the rum comes off the still. Examples

of modern hybrid stills can be found at St. Nicholas Abbey (see pages 74–77) on Barbados and at Cayman Spirits Co. (see page 83) on Grand Cayman.

MATURATION

Ask someone to picture "rum" in their head, and it's quite likely they will think of an oak barrel. Barrels or casks are linked to rum's history, just as they are to its flavour. Since its earliest conception in the 17th century, rum has been shifted around in barrels, from island to mainland, from sugar mill to port, from distillery to blender. Before the dawn of of the forklift truck and pallet, the oak barrel was the trustiest of vessels to store your goods. It's been around since Roman times, and for some 2,000 years it has been the go-to method of transportation for pretty much everything – be it fish, nails, coins, booze, or dead admirals (in the case of Admiral Horatio Nelson): the unique shape of a wooden barrel – that pinches inwardly at both ends – makes it surprisingly easy for a single person to move hundreds of kilograms of cargo around by themselves. Barrels are watertight, relatively cheap to "raise", highly durable (some last over a century before being decommissioned) and easy to store. The unique nature of wood as a storage material also means that air and vapours can move freely in and out of the cask, while the liquid stays safe inside. This is a key element of the maturation process. Best of all, though – they can turn fiery white rum into a spirit of nuance and distinction.

LEFT Hybrid German stills are very popular with gin distillers, and we're starting to see them used to make rum too.

BELOW Fermented molasses bubbling through one of the plates on the column still at Antigua Distillers.

TYPES OF OAK

To better understand how oak affects a white rum, we must get to grips with the material itself.

Most of the barrels in the spirits industry are made in the US and intended for the production of Bourbon whiskey, or constructed in Spain and France, where they are used to age sherry, wines, and brandy. The rest of the spirits-producing world (including rum, Scotch, and Tequila) purchases second-hand barrels from these producers in the US, Spain and France in order to age their products. This system of *build, use, sell, use*, is born out the economics of availability and the trading patterns that were established centuries ago. But the use of new barrels in the Bourbon and Cognac industries has in turn defined the style of those spirits, with their up-front, concentrated, oak characteristics.

Bourbon casks make up the vast majority of the barrels used by the rum industry and are made from a variety of oak known as "white oak" (*Quercus alba*). This type of oak has a paler-coloured bark than other varieties, although the colour of the cut wood is indistinguishable from any other. White oak is a fast-growing variety, rising straight and true and reaching maturation in only 60–80 years. The result is wood influence that we commonly associate with rum: plenty of vanilla and other associated "white" things, such as banana, white chocolate, buttermilk and custard.

White oak casks are built in the US, filled with Bourbon, emptied and then sold to rum makers. US law prohibits the refilling of these casks, so Bourbon producers are legally obliged to move them on to other industries. Second-hand goods they may be, but having been stripped of some of their flavour, they are less aggressive in their delivery of wood characteristics and easier to control than new casks – think of it like a tea bag that, after brewing a cup, still has plenty of flavour to give to a second, third, or even fourth cup… if left to brew for long enough.

European oak casks are generally used and sold in much the same way as Bourbon casks are: filled one or more times, then sold on to other industries. European oak casks can be made from white oak or red oak (*Quercus robur*) which is a slower growing tree, that twists and turns and only reaches maturation after 150 years. The resulting spirit tends to be more tannic (a trait of the slow growth), peppery and spicy with, rather fittingly, flavours of red-coloured things like dried plums, grapes, cloves and red wine. The wine or brandy that previously filled the cask will have stripped some of the flavour out (just as Bourbon does) but the cask still has plenty left to give, as well as some residual flavours from the wine (or spirit) that it previously contained. Ex-wine and sherry casks are prized by the Scotch whisky industry, but have made little headway into the rum world. Distillers such as Foursquare (see pages 68–71) in Barbados, Brugal (see pages 94–95) in the Dominican Republic and St Lucia Distillers (see pages 159–61) in St Lucia are among the pioneers of these new premium offerings – more to come in the future, I hope.

In the French-speaking islands of the Caribbean, it's quite common to encounter French oak casks, made from *Quercus sessliflora* that grows in the Limousin Forest. These have often passed through the Cognac industry first, but in certain distilleries, like Barbancourt in Haiti (see pages 117–18), it's the new cask that's used. These casks offer up zestiness, spice and plenty of grippy tannin.

BELOW LEFT Although any type of barrel can be used to age rum, the most common varieties are French and American oak.

BELOW Depending on how they'll be stored, some barrels are filled from the top – others through a bung hole on the side.

New American oak casks are rare to find in rum distilleries, although some producers are experimenting with them on a small scale, curious to find out what a new-oak cask can contribute to a rum blend.

Whatever the type of oak, the barrel will be charred (in Bourbon barrel production) or toasted (in European oak barrel production) at the time of its construction, and possibly again, later in its life. The origins of this practice are not entirely clear, but some historians suggest that it was a means of removing the taint of the product that the barrel previously held (fish, for example) before filling it with wine or spirit. Bourbon's alleged inventor, Reverend Elijah Craig, is sometimes credited as the originator of the practice. That's also an alleged claim.

Charring is an all-out flamethrower assault in the interior surfaces of the barrel, as ruthless licks of heat blast the wood for 30–60 seconds, causing the surface to bubble and writhe as it catches fire. When a cask is toasted, the heat is applied more gently, sometimes through convection rather than direct flame, and over a longer period of time – up to and around 6 minutes. Think of it like frying versus baking. Baking the barrels like this results in the degradation of wood polymers into flavoursome compounds, the destruction of unpleasant resinous compounds in the wood, and in the case of charring, the forming of a thin layer of active carbon. The two different approaches also play to the flavour palates of the associated spirit industries.

THE MATURATION MECHANISM

Ageing rum is not as simple as "the longer you leave it the more woody it gets", and certainly not as simple as "the older the rum the better it tastes". An age statement on a bottle can be useful, but it only really becomes relevant if the other variables are made aware to us: the type and condition of wood, age of the cask, how many times it has been filled and various environmental factors.

Newer casks will give a rum more flavour, and it's for this reason that you may encounter an amber-coloured 3-year-old next to a straw-coloured 10-year-old (using the same teabag three or four times will produce similar results). That's not to say that refill casks are worthless, in fact it's sometimes a more pleasantly subdued and considered flavour that we find from these older barrels.

ABOVE Deciphering the complex nature of spirits maturation is a skill that took decades to master.

Much of what goes on in the perpetual twilight of a warehouse, however, is unpredictable without the analysis of every stave of wood that makes up every cask and every drop of liquid that goes into it. The changes that take effect in the murky realms of the vessel are, even today, still being scrutinized and tested to better understand the effects of the barrel and the optimum maturation conditions.

We're not completely in the dark though. Oak itself contains over 100 volatile components capable of contributing flavour in a rum. Additionally there are other compounds formed through the oxidation of wood extracts and compounds already present in the freshly made spirit. It's these factors that broadly affect the flavour of an aged spirit.

Looking at this in more detail, there are four components of oak structure that contribute flavour to rum: lignin, hemicellulose, extractives and oak tannins. Once charred or toasted, the lignin in the oak contributes to flavours of toast, coffee, vanilla and then caramel, chocolate, toffee and cream. Hemicellulose is the breeze block of oak's secondary cell walls. It is thought to react with complex acids in the spirit, causing simple un-sweet wood sugars (around 200 different types) to be extracted that provide body and "smoothness" to the liquid. Extractives are free-running solubles that get washed out by the rum. They include a whole host of flavour compounds that can provide grassy, baked, wood-sap, peachy, floral and even greasy aromas. Wood tannin gives the familiar drying sensation on the palate, and when managed correctly, balance and grip to an otherwise flabby spirit. Tannins also impart colour and astringent flavour, at least in the early phase of maturation, and take part in various oxidative reactions removing sulphury off-notes and promoting colour stability, lignin breakdown and oxidation of alcohol into acetals, producing ethereal top-notes.

Last, but certainly not least, is the chemical degradation of the liquid through oxidation. Besides ethanol, there are numerous other trace alcohols present in rum, each with its own weight and flavour and each capable of being turned into aldehydes and acids. For example, the oxidation of the ethanol (alcohol) in the cask forms acetaldehyde and acetic acid. Aldehydes play an important role in rum aroma, like benzaldehyde (oxidized benzyl alcohol), which smells like almond.

Acetic acid, along with other oxoacids are crucial for the formation of esters. Esters provide all of the fruity and floral top notes in rum aroma, everything from geranium or jasmine right through to apple, sage, pineapple and strawberry.

ABOVE These vertically-oriented barrels at Brugal in the Dominican Republic are typically aged for 1–3 years.

CLIMATIC CONSIDERATIONS

Climate affects rum at virtually every stage of production, from the cane to fast ferments and accelerated maturation.

Casks are organic containers, each one like a wooden lung that "breathes" in its immediate environment through the course of the day. Alcohol and water are in a constant state of evaporation, and they both move out of the cask, making way for the incoming air. The hotter the climate and the greater the variance between day and night, the faster this process occurs. Over time, the volume of the cask depreciates and the liquid dissipates, and in the tropics this occurs at a rate of 5% to 10% of the total contents of the barrel every year. In particularly hot climates, like Venezuela and Guyana, a distillery might expect to lose half of the barrel in the space of five years.

On some French-speaking islands, *rhum agricole* producers "top-up" casks with similar-aged rum as the level in the barrel drops. This physical intervention in the maturation process is known as élevage ("breeding"). It's a canny way of reducing the number of casks that the distillery needs to store, but it also reduces the angel's share and affects the flavour of the future rum by minimizing oxidative reactions.

I have heard it said that spirits aged in the tropics mature five or ten times faster (depending on who you speak to) than in the chilly climes of the whisky or Cognac industries. But I think that statements like these can be a little misleading and are founded upon unscientific principles. Certainly, the interactive effect of the oak is accelerated, as the contraction and expansion of the cask is amplified by hot days and cool nights. This is why the spirit colours so quickly, as tannins are quickly drawn out of the cask. Evaporative losses are much higher in the Caribbean, so the spirit concentrates much faster, and this also has the apparent effect of speeding up maturation. The increased headspace in the cask (as the liquid evaporates) also increases the rate of oxidation, because when the cask empties, the area of exposed liquid increases until the cask is half full. But the increase in surface area alone is enough for a five-fold increase in oxidative degradation.

So in some respects the maturation is accelerated significantly, and in others it is but a slight change. The point is, that a rum matured for five years in the Caribbean and a rum matured for 15 years in France, will not taste the same. Climactic considerations have too great an influence here for us to be able compare one age statement to another, even if the starting liquid and cask are identical. The fact that even subtle shifts in temperature, air pressure and humidity can affect rum quite dramatically is certainly something to be celebrated, and comes as no surprise for a product born out of such humble origins as cane and wood.

SOLERA AGEING

The process of solera ageing has its origins in the production of sherry, so it's not surprising that it should find its home in some of the Spanish-speaking distilleries in the West Indies, and it's brands like Santa Teresa (see pages 188–89) and Zacapa (see pages 172–73) that have found the most fame in this particular field.

A solera traditionally comprises three or four horizontal "layers" of casks, which are all filled with rums of the same average age. Rum for bottling is vatted from liquid drawn from the casks on the bottom layer, nearest the ground ("suelo" means "ground" in Spanish, which is where the term "solera" is taken from) but these casks are never completely emptied. The bottom layer is then topped up with rum from the second layer, which is topped up from the next layer, and so on. The top layer is topped up with other aged stocks from outside of the system, or with white rum.

Solera is a system of both maturation and blending that maintains consistency and balances old with new and the rum drawn from the solera system will contain some small percentage of rum that is as old as the system itself. Well, that's how the system is supposed to work, anyway.

In reality, it isn't always practical to store barrels in layers on top of one another. The "layers" may constitute entire warehouses, where the rum is vatted in between each step. With some distilleries, the term "solera" has only vague similarities to the sherry-making process, such as with Ron Zacapa's incredibly convoluted *sistema solera*, which mixes static ageing, the French practice of élevage (see page 54) and some elements of Spanish solera all into one system.

BLENDING

Blending is nigh-on impossible to avoid in the world of rum. Almost all rums are blended in some shape or form: a blending of casks, ages, distillates or distilleries. Blending balances flavour, defines a product's style, and hedges bets, like an insurance policy against the possibility of certain rums becoming unavailable, if you will. It also stretches volumes, lengthening flavoursome

RIGHT Diversifying the flavour of rum stocks is the best way for a master blender to compose a balanced product.

heavy rum with lighter-style spirit. Imagine a finished bottle of rum like a piece of music, where all of the component parts form a harmonious balance of flavour. Sometimes it's nice to experience an unblended rum – a solo piece – but for the most part we are looking for balance and synergy. In this analogy, different styles of rum are representative of different musical instruments – from the bass notes of Demerara or Jamaica, to the high-pitched treble of column-still Spanish rums. Orchestrating these separate components into a finished composition – whether from the same distillery or not – is where the artistry of the blender comes into play.

Further difficulty arises when re-creating that composition time and time again. In an orchestra you would find the best musicians of their time to play the piece, but as any concert-goer knows, there will always be subtle changes to the arrangement in each subsequent portrayal. The blender (or conductor) has similar challenges in the form of changes in distillery character and – if the rum is aged – price and availability of casks.

Practically speaking, the master blender will nose and taste cask samples, then compose a blend based on his or her findings. The distillery staff will then be tasked with dumping the liquid from all the relevant casks and mixing the liquid together in stainless steel tanks or occasionally large wooden vats.

FILTERING

All rum undergoes some degree of filtration, through steel, cellulose or nylon mesh, to remove particles attracted during the distillation process, or from time spent in cask.

Some rums are also chill-filtered. This process is the same as any other mechanical filtration method, except the spirit is chilled to approximately 0°C (32°F) (and sometimes much lower) prior to filtration. The chilling

is necessary to draw certain fatty-acids and long-chain esters out of solution, which would turn the liquid cloudy if it is subjected to particularly cold (sub-zero) storage conditions, or if served over ice or from the freezer. While this is thought to only subtly change the flavour of the spirit, it would appear to be an acceptable compromise for a brand that doesn't wish to have their liquid turn cloudy on store shelves. Not everyone agrees that chill-filtering has a positive impact on quality, however. Some rum producers are beginning to follow the lead of the Scotch whisky industry and labelling their product as non-chill filtered – their belief being that process diminishes mouthfeel and removes precious flavour-giving components from the rum.

Cloudiness can also be a sign of a potentially dangerous product, but assuming you are assured of the provenance of the bottles, it's nothing to worry about.

Some rums, especially those of Spanish origin, may be filtered through charcoal prior to blending and bottling. This process is intended to soften flavour, but also to remove colour. Bacardí Carta Blanca is perhaps the best example of such a rum, as this spirit is matured for around two years, yet in the bottle it is crystal clear. The process also irons out discrepancies in colour, in some respects achieving the same effect as adding distiller's caramel but by removing colour instead.

Activated charcoal is a type of carbon that has been treated with oxygen. These lightweight black granules are unique and unrivalled in their surface area-to-mass ratio – a single gram can have a surface area in excess of 500 square meters! The more surface, the better the chance that large impure molecules adsorb onto the mass of the charcoal; activated charcoal can adsorb up to 20 times its weight. This can be a good or bad thing, since charcoal is not great at discriminating between "bad" and "good" flavour molecules. Either way, it's been used in spirits production for over two centuries, and is especially important for vodka, where flavour-free is often the goal.

SWEETENING

Although rum is inextricably linked with sugar, and many rums do indeed smell of "sweet" things (honey, toffee, treacle, etc.), rum will never taste truly sweet unless it has been sweetened before bottling. Virtually all of the sugars provided by molasses or cane juice are converted into alcohol during fermentation, and any residual sugars that are left behind do not carry over during distillation. And it's because of this fact that rum bottled fresh from the still will have no sugar in it whatsoever. Even barrels, with all their associated caramels and vanilla contribute only trace quantities of actual sugar.

With that in mind, it may be surprising to learn that at least half of the rums in this book do contain sugar and therefore have been sweetened. This goes for white rums as well as darker expressions, although it is in the latter that we tend to find the most liberal use of sweetener. This is nothing new – sugar has been added to rum for centuries – which is hardly surprising given the availability of the stuff in and around rum distilleries. Sweetening rum has the effect of softening alcohol burn and highlighting selected characteristics, as well as thickening the texture and the apparent concentration of the liquor. And it's for this reason – to make the rum more approachable – that sweetening has become an industry-wide practice. The problem is, some rums are so sweet that they are in danger of approaching a liqueur level of sweetness, and in my opinion, too much sugar can also muddy flavour and flatten nuance.

Most distillers that admit to adding sugar claim to do so because they are trying to iron out discrepancies in flavour from batch to batch. In other words: to ensure consistency. I'm fine with this – it's something that's practised in other spirit categories besides rum, most notably in the Cognac business, which refers to the sweetening of their liquids with the innocent sounding term "dosage". With Cognac, the legal limit is 2 g of sugar per litre of spirit – a barely detectable quantity.

But what is more frustrating than the act of sweetening itself, is the reluctance of distilleries to own up to it. "Do you add sugar?" is a question I often ask when touring distilleries, and it's often followed by a period of

LEFT Testing the organoleptic properties of some cask samples in the lab at St. Lucia Distillers.

awkward silence. The producers that do add only a little (less than 5 g/litre) are usually quite honest about doing so. Conversely, it's the rums that are noticeably sweet (I'm looking at you, Central America and Guyana) that are keeping tight-lipped. Transparency has never been more sought-after in food and drink than it is today, both for the health conscious seeking assurances and for those interested in provenance and the integrity of manufacturing.

In 2014 the government-owned Swedish liquor store chain Systembolaget, and Alko, a similar chain of stores in Finland, ran a series of tests on a range of over 30 popular rum brands. The products were mostly from Spanish-speaking islands in the Caribbean, and Central and South American countries. Their results were, for the most part, quite consistent, and both studies made for a rather disturbing read. At the lower end of the scale, the younger island rums, such as Havana Club, Brugal and Bacardi, contained around 3 g sugar per litre of spirit. At the higher end there were some rums, like Ron Zacapa 23, Diplomatico Reserva Exclusiva, and Rhum Quorhum Solera 23 that each contained over 40 g sugar per litre of spirit. These figures are difficult to discredit, since testing was rigorous and conducted by two independent bodies.

Some of these producers still insist that the sugar in their rum comes from the barrel or from some proprietary production technique, relating to still shape or fermentation procedure.

The issue lies in the fact that adding sugar to rum, just like adding colour, is unregulated. Producers can choose to sweeten as they wish, and it's consumers that will make the final decision with their wallets on whether the rum is enjoyable or not. I personally think that some sweet rums are really rather delicious, but that certainly doesn't mean that good rum has to be sweetened aggressively, or that an amazing rum need have any sugar adding to it at all.

It's unlikely we will see an end to sugaring in rum, and I'm not sure that it needs to stop. What would be nice though, is some transparency on the matter. Labelling that clearly defines how much sugar has been added to the rum. With that information we can better understand why we like certain rums, and how we assign value to that.

COLOURING

Colouring is common among virtually all of the aged (and some of the un-aged) rums in this book. In fact, it's common among almost all spirits, as a means of standardizing the appearance of bottles on the liquor store shelf, and suggesting a little more time in oak than the natural spirit's colour might communicate.

This is achieved using distiller's caramel (E150a), which is obtained through the heating and caramelization of carbohydrates (sugar). So, it is in fact, just caramel. E150a has no sweetness to it however, since the process is carefully controlled so as to caramelize all of the available sugars, resulting in a very thick, black syrup. By itself the flavour is bitter, if anything, and a little goes a very long way. A pinprick of caramel is enough to muddy a sink-full of water.

Judging the rum by its colour is futile at the best of times, but once the element of colouring is introduced, the relationship between the colour of the liquid, its time spent in oak and the flavour one might expect of the liquid, is misleading to say the least. In fact, it's designed to fool you. The practice of adding colour to suggest long years in casks is one of the longstanding hallmarks of the Black Rum style. The irony being that, while these rums may appear to be long in years, they are generally a blend of either very young or even un-aged spirits. Mutton dressed as lamb, you might say.

Think about it enough (as I have) and it eventually leads one to question whether the colouring of rum really matters at all. Scientific studies on this subject suggest that the associated flavours of oak are perceptible in both spirits that are aged in oak and those that only appear to have been. It's a great example of how the colour of a drink can have profound influences on our perception of its flavour: "eye appeal is half the meal", so the saying goes. Take a nose on a glass of Navy rum and it's difficult to stifle similarly coloured flavour descriptors like "oak", "toffee", "molasses", "coffee" and "spice". The same rum without any adulteration of colour would not attract the same vocabulary. Ignorance is bliss. At the end of the day we are only fooling ourselves though, and blenders have been perfecting this art for at least two centuries.

RUM CLASSIFICATION

The single greatest challenge that rum faces in the 21st century is how it should be labelled. Whisky has its single malts and blends, brandy has age designations by VS, VSOP and XO. Even that most abused of spirits, Tequila, has strict classification terms that make it a relatively easy category to navigate around. Rum has never had an effective system of classification, and it's certainly about time it did.

The problem stems from the fact that there are no universal regulations concerning how rum should be labelled. Rum is made across five continents and in as many as 50 countries, many of which have their own regulations and rules regarding how the liquid is produced and how long it is aged for. Getting them all to agree on an overarching labelling policy is simply not going to happen.

So we make up our own rules around classification, as a means of communicating rum style and finding some orderliness amongst all the confusion.

In the past, many of us have communicated rum style in colours: white, light, silver, blanca, gold, oro, dark etc. But basing flavour on colour alone is an ill-defined and often misleading way of communicating rum flavour. Many budget "gold" or "dark" rums are in fact un-aged or very young rums that get much of their colour from caramel colouring, while some rums that are aged in barrels are filtered to remove their colour. These production elements are poorly legislated at best, and open to blatant abuse at worst, so they skew the whole system, creating broader misunderstanding of rum in general, which in turn makes it a difficult category of spirits to engage with.

More recently, we have found a better way of breaking down rum style, which is by classifying it according to the island or region that originated the style: Jamaican (pot-still heavy rum), Barbados (a blend of column and pot), Cuban/Spanish (column-still), French (made from cane juice rather than molasses) and so on.

Obviously there are producers that don't sit geographically in any of these regions, but it's likely that the rum they make has taken a lead from one of these styles. This is a system that works alright, but it requires that the drinker has some knowledge of the traditional practices of each region. It also assumes that the rum in question adheres to the expected style of its region. But this often isn't the case. Take Dominica for example, the island's only remaining rum distillery makes rum according to the French standard and yet it is a former British colony. And what about the US, with its hundreds of craft distilleries that produce a whole range of styles. Finally, and perhaps worst of all, it shoves a great number of proudly independent Caribbean and Central American nations under the title of their (generally) former colonial administrator, which is more than a little disrespectful, in my view!

I am of course not the first to recognize this need for new classification, and quite recently there have been great steps towards establishing a global standard for rum categorization. The aim of a new system is simple: build a framework of rum classification that clearly informs the consumer how the product has been made and what it is likely to taste like. With the information clear on every bottle (or from the mouth of every bartender), the consumer will then have everything they need to place a value on the product.

One such system has been developed by two of the biggest names in the rum industry: Luca Gargano of the Italian rum bottler Velier, and Richard Seale of Foursquare distillery (see pages 68–71) in Barbados. Their system goes something like this:

Single Pot-Still Rum – A pot-still rum that is the product of a single distillery

Single Column-Still Rum – A single column-still rum that is the product of a single distillery

Single Blended Rum – A blend of pot- and column-still rum that are both the products of a single distillery

Blended Rum – A rum containing pot-still rum that is the product of more than one distillery

Rum – A multi-column distilled rum that contains no pot-still rum

This is a classification system that places a great deal of emphasis on the distillation process and whether the rum is a product of a single distillery or not, and follows closely to the Scotch whisky model. The main intention is to highlight the different approaches to making rum these days: in a traditional distillery (with a pot-still) and in a modern ethanol plant (with multi-column stills). This is important information for consumers, because it highlights the value of rums that are produced in the more traditional, more costly, manner. On the other hand, it fails to effectively communicate flavour. There is no mention of base material, country of origin, maturation or fermentation.

For this book, I have devised my own classification system, that is built upon the above system and the system detailed in Martin Cate's excellent *Smuggler's Cove* cocktail book. This system is not as exacting as Seale and Gargano's in its treatment of rums that are the product of a single distillery vs. rums blended from various sources. It also makes no distinction between single-column (Coffey) distillation and multi-column distillation. While I recognize that the two methods can and do make different styles of rum, I also believe that a good system also needs to be a simple system.

All the rums in this book can be categorized based on three key criteria:

• How long (if at all) the rum has been aged

• What base material the rum is made from

• How the rum has been distilled and/or blended;

The first of these is the age of the rum. Classifying rum by the time it has spent in barrels is quite often misleading. This is because not all producers adhere to the EU and US rules of stating the age of the youngest rum in the bottle, and regulating this is a difficult if not impossible task to undertake. There are also rums in this book that are matured for only a few years, but thanks to the addition of sugar, colourings and other flavourings (see pages 56–58), simulate the characteristics of an older rum. I have debated these practices in other sections of the book, but for the sake of classifying flavour, we are forced to lump them in with rums that are genuinely old, as they taste pretty damn similar. With that in mind, we will be using four different descriptors to communicate maturation: **un-aged**; **aged white**; **aged**; and **extra-aged.**

The second section of the classification concerns the raw material that the rum is made from. Rums made from cane juice (also known as *agricole*) have a different spectrum of flavour and aroma from those made from molasses or cane syrup (cane honey). In this book, we will single out rums that are produced from the fermentation of cane juice, by placing "**Cane Juice**" at the start of the rum's category identifier. I think that it's very difficult to distinguish between cane syrup and molasses as a base material in a finished product, and a category system with "molasses" or "syrup" in front of every title is too clunky. So these two will be lumped in together and identified by the fact that they do not stipulate "Cane Juice" as their base material.

Distillation is the hardest of the three classification components to communicate, partly because of the diverse range of rum production techniques out there and the blending that follows. But also because these pieces of machinery don't communicate flavour effectively for the average consumer. Too much detail and the system becomes baffling and ineffective, but too little detail and major deviations may get missed and there will be too little information to form an accurate assessment of the product.

This system will make three separate distinctions for distillation: **column-still** (but rather than explicitly state that a rum is made in a column-still, we will simply refer to these spirits as "rum"); **pot-still**; and **blended** (being a blend of pot and column-still rums). The most important distinction here is the pot still, which produces a very different type of liquid when compared to the column. Naturally, a blend of both will offer something, somewhere in-between.

In practice, our system now offers a complete solution for describing any of the thousands of rums that are out there, produced by hundreds of distilleries, across dozens of unique territories. Whether it's an "Extra-Aged Rum" from Nicaragua, an "Aged-White Blended Rum" from St Lucia, an "Aged Pot-Still Rum" from Jamaica, or an "Un-aged Cane Juice Rum" from Martinique.

BLACK RUM/NAVY STRENGTH/OVERPROOF

Here are three additional classifications of British origin that, although capable of fitting into the above system, are better singled out, as they are more heavily stylized by their strength or the liberal use of colourings than they are by base product, distillation or maturation.

Black Rum is a style of lightly aged or un-aged rum that has been heavily coloured to simulate what might have once been a long-in-barrel style consumed aboard ships. They are typically coloured with caramel or molasses to recreate the effect. This produces a unique rum format, that is both hot and light, yet appearing dense and rich. It's very important to draw a distinction between these rums and extra-aged examples that may have a similar hue, but taste rather different. Some good examples of this style are Gosling's Black Seal, Captain Morgan Original, and Lamb's. The point is, they are still young rums, but their darker appearance has a peculiar effect on our sense of flavour perception, being simultaneously "old" tasting and light.

Navy Strength is an extension of the Black Rum style, and refers to rums that have been coloured and that are stronger than 50% ABV. Traditionally these rums would have been at least 57% ABV, which is equivalent to the imperial measurement of 100% proof (see page 25). Some examples of Navy Strength rums are: Wood's, Rum XP, Pusser's Overproof and Gosling's 151.

Overproof is a term that can also be used to describe Navy Strength rum, but I tend to use Overproof when referring to un-aged or very lightly aged spirits that are bottled above 50% ABV Some good examples of this style are: Wray & Nephew White, Sunset Very Strong Rum, and Clarke's Court Pure White Rum.

AGRICOLE AND AOC

For all my moaning about a lack of overriding legislation when it comes to rum-making, this is not the case as far as *rhum agricole* is concerned. This style of rum is known to few people and enjoyed by even fewer, but it is one of the most exciting areas of the rum category and one that is carefully defined by law.

Under EU law, *rhum agricole* must be produced from the freshly pressed juice of sugarcane and must be made in one of nine listed territories including the likes of Guadeloupe, Grenada, Madeira and Réunion. In addition to this, the island of Martinique has an Appellation d'Origine Contrôlée (AOC), which is similar to the EU's Protected Designation of Origin, that sets out rules concerning production practices, distillation equipment, and even cane-harvesting periods for any product wishing to class itself as AOC Martinique Rhum Agricole (see right).

The only problem with the EU's *rhum agricole* definition is that it doesn't capture all rums made from sugarcane juice as a base material, which can leave some rums locked in a state of limbo if they don't comply with certain aspects of the edict. To make matters more confusing, the term *agricole* was not historically used to describe sugarcane juice-based spirits, but to signify a plantation-based distillery versus a larger urban distillery regardless of the material used. The plantation distillery with its immediate source of sugar was *agricole* (agricultural) and the large urban distillery receiving molasses was *industriel* ("industrial").

For me, any rum produced using fresh cane juice as the base material and where the use of cane juice is perceivable in the final product (I'm looking at you, Barbancourt distillery — see pages 117–18) can reasonably be called a *rhum agricole* according to the modern definition — regardless of where it actually comes from. To make a rum from cane juice, it's essential that the cane grows nearby, and that physical link to the land — irrespective of distillery size — is what really exemplifies the style.

AOC MARTINIQUE RHUM AGRICOLE

This classification is by far and away the most rigorous among any legal classification of rum. It starts with the plantation itself, which must be on the island of Martinique and must fall within one of 23 designated municipalities that lie mostly in the centre of the island. Cultivation yields are limited to 120 tons (132 US tons) of sugarcane per hectare, which is designed to limit the amount of fertilizer used and to keep agricultural practices sustainable. Harvest must take place between January 1 and August 31 every year, and only certain chemicals are permitted to be used.

The wort used for fermentation must be composed only of the juice of the plant (and water) and must be a minimum of 14° Brix and a pH of at least 4.7 – both of these measures are there to promote the harvesting of fully ripe cane, but they also limit fermentation problems due to insufficient sugars. Distillation takes place in a column still comprising 5–9 rectifying plates and at least 15 copper or stainless steel stripping plates. The spirit must come off the still at an average of 65–75% ABV. These measures are aimed at limiting undesirable heavy alcohols in the final product.

RIGHT Just your average Martinican supermarket where a litre of AOC Martinique *rhum agricole* costs a mere €4.95 (£4.20 or $5).

BELOW If badly managed, a bottling line can easily become the "bottle neck" of rum production.

The legislation also stretches to label, where *blanc* must be rested in steel for at least 3 months; *élevé sous bois* must be aged for at least 12 months and contain at least 20 g (0.7 oz) of congeners (flavour-giving compounds) per 100 litres (26.5 US gallons) of pure alcohol; *vieux* must be aged for at least 3 years in casks no larger than 650 litres (172 US gallons) and contain at least 325 g (11.5 oz) congeners per 100 litres (26.5 US gallons) of pure alcohol.

PART THREE
THE RUM TOUR

THE CARIBBEAN

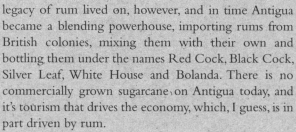

The Antigua Distillery

ST JOHN'S

ANTIGUA

The story of sugar on Antigua begins with Colonel Christopher Codrington, the Captain-General of the Leeward Islands, and a successful sugar planter with holdings in Barbados and St. Kitts. European colonization of Antigua and Barbuda began in earnest in 1634 with the arrival of English colonists from St. Kitts. But it was the arrival of Codrington in 1674 that would change the course of history on the islands. Codrington brought sugarcane to the island from St. Kitts, and established a plantation named "Betty's Hope" in honour of his daughter. The plantation covered 350 hectares (870 acres) and at its height was worked by nearly 400 slaves. Other planters, who had previously been focused on tobacco and indigo crops, took Codrington's lead, and by the 1750s, over half of the arable land on the island – 28,000 hectares (70,000 acres) – was occupied by 150 sugar mills. Most of them ran a distillery too. Betty's Hope remained in the Codrington family for 250 years, and was eventually sold in 1944 and closed shortly thereafter. The two original windmills can still be seen today, and there is a visitor centre and museum that give guests a good taste of what plantation life on Antigua was once like.

Sugar slowly declined through the 19th and 20th centuries, and Antigua slid into a state of economic stagnation. By 1939 there were just two distilleries. The legacy of rum lived on, however, and in time Antigua became a blending powerhouse, importing rums from British colonies, mixing them with their own and bottling them under the names Red Cock, Black Cock, Silver Leaf, White House and Bolanda. There is no commercially grown sugarcane on Antigua today, and it's tourism that drives the economy, which, I guess, is in part driven by rum.

Visitors who stray far enough from their cruise ships or yachts will discover an island of rich contrasts. Exiting the pastel confines of St. John's Heritage Harbour (which is effectively an American shopping mall touting branded goods, diamonds and overpriced sandwiches) it's all cracked pavements and broken-down vehicles until you hit one the islands 365 beaches – one for every day of the year! In a backstreet of one neighbourhood, I visited a bar that stated on the door in no uncertain terms, "No drugs, no weapons, no bareback." At some time, later, the proprietor felt the need to add, "No children."

One bar that doesn't see the need for such signs and that should certainly not be missed, is Papa Zouk's seafood and rum shack. The bar stocks a fantastic range of international rums, good seafood and a compelling backstory. Calamity struck this little restaurant back in 2009, when a fire completely burned it to the ground. At that time Papa Zouk's had one of the greatest rum collections in the West Indies, and in the aftermath some of those bottles were salvaged. With the labels burned to a cinder, proprietor Bert Kirchner saw an opportunity and blended everything into a single vat. Visitors to the rebuilt Papa Zouk now have the opportunity to buy a 15-ml (0.5-oz) sample of Bert's "Fire Rum" and taste some of the world's finest rums brought together by tragic circumstances.

LEFT Crumbled remains of old sugar mills, like the ones at Betty's Hope, are a regular sight across Antigua.

THE ANTIGUA DISTILLERY

The Antigua Distillery is situated on a small peninsula of land between two main harbours in Antigua's capital, St John's. There's a container yard there and the coastguard's office, and then there's Antigua Distillers Limited (ADL), with a full distillery and separate building that handles logistics for their brand agency subsidiary, Premier Beverages. Despite being enveloped by Caribbean waters and the close proximity to the Fort James beach, don't be fooled by the picturesque setting that a map might suggest. It turns out that once upon a time, this wasn't a peninsular at all, but an island, linked to mainland Antigua by a causeway. Rat Island, as it was known to the locals, was not riddled with vermin as the name suggests, but shaped like a rat.

Thanks to the dredging of Deep Water Harbour, and the widening of the causeway, a modern satellite view shows up only a very normal-looking strip of land.

Rat Island probably wasn't the first-choice location for the three Portuguese entrepreneurs who set up the distillery. These men were ex-indentured servants from Madeira, who had each established their own rum blending houses in St. John's, in the north of Antigua. Business was good, and in 1932 they clubbed together and built their own distillery that would secure a good supply of quality rum for the future. The authorities were reluctant to site a distillery on the mainland, deeming it both noisy and smelly, so offered them "Rat Island" as an alternative, which at the time was home only to a leper colony.

Undeterred, the distillery was constructed, complete with pot stills, and began to make Caballero-branded rum. A few years later, in the 1940s, they set up the Montpellier Sugar Factory on the east coast of the island, near Freetown, and replaced their pots with a multi-column Savalle still. The sugar estate provided the distillery with all the molasses it needed, including "fancy molasses" and muscovado sugar, which they used to launch their Cavalier brand of "Muscovado Rum" in 1947. The plantation closed in the 1950s, at which point Antigua Distillers switched to using standard blackstrap molasses from the Antigua Sugar Factory. In time, the sugar factory closed too, and the distillery began sourcing molasses from St. Kitts and then Guyana. These days, deliveries of molasses arrive from Guyana by boat, which moor up in Deep Water Harbour and pump a 1,000-ton (1,100-US ton) parcel of black syrup through

ABOVE The copper portholes on the Antigua Distillery's beautiful column still offer a striking perspective of alcohol being stripped from molasses wine.

RIGHT For all the technological advances that the spirits business has witnessed over the past 50 years, some processes are still undertaken by hand and nose.

ENGLISH HARBOUR 5-YEAR-OLD (40% ABV) AGED RUM

Glacé (candied) cherry, tobacco, coffee liqueur and almond frangipani. Palate has restrained sweetness, with brittle cacao, burnt caramel and creamy vanillin. Finish is light and softly sweet.

ENGLISH HARBOUR 10-YEAR-OLD (40% ABV) AGED RUM

More fruit than the 5-year-old; soft dried apricot, peach nectar and butterscotch sauce. There's gentle wood spice there too — mace, nutmeg, dried ginger and coriander seed. Palate is thicker, but remains light enough to slip down easily. Gentle and elegant, lingering on dried prunes, sandalwood and cigar.

ENGLISH HARBOUR 1981 (40% ABV) EXTRA-AGED RUM

Banana bread, malt loaf. Lots of nutmeg and ginger, mace and toffee sauce. Thicker still, but juicy. Jammed full of tobacco, old pipe taint and bitter chocolate.

ENGLISH HARBOUR OLOROSO SHERRY CASK (46% ABV) EXTRA-AGED RUM

Fruit and nut milk chocolate, dried raisins. Palate is big on sherry — dry and unctuous. The spice draws things out, but erases some of the fragile distillery character.

ENGLISH HARBOUR PORT CASK (46% ABV) EXTRA-AGED RUM

Jammy and soft on the nose — soft strawberry, plum pie. Sweet and spice and all things nice. Confected and slick, with black pepper and grenadine taking the finish away.

underground pipes and into an enormous receiver on the hill top. Building your distillery on Rat Island does have some advantages.

The highlight of this distillery is the triple column still that replaced the older column in 1992 – if you want a taste of what the previous still was capable of, look no further than English Harbour 1981. Due to the high risk of tropical storms in the area, someone decided to chop up the still into smaller pieces, then line them up next to each other (and in some cases on top of each other) to lower the height. This means that there are in fact five columns that operate as if they are three. Confused? I know I am. As with all column stills, this one is steam-powered, with much of that steam being generated through the burning of waste oil from cruise ships.

But the really interesting thing about this still is what it's made from: copper. From the main structure of the columns, to the internal bubble plates, the porthole frames… even the bolts – it's all copper. The condensers are copper too. With all that copper column going on you can be sure that the spirit is high in strength, and it is – 95.5% ABV – so very nearly neutral in taste.

But that doesn't matter too much to ADL, as it's during the maturation process that they build their flavour profile. Their English Harbour brand is named after the small settlement on the south of the island that was formerly a Royal Navy base of operations. English Harbour rum has had its share of the awards over the years, and I can see why; it features complex, unsweetened maturation characteristics that you only encounter when good wood is matched with a great blender. Most of the barrels arrive via Kentucky, but the distillery is also experimenting with European wine and sherry casks, the first releases of which we are just starting to see.

BARBADOS

Unlike the other islands in the eastern Caribbean, which are volcanic in their geological origins, most of the island of Barbados is formed from a coral reef limestone cap. Over a period of about a million years, the gradual accumulation of the oceanic sediments and regular tectonic uplifts caused by the Atlantic plate being pushed under the Caribbean plate, literally forced Barbados to surface. The end result is a much flatter island than the others in the Lesser Antilles belt, and when coupled with strong Atlantic winds, this made Barbados easy to colonize, setting the stage for one of the first great sugar islands of the Caribbean, as well as the birthplace of Caribbean rum.

Barbados was named by Spanish colonists, who briefly claimed the island in the 16th century. It's thought to mean "the bearded ones" which may be either in reference to the bearded fig-trees that were indigenous to the island, or perhaps to a particularly hairy tribe of Carib Indians who lived there at the time. By the early 17th century, the Spanish had effectively given up on Barbados (no gold), which allowed the English to settle its uninhabited land, in the 1620s.

Barbados started out growing tobacco and indigo, but Barbadian tobacco couldn't compete with the quality of the Virginian offering, being described once, in 1628, as "foul, full of stalks, and evil coloured". A new commodity crop was needed. And so the island began cultivating sugar in 1640. It was a Dutchman, Pieter Blower, who, in 1637, brought cuttings to the island by way of Brazil.

The calcium-rich coral-island soil proved to be good for the cane and the flat swathes of land made harvesting easy. Barbados was the first island in the Lesser Antilles to fully embrace sugarcane, and the industry expanded at an exponential rate. In 1645, there were 4,000 hectares (10,000 acres) of arable land on the island, but the forest clearing in the years that followed meant that by 1667 there were 10,000 hectares (25,000 acres) operated by 750 land owners. By that point, there were around 300 sugar mills, together producing 4.5 million litres (1.1 million US gallons) of rum a year. Soon, up to 70% of the land was reserved for cane growing, so much so that almost everything, including food, often had to be imported from New England. This relationship with the American colonies proved fruitful for both sides

however. By the mid-1700s Barbados was exporting over 6.8 million litres (1.8 million US gallons) of rum a year, and at least half of it was heading north, to New England, Philadelphia, Virginia and the Carolinas. Like the Irish and Canadians, the colonists of north America favoured the lighter style of rum. Evidence suggests that the earliest Barbados rums were double-distilled in pots, resulting in a purer, and cleaner-tasting rum.

But trade relations with North America turned out to be Barbados' Achilles' heel, as embargoes placed during, and following, the American War of Independence kicked in. Not that they stopped George Washington tapping a barrel of Barbados rum at his presidential inauguration. With Barbados' largest export market all but neutralized, export rum volumes to America dropped to just 91,000 litres (240,000 US gallons) in 1788, compared to 4.5 million litres (1.2 million US gallons) in 1768.

Falling sugar prices and the decreasing demand for Barbadian rum, along with the looming threat of the emancipation of slavery which would lead to increased labour costs and social unrest were all factors that played a part in the slow collapse of the sugar industry on the island. In the 1820s, Barbados exported just 60,000 litres (15,500 US gallons) of rum a year, compared to Jamaica which exported three times that volume every

BELOW The most obvious difference between the geography of Barbados and the other islands that comprise the Lesser Antilles is the distinct lack of hills.

day. However, in 1834 there were still a total of 340 sugar mills, and 82,807 slaves on the island. Molasses was still being shipped north, and domestic rum consumption rocketed. The rum industry on Barbados was still very much alive.

Towards the end of the 19th century, the sugar industry became more commercialized as wealthy plantation owners consolidated the farms that were too small to make a decent living from. Soon, the average plantation on Barbados comprised hundreds of acres of land managed by a workforce of at least 100 slaves. As well as processing the sugar, many of these plantations would have been distilling rum from the leftover molasses too.

Further consolidation and new legislation stripped the industry back further. The 1938 *West Indies Yearbook* lists only four rum manufacturers on the island: Batson's, Mount Gay, West Indies Rum Refinery and Barbados Distilleries Ltd. By the 1980s, only Mount Gay and the West Indies Rum Distillery remained. The good news is that we're back to four again now, thanks to the (re)construction of Foursquare (see right) in St. Philips and St. Nicholas Abbey (see pages 74–77) in St. Lucy.

With the exception of St. Nicholas Abbey (which actually uses a hybrid column/pot), all of the distilleries on Barbados use column stills in tandem with pots to make blended rums. This is the hallmark of the Barbados style, which has been mixing column and pot rum longer than any other nation. Just like Jamaica, St. Lucia and Guyana, this in-house blending of opposing distillates produces a balanced product that is difficult to replicate with one or the other alone. There is no legislation that defines this, it's more like a secret covenant between distillers – a solemn vow of responsibility towards authenticity of taste, and transparency of production. It sounds like a cliché, but there really are no bad rums from Barbados, just rums that are good and rums that are very good.

For me at least, Barbados remains the spiritual home of rum in the Caribbean. It was the first, it was for a long time the biggest, and there still exists a certain holiness to the island where rum is concerned. There are something like 1,500 rum shops on the island, where the delicate art of knocking back a 200-ml (7-oz) bottle of E. S. A. Fields with some coke or ginger is practised by both locals and tourists alike. Like Guyana, the ritual of eating "cutters" alongside a glass of rum is alive and well here. In Barbados this is typically something fatty, like chicken liver pâté, or a stew containing some unidentifiable meat and altogether too much chilli (chile).

FOURSQUARE

The story of the Foursquare Distillery is not really a story of a distillery at all. The estate was once known as "Square Pond" and is referenced as far back as 1636. This preceded the arrival of cane in Barbados, however, and the Foursquare sugar mill wasn't established until much later, in the 1730s. The oldest building on the site is dated to this time too. Known as the "still house", it carries historical and architectural designations from the Barbados National Trust. Interestingly though, Foursquare was never particularly well renowned for its "stills", even though rum was certainly made there during the 18th and 19th centuries. The mill was well known for the quality of its sugar, though (especially

THIS PAGE Less than a 10-minute drive from the airport, the visitors' centre at Foursquare is a must-see. Foursquare produce everything, from £8 ($10) bottles of Old Brigand, to single pot-still rums that fetch hundreds of dollars at auction.

THIS PAGE The long neck on the pot still (top left), plus its two retorts, results in a relatively light, yet characterful, pot-still distillate; the steel Coffey still, (bottom left) which produces an even lighter style of spirit, is showing some signs of buckling under (low) pressure! Between them, these stills make dozens of rum expressions.

"fancy molasses"), and it won awards for its vacuum pan sugar in 1886. In the 20th century, the mill, like many others, acquiesced to economic change and the growth of tourism on the island. It finally closed in 1984.

But the real story of Foursquare is not really a story of a distillery at all. It's a story about blenders.

In the British Caribbean, it was blenders that elevated rum from hard white spirit, to a consistent, reliable and delicious-tasting thing that could be called a "brand". This is especially true in Barbados, where the 1906 Rum Duty Act made it law that distilleries could only sell their rum in quantities of 10 gallons (45 litres/12 US gallons) or above. Ten gallons is a little too much for one person, or even for 10 people, but rather than damaging rum sales, this single piece of legislation helped to establish the blender's profession and introduced a personal touch to the category when it was needed. There were dozens of these blenders in Bridgetown and traders like Martin Doorly & Co, E. S. A. Field, and R. L. Seale's all centred themselves around the busy trading thoroughfare of Roebuck Street. These men dealt not just in rum, but in textiles, metalware, rice, potatoes and anything else that could be bought and sold. Selling potatoes and rice is quite unlikely to write your name in history, but blending rum might. One such blender was Reginald Leon Seale, who, in 1883 at the ripe old age of 13, was apprenticed

with a trader who taught him how to blend. Some years later, Seale established his own trading company, which also practised the art of rum blending, only this time it had his name on it.

R. L. Seale's was incorporated in 1926, and the company passed from father to son, through Reginald Clarence Seale, who ran the business until 1972, and on to Sir David Seale, who in 1977 broke the business away from Roebuck Street and built a blending and bottling facility in Hopefield. At that time, the Seales were buying rum from the West Indies Rum Distillery (see page 78), but after acquiring Alleyne Arthur & Hunte in 1993, a distillery of their own was needed. The site of the former Foursquare distillery was chosen, and in 1996 Sir David Seale opened a state-of-the-art operation, splicing together the history of sugar and rum-making in Barbados, with the flourishing tourism industry, into what it is today – a glorious theme park dedicated to making and promoting rum. An equally monumental event took place the following year, when David's son, Richard came on board as the new managing director.

Richard is among the most vocally passionate people in the rum industry today, and true to the blender's constitution, he is a balanced mix of knowledge and opinion when it comes to the history and current state of the category. That's fair enough if you ask me. In a category that is as fragmented and confusing as rum can be, rum needs patriots who can speak with authority and shepherd the ill-educated through the various pitfalls that await them.

Alongside his work as a self-appointed educator, Richard (and his father) manages a veritable "sticker book" of rum brands that have been amassed by Seales over the years. These brands include some of the oldest and best-loved names in Barbadian rum history. Naturally, there's R. L. Seale's "Finest Rum" with its iconic black bottle and bent neck. Then there's the prestigious Doorly's "Macaw" brand, E. S. A. Field (Barbados's most popular white rum), Old Brigand (Barbados's most popular aged rum), Alleyne Arthur's "Special Barbados Rum" and countless special releases under the Foursquare brand name. You can also add to that list the various contracted brands that are produced at Foursquare, like Mahiki Rum (from London's famous tiki club) and Rum Sixty

Six, not to mention independent bottlings such as those from Luca Gargano's Velier (see page 207).

The distillery uses molasses from Guyana to produce its rums, although there are small-scale experiments taking place that use cane syrup sourced from St. Nicholas Abbey (see pages 74–77). Fermentation is conducted in four vessels, each of them 44,000 litres (11,500 US gallons), and the same parameters (including yeast) are used across all the expressions. In terms of distillation equipment, Foursquare has all the bases covered. The higher-ester rum is made in a 1,760-litre (465-US gallon) copper pot still made by Forsyths in Scotland. It has a long neck and two linked retorts. This still produces a distinctly characterful spirit at roughly 82% ABV, which is similar in style to Jamaican pot-still rums. Interestingly, the spirit vapour passes through two separate condensers: one that converts most of the vapour into a liquid (like most other pot stills) and another that cools the distillate down to 8°C (46°F). This improves the efficiency of the distillation process by alleviating the airspace of warm spirit vapour and thereby lowering the air pressure in the system. The air pressure is also lowered in the Foursquare Coffey still, though in this instance, it's with a greater sense of purpose. The still comprises two linked columns and an aldehyde stripper. The first two columns produce a light rum at 92% ABV, and when the aldehyde stripper is incorporated, it serves as a third column, and is only used to make very light, high-strength, rum. The whole system is run under a partial vacuum, which lowers the temperature of the steam down to 80°C (176°F) and the boiling point of ethanol even lower. It's an energy-saving solution more than a secret recipe for incredible rum, but it's commendable nevertheless.

All of the rums produced at Foursquare are a blend of column and pot-still spirits, with the exception of one or two limited pot-still releases. Richard Seale is determined that rum should be made this way, but after four generations of blending, that's hardly surprising. The urge to blend white rum is also too great a temptation, so with few exceptions, Foursquare mature two types of rum: a high-strength, column-still spirit, with a little pot-still rum added to it, and a fruitier pot-still rum with a little column-still spirit added to it. During maturation, the chemical makeup of the spirit, along with the cask itself, determines which direction the flavour profile will follow. By acquainting these two disparate spirits with one another prior to ageing, Seale can be more confident of an affinity later down the line.

DOORLY'S 3-YEAR-OLD (40% ABV)
AGED WHITE BLENDED RUM

A Thai curry of softmints and coconut, with light herbal notes and cool fenugreek. Taste is soft and creamy: baking spices, lime leaf and vanilla seed. Gentle white pepper on the finish.

DOORLY'S 12-YEAR-OLD (40% ABV)
EXTRA-AGED BLENDED RUM

Papaya salad, green oak, nutmeg and brown sugar. Juicy and concentrated flavour, but not at all heavy. Finish is clean and the alcohol soft. More please.

DOORLY'S PORT CASK (40% ABV)
EXTRA-AGED BLENDED RUM

Ripe and red, with soft juice of cranberry. Finessed. Cola bottles and cherry on the palate. Grippy and tight, with chocolate-coated raisins and strawberry jam.

DOORLY'S ZINFANDEL CASK (43% ABV)
EXTRA-AGED BLENDED RUM

Coffee and cinnamon, strawberry latte and vanilla. Milky and sweet at first, like strawberry milk. Tannin kicks in through the finish, with a lingering tightness and red wine grip.

FOURSQUARE SINGLE BLEND 2004 (59% ABV) EXTRA-AGED BLENDED RUM

The aroma here is boisterous and wild, and the concentrated Barbadian finesse quite confusing! On the palate, it's a big hit of tropical fruits: passion fruit, guava. Wood spice holds the texture on the palate and clutches out the finish. Intense and big.

R. L. SEALE'S EXPORT (46% ABV) EXTRA-AGED BLENDED RUM

Starts with mint humbugs but quickly turns to pink peppercorn and slick caramel sauce. Taste is part green sappy spice and part resinous oak lactones. Finish is balanced by a complex flitting between cut wood and sizzling aromatic spice.

MOUNT GAY

The Mount Gay Distillers experience is just a 10-minute walk from the port in Bridgetown. Set in a colonial-style property, it's an all-singing, all-dancing, tribute to the world's oldest rum distillery. Thirsty tourists are taken on a multi-sensory tour of the history of the refinery, the history of rum in Barbados and invited to partake in a full tasting of the range of Mount Gay rums at the beautiful mahogany bar. What visitors won't see, however, is any rum being made. And that's because Mount Gay isn't made in Bridgetown. It never has been. The distillery, formerly known as the Mount Gilboa Distillery but often referred to as the Mount Gay Refinery, is actually in the far north of the island, cleverly concealed for such a sizeable operation, and accessible by invitation only.

The distillery is one of the oldest in the world, and it's claimed that rum was being made here as far back as the 17th century. The earliest written evidence is a deed of sale from February 20, 1703, which details some of the equipment on the site at that time: "Two stone windmills... one boiling house with seven coppers, one curing house and one still house." The remains of one of those windmills can still be seen there today.

The Mount Gilboa estate was officially formed by William Sandiford, who consolidated a number of small sugar plantations in the early 18th century. The estates all lay on a ridge of land to the north of the St. Lucy parish of Barbados called Mount Gilboa, so Sandiford used that name for his 113-hectare (280-acre) plot of land. In 1747, the Sandiford family sold the mill and distillery to John Sober (never to be sober again!), and the distillery stayed in the family for the next 100 years. During this period, Cumberbatch Sober (John's son), who lived in London, asked his good friend Sir John Gay Alleyne to manage the operation for him. Alleyne owned the nearby Nicholas Plantation (see pages 74–77) so had some experience in these matters, and whatever he did,

he did well. In 1852 the Sobers renamed the plantation Mount Gay in honour of their friend (Mount Alleyne was already taken).

Mount Gay launched their best-known blend, "Eclipse" in 1910, thought to reflect the total eclipse of the sun that occurred that year. This eclipse would have been a very different product to the present-day blend however, as the distillery comprised only pot stills in 1910. It was shortly after the launch of Eclipse that the next major player in the Mount Gay story was introduced: Aubrey Ward, a highly successful English/Irish businessman, who bought the distillery in 1918. He set about upgrading the old equipment with newer pieces, including the addition of a Savalle column which operated up until 1976. Along with his business partner and marketing specialist John Hutson, Ward opened up Mount Gay to the international market, and by 1958 it was sold in 19 countries. Aubrey Ward's efforts were continued by his son Darnley DaCosta Ward until his death in 1989. At the time of Darnley's death, the French spirits company Rémy Martin (later becoming Rémy Cointreau) bought a majority shareholding in Mount Gay Distillers Ltd., but the Ward family retained a shareholding in the company as well as ownership of the physical Mount Gay Refinery. Consequently, the refinery (which is actually the distillery) is licensed to produce rum for Rémy Cointreau, who upon receiving fresh rum, take care of the ageing and blending of Mount Gay rums. The bottling is done in Bridgetown.

This slightly awkward arrangement forms the preface of the Mount Gilboa brand. Named after the former title of the Mount Gay Refinery, Mount

BELOW LEFT Master Blender Allen Smith assesses the job at hand – a forklift truck may be required.

BELOW The black stuff that you can see on the walls of the warehouse is the ethanol-loving *Baudoinia* mould.

Gilboa was launched by Frank Ward (a descendant of Aubrey Ward) in 2006. A triple pot-still rum, distilled in the same pots used in the Mount Gay blends, Mount Gilboa seems to have struggled to gain traction among connoisseurs despite being a rare artefact: 100% pot-still Barbadian rum.

The Mount Gay estate currently owns 134 hectares (331 acres) of cane-growing land, which is good for 5,000–6,000 tons (5,500–6,600 US tons) of molasses per year. That represents a little over half of the molasses required for their annual rum production (the balance comes from Guyana and other sources on Barbados). There's no sugar refinery at Mount Gay, so the molasses arrives by truck from the local sugar factory, or from the docks. Once the molasses has been pumped into one of the underground storage vats, it is mixed with water that's tapped from a 90-metre (300-ft) coral limestone well, which is owned by the estate. A proprietary yeast strain is added to the molasses, which is fermented in oak fermentation vats for around 36 hours.

Distillation at Mount Gay is conducted in two separate still houses. The first of which contains four large pot stills, manufactured by coppersmiths from Forsyths and Macmillan in Scotland and Forgassa in Spain. The oldest of the bunch (a Macmillan still) was probably installed at the turn of the 20th century, but even Mount Gay aren't entirely sure of this. What is known, is that when "Blues", the oldest employee at the distillery, joined in 1965, the still looked old even then. The pots are all very similar in their design, however, following the typical rum setup of one large pot followed by two linked retorts. The pot-still rum is distilled twice, which takes it up to a strength of around 85% ABV.

The second still house is for the two-column copper Coffey still, which churns out the vast majority of the spirit made here, at a strength of over 94% ABV. As you might expect, this is a far lighter spirit than the pot-still stuff, but this balancing of pot and column is the defining characteristic of the Barbados style. The freshly made pot and column rums are each diluted to around 65% ABV and matured separately to one another for a period of one to 10 years, depending on which blend it will finally end up in.

RIGHT Mount Gay Black Barrel: while harder to track down, this rum contains a higher proportion of pot-still spirit compared to "Eclipse", and it is finished in heavily charred ex-bourbon barrels.

MOUNT GAY ECLIPSE (40% ABV)
AGED BLENDED RUM

There's a pleasant (albeit soft) brown sugar syrup that emanates from this, though not a lot else. Perhaps a suggestion of pot-still weight, but it's well concealed by light spirit and those gentle maturation characteristics. The taste is even lighter, and only the softest hint of milky latte and banana candies is there to inform us that this isn't vodka.

MOUNT GAY XO (40% ABV)
EXTRA-AGED BLENDED RUM

A fruity and nicely balanced little number: leather tobacco pouch, Rolo candies, pudding wine and soft sherry conspire to make this a very much whiskey-esque style of rum. The honeyed palate is balanced by an interjection of prickly spices along with molasses and coffee and walnut cake.

When the brakes are released and the pedal pushed firmly to the metal, this distillery can fill 250 x 200-litre (53-US gallon) barrels in a single day. The casks are stored upright here, and loaded onto a conveyor belt for emptying followed by immediate re-filling. The effect is something like a Formula 1 pitstop. Almost all of the casks at Mount Gay are ex-bourbon, but Allen Smith, Mount Gay's master blender, is also conducting some experiments with European wine and sherry casks. I even spotted some virgin oak barrels on my tour of the distillery. But this goes beyond the simple finishing of rums in glamorous casks. Smith is trialling different toast levels with his rum, and running entire maturation cycles in wine casks.

It's all part of a wider project that Mount Gay are pursuing, to explore the two main variables in rum-making: the distillation process and the maturation process. Besides releases from selected casks, we can also expect to see 100% pot-still and 100% column-still bottlings in the not-too-distant future.

These bespoke offerings are welcome additions from such a large producer. Mount Gay won't divulge exactly how many casks of rum they are currently holding, but with four enormous bonds, and anything from 10,000 to 20,000 casks in each bond, I wouldn't be surprised if there were 50,000 casks of rum on site. And they're going to need it – Mount Gay currently fills the equivalent of six million 70-cl (24-oz) bottles of rum in a year. Around 30% of that is white rum, but accounting for evaporative losses of 7–12% per year, the distillery needs to empty (and re-fill) in excess of 15,000 casks of rum every year to keep up with demand.

ST. NICHOLAS ABBEY

St. Nicholas Abbey is Barbados's youngest distillery. Under the supervision of the Warren family, bottling of rum started here in 2009 and distilling in 2013. But paradoxically, this abbey (which is actually not an abbey at all but one of only three surviving Jacobean mansions in the Western hemisphere) has a reasonable claim to being the oldest surviving sugarcane plantation in Barbados, and possibly, the Caribbean.

The house and plantation were first established by Lieutenant-Colonel Benjamin Berringer, who arrived in the fledgling British colony of Barbados in 1634. He had £8,000 (£1.4 million/$1.75 million today) in

ABOVE St. Nicholas Abbey has a strong claim for being the most beautiful distillery in the world.

RIGHT The hybrid still at St. Nicholas Abbey produces a spirit that sits somewhere between column and pot; soft, but not devoid of personality.

his bank account. By the 1650s, a plantation had been established, and like most others on the island by this time, it was turning to sugarcane cultivation. Although no conclusive evidence currently exists, it is quite possible – likely, even – that rum was being made at the Nicholas Plantation during the 1650s. The old mill house is architecturally very similar to some of the earliest rum distilleries of the time, and just recently, the archaeologist and spirits writer Professor Frederick H. Smith has retrieved currently unidentified copper artefacts from the grounds of St. Nicholas Abbey. If investigations can demonstrate a history of distilling activity during the late 17th century, there could be a new contender to the claim for "world's oldest rum distillery".

Benjamin Berringer died in 1660, the rumour being that he was poisoned or possibly killed in a duel (accounts vary) by his business partner, Sir John Yeamans. Yeamans was an infamous colonist, described in his day as "a pirate ashore", who had arrived on the island with 200 African slaves. After Berringer's death, Yeamans changed the name of the plantation to "Yeamans Plantation" and the following year he married Berringer's widow. Berringer's children took the matter to court, and were awarded ownership of the property in 1669, about the time that Yeamans emigrated to America and founded the colony of Carolina. When Berringer's grand-daughter married George Nicholas in the late 1600s, the Yeamans name was finally changed to "Nicholas Plantation" in his honour.

The Nicholas family ran the operation until 1725, when falling sugar prices forced the family to sell the plantation to Joseph Dottin, who was Deputy Governor of Barbados at the time. Dottin gave the plantation to his daughter, Christian, upon her marriage to Sir John Gay Alleyne in October 1746. Sir John might have been the greatest plantation manager of his generation. In his time he managed various successful operations on Barbados, including the Mount Gilboa plantation, which would later take his name (see page 72). Perhaps the most significant contribution Sir John made to St. Nicholas Abbey was expanding the company's rum distillation as a mean of economic sustainability.

Sir John and Christian died at the turn of the 19th century with no surviving heirs. The following years were spent trying to track down European members of the Dottin family and the property incurred considerable debt until it was taken over by the Chancery Court in Bridgetown in 1810. It was sold to the Cumberbatch family for £20,500 (£1.75 million/$2.2 million today) and passed from father, to son, to daughter, ending up in the hands of Sarah Cumberbatch and her husband, Charles Cave. It is believed that the plantation was named St. Nicholas Abbey by the couple, who were married in "Bath Abbey", and whose ancestral home was "St. Nicholas Parish" in England.

St. Nicholas Abbey remained in the Cave family for some 200 years, and continued to produce sugar up until 1947, after which the doors were opened for tourism. In 2006 it was purchased by Larry Warren, a renowned Barbadian architect. And it's under the Warrens' guidance that St. Nicholas Abbey has been beautifully restored to a state that is quite likely better than its original glory. Every square inch of the house and grounds has been sensitively refurbished to pristine condition and I cannot imagine a grander place to spend an afternoon drinking rum and enjoying the nature of the island.

The rum side of the estate is managed by Larry's son, Simon, who has recently purchased 90 hectares (225 acres) of adjacent land. This means that all of the future rums produced here will be made from estate-grown sugar. That'll be the thin end of a fat wedge of sustainable practices that are taking place here: everything, from the milling of the raw cane to stencilling of the bottles, is

THIS PAGE A growing collection of casks, an old sugar mill, and the future promise of estate-grown cane: St. Nicholas Abbey is definitely one to watch.

WHITE RUM (40% ABV) UN-AGED BLENDED RUM

Peachy liquorice (licorice), oak moss, and sweet florals. Sweetness continues on the palate. Cream cheese, peach melba, coconut water and sake. Elegant and crisp through the finish.

5-YEAR-OLD (40% ABV) AGED BLENDED RUM

Soft wood caramels, sticky toffee pudding and a touch of fragrant coconut. Wood is crisp and succinct. Well-structured and unctuous and big on the palate. Tobacco and stewed tropical fruits on the finish.

12-YEAR-OLD (40% ABV)
EXTRA-AGED BLENDED RUM

Fruity and full, clean mineral notes, with nutty spices and thick caramel notes. Tropical caramel pastry and rich resinous woody notes. Pipe residue and a lick of cane honey on the finish.

18-YEAR-OLD (40% ABV)
EXTRA-AGED BLENDED RUM

Melon and more tobacco. Sweet and juicy on the palate, where tannins play an almost acidic role, balancing sweetness and holding the finish. Banoffee, treacle tart and ripe stone fruits.

1,500-litre (400-US gallon) steel vessels. The yeast is first propagated with a small batch of the cane honey, to promote growth and commence fermentation. After a while, more of the diluted cane syrup is added and air is percolated through the tank. From start to finish, the total fermentation lasts 48–60 hours, producing a cane wine with a strength of 9–12% ABV.

Next, the cane wine is passed over to one of the youngest pot-stills in the West-Indies – a German-manufactured 600-litre/160-US gallon) copper pot. The still is powered by that same *bagasse*-burning steam boiler, and has a rectifying column attached to it, resulting in a clean yet characterful spirit that is collected between 88–94% ABV. The spirit is cut back to 65% before being matured exclusively in ex-bourbon casks.

The distillery currently has 150 barrels of maturing stocks and these days, St. Nicholas Abbey bottle their own white rum and 5-year-old rum, both of which were made entirely on the grounds of the abbey itself. Back in 2009, when the first rums were released, the Warrens had no aged stocks, so the original "5" rum was bought in from the Foursquare Distillery (see pages 68–71). As time has progressed, so too has the rum, and St. Nicholas Abbey still bottle two older expressions – a 12-year-old and an 18-year-old – which are in fact products of Foursquare Distillery.

conducted on site. The leftover *bagasse* from crushing is compacted into manageable briquettes, which are used to power the modern steam boiler that powers the mill and heats the evaporators and the still. All that's needed are some oak trees and a glassblower, and this little operation would be entirely self-sufficient.

The rum is made from sugarcane syrup, rather than juice. Under the not-so-watchful eyes of the resident bat colony, the freshly pressed juice is passed through a series of evaporators, reducing the volume down by approximately 70%. Once reduced, the syrup is stable enough to be stored for months, which is necessary to ensure all-year-round production of rum outside of the typical February–June Barbados harvest.

Before fermentation, the syrup is diluted and acidulated, then fermentation takes place in one of two

RIGHT Labels are applied by hand, glass is engraved by hand – even the leather seal on the bottle cap is hand-stamped.

THE WEST INDIES RUM DISTILLERY

With a name like the The West Indies Rum Distillery (aka W.I.R.D), you might imagine that this Barbados rum producer sits on the edge of a white sandy beach, surrounded by palms, and a breeze that carries the faint smell of rum and coconut – and you would be right! This distillery even has its own beach club. But while the sand on Brighton Beach, to the north of Bridgetown, is unquestionably sand, the palms and the coconuts are slightly less literal. Along with the Cockspur brand of rums, this distillery makes the famous "Malibu" coconut liqueur on behalf of French spirits giant Pernod Ricard: all 30 million litres (80 million US gallons) a year of it. Welcome to Barbados's biggest distillery.

The distillery was built in 1893 by George and Herman Stade, who had emigrated to Barbados by way of Trinidad. George was an engineer, and it was he who sourced the machinery and introduced the first column still to Barbados (in fact, this still might have been only the second column still in the Caribbean (after Bacardí) and likely remains the oldest in use today).

Meanwhile, Valdemar Hanschell, a Danish merchant based in Bridgetown, was busy adding rum blending to a diverse list of marine services that already included chandlery, rope braiding and sail making. Around a decade later, he launched Cockspur rum, named after the island's traditional emblem of a rooster. Hanschell went on to merge with various other companies through the 20th century, becoming Hanschell Larson in 1928, then Hanshell Innis Ltd in 1971.

Meanwhile, the Stade distillery was nationalized under the name West India Rum Refinery in 1918 and remained that way until it was sold in 1973, to the Goddard family. Goddard Enterprises is a major Caribbean conglomerate, with subsidiary companies in over twenty countries, as well as a few rum brands to their names like Gold Braid and J&R. The Goddard's bought Hanschell Innis too, which was already being produced at the distillery.

The distillery is one of only a handful in the rum world that uses a semi-continuous fermentation process, rather than fermenting in batches. This approach started in 2002, when the old open-air fermenters were replaced with four high-spec new additions, each of them with a 230,000-litre (61,000-US gallon) capacity. To put that into context, these fermenters are five times the size of

the ones at the Bacardí distillery in San Juan, although there are only four of them compared to Bacardí's 20. The process involves breeding massive cultures of flocculating yeast (dense clumps of yeast) that are harvested in settling tanks, washed with sulphuric acid, and stored until such a time that they are needed. In this way, the distillery can amass staggering numbers of yeast cells and run back to back fermentations for days on end. Moreover, fermentation time is significantly reduced, down to as little as 12 hours for a 60-ton (66-US ton) batch of molasses. For this to work, and for the yeast culture to remain consistent, all of the equipment must be maintained to a surgical level of cleanliness, so at all times one of the four fermenters is cleaned by an automated CIP (clean in place) system while the other three are in use.

The distillery uses four stills in total, two column configurations, one pot still, and one pot still connected to a column: The #79 still is a modern four-column continuous still that runs 24 hours a day, 365 days a year, producing 45,000 litres (12,000 US gallons) of spirit a day. The slightly older John Dore multi-column still (#77) was installed in 1975, and depending on which of the four columns that are used it can produce medium- to light-bodied rums for blending. The #62 still is a wash still, which feeds a low-strength distillate into the distillery's original 1893 column still. This still produces a medium-bodied rum at 55–60% ABV. This distillate is then redistilled in the fourth still (#73) which is a copper pot with a rectifying column on top that produces a distillate of around 85% ABV.

Only the former are used to make the base spirit for Malibu, but true to the Barbadian style, it's a combination of pot and column that is blended to make the rum you find in a Cockspur bottle.

BRITISH VIRGIN ISLANDS

ANEGADA

TORTOLA

VIRGIN GORDA

Callwood Distillery

ROAD TOWN

Sixty tiny islands make up the British Virgin Islands, of which only 16 are permanently inhabited. The largest of those is Tortola, which comprises around 55 square kilometres (21 square miles) of land. The hills here are steep, rising up to over 500 metres (1,650 ft), and the roads are intestinal, like a rollercoaster ride through some wretched animal. Worse still, as the "British" part of the name dictates that everyone drives on the left-hand side of the road, but the close proximity to the US means that all the cars are imported left-hand-drive vehicles. Throw in an almost complete lack of road signs, and it means driving on the island can be quite frightening.

The terror of driving around the place is certainly worth it, though. They call the British Virgin Islands "nature's little secret" and you can see why: white sand beaches, turquoise waters and a persistent vista of tropical islands plonked perfectly in the sea. It's surprisingly easy to find your own stretch of pristine beach on Tortola, so along with the tax breaks, it's little wonder that so many people consider it as paradise.

It's for the above reasons that I assumed they were named the Virgin Islands: being unspoilt, flawless. They were in fact named by Columbus, who sighted them on his second voyage, in 1493. Columbus gave them the fanciful name *Santa Úrsula y las Once Mil Vírgenes* ("Saint Ursula and her 11,000 Virgins") after the legend of Saint Ursula, which was shortened to *Las Vírgenes* (The Virgins). The islands were captured by the English (from the Dutch) in 1672, who introduced cotton and sugar. The cotton industry in the Caribbean couldn't compete with that of Egypt and eventually America, so when it collapsed, the Virgin Islands became a monoculture set of islands and sugar was king.

Following a similar course as many other Caribbean islands, sugar remained dominant until the middle of the 19th century, when a combination of the abolition of slavery and the development of European sugar-beet put an end to the party. For the British Virgin Islands it was even tougher, after a series of Hurricanes, the worst of which occurred in September of 1819, destroying many of the sugar factories. In 1819 there were over 100 sugar mills on the island, but just 30 remained in 1845. Many old mills still dot the islands' hills and coastlines of Tortola, such as the one on Brewer's Bay, which even has two small, and rather broken pot stills embedded in its tumbled-down wreckage.

There's only one distillery left on Tortola, and amazingly many of the islands' residents are unaware of its existence. This is partly due to the vehement consumption of Pusser's Navy Rum (see pages 202–03) on the island, which accounts for some 85% of all the rum drunk on Tortola. Much of the consumption is centred around "Pusser's Outpost" in Road Town. Big and garish, the outpost is colonial styled on the outside but more like a Victorian pub for sailors on the inside. The food is bad and the drinks just about passable, but it's required viewing for cocktail geeks on account of being the home of the Painkiller cocktail (see pages 238–39).

BELOW A visit to the island of Tortola is incomplete without drinking rum at Bomba's Beach Shack – but watch out for the mushroom tea…

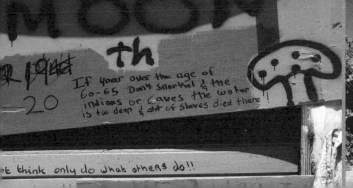

CALLWOOD DISTILLERY

ABOVE A nice day for patching holes in the still neck (while it's in operation). It's back to basics at Callwood, which is part of the charm and also part of the frustration.

The Callwood distillery on Tortola is old. Very old. Indeed, its owners have been known to claim a 400-year ancestry, which takes us back to the earliest known records of sugar farming in the area (so should likely be taken with a pinch of salt). But the original distillery buildings are in keeping with other pieces of architecture from the 17th century, and with other, defunct, sugar mills on the island, so a foundation date in the late 1600s is plausible. There is no documentation to back any of this up, however, and the best we've got is 18th-century references to a 17th-century sugar mill, known as the Arundel Estate.

The estate changed hands in the late 1800s, although no firm date is known. It would, however, certainly have been after the emancipation of slavery, in 1834. It was sold to the buccaneer Richard Callwood, who owned the nearby Thatch Island. Callwood gifted the estate to his son, Richard Jr, who was the progeny of one of Richard senior's former slaves. Sections of the Arundel Estate were sliced-off and sold on over the years (a 1.5 hectare/3.5 acre plot is on the market right now) but the sugar mill and distillery remained in the Callwood family, right up until present day Michael Callwood, Richard Jr's great-grandson.

The methods and equipment have been left mostly unchanged during the past 200 years, which makes Callwood a truly unique distillery, but more important still, is the significance of this place to the history of rum distilling in the Caribbean. In the early 19th century there would have been over a thousand operations just like this scattered all over the Caribbean, but it just so happens that this, along with the likes of Shillingford (see pages 89–90) and River Antoine (see pages 99–100) is one of the last remaining examples.

The staff, and Michael Callwood himself, perform their roles faithfully, but more as caretakers to tradition than as skilled craftsmen in their own right. Like puppets who are controlled by thin threads of history that connect them to the rum makers of old, they are powerless to change, or even appreciate, the delicate nuances of their own rum making routine. It is an inevitability, I suppose, that those who are most faithful to historical practices should also be the ones most ignorant to understanding it. Rum-making was not always the artful undertaking that we think of it as being today, and for the Callwood distillery it is still that way. This probably makes for a slightly inconsistent product, which is all part of the romance of course, but the bigger problem here is that nobody seems to know any technical details concerning how the rum is made! Here, though is what we do know:

Young "green" sugarcane is cut by hand between March and July. It is pressed by a tiny old diesel-powered mill that feeds into a large stone receiver, about the size of a bathtub. The juice is then diluted slightly with water, and boiled for around three hours in big copper kettles. This step helps to preserve the cane juice so that it doesn't need to be fermented immediately. When it's time to ferment, the juice, which is now slightly concentrated, is fed into 200-litre (52-US gallon) "open top" oak casks, where it is naturally fermented by wild yeasts for 10–20 days. Nobody knows what strength the fermentation is when it's finished, but what's perhaps more significant is that nobody cares either! As with much of the process, it is a mystery.

The fermented cane wine is then directed into an old copper pot still of approximately 100 litres (26 US gallons), which is at all times outside and completely exposed to the elements. The still is directly heated by a wood-burning furnace, and most of the fuel is old coconut husks, *bagasse* and bits of wood pallet – I even spotted rotten papaya being thrown in there! A chimney on the side of the furnace vents out the smoke and the contents of the still bubble away. The spirit vapours travel up to the head of the still and down the swan's neck, into a worm-tub condenser. From start to finish, it can take 10–14 hours for the full distillation run to complete and it's controlled only by the intensity of the fire.

Nobody I questioned knew the strength of the resulting distillate, including Michael Callwood, who simply chuckled to himself, considered the question for a moment, and then shrugged. I think it's quite possible that Michael doesn't know, but I hope somebody does if we're to trust the ABV percentage that's written on the bottle!

The good, if somewhat miraculous, news is that the rum is really rather tasty. But perhaps I shouldn't be so surprised. Cane juice is packed full of flavour, and that prolonged fermentation builds up plenty of big fruity esters and aldehydes. Then the low-strength, single distillation ensures that they are retained in every single drop of rum. The distillery currently bottles four products; an un-aged white rum, a 4-year-old, 10-year-old, and a rum liqueur that is sweetened using fresh sugar cane juice… it's called "The Panty Dropper". None of these rums are exported, so you will need to take a trip to the Virgin Islands if you wish to taste them.

RIGHT The methodology used at Callwood is undoubtedly crude, but the rum speaks for itself. My recommendation is the Arundel 4-year-old.

ARUNDEL WHITE RUM (40% ABV)
UN-AGED POT-STILL RUM

Orange! So much orange, it's a wonder the rum isn't flavoured with the stuff. Over time, other fruits slip in too; blackcurrant, apricot and grapefruit. Punchy florals, with peony, hibiscus and big zesty orange. Orange zips through the palate. Zesty and ripe. It's balanced, slightly bitter and rather tasty.

ARUNDEL 4-YEAR-OLD (40% ABV)
AGED POT-STILL RUM

Golden and zippy. Fizzy fruits, burnt butter, and shiny wood. Big acetone notes, it's almost painful to sniff – but it feels intentional. More watery than the nose suggests. But there's fruit, vanilla and toffee, leading to white pepper thrashing through the finish.

ARUNDEL 10-YEAR-OLD (40% ABV)
EXTRA-AGED RUM

Slightly more subdued than the 4, more waxy, with lemon, fruits slathered in toffee and peppered banana peel. Taste is very soft, with some gentle floral complexities developing, and finishing on brown butter and hazelnut.

CAYMAN ISLANDS

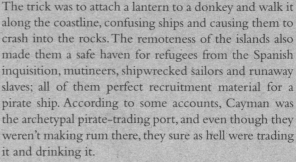

There are some Caribbean islands that have virtually no history of cultivating cane or making rum. The one thing these places all have in common is that they're small, with far too little workable arable land to make a sugar mill and distillery economically viable. Grand Cayman, the largest of the three Cayman Islands, is one of those places. It's a mere 196 square kilometres (76 square miles). Not as small as Tortola or Marie-Galante, but impractical for running a plantation due to its claw-like shape. The Caymans are also fairly remote, being 240 km (150 miles) south of their closest neighbour, Cuba. But there's another very good reason why sugar production – or indeed any kind of production – never really managed to establish itself in Cayman: Pirates.

Columbus first sighted the Caymans on May 10 1503. Spotting the two smaller islands Cayman Brac and Little Cayman, he named them Las Tortugas ("The Turtles") after the numerous sea turtles that inhabited their waters. The islands themselves are long rather than round, however, so the name was later changed to *Caymanes* after the Carib word *caimán* meaning "crocodile". Marine crocodiles did once inhabit Cayman waters too, and it was these along with the turtles that attracted the attention of hungry sailors and fishermen.

The islands remained mostly uninhabited until the 18th century, but soon became a popular hangout for wreckers, salvaging from and plundering distressed ships.

The trick was to attach a lantern to a donkey and walk it along the coastline, confusing ships and causing them to crash into the rocks. The remoteness of the islands also made them a safe haven for refugees from the Spanish inquisition, mutineers, shipwrecked sailors and runaway slaves; all of them perfect recruitment material for a pirate ship. According to some accounts, Cayman was the archetypal pirate-trading port, and even though they weren't making rum there, they sure as hell were trading it and drinking it.

There are no pirates there these days, or at least only of the tax-avoiding kind, but the Cayman Islands still celebrate the memory of the marauders in Pirate Week, every November.

SEVEN FATHOMS

When I first heard about a new rum from the Cayman Islands that was supposedly aged under water I had to laugh. It was 2009, just two years after Cayman Spirits Co. had been founded, and around the time of their first release of "Seven Fathoms Rum" – see what they did there? When I was planning my rum tour, I decided it was definitely worth a trip to the Cayman Islands to get to the bottom of this murky story.

Founded in 2007 by Walker Romanica and Nelson Dilbert, the distillery relocated to larger premises in George Town in 2013 and it's now a fairly serious operation.

The distillery makes a selection of rum bases fit for blending, depending on the time of the year. Most of the rum is made from molasses, but in the past they have also used evaporated cane juice as well as fresh cane juice in concert with brown sugar to produce an *agricole*-style rum. The molasses is cut to 20° Brix then fermented for 6–7 days in 4,500-litre (1,200-US gallon) steel fermenters. The 8% ferment is then used to make two types of rum; a 93% ABV "light rum" and a 87% ABV "heavy rum". The light rum is distilled twice, first

LEFT The all-singing and all-dancing visitors' centre at the Cayman Spirits Co. If you ask for Jordan, he will actually sing and dance for you.

in a 5,900-litre (1,560-US gallon) Vendome stripping still, which pulls out a low wine of around 40% ABV, and finally in a smaller Christian Carl pot still with an eight-plate rectification column. The "heavy rum" is distilled just once in the Christian Carl still. These two liquids are then blended together ready for maturation. Maturation *underwater*.

You're probably wondering how they do it, and I'm going to tell you, but first a little backstory: besides being the proprietor of a distillery, Walker Romanica's family also own a company called Divetech, who specialize in diver training and equipment retail. This means access to lots of technical equipment too, like winches and cranes – you know, the kind of stuff you might need if you wanted to drop barrels of rum into the ocean (and pull them back out again).

The first stage of the process is locating a suitable place for storing the casks. Diving is a very popular sport in Cayman, so barrels need to be hidden in quiet spots where they will remain undisturbed for years to come. Stage two involves laying concrete foundations under the water, which will be used as anchorage points for the barrels. Each foundation will be good to hold three casks, and Cayman Spirits Co. now have a bunch of these points plotted all around the bays of Grand Cayman. The barrels themselves are protected from the water, though the distillery will not divulge exactly how this is done. Next they're hauled on to the boat ready for dunking. Most barrels contain enough air in them so they will float to the surface, but when the crane drops the cask, its momentum causes it to sink before resurfacing. It's at the point where the cask has sunken near the bottom that a waiting diver secures it to the foundation.

According to Cayman Spirits Co., Seven Fathoms rum is a blend of one-, two-, and three-year-old rums,

all of which have spent some time maturing underwater. To meet that demand they claim to have approximately 100 casks of rum currently anchored in Cayman waters. There are further experiments taking place too, with older rums, smaller casks and one highly sought-after Modern Cooperage cask. At £2,400 ($3,000) a piece, these steel barrels are sealed units that simulate the effects of a wooden cask by using racks of barrel staves that can be manually "stirred" through the liquid. The theory is that it provides superior control and repeatability, as well as virtually eradicating the angel's share and therefore increasing profitability. Immersing wood into rum seems somehow fitting for a company which has made a name for itself by drowning wooden barrels in the sea.

GOVERNOR'S RESERVE (40% ABV)
UN-AGED RUM

Aroma is fairly neutral but still displays some cheap white chocolate, greasy cake mix, almond and creamy pepper. Taste is light, with just a touch of chewy lime zest and butter.

SEVEN FATHOMS (40% ABV)
AGED BLENDED RUM

Musty tobacco, cedar wood, butterscotch and slick caramel. The aroma is more bourbon than it is rum, but it's pleasant nonetheless. Good body on the palate, with all the usual white oak culprits: coffee, toffee, vanilla, coconut, and white chocolate. The linger is glossy and seductive.

CUBA

The name Cuba comes from the Taíno Indian word *cubao* ("where fertile land is abundant") and it's certainly an apt description of the Caribbean's largest island. If Barbados dominated 17th-century sugar cultivation, and Jamaica dominated the 18th century, it was undoubtedly Cuba that laid claim to the 19th century.

Sugar production got off to a slow start here, impeded by failures on Spain's behalf to take note of British and French innovations in cane cultivation, and by decades of declining Cuban population. Local rum production was stifled during the 18th century, thanks to Spanish paranoia that the new spirit might compete with Spain's native wine, sack (sherry) and brandy. The Real Cédula ("Royal Decree") of June 8 1693 actually prohibited rum-making, but the effect was the establishment of numerous illicit distilling operations and the rise of *aguardiente de canne* – rum's tearaway younger sibling. The blanket ban continued through the first half of the 18th century, and in 1754, offenders were ordered to work on public buildings with no pay, which typically landed them with a life lived on the street.

As the old Cuban saying goes, "sin azúcar no hay país" ("without sugar there's no country"), and this is certainly true of Cuba. The change – for both sugar and rum – came during the Seven Years War (1754–63), when the British briefly occupied Havana. By that time, rum drinking was fully ingrained in Royal Navy culture, and the necessary stills and expertise quickly disseminated through the island. Following the return of the Spanish, the policies surrounding rum production and trade were relaxed, but more important still were the revolutions in both America and Sainte-Domingue (Haiti), which established new trade and attracted new expertise and slaves respectively. Cuba, an island that accounts for almost half of all the farmable land in the Caribbean, comfortably filled both voids. Consequentially, the island exported 5 million litres (1.5 million US gallons) of rum in 1802 – 30 times the quantity exported in 1778.

Technological advances throughout the 19th century, including the mechanization of the refining process and the establishment of railways, saw Cuba's share of the world market more than double and the crop become the primary focus of the economy. With sugar in increasingly high demand, and molasses exports to North America increasing too, Cuban cane was making money on three separate fronts. By the mid-1800s, Cuba had become the most valuable island in the Caribbean.

Besides its landmass, there were a number of other factors that contributed to Cuba's dominance in the industry, not least of all its trading relationship with the US and its reluctance to abolish slavery. Cuba was also the only major island in the region that was free of mountains. Nearly three-quarters of its land formed a rolling plain – ideal for planting crops. Cuba also prospered above other islands because they used better methods when harvesting the sugar crops: they adopted modern milling methods such as watermills, enclosed furnaces, steam engines and vacuum pans.

Following the Cuban War of Independence, the island began the 20th century under indirect US control,

THIS PAGE The barrel bus at Havana Club's San Jose distillery (below left) and a number of column stills at work (below right). Cuban-style rum is a blend of column-still distillates.

culminating in the brutal dictatorship of Fulgencio Batista, a man who was popular with the US thanks to his anti-Communist position and because the situation furthered US business interests on the island. American money built huge factories known as *centrales*, able to process cane for a large number of different plantations. Batista encouraged large-scale gambling in Havana, by granting tax exemptions for new casinos and assigning public funds as grants for construction. Havana became a playground for American pleasure-seekers who quaffed back Daiquiris and Mojitos by the dozen. Rum production increased steadily, barely affected by US prohibition in which Cuba, just 90 km (55 miles) from Key West served as a handy stop off for the committed drinker. Just prior to World War II there were over 100 distilleries on the island, the main producers being Matusalem ("the Cognac of Rums"), Bacardí, Caney and Arechabala (now Havana Club). By 1959, US companies owned about 40% of all the Cuban sugar plantations.

It was a golden era of Cuban cocktail culture, but a dark time for the Cuban people. A time where Ernest Hemingway could be found propping up the bar at La Bodeguita del Media or La Floridita – he still does, but only in the form of a roped-off statue – and when the Club de Cantineros de Cuba (today known as the Cuban Bartenders' Association) would meet at their three-storey headquarters on Paseo del Prado. Cuba remains one of the only nations in the world that celebrates a National Bartender's day every year, which it does on October 7.

After a campaign lasting several years, Fidel Castro took control of Cuba on January 1 1959. The revolution was sold as a democratic one, but within a matter of months the extreme economic and social crisis that Cuba faced forced Castro to go a lot further than perhaps he first intended. First he took control of the media, then nationalized commerce, seizing 105 sugar plants and the 19 remaining distilleries on October 13 1960. The act infuriated Washington, which imposed an economic embargo which still stands today. There's nothing like a spot of communism to get the citizens thirsty, however. Distilleries worked around the clock, and between 1986–87 alone, Cuba produced 8.3 million litres (22 million gallons) of rum. And since there was nobody but the Soviets to trade with, only a fraction of that figure ever left the country. Equally impressive was the volume of industrial ethanol produced during the same period – over 1 billion litres (2.6 billion US gallons) through the 1970s and 1980s. The shift of Cuba's attention from spirit to steak in the late 1980s diverted molasses away from the distilleries and into cattle feed, shrinking the alcohol industry to its present day form.

These days, Havana Club is the only widely exported Cuban rum brand, and is produced across two separate distilleries near Havana. But other regions also contain distilleries that make numerous smaller brands for local consumption. Among the biggest of these are Roneria Central in Villa Clara in the centre of the island; and Roneria de Santiago de Cuba, the former Bacardí distillery on the island's southeast coast. The island is big enough that each region tends to conform to a specific style of rum – western is very dry, central style is balanced and eastern rums are fruity – a remnant of a time when there were dozens of such operations across the nation.

In total, Cuba drinks around 55 million litres (14.5 million US gallons) of rum a year, but the vast majority of this comes from lesser-known brands. Browsing the shelves of the local shops reveals tempting lesser-known varieties such as Cubay's pleasantly sweet dark rum and Ron Palma Mulata – a good white rum.

THIS PAGE Cuba can't buy casks directly from the US, so Havana Club barrels are usually on their third or fourth fill when they arrive here (below left); *cantineros* working on a mojito production line (centre); the barrels may be third-hand, but they can still create some exceptional liquids (below right).

all of Cuba's distilleries were seized and nationalized, including Havana Club and Bacardi – which had by that point already established distilleries in Puerto Rico and Mexico and later a headquarters in Bermuda. The Arechabalas also left Cuba during this time, but failed to reestablish production of their rum. Back in Cuba, Castro started making "Havana Club" rum (to a new recipe), which was sold locally, as well as to his comrades in the USSR. By the mid-1990s, and after the collapse of the Soviet bloc, Castro was keen to get a little more out of his rum brand, so he teamed up with the French spirits giant Pernod Ricard, who in a joint partnership known as Havana Club International now market Havana Club across the entire world. Well, except the US, owing to the long-standing trade embargo. But if you live in the US, you might at some point have seen bottles of Havana Club rum for sale, which begs the question – where are they coming from?

While Castro was negotiating terms with his new partners in 1993, another negotiation was going on in a boardroom in the Bahamas. Remember the Arechabala family? Well they certainly remembered, and as far as they were concerned, they had never been compensated for the illegal seizure of their assets in Cuba, or for the continued marketing of their Havana Club brand. Havana Club was – to all intents and purposes – still their brand. So they sold the rights and the recipe to another company – Bacardi. The same Bacardi that still held a sizeable grudge against the Castro regime on account of the seizures of their own Cuban operations, along with the distilling clout to easily launch a rum-based revenge project. And so it was, that from 1995 onwards, Bacardi began marketing a Cuban rum brand, produced in Bermuda, sold in only the US, called Havana Club.

Lawsuits followed, of course, and Bacardi's Havana Club disappeared for a time, but in 1998 a new piece of federal legislation now commonly known as the "Bacardi bill" came into effect, which effectively banned trademark registration for brands that have been confiscated by governments, like, say, Havana Club in Cuba.

These days, Bacardí Havana Club is made at their Puerto Rico distillery, and the brand maintains that the Arechabalas passed them a legitimate trademark to the brand name, for its use in the US and the rest of the world. But more recently, US–Cuba relations have been

HAVANA CLUB

Havana Club is one of those brands that makes rum an easy subject to get excited about: a name that paints a picture of jazz music, cocktails and cigars; branding that conjures up the golden age of Club de Cantineros de Cuba; and liquid that – somewhat ironically considering its country of origin – mixes very well with others. Havana Club is the darling of the current generation of bartenders; a brand that has salsa-danced the Mojito from the depths of obscurity to the lips of every drinker in every continent of the world.

A rum called "Havana Club" was first registered by José Arechabala in 1934. The product was sold primarily in Cuba, although the popularity of the island in the US at that time ensured that many bottles made their way to the States. Following the Cuban Revolution, in 1960, thawing, and Pernod Ricard have had a Trademark re-application accepted by the US Office of Foreign Assets Control, which now gives them the rights to market Havana Club – that is the one produced in Cuba – on US turf. As a backup plan, Havana Club International have already begun bottling rum under the "Havanista" brand, which is indistinguishable in appearance and taste from standard Havana Club rum.

If it all sounds a little convoluted, it's worth noting that this is just the tip of the iceberg where it comes to the complex relationships between the US and Cuba and between Bacardi and Castro. But since most of the world, for the time being at least, is drinking Havana Club that's made in Cuba, it's there that we'll focus our investigations.

Since 2007, Havana Club has been made in two separate locations in Cuba. The oldest distillery, Santa Cruz del Note, was built in 1993, after the formation of Havana Club International. Ten years later, demand for authentic Cuban rum was high and Havana Club rum had won itself a serious international following. So a new distillery was built, this time closer to Havana and featuring improved facilities for visitors (though it's still only accessible with an invitation). Santa Cruz is still the brand workhorse, producing the younger rums in the portfolio, Anejo Blanco and Havana Club 3-year-old, which together account for just over 60% of the four million 9-litre (2.4-US gallon) cases of Havana Club that ship every year. That leaves the newer San Jose plant free to focus on the aged and super-premium expressions.

Havana Club rums are legally required to be made from Cuban molasses only. But with around 50 Cuban sugar refineries to choose from, they can still be selective where it comes to sugar and mineral content. The production process is the same no matter which distillery you visit. Once the molasses has arrived, it's cut with water and fermented for 24 hours using Havana Club's proprietary yeast strain. The molasses wine is then distilled in a single steel column still, with copper bubble plates, up to a strength of 74–76% ABV. The resulting distillate is known as *aguardiente* ("fire water") and it's this slightly floral, slightly honeyed stuff that forms the basis for all Havana Club products. The *aguardiente* is next matured in American oak for two years then filtered to remove most of its colour. Following on from that, there is a new arrival in the form of neutral molasses spirit. This high-strength ethyl-alcohol is bought in from one of Cuba's industrial alcohol plants and is mixed to a

HAVANA CLUB 3 AÑOS (40% ABV)
AGED RUM

The soft lemon colour is reflected in the slight citric aroma of this rum. Oak takes on a greener, cedar-style aroma, with toasted pine nut and a murmur of treacle also making an appearance. Taste is light, effeminate and crisply dry.

HAVANA CLUB 7 AÑOS (40% ABV)
AGED RUM

Unsurprisingly, for a Cuban rum, this classic aged rum is all aspects of cigar: peppered dried fruit, sour nut, earthy funk, and all the time a warm citrus note that's best described as "hot orange juice". Gentle tannin on the palate reveals some bitter cacao notes, as well as that lingering hum of dessert fruits and spice drawer.

HAVANA CLUB SELECCIÓN DE MAESTROS (43% ABV)
AGED RUM

A fruit and nut rum that starts with yuzu zest and soft caramel before drifting into the heady florals of honeysuckle and toasted almond syrup. Wood here is pencil sharpening and cigar box, which carries through to the palate where that little extra alcohol gives a lick of toasted wood spices and dried pomegranate seeds.

specific ratio with the *aguardiente*. If it's bottled straight away, it is done so as Havana Club Anejo Blanco. For all other marques, further maturation is required.

Unlike most rum-makers, Havana Club get their casks from Scotland, Ireland or Canada rather than the US. The barrels are still American, but the trade embargo between Cuba and the US means that even barrel purchases must be made in a round-about way. Curiously though, this work-around approach will have surely shaped a different style of Cuban rum to the ones that might have been made there prior to the Cuban Revolution in 1959. A white oak barrel can't go on dishing out flavour forever, and by the time Havana Club get their hands on them, they are invariably on to their fourth or fifth fill. This means that this particular rum needs a lot of time in oak before it becomes rich in maturation character – that, for me, might be one of the reasons that even the older expressions retain their mixability.

DOMINICA

Shillingford
ROSEAU

On November 3 1493, just 20 days after departing the Canary Islands, Columbus sighted a small volcanic island that he named Dominica after the Latin word for Sunday. In the light of present day, Dominica is still a feral and rugged land, so one can only imagine the sights that Columbus beheld over 500 years ago. Dominica is nicknamed the "Nature Island" on account of the dense rainforest and network of rivers that dominate the interior island. Driving through the black heart of the jungle at night is a solitary and intimidating adventure. Ever curious, I once stopped my vehicle at the side of the road, stepped out, and cut the lights. The experience was like being instantly transported to a dream world, where blackness only served to thicken the humidity, skewing your perception of time as the deafening scream of wildlife envelopes you.

That dense centre of the island remained one of the last strongholds of the fierce Caribs, through most of the 18th century until Britain took it over in 1763. Plantations operated around the coast of the island, but they favoured coffee, and by the end of the 19th century, sugar accounted for less than 15% of total exports. This alternate approach to agriculture bred a unique culture of slavery too. Slaves on Dominica were permitted to grow their own provisions and trade them at market. Some bought their freedom with the proceeds, which established communities for free black inhabitants, some of whom bought slaves of their own. Later, Dominica became one of the first islands to have black members in the House of Assembly, and by the time slavery was abolished in 1838, the majority of the house was black. Dominica was the only island in the British West Indies where white rule was successfully challenged.

Today Dominica is a rich blend of its French, English and African heritage. But more than anything, the people here are Dominican. In the 17th century,

the French considered the spirit made from sugarcane grown in this rich, volcanic soil to be unique. Today, none of the rum bottled on this island is exported but conditions still exist to produce exceptional cane spirits.

Dominica does a big domestic trade in flavoured rums, which are typically unsweetened infusions of herbs, barks or spices, steeped into white rum, and referred to on the island as "cask rum". One of the island's most famous blends of cask rum is *bois bandé* which, like the Dominican Republic's Mama Juana and Grenada's Woodman, is said to have a tumescent effect on the males who consume it. It's made by infusing the highly prized bark of the bois bandé tree in white rum for a number of weeks or even months. It's harder to come by these days as the drink became so popular with the locals that it threatened to kill off all the trees. The authorities have subsequently declared the stripping of bois bandé bark a criminal activity.

If you find yourself driving north of Roseau towards the Macoucherie Estate (operated by Shillingford Estates Ltd) you can't help by pass the so-called Belfast Distillery. This distillery, which once blended rums from a copper pot and column, closed in the late 1980s. There have, ever since, been rumours of the equipment

THIS PAGE The colourful capital of Dominica, Roseau, houses the iconic Ruins Rock Café (centre) – an ideal spot to test how much rum punch you can consume in a afternoon.

being reinstated, but currently Belfast blends rum from Guyana, Trinidad and Barbados and bottles the Soca White and Red Cap brands under the Belfast label. It's a wonder that the word "distillery" is permitted to be used, as the reality of the operation is one of a distribution and packaging point for canned fish, soft drinks, and just about anything else you care to imagine.

There are two rum bars that are definitely worth a visit in Dominica. The first is actually a restaurant called "Islet View", which is all on its own on the outskirts of Castle Bruce on the island's east coast. The bar stocks over 100 beautifully presented proprietary rum infusions. The second bar is Ruins Rock in Roseau, which looks like a small fortress. They serve a damn good rum punch.

SHILLINGFORD

Hurricane Erika struck Dominica on August 27 2015. On the west coast, 2.5 cm (1 inch) of rain fell every hour for 12 straight hours, turning rivers into torrents and green hills into deadly mudslides. The sea overflowed onto the shore, engulfing small villages and killing dozens. On the northwest of the island, near the mouth of the Layou River, the 250-year-old Macoucherie Estate suffered badly. The original stone buildings – some of them with walls 60-cm (2-ft) thick – were almost completely submerged in water. The stills and fermenters got their feet wet too, and the cane press, staff housing and staff cricket field were obliterated. The barrel store was also hit hard and all but 40 casks of rum were lost. As the carnage unfolded, Don Shillingford could do nothing but watch, open-mouthed from his old plantation house on the hillside.

The Shillingford brothers (Thomas and William) were blacksmiths, who first set foot in Dominica in the mid-18th century. The blacksmith craft was an essential cog in the engine that was the sugar industry. Horses needed horseshoes; the sugar mills and crystallization pans were in regular need of repair; molasses barrels required metal hoops to hold the barrels together; and slaves needed shackles. From their base in Newtown, the brothers prospered, expanding their business almost as quickly as they expanded their families. As with many industrious white colonists of the time, racial hierarchy soon succumbed to the pull of human desire. Thomas Shillingford became the first in his family to depart

ABOVE The oldest remaining building on the Macoucherie Estate is thought to date back to the 18th century. Fortunately it survived the floods, which is more than can be said for the barrel store.

from the social expectations of the time by marrying a black woman who was originally from Sierra Leone.

Over the years that followed, the Shillingfords evolved from a small house of white British colonists to a sprawling family of Dominicans, with influence in virtually every aspect of island society. From the membership of the legislature to landholding, insurance brokering, media, schools, the importation of food and other merchandise and the exportation of cassava, arrowroot, cocoa, bananas, coffee, citrus fruits, sugar and rum. Although the powerful influence of the family began to decline from the 1960s, with the rise of Lebanese immigrants and political change on the island, the Shillingford name is still identified all over the Caribbean as a Dominican name.

The Shillingfords owned and operated plantations on Dominica through the 19th and 20th centuries, but it was

LEFT Once they're back on their feet, I believe there is huge potential for the Shillingford rums. And given Don's commitment to premiumization, I expect to be enjoying them in five to 10 years' time.

MACOUCHERIE WHITE (40% ABV)
UN-AGED RUM

Underripe melon, candle wax and oil. Sweet and fruity on the palate, not too hot, creamy and full. Sweetly floral through the finish.

MACOUCHERIE RED (40% ABV) AGED RUM

A nicely balanced product on the nose – yellow caramel and oak lustre plays nicely with the bright funky vegetal notes. Expect to find banoffee pie, cinnamon churros, treacle tart and fermented mango. Great bitter/sweet balance, plummy, candied and very moreish.

MACOUCHERIE OVERPROOF (64% ABV)
OVERPROOF RUM

Bubblegum and sweaty banana, the nose is part industrial oil and grease, and part agricultural ferment. There's dried apple, soft mango, banana, and petrol there. The taste is spicy, but not overly so, then sweet pungent fruits take hold.

Howell Donald Shillingford, CBE who, in 1942, bought the bankrupt Macoucherie Estate on the island's west coast. A mill was first founded on this site (which takes its name from the nearby river) as far back as the 1770s, and by 1827, when the estate was owned by James Laing of Scotland, the business owned 113 slaves. In the same year Macoucherie produced 89,000 kg (196,000 lbs) of sugar, 18,500 litres (4,850 US gallons) of rum and 33,000 litres (8,650 US gallons) of molasses.

The abolition of slavery in 1838 marked a slow decline in sugar production on Dominica, but rather than close up shop completely, Macoucherie took the same approach as the French islands, and in 1890 switched its attentions to producing rum from cane juice. When Howell Shillingford bought the plantation he expanded sugarcane cultivation on the property and rebuilt the mill and distillery. In time, the estate passed on to Howell's son, and his son, Clifton "Dense" Shillingford, and the recovery of this distillery is being handled by his son, Howell's great-grandson, Don.

The Shillingfords are the only cane growers on the island today, but over 70% of Don's 14 hectares (35 acres) of sugarcane was wiped out by Erika. Cane grows back of course, but stone does not. The destruction of the distillery's aqueduct was a major blow. Shillingford is one of only two rum distilleries in the world that still uses a water wheel to turn their cane cutter – the other being River Antoine (see pages 99–100) in Grenada. Water is collected in a reservoir 3 km (2 miles) up in the green hills of the Shillingford Estate, and by controlling the flow, the distillery team can adjust the speed of the Pelton water wheel, which has been clocked at up to 95 kph (60 mph). When operational, the mill cuts 1,800–2,700 kg (4,000–6,000 lbs) of cane in a day, and the distillery goes through about 61,000 kg (135,000 lbs) during a normal season. Fermentation of the cane juice (which is adjusted to 7° Brix through the addition of water) takes four to seven days to complete, and then the fruity wash is distilled in a single small column up to a strength of 70–75% ABV, retaining a good deal of the cane's original characteristics with it. The estate usually has about 25 full-time employees and an annual production capacity of around 19,000 litres (5,000 US gallons).

The Macoucherie rums made here are all of the cane juice variety, but Don also makes Prime Star rum, which is distilled from a wash of molasses, sourced from Trinidad. Don still sells his overproof rum too, which is also molasses-based and matured for a couple of months in oak. Local drinkers turn up with a container and pay for whatever they take. The distillery shop currently feels like the de-briefing area in a war zone, but there are big plans afoot. More of the 180-hectare (450-acre) Shillingford estate will be allocated to cane growing in the future, and more aged rums will be produced. Don plans to release 5- and 10-year-old single-cask expressions, which will tap firmly into the premium end of the market.

DOMINICAN REPUBLIC

The island of Hispaniola is shared between the Dominican Republic in the east and Haiti in the west. It's often referred to as a microcosm of Latin America, which it has more in common with than any of the Caribbean islands. The Dominican Republic has both the highest and lowest elevations in the region and this is likely one of the reasons that it garnered interest from a certain 15th century explorer. When Christopher Columbus landed on the island, on his first voyage across the Atlantic in 1492, he named it "Insula Hispana", meaning "the Spanish Island" in Latin or La Isla Española, in Spanish. Columbus transported cane cuttings to Hispana on his second voyage, in 1493, but the fragile plants died during the crossing, and the newly founded colony of Santo Domingo would have to wait another seven years until Pedro di Atienza arrived with living plants in 1500. Once planted the cane did rather well and it wasn't long before it was being pressed and fermented, the earliest known reference of this being in 1511. Five years later, in 1516, the first known mill in the West Indies dedicated to producing sugar was built in the colony of Santo Domingo in the south of the island. Exactly when the first distillation on Hispaniola took place remains a mystery.

As with most Spanish colonies, the focus was mainly on finding gold during the early years of colonization. The popularity of *aguardiente* grew too, becoming a particular hit with the Spanish *buccaneros*, where it was a staple piece of merchandise in their contraband economy. This eventually led to the King of Spain banning rum production in 1720, and it remains to this day the only Caribbean island ever to do so, besides Puerto Rico (see pages 148–49). The prohibition was lifted in 1778 and a permit system was introduced. Just 15 years later there were 173 distilleries in the Dominican Republic, each of them gobbling up molasses from the 792 sugarcane plantations that populated the eastern side of the island. Many Cubans travelled to the Dominican Republic in the 1880s and 1950s ahead of the Cuban War for Independence and the Cuban Revolution. On both occasions, they brought with them a taste and a passion for making Cuban rum, and it's the legacy of this that sets the Dominican style.

These days the sugar industry has consolidated significantly, and most of it in the southeast of the country and controlled by a handful of powerful families. Virtually all of the sugarcane in the Dominican Republic is cut by hand, by a workforce comprising mostly men, women and children of Haitian descent, who toil for 14-hour days in the fields for the equivalent of less than £1.60 ($2) a day. For almost 80 years, the Dominican sugar barons have been luring poverty-stricken Haitians across the border with promises of a better life. They're housed in plantation communities known as *bateyes* and compensated for their efforts with food tokens. Most of the time their documentation is confiscated, rendering them stateless and illegal. Many of the workers are born into this life of indentured servitude, starting in the fields as young as seven-years-old. Nobody knows how many Haitians currently live within this system, but it's

estimated that up to 20,000 fresh souls are smuggled across the border every season – and there are two cutting seasons a year in the Dominican Republic.

There are three major rum-makers in the Dominican Republic, and they all conveniently start with the same letter: Barceló, Bermúdez and Brugal. All the rums made here are multi-column distilled, achieving vodka levels of neutrality in the process. For better or for worse, this has firmly placed the emphasis on maturation, to the point where a visit to a distillery is in fact a visit to a barrel store and bottling line. Though it has to be said, the distilleries themselves, which are little more than industrial ethanol plants, are not inspiring setups. Most of them are located in the low-lying southeast of the country, like oil rigs amongst a sea of sugarcane.

Bermúdez is the oldest of the three producers, dating back as far as 1852. They're also the only one of the trio that doesn't really export their product, but instead choose to focus on producing budget whiskey and vodka brands for the local market. Speaking of the local market, Brugal dominate 75% of the share in the Dominican Republic to the extent that many of the street and road signs are sponsored by them.

By Dominican Republic law, all rum labelled as being from the Dominican Republic must be distilled there and matured for no less than 12 months. Even white rums must abide by this rule, and are filtered to remove colour after maturation.

BARCELÓ

As is consistent with most of the rum brands arising in Spanish colonies, Barceló (bar-SEL-oh) was established by a Spaniard too. Julián Barceló emigrated to the Dominican Republic from Majorca, Spain, in 1929 and established a blending house the following year. The 1930s was the dawn of the iron-fisted dictatorship of Rafael Trujillo, which saw 30 years of enormous industrial growth for the Dominican Republic, and Barceló certainly made the most of it, working with local distillers around Santo Domingo to launch the "Carta Real" brand. Unlike Ron Barceló itself, Carta Real is still owned by the Barceló family, who, headed up today by José Barceló, still bottle rums in Santo Domingo under the brand names "Columbus" and "Dubar Imperial".

The first rum going by the name of Barceló was launched in 1950, starting with Blanco and Dorado ("golden") expressions. These were joined by an Anejo and Imperial in the 1970s. Over the past 20 years the brand has gradually been bought out by Spanish investors, and merged with Varma International. This has prompted further releases of extra-aged rum expressions (see below) as well as enormous export trade in Spain and a further 55 countries besides. Nowadays Barceló own barely 20% of the Dominican rum market, but thanks to the 20 million litres (5.2 million US gallons) of rum that they export every year, the brand ranks behind only Bacardí, Havana Club and Captain Morgan in the West Indies.

Barceló is the only rum in the Dominican Republic to use cane juice as their base material. In fact, as far as I am aware, it is the only Spanish-style rum made exclusively from sugarcane juice. So we're looking at an *agricole*-esque product then? Nope. The use of cane juice in this instance is neither here nor there, since the distillate comes off the still at around 95% ABV and any trace of base material has been stripped out completely. The producer of that spirit is the sexy sounding "Alcoholes Finos Dominicanos", who are based just north of the south coast town of San Pedro de Marcolis, and not far from Batey Consuelito and Batey Vasca. Constructed in 2009, the distillery comprises both copper and stainless steel column stills, as well as cane-milling equipment sufficient to produce 50,000 litres (13,000 US gallons) of alcohol a day.

Heading west 18 km (11 miles), we find the Barceló ageing and bottling facility. It's as far removed from the tribulations of cutting sugarcane by hand as could be possible. A polished visitors centre, rum museum and

FAR LEFT The humble beginnings of one of the world's biggest rum brands.

LEFT When you're producing rum at this kind of volume, barrels don't remain empty for long.

ABOVE The Barceló visitors centre features dozens of old bottles, including rums blended by Julián Barceló himself.

tasting room prove a tempting opportunity for tourists visiting the south-coast beaches. The high-strength alcohol is tankered over to the ageing facility, where it is cut down to 70% ABV in preparation for filling American white oak casks. Under Dominican law, all rum must be aged for a minimum of 12 months, but Barceló prove they're in it to win it by maturing for a minimum of 18 months on all of their expressions. There's an on-site cooperage that conducts repairs and reconditions casks by stripping the inside and re-charring the wood. The coopers use thin strips of bulrush (known locally as *enea*) to plug minor cracks and fissures in the casks.

The Añejo and Gran Añejo expressions are blends of 2- and 3-year-old, and 4- and 6-year old rums respectively. Gran Platinum is the brand's answer to vodka drinkers: a 6-year-old rum filtered to remove any trace of colour. Then there's Imperial: the flagship of the brand, comprising 8–10–year old rums aged in ex-bourbon casks.

There are some Bordeaux wine barrels taking up space too, which are used only for the 9,000 bottles of Imperial Premium Blend that are released annually. Also hidden among the production space is a filter packed with Mexican onyx stones. The Barceló Imperial Onyx expression is presented in matt black packaging and after undergoing maturation in "extra-charred" casks, the liquid is passed through this filter. I'm not entirely sure what it is supposed to do, but releases like these don't come cheap. It's for perhaps that reason that they have enjoyed some success in the Russian and Chinese luxury markets. I'm always wary of brands that boast ludicrous production practices and overly showy packaging, as they're all too often marketing a

AÑEJO (38% ABV) AGED RUM

Burnt orange and tobacco, dry and quite pleasant on the palate. Charcoal, vanilla bitters and mineral finish. Nice.

GRAN AÑEJO (38% ABV) AGED RUM

Aerated chocolate, vanilla custard, coffee ice cream, caramel swirl. Docile and lacking guts, flabby chocolate indulgence, cake. Finish is mildly sweet, greasy and a bit flat.

GRAN PLATINUM (37.5% ABV)
WHITE AGED RUM

Suspiciously lemony: green sherbet and cheap lemonade. No trace of maturation, only lemon essences. What a disappointment, and what a waste of six years!

IMPERIAL (38% ABV) EXTRA-AGED RUM

Stale tobacco, fruity caramel, wood char, oak lactones and maple syrup. Honeysuckle and raspberry cream. Slightly sweet, juicy, slick and full of winey oiliness. Indulgent and damn smooth.

IMPERIAL ONYX (38% ABV) EXTRA-AGED RUM

Soft cherry, more chocolate, vague marzipan heaviness, with coconut and white chocolate. Almost bourbon-like. Taste is full of vanillin; bright white chocolate couples with dark, toffee and tobacco on the finish. Intense and concentrated.

IMPERIAL 30TH ANNIVERSARY (43%ABV)
EXTRA-AGED RUM

Fine fleshy fruits, cacao, burnt vanilla and heady esters. Cognac finesse, sweet grapes, dried mango and sugared coconut. Sweetness builds slowly and lingers through the finish. Dessert fruits, gentle cake spices, muscovado sugar and just big concentrated fructose.

brand of lifestyle than truly delicious rum. In the case of the super-premium Bareceló offerings however, I can't bring myself to hate them, because they're damn tasty rums.

BRUGAL

Andrés Brugal Montaner was only 18 when he emigrated to the Caribbean from Catalonia in 1868. His first choice of tropical island was not the Dominican Republic however, but Cuba, where he settled in the southern coastal town of Santiago, later opening a hardware store. Naturally he was aware of sugarcane cultivation, and at some point he also became aware of the rum manufacturing process too. This was during the time of José Marti, the "Apostle of Cuban Independence", and a period of great social change in Cuba as a colony, and eventually a nation. The Ten Years' War (1868–78) fought against Spain had already sent many planters packing their bags and heading to the relative stability of the Dominican Republic to ply their trade. Then the abolition of slavery in Cuba in 1886 saw the freed men of Cuba join the ranks of the working classes. Security fears plagued business owners and many more left Cuba never to return. Among them was Andrés Brugal, who moved to Puerto Plata on the Dominican Republic's north coast in 1888, which would have seemed like sugar nirvana to the arriving planters and rum makers. Cane was booming thanks to President Ulises "Lilís" Heureaux's subsidising of plantations (with European-borrowed cash), which sought to curry favour with the quickly expanding populace. These subsidies along with the drop in market value of sugar, would ultimately lead to the country's bankruptcy (and Lilís's assassination) in 1899, but by that point Don Andrés Brugal was already well-established as one of the country's greatest rum blenders.

Today, there are estimated to be more than 1,500 Dominican people, scattered over seven generations, who descend from this Spanish immigrants who had come to Puerto Plata to start a rum revolution. Don Andrés himself oversaw production of Brugal rum up until his death in 1930, and despite the Scottish-based Edrington Group buying a majority shareholding of the business in 2008, the day-to-day operations remain in the safe hands of Brugal's fifth generation of Maestros Roneros: Gustavo Ortega Zeller and Jassil Villanueva.

Brugal employ the services of no fewer than three distilleries to produce their spirit. They are all located in

THIS PAGE Brugal Extra Añejo is the No. 1 bestselling rum in the Dominican Republic (top); a snapshot of the enormous bottling hall at Brugal's Puerto Plata blending facility (middle); Brugal cask samples taken at one-year intervals. (bottom).

the ocean of cane that dominates the east of the island, and between them they can produce up to 75,000 litres (20,000 US gallons) of pure alcohol in a day. The spirit comes off the still at 95% ABV and by master blender Jassil Villanueva's own admission, "all of the character comes from the cask". Once it arrives at one of Brugal's ageing facilities, the spirit is cut to 65% ABV ready for filling in batches of 108 casks at a time.

There are two ageing and bottling facilities used by Brugal, a "small" customer-facing operation in the centre of Puerto Plata that offers tours and tastings, and a larger warehouse to the west that handles 85% of the products. The warehouse in Puerto Plata is a colourful place thanks to an old cask management system that Brugal used to employ, which involved painting the chime (outer) hoop red, yellow, blue or white to denote how many times it had been filled. The system has been replaced by barcodes, but the barrels still bear the colour. Besides ex-bourbon casks, Brugal also have healthy stocks of *olorosso a Pedro Ximenez* sherry casks. These are a relatively rare in the rum world, but there are few companies with better access to this quality of wood than the Edrington Group, who have built a reputation for top-quality malt whisky through a liberal use of sherry casks.

This top-level oak really comes into its own in the older expressions that Brugal produce, where wood spice, dried fruits and sweet dairy notes win me over. The 1888 expression is my pick of the bunch, it spends 6–8 years in ex-bourbon casks before being finished for a few years in ex-oloroso casks. Layenda is sort of the reverse of 1888, spending the majority of its time in sherry wood. Brugal Extra Viejo is a blend of rums aged 3–8 years in ex-bourbon casks. XV is also a blend of 3–8-year-old ex-bourbon cask rums, mixed with 2–3-year-old Pedro Ximenez cask rums. Brugal Añejo is aged for 2–5 years, and so too is Especial Extra Dry (which is filtered to remove colour). And if you're feeling flush, why not splash out on a bottle of Brugal "Papá Andrés"? It carries no age statement as, according to Jassil, "the ages are irrelevant". Prior to 2013, Papá Andrés was available only in charity auctions, but Brugal are now releasing 1,000 bottles annually. At £1,200 ($1,500) a bottle though, you'll probably need only one...

It would be neglectful of me not to mention the Brugal Foundation, a charitable organisation set up in 1988 to promote quality education in the Dominican Republic through opening schools and investing in scholarships for talented students who face financial hardship.

ESPECIAL EXTRA DRY (40% ABV)
WHITE AGED RUM

Faint citrus and a fuller hit of the vegetal; coconut water, candy floss and soft, sweet marshmallow. On the palate it's big and round – almost mushy. More vegetal through the finish, little in the way of citrus. Cold vanilla latte.

AÑEJO (38% ABV) AGED RUM

Vanilla resin, caramel cup, bourbon characteristics. Little in the way of fruitiness, but plenty of the more obvious dessert qualities that wood provides. Soft melted wood on the palate, a little spice kicking in to hold the mid palate, fades off quite quickly. Like diluted bourbon, but nicely balanced.

EXTRA VIEJO (38% ABV) AGED RUM

Gives away less on the nose. Gentle orange peel, some "char" bitterness, nutmeg, cinnamon. Elegant. On the palate there's Christmas cake, orange marmalade top notes, with mace, nutmeg and allspice, and just a hint of potted fruits. More baking spices through the finish.

XV (38% ABV) AGED RUM

Buttery dried fruit, like unbaked cake mix. Second sniff brings rum and raisin ice-cream, dessert chocolate, gentle florals and heady stone fruits. Sophisticated and soft. More concentrated and sweet on the palate, but never maturing into anything with too much depth.

1888 (40% ABV) EXTRA-AGED RUM

Elegant, winey, Christmas dinner brandy, soft praline, dried plums, dates. Sticky. Dry sherry fruits does battle with concentrated oak lactones. Wood spices integrate with plump fruits, biscuit (cookie) and butterscotch. Finish is long with flutters of spiced fruit compote and cacao. What a difference 2% of alcohol makes.

LEYENDA (38% ABV) EXTRA-AGED RUM

Massive concentrated raisins and sultanas (golden raisins), deeply rich stone fruits. Candied orange and grapefruit peel. Very sweet on the palate: orange candy and sweaty old raisins. The rum actually loses complexity due to the sweetness, but is delicious nonetheless. Perfect with a cigar.

GRENADA

Britain took permanent control of Grenada from France in 1763 under the terms of the Treaty of Paris. Included in the deal were 100 sugar mills along with 12,000 enslaved Africans. The British took little time colonizing the island, and just seven years later there were 1,500 colonists and 25,000 slaves. That same year the island exported 2.5 million litres (660,000 US gallons) of rum. The number of plantations continued to grow over the following 50 years, until the island became almost completely dependent on sugar, with as much as 83% of the slave workforce involved in sugar production by 1819. Things were set to change however, as the emancipation of slaves in 1833, followed by Europe's steady transition to sugar beet, meant that making sugar was no longer a viable economic activity.

Grenada remained prosperous thanks to an agricultural program in the latter half of the 19th century that saw the island shift from large-scale sugar production to small-scale peasant cultivation of cocoa and spices. Sugar was out, and nutmeg, mace, cinnamon, cloves and ginger were in. Today, this tiny island, which was only introduced to nutmeg in 1843, now produces around one-quarter of all the world's supply. Nutmeg even features on the country's flag. Grenada is the 10th smallest country in the world, and the second smallest in the Caribbean. For me, it serves as a fantastic résumé of all the best bits of the Caribbean: sun-bleached sand and clear waters;

steep mountains that play host to wildlife from iguanas to armadillo; a varied agriculture with enough spices to single-handedly service the Americas; and strong rum.

The island was devastated by Hurricane Ivan in 2004, but the rebuild was swift and the architecture has remained sympathetic to the historical designs. The main town at St. George's is almost suspiciously pristine given the apparent authenticity of the pastel-coloured buildings and thriving market place. Fishermen busy themselves with nets, or with bottled beer. Rum makes an appearance too, but it is a drink consumed mostly by the older generation at present.

There are two rum distilleries on Grenada: Grenada Distillers Ltd. and River Antoine. Twenty-five years ago

THIS PAGE If it's cane harvesting season, you won't be short of sugary treats (below left); Grenada has done a fairly good job at capitalizing on rum tourism (below); Clarke's Court branding above liquor stores reminds us of the top-selling brand; (below right) cane fields and palms near River Antoine Distillery (far right).

there were four, but among the casualties of Hurricane Ivan was the Dunfermline Estate, which was originally established in 1797 just a few miles away from River Antoine in the north.

Grenada's Westerhall Estate was founded in the 1700s, but was originally a citrus fruit and banana estate, before turning to cane-growing and rum-making when Sir William Johnstone bought it in the late 1700s, changing the name to Westerhall in reflection of his hometown in Dumfriesshire, Scotland. This distillery also harnessed energy from the river (the St Louis, in this instance) which turned two wheels, one for crushing cane and the other for crushing fruits. The distillery was retired in 1994, and exactly a decade later, Hurricane Ivan took care of demolishing the walls. Nowadays, visitors are invited to walk the grounds, which are somewhat of an open-air museum of rum history. Westerhall still bottle and blend rum that is sourced from the Angostura distillery in Trinidad.

Moonshining is alive and well in Grenada also, where it's estimated that over 50 illegitimate stills are secluded among the dense hills and steep valleys. Here, they call it *babash* or "mountain dew" and it's made from imported molasses. Those that are not making their own are at least flavouring bought stuff. Spiced rum is known as "woodman" on Grenada, which can be infused with anything from borbondi bark and cola nuts right through to centipedes. If you're wondering why someone would be inclined to drink such a concoction, it's worth knowing that the name "woodman" is not in reference to someone in the profession of felling trees, but rather in the "sexual potency" it supposedly bestows upon the drinker.

Sex sells, and on this particular island so too does Campari… for some reason. Advertising for the Italian aperitif is everywhere, but booze of all sorts is commonplace. Around 5% of the population of Grenada are degree-level students, attending medical courses at St. George's University (it's always the medics that drink the hardest) so it may not come as a surprise to learn that Grenada has the highest alcohol consumption per capita in the Western Hemisphere, rattling through the equivalent of 31 bottles of 40% ABV rum per person, per year. The problem is, nobody is drinking 40% alcohol spirits here. Both of the islands' distilleries bottle super-high strength spirits as standard and I can assure you that it remains that way (undiluted, unmixed) as it claws its way down your throat.

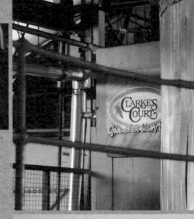

THIS PAGE The Grenada Sugar Factory has undergone some major changes in the past 20 years, but Clarke's Court is just as popular as ever among the Grenadians.

GRENADA SUGAR FACTORY

By the turn of the 20th century, Grenada's sugar industry was already in serious decline. Spices had proven a more lucrative crop and cheaper to manage. The only issue was that nutmeg and cinnamon trees could take decades to reach full maturity, while cane can be grown and cut in a matter of months. Grenada was no longer dependent on sugar, like so many of its neighbours, but there was still money to be made from this fast-maturing cash crop.

This is evident in the construction of the Grenada Sugar Factory, which was built in 1937 on the site of an even older mill that dates back to the 18th century. At that time, the island was still growing in excess of 30,000 tons (33,000 US tons) of sugar every year, but it was becoming increasingly impractical for each plantation to operate their own mill and distillery. So a collective of sugar planters formed the Cane Grower's Association, and consolidated their production in a new company in the Woodlands Valley. They named it the Grenada Sugar Factory Ltd. As with most other sugar-processing plants of the era, a distillery was built alongside the plant to process the leftover molasses into rum.

War was just around the corner, so the first bottling of rum was delayed until 1947, when the Grenada Sugar Factory launched the Red Neck Rum brand. Later, the

LEFT At 69% alcohol by volume, it's advisable to approach Clarke's Court Pure White Rum with caution. I advise having a glass of water close at hand. And perhaps a fire extinguisher, too.

CLARKE'S COURT SUPERIOR LIGHT (43% ABV) UN-AGED RUM

Faintly mushroomy, but very light indeed. Dirty fungal notes on the palate, sweet too, with nutmeg, vanilla and more mushroom. Finish is slack and still fungal.

CLARKE'S COURT PURE WHITE RUM (69% ABV) OVERPROOF RUM

Big, bright – almost jumps out at you. Juicy and citric on the palate, still full of character but remaining fresh and lively. It's hot, but it comes as no surprise. Finish is liquorice (licorice), white pepper, bitter almond and lime peel.

CLARKE'S COURT "SPECIAL DARK" (40% ABV) AGED RUM

Brown sugar and dried coconut sugar cake. Guava, cheese, molasses and sweet vanilla. The palate is sweet and soft, with vanilla and gentle bourbon. Finish is vanilla fudge.

CLARKE'S COURT 5-YEAR-OLD (43% ABV) AGED RUM

Banana milkshake and sweet nutmeg on the nose. Simple and confected. Artificial banana, flabby, sickly and boring.

CLARKE'S COURT #37 (40% ABV) EXTRA-AGED RUM

Baked sponge cake, coffee and bittersweet chocolate. The palate is slick, fruity, but still quite light. Fruit continues to grip, with bitter salted chocolate and alcohol heat.

factory produced another rum under the Tradewinds brand, and this went head to head with products from Dunfermline Estate, River Antoine and Westerhall. All of them, however, were forced to compete with a rapid decline of sugar on the island. Unperturbed, the distillery's best known brand, Clarke's Court, was created in 1973. This rum was named after nearby Clarke's Court Bay, which gets its name from Gedney Clarke, who purchased much of the Woodlands estate in the late 19th century, including the original "Court Bay" that was named by the Dutch. The early Clarke's Court rums would have been quite different to the ones bottled today however.

Following Maurice Bishop's political revolution in 1979, the company was privatized in 1982 and renamed Grenada Distillers Ltd. It was a subtle change of title from the "Grenada Sugar Factory" (by which it is still known by locals) but an important one, as it coincided with the termination of sugar manufacturing. The year 1983 also saw the original alembic stills stripped out of the distillery and replaced with a column still. The raw material changed too. Up until the 1980s the distillery was producing rum from three different Grenadian base materials: sugar cane juice and molasses during the February to June harvest season; and sugarcane syrup and molasses for the remainder of the year. With sugar production coming to an end there was no molasses, so it began arriving by boat from Guyana. The cane syrup continued to be processed using the local crop, but both products were (as they are today) distilled to above 95%, so any trace of character was stripped out. Another 10 years passed, and virtually all of the sugar plantations on the island had shut up shop. Now the distillery uses imported molasses from Guyana and Panama.

The ability to adapt is what's kept this operation alive for the past 80 years, but much has been lost along the way. What we're left with today is, in truth, a ghost of rum's past. Present in spirit, but lacking in body and character.

Molasses is not the only Guyanan import hanging around at the distillery. The master blender at Grenada Distillers is Ahmad Rasheed, a veteran chemist and former operations manager at the Diamond Distillery in Georgetown (see pages 175–78). Under Mr Rasheed's exceptionally experienced gaze, fermentation takes place in 36,500-litre (9,500-US gallon) tanks, of which there are six. The spirit is distilled to 95% ABV and either cut for bottling one of the high-strength products, or sent for filling ex-bourbon casks.

RIVER ANTOINE DISTILLERY

The River Antoine distillery on Grenada's north-east coast was first established in 1785. At that time there would have been dozens of small sugar estates across the island, each of them busily processing the island's chief commodity and producing their share of rum with it. But the sugar industry soon began to decline, and was hit especially hard by the emancipation of slavery in 1834, which made the sugar factories unsustainable.

Milestones in the island's history include the building of Grenada's first school (1872), the arrival of the first motor vehicle (1907) and the introduction of electricity (1928). During this time, the agriculture of the island began to look beyond sugarcane, to the spices that it is now renowned for. But through all that change, through rebellion and independence, one thing has remained almost exactly the same: River Antoine distillery.

The operational practices at River Antoine are old-fashioned to say the least. The distillery is one of only two rum distilleries in the world (the other is Shillingford on Dominica – see page 89) that is powered by a water wheel, which claims to be the oldest working example in the whole of the Americas. The wheel is turned by an aqueduct fed from a nearby reservoir, which is in turn filled by the River Antoine itself. This wheel powers the distillery's conveyor belt and cane mill, processing the raw sugarcane into fresh juice and *bagasse* (the leftover dry husk). The cane itself is all of the "hand-cut" variety, arriving in bundles wrapped in green cane leaves, from one of the 50 or so family farms that supply the distillery.

The freshly pressed juice travels along a narrow, tiled aqueduct and into the boiler room. In here, the juice is filtered and then transferred between consecutive copper pans (four in total) which each hold up to 1,820 litres (480 US gallons) of juice. The pans are gently heated from a furnace operating below, which is fuelled by the *bagasse*. As more fresh juice flows in, an attendant ladles liquid from the cooler pans to the hotter ones, reducing its volume until it reaches 19–21% sugar – somewhere in-between juice and syrup. The volume of juice is recorded on a blackboard and the farmer is paid at a

TOP AND MIDDLE When the conveyor belt breaks down, cane is loaded into the mill by hand. They only press cane in the morning – the reservoir feeding the wheel dries up by noon.

ABOVE Cane juice simmering in copper pans gives us a snapshot of how sugar was once made across the region.

in the US in the middle of the last century, and their design is reminiscent of a whisky still. The distillate passes through two steel retorts and then a heat exchanger, which pre-heats the next batch of wash and kicks off the condensation of spirit vapour. Then the distillate is partially condensed, the vapour travels down through a worm-tub style condenser before it is cut and collected. The machinery and process here is primitive enough that the end results are inconsistent in strength, so it's not unheard of for the rum to be re-distilled to bring the strength up to a minimum of 75% ABV.

The rum made here is bottled straight from the still, and although it says 75% on the bottle, I suspect that at times it could be even higher (but never lower). Passenger aircraft will not carry spirits above 70% ABV and even freight planes require specialist licensing, so it's for this reason that you're unlikely to ever see a bottle of "Rivers" outside of Grenada. If you do, it would have travelled by boat. River Antoine recognized this as a problem for tourists, so these days they also bottle at a comparatively tame 69% ABV, too.

The rum made here is strong by anyone's standards, but the observance of historical methods is stronger still. It's hard not to get caught up in the emotion of the whole thing, as centuries of rum-making are recounted through the wearing of hard stone and timber, and through the subjugation of weary machines. Perhaps I'm a romantic, but when I taste the rum made here I feel like I am drinking the distillery itself. I pray it never changes.

ABOVE Both of River Antoine's products are twice the strength and half the price of Bacardi.

LEFT The fresher the cane, the more juice it gives up. This blackboard records the volume of cane juice each farmer's crop yielded.

rate of $1.75 East Caribbean dollars (45p/30¢) per gallon. One gallon (4.5 litres) of juice is enough to make about ⅕ gallon (1 litre) of 69% ABV rum.

The next step is fermentation, which takes 6–8 days. No yeast is added to the juice; instead the distillery allows its open windows and ensuing natural airborne yeast to take care of proceedings. This, along with the cocktail of bacteria that cling to the side of the tanks, and pirouetting shafts of Grenadian sunshine, makes for wacky alcoholic soup of around 17% ABV, although this is prone to shifting up or down.

Distillation is carried out in one of two 1,365-litre (360-US gallon) copper pot-stills that are each heated by a wood-burning furnace. These stills were manufactured

RIVERS (69% ABV)
OVERPROOF POT-STILL RUM

Petroleum and hard-working grease. Soft raw plantain, clove, mace, dirty papaya. Big and greasy on the palate, hot pepper, green banana, bitter roots and just a zip of lime peel.

RIVERS (75% ABV)
OVERPROOF POT-STILL RUM

More fruit alongside the fuel, with red chilli (chile) jam, cayenne pepper, raspberry syrup and more of those aromatic spices. Raw and bone-dry on the palate with supercharged heat and palate-stripping ripeness. Hard and juicy through the mid palate. A genuinely moving experience.

GUADELOUPE

Known as the "butterfly island" on account of its lepidopteran shape, Guadeloupe is in fact two islands separated by a salt water river. The western wing is called Basse-Terre, and it's dominated by lush green volcanic hills stitched thick with banana trees. The lower-lying land reaches towards the sea, and it's in those areas you tend to find all the sugarcane. Five of Guadeloupe's six distilleries are on Basse-Terre. The eastern wing, Grande-Terre, is lower lying and hotter, and along with lots of chalk-rich soil, it makes for perfect growing conditions for the cane. The island's largest distillery, Damoiseau, is situated here, near the tip of the wing. In the thorax of the island, where the two regions join, is the islands largest city, Pointe-à-Pitre: a busy port and industrial town during the daytime but rather more edgy after dark where the *rhum* flows freely.

During the harvesting season, Guadeloupe is teeming with shifting swathes of leafy sugarcane. There are 12,000 hectares (30,000 acres) of land dedicated to growing cane on the island, which translates to around 800,000 tons (880,000 US tons) of raw cane harvested annually. And since a single ton of cane yields 200 litres (53 US gallons) of *rhum agricole*, it's safe to say that Guadeloupe is future-proofed for any rise in demand. The island actually produces more *rhum* than its more famous southern neighbour, Martinique, but unlike Martinique there is no AOC. There is a Geographical Indication associated with Guadeloupian *rhum*, however, but that doesn't prevent the distilleries on Guadeloupe going about their business as they please. In general, they use the Martinique rule book as a guideline, tweaking bits and pieces to suit their own preference. This also means that distillers on Guadeloupe make more molasses-based *rhum*, or *rhum industriel* as it is known there, although most of it is exported for blending and none is bottled for sale on the island.

Every bit as relevant to the rum aficionado as Guadeloupe itself, is the nearby island dependancy of Marie-Galante. The island is accessible by a one-hour boat ride, heading south-east from Pointe-à-Pitre. For me, Marie-Galante represents the epitome of the Caribbean idyl: white sandy beaches, coral reefs, lazy sun-bleached waterfront towns and generally not a lot going on to distract you from the beauty of the whole thing. Not a lot that is, except for *rhum*-making. There are three distilleries on this island, which measures only 15 km (9 miles) from tip to tip; with a population of just 12,000 souls, nobody's short of a bottle of *rhum* on Marie-Galante.

Besides the quantity of distilleries on Marie-Galante, visitors will notice that the *rhum* produced here is bottled at a rather alarming strength of 59%. The French government have legally sanctioned this bottling strength, which is two degrees above the normal legal limit and almost half as strong again as the industry standard of 40% ABV. "Why?" you might ask. During one *rhum*-fuelled encounter, a local musician told me it's because the island has historically been quite short on water. The distillers made a plea for a higher bottling strength, which meant less water was needed to dilute the product.

Due to the size of Marie-Galante, the distilleries have become popular tourist attractions. By far the most interesting of the three is Bielle, which is producing some of the finest *rhums* in the Caribbean right now.

FAR LEFT Young cane flourishing on the fertile volcanic soils of Basse-Terre.

LEFT Marie-Galante is far less frantic than the towns of Guadeloupe. There's a good tourism trade, great bars and some fantastic *rhum agricole* for lubrication.

BELLEVUE

As the 19th century came to a close, there were 106 windmills on Marie-Galante, which, on an island with a landmass of just 158 square kilometres (61 square miles), means you could never stray far from somewhere that was refining sugar. A few were dedicated only to producing raw sugar, but most were making *rhum*, and if not from sugarcane juice then certainly from the molasses by-product leftover from the sugar-refining process. The empty stumps of many of these forgotten plantations are still dotted around the hills of Marie-Galante, like nagging gravestones reminding us of a once thriving cottage industry. Today, this island which was once known as *l'île aux cent moulins* ("the island of a hundred windmills") has only two windmills that are still turning, and they are said to be the only working windmills in the West Indies. One of them, which was built in 1821, is at the Bellevue distillery.

Hubert Damoiseau has been at the head of this operation for 42 years now, which was originally bought by his great-grandfather, in 1924. As a cousin of Hervé Damoiseau, proprietor of the Damoiseau distillery in Grande-Terre on Guadeloupe's mainland, there's *rhum* in the blood of this family and there's a heartiness to the *rhum*, too. Hubert inherited the distillery from his uncle in the 1970s and impassioned the locals to help him pump some life into the business. Hubert is something of a local hero today and the distillery employees loyally state that it's the man they work for, not the distillery. This is because, in 1995, Hubert merged the operation with the Erstein group, a French sugar conglomerate. Erstein later passed their interest on to the La Martiniquaise group (France's second largest spirits group) who own a whole bunch of brands and distilleries, including Depaz (see pages 133–34) and Saint James (see pages 145–147).

All too often these mergers and acquisitions can turn out a little toxic, especially when humble old distilleries are concerned, but this partnership has proven to be a fruitful one. Over the years that have passed since the acquisition, significant investment has been channelled into the Bellevue distillery and it now holds a position as one of the "greenest" distilleries in the world. This begins with cane that is sourced only from the fields adjacent to the distillery, reducing transport costs and minimizing the carbon footprint. All of the waste water from the distillery is oxygenated using cutting-edge technology then, after seven months, used to irrigate the cane fields. Just like many other *agricole* distilleries, the *bagasse* is burned to produce steam, and the leftover ash is turned into fertilizer.

On top of these sustainable agricultural practices, Bellevue has taken further measures that go above and beyond the normal remit of a spirits producer. Four acres of solar panels were installed in 2010, which overnight made Bellevue the largest solar farm in the Caribbean; and what with being in a part of the world where the sun shines all day long, these panels are good for generating over one-third of all of Marie-Galante's energy needs.

It's thanks to all of the measures listed above, along with a generally fierce culture of sustainability, that Bellevue, a distillery that produces 1.2 million litres (317,00 US gallons) of bottled *rhum* a year (placing

THIS PAGE With its 20-plate column and truckloads of cane, Bellevue is a relatively normal-looking distillery on the face of it, but scratch the surface and there's a wealth of environmental considerations lurking underneath.

BELLEVUE (50% ABV) UN-AGED CANE JUICE RUM

Slightly floral; peach and peach blossom, dried banana skin and leather on the nose. Potent and rich, while remaining elegant and light. Crisp and fresh on the palate, with gentle peppered spice cut by lime oils and coriander seed.

BELLEVUE (59% ABV) UN-AGED CANE JUICE RUM

More restrained on the nose, showing signs of vanilla ice cream, dried yogurt, fresh plum and plantain. Big and luscious in the mouth: green chilli (chile) hot sauce and fleshy fish. Savoury and spiced through the finish, showing brawn and masculinity.

TRES VIEUX XO RÉSERVE ALBERT GODFREY (45% ABV)
EXTRA-AGED CANE JUICE RUM

Maple, vanilla and lots of ripe stone fruit: peach, cherry. Dried coconut, toffee apple and Demerara sugars. Some floral notes of elderflower and jasmine too. Drier than expected, with soft tobacco, rancio, cigar smoke and liquorice (licorice). Finish is all toasted wood and incense.

it third in the production rankings of Guadeloupean distilleries) is in fact carbon negative – a claim that only a handful of spirits producers in the world can make.

Ironically, the windmill is little more than an ornament (ok, a very large and impressive ornament) and it plays no part in the operation whatsoever.

Bellevue *rhum* is made from red and white cane varieties, the juice of which is fermented for 30–40 hours using a conventional baker's yeast. The *rhum* is distilled in a 20-plate stainless-steel column still, up to a strength of 79% ABV. Around 95% of production is bottled as *rhum blanc* at either 50% ABV or, in accordance with the Marie-Galante Trademark, 59% ABV. The remaining 5% is sent for maturation in ex-bourbon and ex-Cognac casks.

THIS PAGE The windmill turns (top), but it doesn't mill anything, unlike this mini-mill (middle right), which juices cane samples to test their sugar content so that the farmer is paid appropriately. The end result is 59% ABV Marie-Galante *rhum*, which packs some heat – but that's the point, right?

BIELLE

I have absolutely no reservations when I say that, of the trio of distilleries on Marie-Galante, Bielle is the most progressive. In fact, it's probably the most exciting distillery in terms of liquid innovation of any of the sixteen distilleries on the French Caribbean islands. This is in part down to a fruitful partnership with Italian rum importer, Luca Gargano, and grappa baron, Gianni Capovilla. It's also thanks to Jérôme Thiery, the distillery manager, whose explorations into cane milling, long fermentations, and pot stills (for some expressions) has resulted in some blinding white *rhums* that exhibit clarity and complexity by the bucketload. But credit must also go to Jacques Larrent, the cellar master, who earned his stripes working for the Martell Cognac house, and has now turned his attention to *rhum agricole*. Between these four men, the rule book is getting somewhat of a re-write.

The Bielle distillery is near the centre of Marie-Galante, around a 10-minute drive north from Grand Bourg. The road gradually becomes less and less passable, but just before you conclude that it's all too much and turn around… the distillery appears from nowhere. On the day that I visited it was a hive of activity. Visitors milled around drinking Ti Punch and sampling the range of *rhums*. Distillery workers busied themselves with the truckloads of cane that seemed to turn up every ten minutes. Authentically dressed local women set up half a dozen market stalls, selling fish-filled pasties, coconut crudités and other pâtisserie items. Wandering the grounds, you're occasional made aware of the aroma of animal sweat and manure. It's the real deal though; carts drawn by oxen plod along the road, loaded high with just-cut cane from the nearby plantations.

Inside the distillery there are roller mills for crushing the cane, fermenters and of course the traditional Savalle column still for making *rhum agricole*. There's also a 500-litre (132-US gallon) German-style alembic pot still that looks slightly out of place in the context of *rhum agricole*. It's of the same cast as those that have become popular in the craft spirits movement of late.

This copper pot hints at some weird goings-on at Bielle, and the deeper you delve the more it becomes clear: Bielle is not a conventional *rhum*-maker, but in truth, two distilleries under one roof. With the exception of "Premium Blanc" (see right), the Bielle branded *rhums* are made in a mostly typical *agricole* fashion: cane (red and white varieties) are hand-cut and milled only twice – this is to avoid the green and sappy flavours that can come about during a third or fourth pressing. Fermentation lasts 36–48 hours and the *rhum* is distilled up to 77% through three linked columns. Then, in a process that (to the best of my recollection) is unique to Bielle, the *rhum* is cut to bottling strength using rainwater – or *l'eau du ciel* ("water from heaven") as Jacques puts it.

Bielle is not the only rum made here, though. The "Rhum Rhum" brand, which has been produced here since 2007, is a little more unorthodox than Bielle products, or as the case may be: very orthodox indeed. It's made in partnership with Gianni Capovilla and Luca Gargano, and this brand has notched up no shortage of awards in its first few years of existence. Production of these *rhums* is at odds with contemporary *agricole* practices, and it's almost easier to think of the *rhums* as fruit spirits, the fruit being the cane itself.

The cane juice is captured only from the first pressing and has no water added to it whatsoever. The juice is then sent for a whopping 7–10-day fermentation, developing all manner of flavourful eccentricities during its mutation into cane wine. This flavourful *vin* is then distilled twice in the copper pot still. Unlike the column still, commonly used by *agricole* distillers, a pot tends to concentrate flavour rather than strip it out, and these rums are certainly no exception to that rule. If the *agricole* category can be criticized for anything, it should be that the distilleries that make it are too consistent to one another, but Rhum Rhum doesn't just fly in the face of that – it swoops in front of your face like a UFO and goes off like a hand grenade. The pot still is also used to

LEFT The sampling bar at Bielle has over a dozen *rhums* to try, so be sure to arrange a taxi home.

BLANC (59% ABV) UN-AGED CANE JUICE RUM

Carrot juice, fermented melon and cracked black pepper. It's minerally and clinical. Bitter orange peels and hot fuel come through after. Bright and sticky, ripped with alcoholic muscle and beefy industrial notes. Heat through the finish.

PREMIUM BLANC (59% ABV)
UN-AGED BLENDED CANE JUICE RUM

More floral than the standard. Iris and violets are chased along by sasparilla and coriander seed, salty breeze, apple mint and wet rocks. The texture is thicker, more unctuous, with cayenne, yellow pepper and raw vegetables. Tried frozen it's sweetly succulent, like honeysuckle and spiced cane juice.

CANNE GRISE (59% ABV)
UN-AGED CANE JUICE RUM

Crystal clear yet dark and brooding, like rotten wood, burnt apple sauce, damp soil and rye bread. Smells of oil, sweat and hard work. Prickly and intense on the palate, big funky ketones, mustard seed. Hairy chest tonic.

RHUM VIEUX – BRUT DE FÛT 7-YEAR-OLD (53.1% ABV) AGED CANE JUICE RUM

Vanilla and oak lactones have tempered the white spirits. This is a honeyed sweet oaky treat. The taste has more depth than expected as every one of those ABVs drills flavour home – fruity liquorice (licorice), more honey, cane syrup and the ever-present oak.

2008 40TH ANNIVERSARY (53.4% ABV) EXTRA-AGED CANE JUICE RUM

Wine-like finesse with the structure of XO Cognac. Selected florals of jasmine and honeysuckle sit atop harder barrel staves, and a selection of juicy yellow fruits. Golden Delicious, mango and grape. Superbly elegant flirting between spice and sweetness on the palate, the finish is long.

RHUM RHUM PMG (56% ABV)
UN-AGED POT-STILL CANE JUICE RUM

A tropical delight. Papaya and pineapple arrive first, fresh and sticky in the sun. Then baked cereal notes, straw and hemp. Taste is concentrated and firm, where fruits quickly dry and do bloody battle with industry spices and mineral-rich soil.

RHUM RHUM LIBERATION 2015 – FRENCH WINE BARREL (45% ABV) AGED CANE JUICE RUM

Big rancio notes, with hot honeyed toast, oak splinters and barrel bung cloth. Palate is drier than expected and quicker to finish, but all the cellar notes remain in check, grape gum and rich. A bold and delicious expression of age in rum.

RHUM RHUM LIBERATION 2015 FRENCH WINE BARREL (58.4% ABV) AGED CANE JUICE RUM

Cleaner and less weighty, which has the effect of drawing out the finish. Fruit remains sharper and lazy cellar notes are held back.

re-distill Bielle's Premium Blanc *rhum agricole*, which is one of my favourite entry-level white *rhums*.

In addition to all the other goings on at Bielle, there's no sign of negligence where matters of maturation are concerned either. Jacques Larrent has indulged in a fine selection of French casks to bolster ex-bourbon stocks, from ex-Cognac through to ex-Sauternes and various other French wine casks. His endeavours have certainly paid off. The Bielle distillery is an exhibition of quality *rhum*-making, and its *rhum* are like works of fine art. With an unusual degree of aromatic precision and great taste balance. It sure makes me glad I'm not a *rhum*-maker who has to compete with witchcraft such as this.

RIGHT Bielle Premium Blanc is possibly the best un-aged *rhum agricole* on the market. It doesn't look too shabby, either.

DISTILLERIE BOLOGNE

Even though Pointe-à-Pitre is both the commercial and literal centre of Guadeloupe, the capital of the two islands is Basse-Terre – a micro-city in the south-west of the Basse-Terre region. This town is a welcome antidote to the tempestuous goings-on of Pointe-à-Pitre, looking and feeling far more like a slice of the French Riviera. Fishing vessels gently sway in the harbour, markets sell fresh fish, and people ride horses on the beach. It's that kind of place. On the northern edge of the town is Distillerie Bologne, a squat green fortress of an operation, set against the smudge of clouds that circle the Soufrière volcano, and peering over rows of ripe sugarcane at the cerulean sea.

The De Bolognes were a Protestant family from the Dauphiné region of France, who had migrated to Holland in the 16th century. Certain members of the family later settled in Brazil, which was a Dutch colony managed by the Dutch West India Company from 1630–54. The family prospered in sugar cultivation, as well as in the trade of sugar and *rhum* in the north-west of France and with Europe. When the Portuguese finally recaptured Brazil, many of the Dutch families were forced to flee. The De Bolognes first headed to Martinique, where they were quickly ushered away for being Protestants, then they arrived in Guadeloupe, in early 1654, with their workers and their gold and their silver, which they were allowed to keep under the capitulation treaties signed in Brazil.

The Bolognes' sugar estates prospered on the southern slopes of of the Soufriére hills. On Christmas day in 1745, Joseph Bologne was born, the son of George Bologne, and Nanon, one of his African slaves. Joseph, who would later be known as "Chevalier de Saint-George", was never involved in the running of the plantation or distillery, but he's worth a mention on account of being one of the most celebrated musicians of his time, being a virtuoso violinist, conductor of the Paris symphony orchestra and the first classical composer of African ancestry. During the

ABOVE The brightly coloured mill at Distillerie Bologne looks as though it's been requisitioned from a travelling fairground.

French Revolution, Saint-George led the first all-black regiment in Europe. He was also handy with a fencing foil, not bad on horseback and an enviable dancer.

Back in Guadeloupe, the Bologne estate fell on hard times during the French revolution, ultimately leading to the sale of the estate. On May 26 1830, Jean-Antoine Amé-Noël purchased the sugar refinery. Born in the town of Bouillante, in the region of Basse-Terre, Guadeloupe, Jean-Antoine was the first free-born man of colour to own a property as extensive (114 hectares/280 acres) as the former De Bologne plantation. Business flourished up until 1848, when slavery was abolished, and despite his efforts to organize paid labour on the plantation, he was crippled by substantial debts. He died in 1850 and was buried on the property. His grave remains marked to this day.

Rhum Bologne is distilled to only 55–60% ABV. This means that less of that juicy cane character of the *vin* (fermented cane juice) is stripped out, and less water is required to dilute the finished product. The newly made spirit is stored in 10,000-litre (2,650-US gallon) oak vats for up to six months during the rainy season, while it awaits bottling. Because of that, even the *rhum blanc* has a slight off-white colour to it.

But it is in Distillerie Bologne's *vieux* (aged) *rhums* that we find the real treasures. Bologne have a policy of using only French oak casks from Cognac and Armagnac houses. The wood offers up fruit and

FAR LEFT Sugarcane in the fields surrounding the Distillerie Bologne.

LEFT Distillerie Bologne is a big operation – dumper trucks are required to load cane into the mill.

BLANC (50% ABV) UN-AGED CANE JUICE RUM

Beefy and ripe, with tomato soup and silage. It smells very much "of the farm". Taste is sweet and more delicate than expected. Peppercorn sauce and cacao through the finish.

2000 (50% ABV) UN-AGED CANE JUICE RUM

Cleaner and light, with citrus top notes and some gentle lavender accents. The taste is gently spiced and herbaceous with cinnamon, tarragon and aniseed. Complex yet light.

VIEUX (41% ABV) AGED CANE JUICE RUM

Ripe grapes and soft fleshy fruit. Sugared almonds, a gentle whiff of tobacco and honey. More tobacco on the palate, sweeter with fruity sugar and delicate baking spices. It shows nice balance.

VO (41% ABV) AGED CANE JUICE RUM

Big tropical fruits, vanilla fudge and soft caramel. Fruit is finessed and Cognac-like. Concentrated sweetness on the palate, drifting between fruit leather, plum jam and sweet liquorice (licorice).

VSOP (42% ABV) EXTRA-AGED CANE JUICE RUM

The fruit takes on a more confected character, but remains intensely concentrated and bright. Apricot, fresh plum and fresh cherry. Taste becomes quite fragile under the stress of the wood; sweet vanilla and toffee are topped with more delicate florals. Sweetness lingers for a long time.

DOMAINE DE DAMOISEAU

Of the six distilleries currently operating on the "Butterfly Island", Domaine de Damoiseau is the only one located on the low-lying countryside of Grand-Terre. In contrast to the water-powered sugar mills of Basse-Terre, it's wind power that was historically used to mill cane on Grand-Terre, and the remains of these structures can still be seen across the countryside. Perched on the tip of the creature's east-facing wing, Guadeloupe's largest distillery might be worthy of an island all of its own. Domaine de Damoiseau bottle a remarkable 3.2 million litres (845,000 US gallons) of *rhum* every year, which accounts for nearly half of all the *rhum* produced in Guadeloupe.

The first Damoiseau arrived in Guadeloupe in 1816, emigrating from France. One of their descendants, Roger Damoiseau, was working in a sugar factory in Grande-Terre when, in 1942, he was told about an old mill up for sale, near the historical port of Le Moule. Damoiseau couldn't afford to buy the property however, but his neighbour, seeing the potential in the man, fronted up a loan and the sale was made. The neighbours cash was safe, so it would seem. The distillery enjoyed great success.

Hervé Damoiseau is the current owner, a man driven by an enormous passion for the *rhum* he makes, with just a light seasoning of 'crazy' thrown in for good measure. When I visited the distillery it took me 20 minutes of searching to track him down, until I eventually found him in the packing area, where he was prying open a bottling nozzle using a screwdriver. In my opinion, it's Hervé's slightly quirky hands-on approach that resonates around the distillery and into the mindset of all the people who work there. Everyone keeps busy in this place, as visitors are invited to wander freely around the plant – "They're fine, as long as they don't fall in the *rhum*!" Hervé informed me with a look of derangement in his eyes, which implied that falling in a vat of *rum* was a real possibility.

These days, the crushing mill is powered by a steam engine. The dismantled 1871 Fives-Lille engine and the vertical engine are at the back of the yard. The rest of the gear is on display in the park in front of the visitor centre. In fact, the Damoiseau distillery is positively littered with decaying pieces of engineering equipment.

spice in spades, but when coupled with that beefy, muscular distillate, you get the best of both worlds – the finesse of a ballerina and the balls of a boxer.

The older of Distillerie Bologne's releases, such as the VSOP (Very Superior Old Pale), which is a blend of *rhums* between four and eight years old, take on an intensely concentrated Cognac quality, with bright florals, a herbal edge, rich fruit and a tobacco finish. Bologne's oldest stocks are unmatched on the island. On any island, perhaps.

Damoiseau produce the lightest spirit on the island, and the lightest of any French *rhum agricole* distillates by my reckoning. This is thanks to the 12-plate Coffey still, which pumps out a white *rhum* at around 88% ABV. Roughly 85% of the output is sold as white *rhum*, but the aged stocks are still enough to fill 3,000 barrels. Works are underway to increase the cask capacity to 8,000 barrels, however.

BELOW Ok, perhaps not everyone is busy, but this is rum-making after all, and a laid back approach is a key ingredient.

BLANC (50% ABV) UN-AGED CANE JUICE RUM

Honey, carob nut, coconut and waxy banana. The palate is light and spiced, less texture and depth than the smell suggests but easy drinking. Finish is rigid and clean; the linger is of mace and white pepper.

AMBRÉ (40% ABV) AGED CANE JUICE RUM

Faintly copper-smelling, mineral-rich and greasy. There's a suggestion of honey and mandarin peel. Orange caramel and forceful vanilla on the palate. Quick to finish.

VO (42% ABV) AGED CANE JUICE RUM

Buttery banana pancakes, soft oak lactones and sweet baking spices. Restrained sweetness and spice on the taste, soft and supple. Maturation seems to have failed to reduce the spice and has upped the texture.

DOMAINE DE SEVÉRIN

The earliest recorded history of the area occupied by the present-day Distillerie du Domaine de Sevérin, in the north of Basse-Terre, shows an 18th-century sugar mill, called Habitiation Bellevue. It's no wonder someone chose to put a plantation here. Lush cane fields prosper happily on the long north stretch, down from the mountain to the coast.

In the early 19th century, Bellevue was bought by Monsieur Sevérin (first name unknown) and the name changed. Jump forward to the 20th century, and sugar-based activities and been wound down, and the buildings had been recommissioned for the canning of pineapples. In 1920, Ms. Beauvarlet purchased the site and re-instated *rhum*-making, placing her nephew, Henri Marsolle, in charge of operations.

Henri operated the distillery for over 40 years, even through the death of his son, Edward, who was tragically killed when he attempted to rescue a co-worker after a boiler exploded in the distillery. Henri handed the reins over to his other son, Joseph, in 1966. In time, many of the day-to-day operations were passed on to Joseph's own three sons: José, Pascal and Thierry.

Sevérin is easily the prettiest distillery of the Basse-Terre collection, and it receives more visitors than any other in Guadeloupe. The operational area and the grounds have been well-maintained. There's an old colonial house that was built by Henri Marsolle in the 1940s, and a small restaurant turns out good Créole food (on the occasions that it is actually open). For those who are unable, or unwilling, to take the short self-guided tour through the gardens, there is even a model train that unceremoniously drags "carriages" of interested parties along the winding gravel pathways.

In 2014 a majority stakeholding of Sevérin was sold to the investment firm, José Pirbakas, so it's unclear what the future holds for this operation. For now at least, Pascal Marsolle still works at the distillery, but more in his capacity as a source of historical information than as a distiller. These days he has a separate company that manufactures Créole cooking ingredients, and he tends to a small retail space in one corner of the distillery building.

Outside, the last remaining paddle wheel in the French Antilles still spins on its axle. It was once used to power the mill that crushed the cane, but was decommissioned in 2008. Time rolls on… the wheel feigns progress... but its unabating motion is superfluous to the Sevérin operation.

Sugarcane is cut by hand here, as the steep slopes make machine-cutting impossible. Once pressed for its juice, it's fermented for 48 hours. If you arrive at the right time of day you can witness the cane wine bubbling over the edges of the 16,000-litre (4,225-US gallon) open-top fermenters and flowing down the sides. Most distilleries toss sulphuric acid to their tanks to quell the gassy expansion, but Sevérin prefer to let things take their natural course. It's another indicator of the graceful acceptance of fate that this distillery seems to have adopted over the years. Distillation is done in a single column, and the resulting spirit is between 65–70% ABV. It's an angry little spirit that they produce at Sevérin, feeling somewhat bitter and warped by the whole ordeal. But there's something strangely pleasant to be found in that, as the liquid grapples with your mouth, trying (but failing) to evade the inevitable. The single aged expression that the distillery is currently bottling tempers some of that aggression, mind you. It's just a shame there aren't any others. That is hopefully set to change however, as the distillery is stocking a range of woods (sherry, French, ex-bourbon) presumably with the intention of blending interesting future releases.

BLANC (50% ABV)
UN-AGED CANE JUICE RUM

Sweet and vanilla-like at first, but slowly, dirty chocolate and agricultural aromas creep in – like a really bad chocolate ice cream. Stiff and highly fuelled on the tongue. Salted liquorice, old rope and molasses. The finish is dry and mineral.

VIEUX XO 6-YEAR-OLD (50% ABV)
AGED CANE JUICE RUM

Sweet and fragrant on the nose. Dried mangoes and apricots, cherry liqueur and booze-soaked dates. Taste is still minerally, with some burn through the finish. Not bad.

THIS PAGE The old water wheel and beautiful grounds at Domaine de Sevérin make it a must-see for rum lovers, or indeed, anyone (below left). Sugarcane is cut by hand at Domaine de Sevérin and transported by tractor to the mill (centre above). The angels return the favour with a spot of music as they enjoy their "share" (centre below). Hopefully we'll taste the fruits of these casks in the not too distant future (below right).

LONGUETEAU

On Columbus's second voyage across the Atlantic, in which he was transporting sugarcane cuttings to the Caribbean, the first island he encountered was named after his own flagship, Marigalante. The fleet spent only a day on the small island, before heading north, where they encountered a much bigger land mass. At that time, Guadeloupe was known to the Carib Indians as "Karukera", which roughly translates to "island with beautiful water". Columbus dropped anchor on November 4 1493 and spent 10 days exploring the island that he named "Santa María de Guadalupe" after the Virgin Mary, venerated in the Spanish town of Guadalupe. Amazingly, the fierce Carib Indians maintained occupation of the island until 1640 when, after over a century of bloody encounters with Spanish and French forces, they relented and the French seized control. They kept the name "Guadeloupe" and named the region where Columbus set to shore Sainte-Marie.

In the early 18th century, King Louis XIV of France granted the title of Marquis de Sainte-Marie to a nobleman, and gifted him a large piece of land on the eastern coast of Basse-Terre. Like most of Guadeloupe, the marquisate specialized in sugar through the 19th century and the estate included a sugar mill and hundreds of acres of cane plantation. Jump forward to 1890, however, and the heir to the original Marquis had developed a penchant for all the noble pleasures that came with his station – drinking, women and gambling – the latter of which he wasn't very good at it. With debts piling high, he was forced to sell the estate to settle his bills. The highest bidder was Henri Longueteau, a local engineer, who, in 1895, turned the mill into a *rhum* distillery. That distillery has since passed through four generations of the Longueteau family, right up to the present-day director, François Longueteau.

Half of the estate's 65 hectares (160 acres) is dedicated to growing bananas and the other half to sugarcane. Between the red and blue varieties, this is enough cane to supply the enitre distillery operation, making Longueteau the only self-sufficient distiller on the island. The cane is crushed and fermented for 48 hours before being sent to the stainless-steel column still, which is capable of processing up to 6,000 litres (1,585 US gallons) of a *rhum* a day. For Longueteau *rhums*, the white *rhum* comes off the still at around 72% ABV, and is then rested in large, inactive, oak vats for three months

SÉLECTION PARCELLAIRE CANNE TOUCHE NO. 9 (55% ABV)
UN-AGED CANE JUICE RUM

More bread and wholesome baked nutty notes on the nose. Powerful fermentation aromas, farm machinery, yeast and silage. Equally agricultural on the palate: date, burnt sugar and green peppercorns.

3-YEAR-OLD AGED CANE JUICE RUM

Mushroom and charred staves. Soft and with faint orange oils and brushed oak. Chewy and full on the taste. Good breadth of oak character, but most of the fruit is lost.

LONGUETEAU 120 ANS (42% ABV)
EXTRA-AGED CANE JUICE RUM

Piña Colada and banana daiquiri. Mushroom funk and black pepper are there too. Some vanilla and a hit of spicy tomato-flavoured potato chips. Green and hot on the palate, with enough grip to asphyxiate a horse.

KARUKERA BLANC (50% ABV)
UN-AGED CANE JUICE RUM

Vegetal and earthy, with fungal notes and sweaty horsehair. Seaweed and brine too. Peppered heat dominates on the palate, like hugely over-seasoned grilled vegetables. Salinity through the finish.

KARUKERA VIEUX (42% ABV)
AGED CANE JUICE RUM

Sweetly floral, with a soapy, bubble bath note too, bringing out violet and jasmine. Oak lurks behind. The palate is wood: freshly sanded balsa wood, slick applewood and glossy lacquer. Raw banana cleans up the finish. A great young *agricole*.

before being bottled. This resting period seems to give Longueteau a slight edge, turning soft tropical fruits into drier, vegetal tones.

The Karukera brand was launched in 2002, when Guillaume Drouin, son to the famous Calvados producer Christian Drouin, had a veritable *rhum* epiphany during a trip to Haiti. He partnered with Longueteau to produce his own version of *rhum agricole*. Only blue cane is used, which is, unusually for an *agricole*, fermented without the addition of anti-foaming or acidifying substances.

For both brands it is the mature *rhums* that really steal the show, and there are certainly plenty to choose from. A strong policy towards French oak casks takes the *rhum* to the realm of citrus fruits, dried berries, and flora.

This distillery is generally hard to access for public tours, but there is a large shop and tasting room that opens throughout the week. There, you can sample the many varieties of *rhum* produced at the distillery, including the Mon Repos (made from cane syrup) Longueteau, and Karukera brands, as well as the usual fruit punches and spiced offerings.

MONTEBELLO

The Montebello distillery, also known as the Carrére Distillery, is a 20-minute drive from the centre of Pointe-à-Pitre, heading south, along the eastern coastal road of Basse-Terre. This is good, because those on a pilgrimage to Montebello will need to use all 1,200 seconds to mentally prepare themselves for what they are about to see.

The distillery is a grey and rust-coloured relic. Half post-apocalyptic shanty town, half steam-punk theme-park, and seemingly constructed entirely from corrugated iron and pipes bonded together with the grease and sweat of nearly a century's hard toil. It is a homage to the industrial age: to steam power, cogs, valves and flames. Along with the near-deafening barrage of noises – hissing, whirring and the occasional scream – one might assume that they are no longer in a distillery, but inside the world's largest combustion engine. There are pressure gauges seemingly everywhere – far too numerous and too dirty to be of any practical function. But it's difficult not to be won over by the industrial craft of the whole thing. Montebello is a mechanical wonder.

The Distillerie Carrére, which was named after the small village in which it is situated, was first established in 1930, by the Dolomite family. It struggled through the early years, hindered by over-production and World War II, until it was eventually closed in 1966 and converted into a cinema. Looking at the operation today, it's hard to imagine how it could possibly have functioned as a movie theatre, and it seems that the endeavour failed to capture the attentions of the locals too. In 1968 the site was sold to Jean Marsolle, the brother of Henry Marsolle: owner and operator of the nearby Séverin distillery. Jean Marsolle's son, Alain, came on board

ABOVE Distillerie Carrére is a corrugated iron metropolis that is equally absurd on the inside.

too, and later purchased the distillery from his father. Alain's legacy was in the acquisition of old distillery equipment, which over time returned the distillery to its original operating condition, including a functioning steam boiler powered by a *bagasse*-burning furnace. The distillery was renamed "Montebello" in 1975, and since December 2011 it has been Grégory Marsolle, Alain's son, who has served as king of this corrugated castle.

The *rhum* produced here is *rhum agricole*, made only from the fresh juice of the cane. Montebello add less water during milling and run a slightly longer fermentation than their contemporaries, claiming that a more complex, fruity cane wine is produced, and that this translates into a finer spirit. The *vin*, which has an ABV of around 12% is distilled in a double-column copper still, and drawn-off at 85% ABV. Perhaps the most interesting element of the production however, is their maturation program. Ever faithful to the gods of grease and steel, Montebello store their casks in sheet metal warehouses. In the Guadeloupean sunshine, these structures are like ovens that softly bake the casks, and forcefully dredging the *rhum* in their flavoursome depths.

Distilleries are factories, and steel and copper can sometimes feel sanitary and cold. Often they are. But

VIEUX (45% ABV) AGED CANE JUICE RUM

Gentle tropical fruits, honeydew melon. Dried mango and sugar-apple. Perfumed and sweet. Waves of candied fruit and finessed wine notes. The palate is refreshingly dry. Prune juice, cacao and gentle spice are lightened with dessert wine qualities, elderflower, lingonberry and grape sherbet.

at Montebello the tangle of shapes and surfaces takes on a different presence, one that feels time-honoured and as relevant as any oak barrel or water wheel. As the Martinican writer Patrick Chamoiseau put it, "Silence is gathered in the sounds of metal. Age, rust, and paint acquire a trembling of skin."

POISSON

The Poisson distillery is near the west coast of Marie-Galante, walking distance from the beach. They make the popular Père Labat brand of *rhum* there, named after the 18th-century Martinican planter who established the standard for sugar plantations in the French West indies. Poisson is my favourite of the Marie-Galante trio, but not because it makes the best *rhum* (that would be Bielle) – it's my favourite because it's also home to a hidden gem of a restaurant called La Table de Père Labat. Eating (and drinking) there should be made mandatory for any distillery visitor. I can highly recommend the *tartare de poisson*, which goes down nicely when accompanied by a Ti Punch.

Back in the 1860s, the Poisson family ran a sugar mill on the current site of the Poisson distillery, though the distillery didn't get its name until Edouard Rameau bought the property in 1916 and installed a distillery there. Besides the aforementioned restaurant and a small shop, not much has changed here. It is the smallest of the Marie-Galante trio (producing just 300,000 litres (80,000 US gallons a year) and production had come to a halt on the day that I visited. Some parts of the building are ancient, some of them so old and worn-looking that you might think it was constructed in the Middle Ages. The production process is true to the standard *agricole* mould. All of the cane on Marie-Galante is cut by hand, and originates from any one of the hundred or so family-owned plots of land. Farmers are paid €60–70 (£51–60 or $63–73) per ton of cane cut, depending on the brix of the juice, which is measured from a sample at the time of delivery. This distillery is a steam-powered operation, where the heat is generated by burning the *bagasse* in a huge iron furnace, which is so battered that it has the look of something constructed a few centuries ago from riveted sheets of dusty leather. Distillation is conducted in the original (101-year-old) copper Coffey still.

The *rhums* produced here vary in quality but one or two are really rather good. It's a nice surprise to find that their standard *agricole blanc* is bottled at three different strengths: 40%, 50% and 59% ABV. In a tasting, this

BELOW Poisson's still is one of the oldest working examples in the whole of the Caribbean. The fact that someone saw fit to slice a piece of metal off the top of Poisson's boiler (centre) is just one of many signs that the equipment here has seen a hard life.

BLANC (40% ABV) UN-AGED CANE JUICE RUM

Sappy, on the nose with hints of coconut resin and palm leaves. There's fried plantain there too, and mace and clove. The taste feels a bit vacant in the face of the *rhum's* stronger siblings, and the lack of heat causes the *rhum* to lose focus. There's generic spicy notes with that watery texture. The finish trails off quickly.

BLANC (50% ABV) UN-AGED CANE JUICE RUM

Much more vegetal on the nose than the lower-strength offering. There's rotten courgette (zucchini) and spiced mushroom soup among other dark, fungal notes. Oregano and dried basil add a herbaceous twist. On the palate, it's zippy and clean. Heavily peppered *duxelles* take away the finish.

BLANC (59% ABV) UN-AGED CANE JUICE RUM

At the higher strength the *rhum* returns to sappy, tropical notes. There's fried plantain, hot banana skin, nutmeg and tamarind. The taste is of fuel, like a hot slap of diesel in your eyes. Mighty.

LE RHUM SOLEIL (59% ABV)
AGED CANE JUICE RUM

This *rhum* even has the colour of ripe banana, but in the aroma some of that ripeness has been sacrificed for generic maturation character. The aroma is like a duller, more tired version of the blanc and smells altogether a little flat. Taste is equally bland, with a gentle lick of pepper and a dry finish. You do have to remind yourself that it's 59%, however.

RHUM BRUN (45% ABV)
AGED CANE JUICE RUM

Subtle on the nose, gently herbal and softly oaked, smells like mocha with a touch of tamarind, vanilla paste and affogato. The taste presents more oak flavours, plenty of cacao, coffee and coconut. Chocolate lingers through the finish.

CUVÉE SPÉCIALE (42% ABV)
AGED CANE JUICE RUM

A richer kind of chocolate on this one. Boozy dark chocolate torte, coffee liqueur and Brazil nuts. Sweet on the palate, drifting along through caramels, simple wood spices and a gentle nudge of fruit compote. Overall a little too tame.

CUVÉE 1997 (42% ABV)
EXTRA-AGED CANE JUICE RUM

The jewel in an otherwise unexceptional crown. Ripe dark and yellow fruits on the nose: banana, certainly, but also honeydew melon and various confected elements reminiscent of dessert wine-soaked sponge. There's a stream of oak lactones at play too, glossy and sweet. Chocolate is back in the taste, as a toasted bitterness (like overdone BBQ ribs) holds the flavour down. The linger wallows in wood and burnt fruit.

offers the opportunity explore the effects of dilution on the product. And in this instance we find three quite different *rhums*; my personal favourite is the 50%. The least desirable *rhums* on the roster are the Doré (gold) and Soleil (sun). Both have been subjected to only short amount of time in cask – two months in ex-bourbon casks and 12 months in a 10,000-litre (2,650-US gallon) oak vat respectively – and in both instances a good deal of distillery character has been lost while the benefits of the barrel are still yet to be found. By far the most special product here is the Cuvée 1997, an 18-year-old *rhum* that is truly a diamond in the rough.

RIGHT Order up a Ti Punch and enjoy some great Caribbean seafood at La Table du Père Labat.

HAITI

Haiti is a country that has struggled more than most in recent years. Struck with natural disaster, political corruption, military coups, trade embargoes and disease; it's easy to misplace the historical and present-day significance of this beautiful country to the *rhum* category. By my estimate Haiti has as many *rhum* distilleries as the rest of the world combined. They call it *clairin* here, and most of its un-aged spirit is made from the natural fermentation of sugarcane juice or syrup on a very small scale. It's hardcore stuff: bright, oily, vegetal and sold at off-the-still strength. Even I was forced to suppress a gasp upon my first combustible sip of clairin. Besides the bottlings listed in the following pages, it's unlikely you'll ever get to taste the fruits of Haiti's 500-or-so distilleries without visiting them in person (most of the clairin never leaves the village it was made in, let alone the country), but it's imperative that we recognize the Haitian culture for sugarcane spirits for what it is: an untainted slice of *rhum* history deserving a book all of its own.

A campaign to occupy the long western coast of Hispaniola was kickstarted by French privateers during the 1630s. The west of the island had been neglected by the Spanish, and by the time they realized what had happened there was no other option than to cede the space to the French crown, establishing more or less the present day border between Haiti and the Dominican Republic. The French were keen cane farmers, and starting in the 1730s, engineers constructed complex irrigation systems to increase sugarcane production. By the 1740s Saint-Domingue (as it was known by the French) together with Jamaica, had become the main supplier of the world's sugar and accountable for over half of all the world's coffee. It's hard to imagine it looking at Haiti today, but Saint-Domingue was the richest colony in the Caribbean during the 18th century.

A hardworking colony like Sainte-Domingue doesn't get by without a large workforce. In 1789, two years prior to the revolution, there were nearly half a million African slaves working in Saint-Domingue, which accounted for roughly half of all the slaves in the Caribbean at the time, outnumbering the white land owners by a factor of twenty. Spurred on by a religious ceremony performed by the *vodou* priest Dutty Boukman, which allegedly prophesied freedom for all slaves, the uprising began on August 21 1791. It would become the greatest slave revolt since Spartacus, making legends out of the likes of Toussaint Louverture, a general of the slave army and a self-educated former slave. On January 1 1804, Haiti was declared a free republic. It was the only successful slave-led revolution of the colonial period.

Freedom came at a cost however. The expulsion of white land owners meant that sugar plantations became mismanaged. Coupled with the ideological threat that Haiti posed to the international community – for whom slavery was still a lucrative economic venture – meant that trade dried up too. Put simply, Haiti never recovered from the revolutionary fallout. Today its economy is in tatters, sugarcane farming is in decline, and its political prognosis best described as "dire".

BELOW LEFT AND CENTRE Cane sold at the roadside costs about 25¢ (1p/1 cent) for more than any person can eat.

BELOW RIGHT Natural fermentation at one of Haiti's countless village distilleries.

LEFT No two stills are the same in Haiti.

ABOVE A clairin pit-stop adds an additional layer of danger to driving.

Port-au-Prince is the poorest city in the Americas. Slum-lined streets are piled high with trash – a problem that is "managed" through the aggressive use of bulldozers – as UN and UNICEF vehicles pick through the turmoil. There is beauty to be found here too. Overcrowded buses are saturated with colour and branded with bible scripture, like roaming fairground rides in a post-apocalyptic metropolis. Motorcycles are loaded with three or more people… Or stacked high with bananas and sugarcane. Pigs casually root through the rubbish for scraps of fermenting vegetables, while their owners conduct business on mobile (cell) phones. Street vendors skilfully shave lengths of cane for children, while others sell tatty cobs of corn, BBQ chicken, watermelon, mango and coconut. On some streets you find men carving up huge ice blocks in the road, the cuttings of which will be used to chill fresh foods where electricity isn't available.

BELOW The tractor at Arawaks, loaded with freshly cut cane (left). Plastic fermenters are not ideal, as they can (and do) taint the spirit (centre). Fritz is hoping to export his Arawaks brand in the near future (right).

Population pressure, poor health, no work, and a non-existent infrastructure have all contributed to the Haitian chaos. But in the rural areas we find serenity, where the human spirit radiates and the distilled spirit does just about the same. If Haiti is to find its way back into the world it will require a concerted effort from international and domestic powers, but for my money, the abundance of interesting *rhum* this country makes is as good a place to start as any.

ARAWAKS

Cavaillon is a small town in the south of Haiti, about halfway along the Les Cays peninsular. Not so long ago there were six clairin distilleries in the region, but in recent times farmers have been lured to other crops like beans, rice and sorghum. One distillery still remains, however. It's run by Fritz Vaval, who took over the role of master distiller from his father 10 years ago. The Vavals are well known in Cavaillon. The town's doctor is a Vaval and two of the streets are named for the family.

The Arawaks' estate pays homage to the Arawak and Taíno Indians that occupied various Caribbean islands prior to the arrival of Christopher Columbus in 1492. Some scholars estimate that on Hispaniola alone there may be have been as many as three million Taíno inhabitants in the 15th century. The Spanish conquistadors put the men to work in gold mines and married their women, but both males and females fell victim to European diseases like smallpox and measles, or to starvation. Whether by disease or by the sword, the arrival of the Spanish ultimately amounted to genocide of the indigenous population. In the 1530s the question came from Spain: "How many Indians are there? Who are the chiefs?" The answer was clearly stated: "None. They are all gone".

Fritz Vaval's estate comprises around 8 hectares (20 acres) of cane-growing land, along with small papaya,

LEFT Formerly a prop in *Star Wars* (ok, not really), the still at Arawaks is not the prettiest, but it gets the job done.

lemon and apricot groves. This is not the site of the original distillery, which moved from the other side of the town back in 2003. The cane mill is diesel-powered, and sends the fresh juice (which is at around 10–12° Brix) into a large trough, where it is filtered and then pumped into one of six fermentation vessels. Here it sits for one to two weeks, naturally fermented by airborne yeast. Next it's pumped into a pot still resembling a trash can with a domed top. The pot connects to a stout rectification column and there's a retort pipe that feeds heavy alcohols back into the main still. Three worm tub-style condensers feed the freshly distilled liquid into collecting vessels.

Fritz sells to the local market in 4.5-litre (1.2-US gallon) containers, but unlike most clairin producers, he also supplies it in 250-ml (9-oz) labelled glass bottles. This aims to add value to the product, removing the stigma of high volume consumption and bringing a degree of discernment to the liquid. The same Arawaks clairin is also bottled independently by the Italian rum company Velier under the Clairin Vaval brand name.

There are experimentations going on at Arawaks too. I tried no less than five fruit-flavoured clairins that are in development, all produced with fruits grown on the Vaval estate. Mango was my favourite, for its sweet vibrancy, but the lemon-flavoured clairin showed how subtle citrus elements can amplify the characteristics we associate with cane juice rums. Perhaps most exciting of all are Fritz's experiments with aged clairin. Having called upon the services of a local artisan barrel maker, Fritz is maturing his *rhum* in a 60-litre (16-US gallon) charred cask made from a local variety of oak. The results, after only a single year, are extremely promising.

In many ways, Fritz Vaval is the ultimate poster boy for clairin. He studied agriculture and natural resources in Mexico, and worked in Canada for most of his younger life. He's a man of the world, well educated, but possessing an endearing sensibility towards Haiti's natural environment. Talking to this man you can sense the ability and determination to instigate a Haitian *rhum* revolution. I, for one, am sold on it.

The next planned works on the distillery will see him change his 2,275-litre (600-US gallon) plastic fermenters for stainless steel. Then he wants to install solar panels so that the distillery becomes carbon neutral or possibly even carbon negative, generating a sustainable energy source for the residents of Cavaillon.

BARBANCOURT

Barbancourt may be Haiti's only internationally recognized *rhum* brand, but just like any other Haitian distillery, you have to drive down a rough pot-holed track to get there. This suburb of Port-au-Prince is no less poor than the rest the city, so the distillery walls are suitably tall (4.5 metres/15 ft) and the gate suitably well guarded. The high walls tell a story of more than just paranoia, however. Barbancourt is a fiercely self-sufficient operation, and a brand name that is revered among the Haitian people. If Port-au-Prince were Rome, Barbancourt would be the Vatican.

Administrating a big business in Haiti's changeable climate (commercial, political and physical) is no mean feat. In one of the most chaotic environments in the world, this family-owned businesses has lasted 150 years, making it one of the oldest companies in Haiti. A few years ago they built a workshop that fabricates replacement parts for the mill, pumps, stills and condensers. They generate their own electricity from two enormous diesel generators, steam from burnt *bagasse*, while water is pumped in from a nearby well. There's the sensation of entering a sanctuary as you pass through the gated portal; the brick-built barrel stores are cleanly maintained and the manicured gardens show off a variety of tropical flora and lawns shaved to a fine green fuzz. It's a normal-looking distillery, but here, in Haiti, it feels almost extravagant. There is cause for celebration though. The presence of Barbancourt can be felt everywhere in Haiti, where 200 ml (7 oz) bottles are available from virtually any street corner or hole in the wall vendor. Today, the distillery produces 350,000 9-litre (2.5-US gallon) cases of *rhum* a year, is employer to 450 people, and is responsible for the livelihood of a further 20,000 people across the country.

Dupré Barbancourt emigrated to Haiti from Charante in France in the 1850s. He purchased the *terres d'étoiles* ("star land") plantation and built his distillery in 1862, applying his methods of Cognac production to cane juice *rhum*. The distillery passed into the hands of Barbancourt's second wife, Nathalie Gardère and it is within the Gardère family that it has remained right up until the present fourth generation owner, Thierry Gardère.

The operation is reminiscent of any other *agricole* distillery. Cane is hand-cut from the 8-hectare (200-acre) Barbancourt estate, and the same quantity again bought in from neighbouring estates. It's milled for its juice and fermented for 72 hours using a brewer's yeast. The fermented *vesou* is then distilled through two linked column stills (one steel, one copper) up to a strength of 94% ABV. The distillery has a policy of using only virgin Limousin oak casks from France, and the spirit is cut to 60% alcohol and joined in the barrel by a selection of spices, including cacao and vanilla. This, for me, is

THIS PAGE Barbancourt fill around 200 barrels a week, and the scale of the warehousing and blending rooms reflect this. The drinking sculpture (below centre) guarding the warehouse door is known to the staff as *le intoxiqué* (the addict).

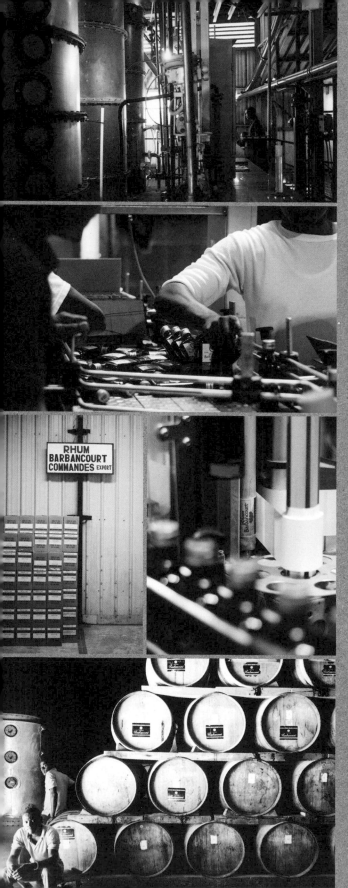

a disappointing stage in the Barbancourt process, and totally unnecessary if it weren't for the fact that most of the characteristics of their base material had been stripped out during distillation. I would love to see what this distillery is capable of with a more robust, lower strength distillate, and no adulteration of flavour.

In reference to the original "star land" plantation and the Cognac categories predilection for using stars to denote age, Barbancourt are the only *rhum* brand that I know of which use a star system on their labels. That's probably because it's a confusing system, but I greatly respect their adherence to tradition. Here's how it works:

"★" matured for a minimum of 1 year
"★★★" matured for a minimum of 4 years
"★★★★★" matured for a minimum of 8 years

LEFT Master distiller Rubens LaFortune produces 13,500 litres (3,600 US gallons) of 94% spirit every day, and a well-oiled bottling line is needed to get it out to customers. Approximately half of Barbancourt's production volume is sent for export.

BLANC (43% ABV) UN-AGED CANE JUICE RUM

Surprisingly bright character on the nose; mild plantain and vegetal notes, gently citric. Lightens up over time and reflects on to the palate. Muggy and tame on the tongue, under-seasoned and soft into the finish.

*** (3 STARS) (43% ABV) AGED CANE JUICE RUM

Mushroomy florals, vanilla, and bitter chocolate. Very light and dry on the palate. Gradual increase in pepper, vanilla oak notes, but altogether quite soft and loose.

***** (5 STARS) (43% ABV)
AGED CANE JUICE RUM

Volatile alcohol, oozy caramel, some vegetal notes creeping back in. Orange oils and fudge. Big pepper, some clean mineral notes and a chewy fruit compote finish.

ESTATE RESERVE
(43% ABV) EXTRA-AGED CANE JUICE RUM

Damp tobacco, sweet toffee, but still quite mineral-y and faint. Taste has more to it: round and full with toffee and dried fruit. Some sweetness threatens to take hold, but the heat keeps things dry and desirable. Linger introduces more tobacco, soft stone fruits, and raspberry lemonade.

CHELO

The Chelo distillery is not an easy place to get to. Located in the town of Saint Michel de l'Attalaye, it's right in the middle of Haiti's northern *Massif du Nord* mountain range. On a map, it's barely 60 km (37 miles) north of Port-au-Prince, but weather permitting it's a five-hour drive through some of the toughest roads on the planet. The track – and that's an overstatement – that scales the mountain is in some sections incomplete, and in others still damaged by the earthquake of 2010. On certain stretches it's even necessary to drive through rivers where children scamper around in the water and locals wash their motorcycles. There are few cars brave enough to attempt it, save for the crazy truck drivers that supply the villages, weaving up the hills with their precariously stacked loads. It's an adventure, and a rewarding one at that, as near to the summit you encounter what is quite likely the highest concentration of distilleries in the world.

These are farming communities, each with small plots of land, growing mostly corn and cane. Every village has a clairin distillery and some have more than one. It's not surprising then, that making clairin is an activity that everyone in the village is engaged with. In one tiny hamlet that I stopped at, children clambered around the pot still as their mothers chatted next to the mill.

Michel Sajous's distillery can be found just outside Saint Michel de l'Attalaye on Chelo farm. Sajous employs half a dozen people at the distillery, and the estate has around 30 hectares (75 acres) of land, planted with different varieties of cane, including the "Crystal" variety – one of the types allowed in the Martinique Rhum Agricole AOC. The mill is diesel-powered and

TOP The wooden vat is both a partial condenser and a wine pre-heater.

ABOVE Spirit-collecting vessels that are big enough to climb in and swim around.

electric pumps channel liquids around the various stages of production. By Haitian standards it's state of the art.

Chelo make their clairin from sugarcane syrup, rather than juice, which means they can distill outside of the harvesting season. After pressing and boiling, the syrup is stored until required. The diluted syrup is fermented naturally in big steel boxes for up to two weeks. The pot still is approximately 500 litres (132 US gallons) and is heated by a *bagasse*- and wood-burning furnace. The distillate is then routed into a short column purifier and then through the first of three worm tub condensers. The middle of these condensers also serves as a pre-heater for fresh wash entering into the pot still. The last condenser is the largest of the tubs and to my surprise is home to a small family of turtles. Yes, you read that correctly. They are fed, of course, but how they survive in the fluctuating water temperature I do not know!

CHELO CLAIRIN AKA CLAIRIN SAJOUS (53.5% ABV) UN-AGED CANE JUICE RUM

Big and herbals, with peppered vegetables, hot rubber, Play-Doh, and diesel. The palate hot, but not hostile, where there's squashed yellow fruits, bitter cacao, and some warming spices, like anise and nutmeg. It's sweet in a dirty kind of way. Finish is oily, spiced and leaves you wanting more punishment.

JAMAICA

Admiral Penn's capture of Jamaica in 1655 established a British colony that would later become the greatest sugar island that had ever existed. Despite being well sighted among the Greater Antilles trading routes, the Spanish had taken little interest in the island, growing tobacco mostly, but most farms were worthless, subsistent smallholdings. At first, the British sought to establish new trading opportunities for their Caribbean interest, so with nails and timber they built the makeshift town of Port Royal, just across the harbour from present-day Kingston. In the space of 25 years, Port Royal became the biggest and wealthiest city in the Caribbean.

The rise of Port Royal can be largely attributed to piracy, for which this town became the de-facto trading outpost for merchants, privateers, and pirates. The residents of Port Royal gained great notoriety for their brazen display of wealth and loose moral parameters. According to one English visitor who promptly left aboard the same ship he arrived on, the demographic was split between, "Pirates, cut throats, whores, and some of the vilest people in the whole of the world". The promise of free trade, a plentiful supply of alcohol and fast women, lured in the pirates, who brought with them gold and silver from plundered Spanish ships. For a 17th-century pirate, there really was no better place on earth to dispense with one's loot than on a fortnight's bender through the rum bars and brothels on Port Royal's Lime Street. The cash and the muscle that these bands of pirates brought to the town convinced the greedy governors to turn a blind eye to all the debauchery. Merchants were happy to have them around too, tasking them with 'forced trade' (robbery) expeditions on Spanish vessels.

The historical accounts of Port Royal during this period are as colourful a picture of pirate culture as you're ever likely to encounter. One 17th-century visitor described it as: "The Dunghill of the Universe, the Refuse of the whole creation...a shapeless Pile of Rubbish confused'ly jumbl'd up into an Emblem of the Chaos, neglected by Omnipotence when he formed the world into its admirable Order."

That negligence on the part of God soon lapsed however. In true "Noah's Ark" style, this rotten city was devastated by an earthquake in 1692, and around half of the buildings were swept away by the ocean. The destruction of Port Royal also marked the beginning of the twilight years of the pirate era, as the agricultural potential of the region demanded that trading waters were properly secured. A new Jamaican history was about to be written, and this one would become equally as legendary.

The early 18th century saw massive agricultural change on the island, as forests were stripped to make way for sugar and coffee plantations. By the mid-1700s, Jamaica competed with only Sant-Domingue for the title of the Caribbean's biggest sugar grower. Sugar mills and distilleries popped up like mushrooms in the night, and exports of rum in the Britain increased linearly through the century (with a notable hiccup during the American Revolutionary War), rising from 910,000 litres (240,000 US gallons) in 1725 to 9.1 million litres (2.4 million US gallons) in the 1770s.

But this was only the beginning. After the Haitian Revolution, Jamaica's rum and sugar production ramped up, and with increasing demand for rum and sugar in Europe, the island became the world's largest sugarcane superpower. By the 1820s, Jamaica was exporting more rum to Britain than all of Britain's other 14 Caribbean colonies combined – over 140 million litres (36 million gallons) a year throughout the decade. Remember, that's only exports to Britain and doesn't include trade with other colonies, or domestic consumption. To put it into perspective, it's as much rum as Martinique's entire annual production during its biggest ever year (1917). It's equivalent to Bacardí's entire annual global output today. Enough rum to fill an Olympic-sized swimming pool every week. If Forbes ran a rich list in 1830, it would have been filled with white Jamaican plantation owners, who were among the wealthiest individuals on the planet.

For a time, the situation was sustainable as the island's varied landscape meant it didn't fall victim to the monoculture mentality. Jamaica was able to ride the ebbs and flows of the volatile sugar market that would be the ultimate undoing of smaller islands. But at the turn of the 20th century, familiar themes began to play out; those of consolidation, oversupply, competition with sugar beet, and disruption during wartime. Jamaica still had 110 distilleries in 1901 and over 12,000 hectares (30,000 acres) of arable land dedicated to growing sugarcane. The island was producing three distinct qualities of rum, intended for the local market, British market and European market (which basically meant Germany). By this time, Germany had developed quite a taste for fruity high-ester rum, so when the German government raised taxes on Jamaican rum the industry responded by manufacturing ever more intense "Continental Rum" that could be diluted to a sensible drinking formula once it arrived in Europe.

The surplus of rum after World War II led many to close or consolidate, as prices hit rock bottom. The number of distilleries in 1948 had dropped to only 25, and in the 1960s, rum manufacturers banded together to coordinate prices and production to attempt to stabilize the rum market – the rum equivalent of OPEC.

There remains only five active distilleries on the island today, and while volumes are still among the highest in the Caribbean, the majority of the rums made in Jamaica is sold on the wholesale market – where it is sent on to one of the blending houses to form a finished product. And it's sought after stuff. Jamaican rum can transform an otherwise dull blend in to a weighty, resonant little number. This is thanks to the island's commitment to the pot still, which despite the laborious batch process is responsible for defining the pervasive style. But in Jamaica, "pot still" doesn't always mean the artisanal little alembic still that it you might see on other islands. Jamaican distilleries are home to some of the biggest pots outside of the Irish whiskey industry, each with a double retort that concentrates the liquor up to high strengths.

Pot-distillation, along with absurd fermentation processes, and the occasional use of dunder (see page 48) means that Hampden Estate distillery (see pages 126–27) has sustained a century-old niche industry supplying high-ester pot-still Jamaican rum to flavour houses. These "espresso" rums are almost undrinkable in their pure form, but highly sought-after when used as a ballsy component of blend that needs a kick in the right direction.

This distinctive approach also means that Jamaica will soon be awarded a Geographical Indication (GI) for its rum. After almost a decade of wading-through-molasses bureaucracy, the island recently passed the first GI in the English-speaking Caribbean. This was for "Jamaica Jerk", which will soon be followed by "Blue Mountain Coffee" and "Jamaica Rum". Under the jurisdictions where the GI is applicable, any product labelled as "Jamaica Rum" (or similar) must be fermented and distilled from molasses, on the island of Jamaica, and possess the organoleptic properties associated with Jamaican pot-still rum. It does, however, not need to be matured in Jamaica.

Contemporary Jamaica is every bit the temple to the drunken gods of rum, but most visitors are sadly only sold the edited version of what true Jamaican culture is all about. The all-inclusive resorts that form the basis of what most tourists experience, might as well be on a separate island. There the cash-fueled propaganda engine would have you believe that staying within their manufactured ecosystem is the safest place for you. But under the veneer of the Jamaica stereotype, Jamaica's "four R's" (reggae, Rastafari, reefer and rum) exist with far more nuance than any tourist brochure can possible illustrate. While Jamaica is not without its dangers, I believe that getting to the heart of British Caribbean culture is worth the risk. How else would I have found myself between Kingston bars, wading through a street filled with revellers at 2am on a Thursday, with a bottle of rum in one hand and a quarter of jerk chicken in the other? But as they say in Jamaica, "Chicken merry, hawk de near."

BELOW Green cane at dusk at the Hampden Estate. No other island identifies with rum and sugar at such a fundamental level as Jamaica and the Jamaicans.

APPLETON ESTATE

We find the Appleton Estate in the southwestern district of Jamaica, known as St. Elizabeth. It's accurate to call Appleton an estate rather than a just a distillery, since there are 400 hectares (1,000 acres) of sugarcane plantation here as well as the Appleton Sugar Refinery. All of the rum that is made at the distillery is produced from one of the 10 varieties of Appleton Estate cane that is grown there, which makes the brand unique among Jamaican rums. But to reach the Estate it's first necessary to penetrate the green heart of the island, through dense forest, up steep inclines, and through Cockpit County, which contains some of the most unique geology in the Caribbean.

The "karst" of Cockpit County are a range of cone-shaped mountains in miniature. Only known to occur in a handful of countries besides Jamaica, these green goosebumps besiege the Appleton Estate's northern front. They whip up odd pressure systems in the area, creating an entirely unique ecosystem. During the wet season, when the cane is flourishing, the rain falls daily in sharp bursts, almost to the same minute. This means the plantation is irrigated on a strict schedule, and over time the sugarcane takes on an unusually vivid shade of green. This, in turn, produces a better quality, higher yield sugar, and even reflects right down to the molasses itself. Tall tales of terroir are too often tenuous in respect of molasses-based rums, but if there's tenability to be found anywhere, it's at Appleton Estate.

Don't believe me? Joy Spence has been Appleton's master blender for 20 years, and she told me that "the orange peel top note that is the hallmark of Appleton Estate rums, is a result of our unique sugarcane plantation". It has to come from somewhere, I suppose, why not the karst?

Perhaps that's why Cockpit County was chosen for the plantation in the first place. The oldest reference to the estate goes back to 1749, when it was less than 4 hectares (10 acres) in size but known to be producing both sugar and rum. A few years later, the estate was bought by the Dickinson family, descendants of Frances Dickinson, an officer involved in the 1655 capture of Jamaica from the Spanish. Appleton was sold in 1845 to one William Hill, and at the time comprised 7 hectares (17 acres). By 1900, it had increased to 23 hectares (56 acres) when it was sold to A. McDowell Nathan, one of Jamaica's most prominent businessmen. Ten years later it had quadrupled in size and, in 1916, the current owners J. Wray & Nephew bought the property. All 1,300 hectares (3,200 acres) of it.

The company began when founder John Wray bought the Shakespeare Tavern in Kingston in 1825, and they later began blending rums. By the 1870s, J. Wray (then headed up by his nephew) was producing some of the most highly respected rums in the industry, winning awards for their 10-, 15- and 25-year-old expressions. Although the brand is most famous for its white overproof rum these days, back in the early 20th century, it was bottles with age statements that drew a crowd. None more so than the legendary Wray & Nephew 17, which was used in the original Mai Tai of 1944 (see page 212). The rum itself has long been discontinued, and when a few bottles of Wray & Nephew 17 resurfaced at the turn of the millennium they were quickly snapped up before being valued at £21,000 ($26,000) a piece.

J. Wray & Nephew were themselves bought out by the Campari Group in 2012. They now command 4,450 hectares (11,000 acres) of plantation land, and operate two distilleries on the island: Appleton Estate and New Yarmouth, the latter being situated in Clarendon, further east. It's there that Wray & Nephew White (overproof) is made. Considering "Whites" is the bestselling rum on the island, the distillery is a bit of an enigma, and

BELOW Elegant lyne arms dip in and out of retorts at the Appleton Estate distillery (left). Only a seriously laidback approach to rum-making can wear out a chair like this (right).

THIS PAGE J. Wray & Nephew is the most popular rum brand in Jamaica, and it's produced at Appleton's sister distillery, New Yarmouth (top). Only a token gesture of rum is matured on-site at the Appleton Estate (above). The vast majority is filled and stored in Kingston.

SIGNATURE BLEND (40% ABV)
AGED BLENDED RUM

Buttered sweetcorn, brioche, banana cake. Taste is full of pot-still funkiness: a battle of light and dark, juicy fruit chewing gum and bitter orange peel.

RESERVE (43% ABV) AGED BLENDED RUM

Spicy fruitcake, ginger, moody and brooding. Peach melba, apricot kernel, tobacco and dark chocolate. There's a dry, leathery note through the finish ending on black pepper and pine.

APPLETON 21-YEAR-OLD (43% ABV)
EXTRA-AGED BLENDED RUM

Gentle crème caramel, coffee, cocoa and vanilla soy milk, then orange sherbet and elderflower. Good dusting of nutmeg. Hot red sand, spiced clove, dates and prune juice. Finish is tickly and tasty with cracked toffee and honeycomb.

ABOVE Old ledgers and leaky casks transport visitors a century or so ago to Appleton's old brick warehouse.

BELOW LEFT Not only a distillery, Appleton continues to operate a sugar mill, too.

every bit the yin to Appleton's tourist-friendly yang. Like Appleton, New Yarmouth has its origins in the 18th century, but the original mill was abandoned at the turn of the 20th century and a new one built on the same site in the middle of the century. Besides producing Wray & Nephew there, this distillery also turns out a gaggle of other, lesser known white rum brands for the domestic market: Coruba, Conquering Lion, Charly's JB and Edwin Charley.

Back at Appleton, we discover a 36-hour fermentation process using Appleton's own proprietary yeast strain. The resulting molasses wine is 7% ABV and this ramps up to 86% through one of Appleton's five 22,750-litre (6,000-US gallon) pot stills. The still house at Appleton is a plumber's paradise, where the trunks of these beastly

pots plunge in and out of retorts like sea monsters. There's a column still at the far end of the still house, and the spirit it produces makes up the majority of the Appleton blend.

Un-aged rum is tankered to warehousing in Kingston, where it is cut to 80% ABV before being put to cask. Column- and pot-still spirits are matured separately and blended just prior to bottling. Close to one-quarter of a million casks of rum are currently held at Wray & Nephew's warehouse, including some of the oldest stocks in the whole of the Caribbean.

Between the Appleton Estate and Wray & Nephew "Whites" Overproof brands, J. Wray & Nephew dominated both the domestic and export market trade. Appleton is the world's fifth best-selling international rum brand, shifting the equivalent of 15 million 70-cl (24-oz) bottles in 2015. The rum produced at the estate makes up around 28% of all the rum made in Jamaica today, yet it accounts for more than 70% of the island's branded export volume. J. Wray & Nephew as a whole command 70% of the local market and the vast majority of that comes from Wray & Nephew "Whites" Overproof – which is as much a part of the Jamaican fabric as Bob Marley.

Appleton means quality; it's a national treasure here, and invokes a deep sense of patriotism in any Jamaican that speaks of it. And trust me, everybody in Jamaica wants to talk about Appleton. When abroad, Appleton is the international ambassador for Jamaican rum, typifying the Jamaican style and flying the flag for pot-still rums in general. In fact, it is the only rum in the world's top 10 sellers that contains a substantial pot-still component.

CLARENDON

Some distilleries are so small, that even in their country of origin it's difficult to track down a bottle. If you visit Jamaica you might think this of the elusive Monymusk Overproof, which was launched by the Clarendon distillery in 2011. Just 5 km (3 miles) from Jamaica's south coast, Clarendon is not a small distillery. In fact, at around 40 million 75 cl (26 oz) bottles of rum a year, Clarendon is far and away Jamaica's biggest rum-maker. But Monymusk rum accounts for only a fraction of the rum distilled at Clarendon, and to understand where the rest goes, it's worth investing in some back-story:

The distillery is owned in roughly equal shares by four separate business interests. The first three fall under an organization known as the National Rums of Jamaica (NRJ), and they are: DDL of Guyana; Goddard Enterprises, whose portfolio also includes the W.I.R.D. distillery in Barbados (see page 68); and the Jamaican government. The remaining slice of the pie belongs to Diageo, for reasons that will become clear very shortly. To make things more interesting, National Rums of Jamaica also have interests in a further two (former) distilleries: Innswood, which operated from 1959 to 1992 and which now serves and an ageing and blending facility for the Monymusk brand rums produced by NRJ; and Long Pond, a mothballed distillery that may be gaining a new lease of life in the near future.

So where is all the rum from this distillery going? Well, 90% of the spirit distilled here is bottled by Diageo for Captain Morgan rum that is destined to be sold in Europe (Captain Morgan in the US is distilled mostly in St Croix – see pages 191–92). That little arrangement alone accounts for 60% of all the bulk export rum from Jamaica. Some of Diageo's cut is also used to make the legendary Myers's brand. The remaining 10% of production is split between NRJ's own Monymusk rum as well as other, small Jamaican brands like Port Royal and Smatt's.

The original distillery at Clarendon was built in 1949, and part of this building is still used to house the two pot stills and associated fermenters. There are two types of pot-still rum made at Clarendon, light (low-ester) and heavy (high-ester). This is controlled during fermentation, where the light rum undergoes a quick 24-hour ferment in steel tanks; and the heavy rum is fermented for up to a month in wooden tuns similar to those found at Hampen Estate (see pages 126–27)

RIGHT This 1961 advert for Myers's Rum, complete with exotic scenery and the promise of adventure, was tailored to the American market. It also included a handy recipe for a Planter's Punch cocktail.

– although much bigger and without the dunder! The older of the two pots is an enormous 20,000-litre (5,285-US gallon) beast with a double retort. It is joined by a newer still, manufactured in India, that weighs in at 25,000 litres (6,600 US gallons) – by my estimations, it is the biggest pot still in the Caribbean.

Around three-quarters of Clarendon's output is taken care of by the column still. It's a cutting-edge example that was installed in 2010, replacing an older model. This still can be configured in a number of ways to produce three different marques of spirit that range from medium-bodied to neutral. It is, itself, fed fermented molasses from four 200,000-litre (52,850-US gallon) open-air steel troughs that can run a complete fermentation in 24 hours.

HAMPDEN

The Hampden Estate is one of the great hidden gems of the rum world. A keeper of lost art of Jamaican rum. The undisputed champion of high-ester rum; the duke of funk; and high-prince of hogo. For many people, the penetrating taste of Hampden rum is the very definition of rum flavour. You've probably tasted it in confectionery and ice-cream. Brilliant, bizarre and capable of transforming the most mundane of spirits into a blend that has character and depth.

In the north of Jamaica we find the most important sugar-growing region, prized by Richard Long in his 1774 book *The History of Jamaica* for its ability to, "yield more sugar, and better in quality [and] produce an extraordinary quantity of rum". Anyone accustomed with the West Country of the UK will recognize the Trelawney and Falmouth place names, which tell a story of how the sugar and rum routes traced a watery bridge between Jamaica and the county of Cornwall (which also happens to be the name of Jamaica's westernmost county). Hampden could tell that story too. The estate was founded in 1756 by Mr. Archibald Sterling, a Scotsman. It has remained in continuous production ever since the time of Sterling, who in 1779, built the Hampden Great House of which the ground floor served as a rum store until the early 1900s. During the 1800s, the estate passed on to the Kelly-Lawson family, and then the Farquharson's, with whom it remained until 2003. During World War I, Hampden Estate constructed the Hampden Wharf in Falmouth, for shipment of its sugar and rums. The wharf is still standing, and is today a major entry port for "The Harmony of the Seas" – which, as of 2016, is the world's largest passenger cruise ship. In 2003 Hampden was bought by the Jamaica Sugar Company, who ran the refinery and distillery until 2009 when it was sold by public auction to the Everglades Farms Ltd. owned by the Hussey family. The estate is today composed of 5,250 hectares (13,000 acres) of cane-growing land, which for the sake of comparison is about the same area of land as the entire island of Tortola.

The smell of the cave-like fermentation house at Hampden is like sticking your head in a barrel of balsamic vinegar and inhaling. Deeply. It's all at once sharp, mouldy and ancient. There are no less than 89 fermenters in total – a record-breaking number – ranging from 9,000–13,500 litres (2,400–3,600 US gallons) in size, and each of them crusty and buckled like an old wooden bucket thanks to long years of microbiological activity. It's these fermentation vats that possess the secrets to the high-ester preparation.

This is in part due to the distillery's use of dunder (see page 48) during the ferment. This acid-rich throwback to the previous distillation helps to promote a long and healthy fermentation by lowering the pH of the mix, as well as forging a link between each subsequent fermentation.

During the fermentation, both alcohol and acids are created through the action of the airborne yeasts and the ever-present bacteria that call the fermentation vats home. Each vat is left to bubble away for a minimum of two weeks, and additional days (up to a month) are then added on to the end of the fermentation to create seven unique marques of rum. This process, which is known as esterification (see page 47) sees the alcohols and acids undergo further reactions, creating wild fruity notes ranging from red berries, pineapple and kiwi, through to geranium and rose. Each of the seven marques are scored according to their ester content, which is measured in parts per million (PPM) with the lowest marque scoring 350 ppm and the highest 1,600 ppm (the highest level permitted by the Jamaican authorities). At the top end of this scale, the massive

RUM FIRE (63% ABV)
OVERPROOF POT-STILL RUM

Where to begin? This is a tropical storm of a rum, summarized with the word "pineapple", but certainly comprising layers of fruits in various states (fresh, dried and rotten). It's strangely appealing, both on the nose and the palate, and it's more-ish in much the same way as bathing in mud is. The finish is packed with funk, banana essence, brioche and bad apple, all of which appear sporadically.

HAMPDEN GOLD (40% ABV)
AGED POT-STILL RUM

Nutty cereal notes, crumbly fudge, and dirty like a soiled stable. Taste is brighter than expected, with ground ginger, car leather and freshly cut sandalwood. The linger revisits banana, but it's more bready, with nutmeg and allspice bringing up the rear end.

concentration of esters takes the spirit far beyond the realms of what could normally be classified as drinkable rum. This is a concentrated, almost perverse level of fruitiness. Not normally bottled on its own (with the exception of DOK – see below) most of the super-high-ester rum produced here is used as flavouring for confectionery, ice-cream and other desserts. If you have ever tried a "rum-flavoured" liqueur chocolate, the base flavour probably came from Hampden.

Hamden employ three pot stills, which all have a 5,000-litre (1,320-US gallon) capacity and are all true to the classic Jamaican configuration: one large pot sequenced by two retorts and a condenser. The middle-cut comes off at around 85–87% ABV, and the distillation process is consistent among all the rums made here, regardless of the target ester count. The water here is supplied not from underground aquifers, but via Hampden's own mountain water collection system, which after use, returns only clean water to the earth.

If you want to try a real taste of Hampden Estate rums, look no further than DOK high overproof rum. Lauded as the highest ester count of any rum in the world, it is an experience not to be missed. Hampden produce the Rum Fire brand, which is difficult to get hold of outside of Jamaica, where it is a direct competitor of Wray & Nephew (see pages 122–24).

Perhaps the best example of Hampden Estate functioning in a blend, is in Smith & Cross (see page 204) where that high-ester trademark carries a finish that dares you to take another sip.

THIS PAGE Hampden Estate manufactures rum like no other and the produce of these pot stills (below left) finds its way into dozens of blends. Rum Fire, the distillery's own brand (below right), does pretty much what it says on the bottle, and a barely legible sign (bottom right) tells us all we need to know about this distillery.

WORTHY PARK

Appleton Estate may be the longest continuously operating rum distillery in Jamaica, but there is another that claims an older (albeit interrupted) history. Worthy Park Estate was patented in 1670, having been gifted by the British crown to Lieutenant Francis Price for services to England during the 1655 capture of Jamaica. Over the 300 years that followed, Worthy Park became the textbook West Indies sugar plantation – literally. Michael Craton's *A Jamaican Plantation: The History of Worthy Park 1670–1970* charts the fortunes and misfortunes of Jamaica's most efficient sugar maker through the island's turbulent history.

Worthy Park first turned to sugarcane cultivation in the 1720s (around a quarter of a century before Appleton), which makes it the oldest sugar factory in Jamaica. The earliest reference to distillation at Worthy Park pops up in 1741, where the equipment used to produce rum is detailed in a land survey document that is still held in nearby Spanish Town's archive. By 1794 the estate comprised 230 hecatres (570 acres) of sugarcane plantation yielding 181 puncheons (66,000 litres/17,500 US gallons) of rum in the year.

The estate grew over the years and passed between three separate families, most recently the Clark family who bought the property in 1918. Since then, four generations of Clarks have managed Worthy Park, starting with Frederick Clark (who made the original purchase) through to the present-day owner, Gordon Clark. Gordon's office is sited in what used to be the on-site slave hospital, which itself is located in a cluster of buildings equivalent to a modest-sized hamlet. Scale is an important thing to get your head around when it comes to Jamaican sugar estates.

After 300 years' experience turning grass into sweet stuff, Worthy Park have got things down to a fine art. The cane is still mostly cut by hand, then processed in the gigantic Worthy Park sugar refinery. Since the late 1960s, this has been the most efficient sugar grower across the entire Caribbean. And they needed to be. The Jamaican rum industry was in a state of oversupply after World War II, forcing prices to unsustainable levels and threatening to cannibalize the entire industry. Action was needed, so the Spirit's Pool Association of Jamaica met with all of the distillers on the island, and in agreement with them, Worthy Park put a cork in two centuries of continuous rum production. Corks can be removed however, and in 2004 the decision was made to recommence distilling. Construction was completed in 2007 – and what a corker of a distillery it is!

Rum is made from molasses, which is pumped along a 1-km (2/3-mile) underground pipe from the Worthy Park refinery. Three types of fermentation are run here: one "quick" ferment, using a distiller's yeast; a medium-ester ferment, pepped up by the distillery's proprietary yeast strain; and three-week high-ester (900 ppm) fermentation that is fermented naturally by airborne yeast. All rums are distilled in an 18,000-litre (4,750 US gallon) pot still with

LEFT A beautiful example of a classic Jamaican pot still, though, as with many of the world's pot stills, this one was manufactured in Scotland. From the right, the still feeds into the low-wine retort, and from there it travels into the high-wine retort, before heading into the cylindrical condenser.

RUM BAR WHITE OVERPROOF (63% ABV)
WHITE OVERPROOF POT-STILL RUM

A heavily concentrated overproof rum, starting with over-ripe banana, nail varnish, and cherry candies. These particularly volatile elements dissipate slowly, which reveals a firmer suggestion of pineapple and brown bread. The taste is hot, hints of PX wine long-in-bottle, cracked cacao, and fierce black pepper.
A fantastic overproof.

RUM BAR GOLD (40% ABV)
AGED POT-STILL RUM

Restrained funk on the nose of this one, as a cleaner style of pot-still juiciness penetrates through. The nose is not without fruit however, delivering Jelly Baby esters, dried mango and peach nectar. Oak influence is more pronounced in the taste, which delivers wood char, banana split and a gentle heat.

a double retort, manufactured by Forsyths in Scotland. It's fully automated, absolutely beautiful, and capable of processing 8,000 litres (2,100 US gallons) of 85% rum a day. I'm told it may be joined by a sister in the near future.

Versatility and scalability is the name of the game here. The distillery, which now accounts for 30–40% of the estate's turnover, adheres to the traditions of Jamaican rum making, but this is a smart operation; one with a fully quipped lab, a state-of-the-art Clean In Place (CIP) cleaning system, and a deep understanding of what makes sugar tick. But more than anything, Worthy Park is a business, run with a solid understanding of the international rum market. This distillery, like most others in Jamaica, relies on a healthy wholesale trade to flog a portion of its rum. At present one-third of all the spirits made here is sold to a third party, and the customer sheet currently includes Main Rum, Hamilton Pot Still Rum, and even Bacardí, where Worthy Park rum features among their "Single Cane Estate" range. You'll also find Worthy Park rum in the Jamaica component of the popular The Duppy's Share blend (see page 204). Of the remaining rum, around half of the spirit is destined to appear in Worthy Park's own "Rum Bar" label, and the remaining rum is tucked away in casks for a "rainy day".

THIS PAGE Worthy Park employs about 30 members of staff in their distillery, although the enormous Worthy Park Estate employs many more than that in sugarcane-cutting and sugar-making activities.

MARTINIQUE

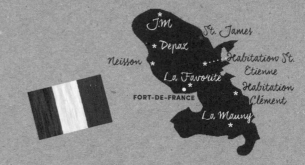

Among all of the rum-producing regions in this book, the island of Martinique is deserving of some special distinction. In part, because it is the only *rhum*-producing region in the world that is regulated by an Appellation d'Origine Contrôlée (AOC – see pages 60–61). Also, because there were once over 500 habitations on the island, each of them tending to small plots of sugarcane and dedicated to the mechanical art of refining it into sugar or *rhum*. Finally, because even today the people of Martinique, its *rhum*-makers or otherwise, are so profoundly assured of the spirit of this island that it would be irresponsible to ignore them. It's been a rollercoaster ride for this island over the past 150 years. The amount of cane-growing land on Martinique has shrunk by two-thirds over the past 50 years, and so too has the number of distilleries. The quality of *rhum* on the other hand, has never been better.

"There are no bad rhums on Martinique." Gilles tells me. He's the owner of a former indigo plantation in Les Anses d'Arlet, in the south of Martinique, who emigrated from France to Martinique – an overseas department of the French Republic – some 20 years previously. At that moment, he was cracking the wax seal on an ancient bottle of XO *rhum agricole* from the late, great "Dillon" distillery. As we toasted to our first sip of the honey-coloured liquid, I pondered the statement. He was right, of course, on the strict proviso that you like Martinique *rhum agricole* in the first instance. As with the other French islands in the Lesser Antilles belt, the *rhum* made here is distilled from the fermented juice of the cane, not the molasses. On Martinique the AOC gets quite specific about the details of this, to the point where quality is more or less standardized across the board. All of the seven remaining distilleries on the island crush their cane as it arrives, and some still use ancient steam boilers, fueled by sugar cane *bagasse* (the leftover crushed husk of the cane), to power their steel-roller mills. The fermented juice of this cane is distilled into *rhum agricole* (literally "agricultural rum") resulting in a full and fruity take on a category that is dominated by the rich and spicy darkness of molasses. Martinicans call molasses-based rums *rhum industriel* ("industrial rum"), and speak of it with either playful indignation or total disinterest.

This mild and slightly seductive form of arrogance is just one of many reminders to visiting tourists that this is still a part of France. It's a tropical island, no doubt, but once you get past all the mosquitoes, bats, coconut palms and 30°C (86°F) heat, the culture and tempo of life is more like a slice of rural Provence. Villagers light up a cigarette in a morning as they head out to collect their baguettes from the local boulangerie, and even though bananas and plantain are available on-tap from roadside vendors, poor-quality coffee and the full range of cheeses can easily be tracked down too.

THIS PAGE Dusk at Les Trois-Îlets in the south-west of the island – the perfect time for a Ti Punch (below left). Cane-cutting at J.M's Préville Estate on the northern shoulder of Mount Pelée (below right).

THIS PAGE Take your pick, but personally I'd opt for three bottles of Depaz (left); a bottle of Rhum Dillon from the 1960s – beautifully finessed and tasting of fresh cherries and orange curd (above); from donkey cart to articulated lorry – when it's harvesting season, a farmer will get his crop to the distillery by any means possible (right).

The French first established a colony on Martinique in the 1640s and the first sugar-refining equipment arrived via the Dutch just a few years later. There were 14 sucreries on Martinique in 1670, 207 in 1690 and 454 in 1742. Like the Spanish, French colonies could only trade with other French colonies, and from 1713, *rhum* (known at the time as *guildive*) produced on Martinique fell under this edict too. The surplus of molasses on the island vastly outweighed the demand for French *rhum* in the motherland however, so this led to clandestine distilling operations, along with the smuggling of molasses into British North American colonies. As the law loosened up in the early 19th century, it allowed for the increased production of *rhum* (still from molasses at this point) to the point that 1 million litres (265,000 US gallons) had been exported by 1847.

Between 1850 and 1920 the Martinique *rhum* industry – and therefore Martinique itself – prospered enormously as a result of war and plague. French soldiers fighting in the Crimean War (1853–56) were rationed with *rhum*, which coincided with the abolition of taxation on the importation of colonial spirits into France. Next, came the *phylloxera* louse, which in its decimation of French vineyards, forced the country to turn to *rhum* when all the wine ran out and brandy stocks ran low. World War I was also extremely kind to Martinique, thanks to the French army once again rationing soldiers with *rhum*,

this time at a rate of 570 ml (one pint) per week. In 1917, Martinique made 30 million litres (7.4 million US gallons) of *rhum*, which accounted for over 80% of the country's total export value.

One natural catastrophe that certainly didn't benefit the industry was the eruption of Mount Pelée. In 1902 the town of Saint Pierre on Martinique's western coast was known as the "Paris of the Caribbean." It was the commercial capital of the island and home to dozens of large plantations, most of which were making molasses-based *rhum*. It was also a busy port town that dealt in shipments of molasses from Martinican refineries without distillation capabilities, as well as those from Guadeloupe, St. Kitts and Demerara. When the volcano erupted on May 5, it wiped out all 30,000 occupants of the town (except one, a prisoner) and destroyed all the refineries and distilleries too. Distilleries could, and were, rebuilt of course (this time far away from any

volcanoes), but a bigger threat was beginning to present itself. France's quick shiftover to sugar beet as a source of raw sugar was dangerous for Martinique, which had up until then profited quite nicely from the tandem industries of sugar and molasses-based *rhums*.

The production of *rhum agricole* probably began – as the name suggests – on farms and rural smallholdings that struggled to deliver their crops to centralized sugar mills. It probably began long before sugar beet became a threat. But as the price of sugar continued to fall, and demand for *rhum* steadily increased, the obvious solution was to skip the sugar-making process altogether and distil *rhum* from the cane juice instead.

The transition didn't take place overnight, however. In 1930 the split between *rhum agricole* and *rhum industriel* was roughly 50/50. At that time, up to 25% of all the spirits consumed in France was Martinican *rhum*, and the Martinicans themselves were drinking 32 litres (8.5 US gallons) of *rhum* per person, per year – more than any other *rhum*-producing island. Over the 50 years that followed, *rhum agricole* grew to became the dominant style as production of molasses *rhum* toppled. But the increase in market share was more a reflection of an industry in decline than a change of taste.

There are a number of reasons why Martinican *rhum* fell so sensationally. Quota systems were implemented after World War I to curtail overproduction. The system introduced a degree of bureaucracy to what had previously been a simple means of an agricultural livelihood. Buy-out and consolidation ensued, and the most dependable brands were the ones that made the cut. Martinican *rhum* lost export trade to France as whisky grew in popularity. In turn, there was a lack of capital to market products, and no means to upgrade old equipment.

Today there are seven distilleries on Martinique. It's only a small island of course, but that's 30 fewer than there were in 1960, and a drop in the ocean compared to 1939, when there were 150 distilleries in operation.

Martinique still produces over a dozen different brands of *rhum agricole*, and some of them, like Dillon, Trois Rivières and J. Bally, are the adopted phantoms (or spirits) of cherished distilleries from the past; their new homes functioning as both holy temples and ongoing life support systems.

During the harvesting season, Martinique is alive with activity. Enormous trucks shift tons of precariously balanced sugarcane along twisting hillside roads, servicing the 3,250 hectares (8,000 acres) of cane-growing land. Those with a more modest crop load pick-up trucks until they're running on their rims and the suspension can take no more. Most of the cane is cut mechanically but on steep hills it's still necessary to do the job by hand.

Surprisingly, dedicated *rhum* bars are scarce on Martinique. The population choose instead to drink at one of the numerous and ever popular "snack" bars. Typically comprising little more than a terrace with some worn-out plastic picnic tables and a garish menu stuck to the wall, these so-called food outlets are your best bet for erasing an entire afternoon in the hot embrace of a *rhum*-fuelled love affair. Generally speaking, if you order *rhum* you will be served a Ti Punch (see pages 226–27). It can arrive as individual components (where you mix your own) or as a completed drink. Sometimes the bottle will simply be left on the table and the waiter will calculate what you owe by gauging the volume that's gone missing. For the power drinker, there is the option of *feu* ("fire") or *petit-feu*: this ritual – which takes place in the early hours of the morning – sees the drinker swallow a shot of *rhum*, which is immediately followed by a glass of water. The idea is that the water "douses" the heat of the spirit, and the game is to see if you can swallow the *rhum* without it touching your lips or tongue.

DEPAZ

On May 5 1902, after days of tremors and sensational plumes of ash, Mount Pelée, 5 km (3 miles) to the north of Saint Pierre, finally gave way. It began with a gruesome "crack", which could be heard across the valley. A river of boiling hot mud flooded into the valley, destroying the cane fields and crashing through dwellings. A mass exodus of wild animals ensued, as giant centipedes and pit vipers fled the hills and descended upon Saint Pierre, killing and/or terrifying people and livestock in the process. The next day, blue flames topped the summit of the mountain, signalling the imminent arrival of lava. Authorities urged everyone to stay put, insisting that the mountain presented no (further) danger. Two days later, on May 8, a sudden and extremely powerful blast of hot gas and volcanic debris killed very nearly every one of the 30,000 residents of Saint Pierre in minutes – the highest death toll of any volcano in the 20th century.

While all this was going on, Victor Depaz, a 16 year old-boy from Saint Pierre, was studying in Bordeaux. Victor's family had, up until that time, operated a very old distillery in Saint Pierre, called L'Habitation Perrinelle. Victor learned of the decimation of his home and death of his entire family by telegram the next day.

With no home to go back to, he completed his studies in France and returned to Martinique penniless, involving himself in the only industry that he knew: distillation. By then the rebuilding of Saint Pierre was underway, but the town was never restored to its former glory, and even today it is little more than a small but pretty town.

The devastation caused by the eruption, along with the danger of further eruptions, meant that it was 15 years before anyone dared to establish a sugar plantation in Saint Pierre. Perhaps it was madness, or perhaps it was a form of closure, but it was the orphan, Victor Depaz, who at the age 28, bought himself 512 hectares (1,265 acres) of land 1 km (2/3 mile) north of Saint Pierre, on the flanks of the mountain that had killed his entire family. On May 8 1917 he began distilling.

It turned out that all that volcanic soil did wonders for sugarcane, and as Depaz's estate flourished so too did his wealth. He went on to have 11 children and built himself an enormous château to house his family. Depaz died in 1960, by which time he had become one of the more prominent members of Martinique society, even at one time serving as Mayor of his beloved Saint Pierre.

The Depaz estate remains intact today, including the perfectly manicured lawns and enormous former

BLANC (50% ABV)
UN-AGED MARTINIQUE RHUM AGRICOLE AOC

Typical Plantain and green banana notes keeping things sticky but fresh. Spicy and sappy on the palate, with black pepper heat and chlorophyl bitterness. Green, hot and bitter through the finish.

BLANC (55% ABV)
UN-AGED MARTINIQUE RHUM AGRICOLE AOC

Showing off more boisterous qualities, this concentrated *rhum* is all about big fermented banana, lime cordial and rotten mango. Spice and lashings of salty sea spray on the palate. Hot all the way down, but still you go back for more.

CANNE BLEU (50% ABV)
UN-AGED MARTINIQUE RHUM AGRICOLE AOC

Pungent vegetal notes, softly fishy with maritime flavours. Weighty on the palate but with incredibly suppressed alcohol.

PLANTATION (45% ABV)
AGED MARTINIQUE RHUM AGRICOLE AOC

A nice balance of maturation and distillery youthfulness. Oak has tempered the green exuberance of the white *rhum* in to baked and charred tropical fruits. There's some dried fruit here too, reminiscent of Pedro Ximénez wine, and a touch of cocoa. Crème brûlée. Rich dried fruits, sultana (golden raisin) and brioche.

VSOP RÉSERVE SPÉCIALE
AGED MARTINIQUE RHUM AGRICOLE AOC

This 7-year-old *rhum* is softer on the nose, with elements of cake batter containing soft baking spices and some remnants of soft, dried fruits too. In the taste it's all dense brown sugar, heavier and richer than the nose suggests. The liquid dries off pleasingly through the finish.

XO "GRANDE RÉSERVE" (45% ABV)
EXTRA-AGED MARTINIQUE RHUM AGRICOLE AOC

Indulgent and dessert like, this is a blend of 8- and 10-year-old *rhums*. Morello cherry, macadamia nut and beurre noisette produce a finely balanced aroma. On the palate this gives way to deeply woody, Rancio notes as complex toasted spices balance bittersweet elements.

XO "CUVÉE DU GRAND SAINT PIERRE" (45% ABV)
EXTRA-AGED MARTINIQUE RHUM AGRICOLE AOC

Waxy honey and meadowsweet fill the nose, leading to ripe red apple and plum. In the taste it's vegetal, with seasoned green tomato and radish leaves. The finish is cedar wood and soft leather.

HORS D'AGE 2002 VINTAGE (45% ABV)
EXTRA-AGED MARTINIQUE RHUM AGRICOLE AOC

There's burnt cinnamon, mace and hemp. In the taste, the alcohol carries the weight of the sweetness and drifts along in to soft spices with balanced bitterness. The finish is clean, and the alcohol impressively well suppressed.

residence of Victor Depaz and his family. The peak of Mount Pelée continues to feature heavily in the branding of the *rhum*. These days, the Depaz distillery is owned by La Martiniquaise, the same company that own Saint James distillery on the east of the island. The Depaz distillery, which also produces the Dillon brand, has a self-guided tour and an impressive faux-Creole reception area that has the only set of automatic doors made from wood that I have ever come across.

Production is a relatively standard affair as Martinique *rhums* go. One point of interest is the working steam- powered mill, which is still fuelled by a *bagasse*-burning furnace. La Favorite (see page 136–37) is the only other distillery on the island that

continues to generate energy in this bygone manner. After fermentation, two stainless-steel stills are used to distill Depaz *rhums* up to 68–70% ABV, producing a broad selection of *blanc* and *vieux rhums* that seem to speak of the nearby Caribbean sea, of salt and sun-bleached timber. There's a copper still there too, which was pilfered from the old Dillon distillery and is still used today to make Dillon *rhums*.

The original Dillon distillery is in the heart of Fort-de-France and it takes its name from Arthur Dillon (1750–94) a soldier with Lafayette's troops in the American War of Independence. The distillery closed in 2005 and it now serves as a central bottling plant for the brand owners.

J.M

The north of Martinique is dominated by Mount Pelée, a volcano that is currently in a quiescent state, which means it is not active, but is registering seismic activity. Despite the widespread devastation during the volcanic eruption of 1902, Martinique's oldest remaining *rhum* distillery, Rhum J.M, survived.

Antoine Leroux-Préville bought the area now known as the Préville estate in 1790 and established a sugar factory there. In 1845, the sugar factory was sold to Jean-Marie Martin, who installed stills and began marketing molasses-based *rhum* under the J.M. Rhum name as a sideline. By the end of the 19th century, J.M's descendants had left the island, and the business – including the sugar works with five boilers, water mill and iron-wheel mill, as well as the "building used as the fermenting shop with a Père Labat-type boiler system" – was liquidated. It changed hands a few times in the early part of the 20th century, as successive owners did their bit to update the distillery. In 1914, Gustave Crassous de Médeuil, already the owner of the Bellevue estate located in the hills of Fonds Préville, purchased the J.M distillery, which by now was dedicated only to the production of *rhum agricole*.

As you drive north on the winding Route de la Trace, banana plantations fill the vista. If cane means cash in the south, it's a peelable type of gold that grows in the north. The slightly higher altitude in the north lends itself better to growing bananas than cane.

J.M grow both crops. In fact, they are the only producer on the island to make *rhum* entirely from their own cane plantations, and between their nearby Bellevue and Préville estates, they have around 200 hectares (500 acres) of the stuff. J.M are quick to preach on the benefits of farming your own and the positive impact that the banana trees have on the local terroir. Sugarcane and banana plantations are rotated every five or six years to create optimal soil conditions for both products. If ever there was an explanation for that tell-tale *agricole* banana aroma, it's here.

Perhaps the greatest benefit of the cut-your-own approach however, is the freshness of the sugarcane. J.M's long-time master distiller and blender, Nazaire Canatous, sets his team the challenge of milling fresh cane within a single hour of cutting it. If the distillery had a catchphrase it would probably be: "you can't get much fresher than that!"

THIS PAGE J.M is high up in the north of Martinique. Contained within a lush green crucible, it's probably the prettiest of all the operational distilleries on Martinique. That 100% copper column, confirms it (bottom right).

ÉLEVÉ SOUS BOIS (50% ABV)
AGED MARTINIQUE RHUM AGRICOLE AOC

Light, honeycomb, funky florals and a touch of sour custard. Brown sugar on the second nose. Taste is tight and bright. Sweet oak melds with youthful aggression.

VSOP (43% ABV)
AGED MARTINIQUE RHUM AGRICOLE AOC

Cappuccino, Brazil nut, chocolate. Fruits appear on second nosing. Less sweetness on the palate than the nose suggests. Tamarind and prune. Bitterness holds the finish nicely.

10-YEAR-OLD (45% ABV)
EXTRA-AGED MARTINIQUE RHUM AGRICOLE AOC

Waxy and honeyed. Less pungent and softer, sweeter, more fragrant. Soft nuttiness: almond. Bright and grippy on the palate, with gentle citrus coupling with wood tannin and vanilla sweetness.

15-YEAR-OLD (43% ABV)
EXTRA-AGED MARTINIQUE RHUM AGRICOLE AOC

Slick caramel sauce, millionaire shortbread and crème Anglaise. It gives way to sugared soft fruits, orange sherbet, grape juice and lemon tart. Well-structured on the palate, with a warmth that's tempered by cane juice, waxy polish and candy shop flavours.

Speaking of Nazaire, this man is one of the longest-serving distillers in the business, having worked at J.M for 45 years. His predecessor was his own father, who first clocked in to work at J.M in 1930. It's fair to say that the the brown-sugar signature style of J.M has been largely shaped by these two men.

Once the cane takes the very short trip down to the distillery, the three-stage mill (which was converted from steam to electric in 2013) starts the rhum-making process. Volcanic spring water from the mountain is used to extract the sugar, and it's this same water that is used to finish the products at their respective bottling strength. There are 17 fermentation vessels all told, with a total capacity of around 300,000 litres (80,000 US gallons). Fermentation lasts only 24 hours then the liquid is distilled through a single copper column. Waste water from the distillery (known as vinasse) is collected in a dirty yellow lake and used to irrigate the banana trees. Spirit destined to be sold as rhum blanc is rested in steel for a full six months – this is longer than most distilleries, and something that J.M believe is reflected in the quality of their spirit. The rest of the spirit is sent to the barrel house which, thanks to the exceptional humidity of the surrounding environment, has its own unique mark to place on the liquid.

LA FAVORITE

La Favorite is the only remaining distillery in Martinique's capital, Fort-de-France. And what with being only a 15-minute drive from the port, you might expect it to be a glossy-facaded tourist magnet, cunningly engineered to lure in cruise ship excursion groups like sphinx moths to a lightbulb. But La Favorite's marketing department appears to have missed that memo. Indeed, this humble little distillery surely offers the most unembellished insight into Martinique rhum agricole of all the island's distilleries.

A sugar mill was founded on the current La Favorite estate as far back as 1843. At the time of its construction, "La Jambette" (named for the bordering river that supplied hydraulic power) consisted of 45 slaves, two sugar refineries and a small molasses rhum distillery with five fermentation vats and a copper pot-still. This refinery operated for 60 years, and while that can be deemed a success, they were certainly hard-earned years. Mainland France progressively shifted towards sugar beets as its prime source of sucrose during this time, then there was the defeat of the monarchists, who the planters all supported, and, just for good measure, Hurricane San Magín, which was the cause of 700 deaths on Martinique in 1891, was the near destruction of La Jambette.

It was only the Caribbean estates that swiftly shifted their attentions to rhum that survived the sugar downturn. Until that point, rhum on Martinique had been almost entirely molasses-based and little more than a by-product of the more lucrative sugar-refining operations. The onset of phylloxera louse, which decimated the French wine and brandy industry in the 1880s, helped rhum gain a foothold in the lucrative folds of the motherland. In the case of La Jambette, the business failed to act quickly enough, and was sold, in 1902, to Henri Domoy.

Domoy put an end to all the sugar-refining activities and turned his attentions to producing *rhum agricole* full-time. This started with replacing the pot-still with a copper column, which was followed by a steam engine to crush the cane and new generators. Domoy also built a railway line through his plantation to transport cane from the fields as quickly and efficiently as possible. By the 1920s, the distillery was in fine form, and Domoy had completed the construction of a grand, imposing manor house called *Château de La Favorite*.

Since then, the distillery has passed through three successive generations of the Domoy family, from Henri, to André, to Franck Domoy: Henri's great-grandson, who took over the day-to-day running of the operation in 2006. It's the longest continuously family-run distillery on the island. But more than that, this is *agricole* in its rawest form – blunt and very much imperfect. The staff barely acknowledge the curious visitors who wander freely around the distillery floor, in and amongst working gears and volatile fumes. It's a health and safety nightmare in the making. It can't go on like this for much longer. It's not to be missed.

La Favorite produce only a small range of *rhums*, and an even smaller range of *vieux* expressions. The distillery is powered by a diesel steam engine that was built in France in 1906. It powers the three-stage mill, and pumps the cane juice into the fermenters, of which there are 10, each 35,000 litres (9,250 US gallons) in size.

TOP RIGHT Not a bottle of *rhum*, but a wide shot of one of La Favorite's 35,000-litre (9,250-US gallon) fermenters.

MIDDLE A stare that could strip spirit from wine and send this curious author running for cover.

BOTTOM Some team members clearly take their job a little less seriously than the chap above.

CŒUR CANNE (50% ABV)
UN-AGED MARTINIQUE RHUM AGRICOLE AOC

One of the more feral of the Martinique set: wet cut grass, hot vinegar, and grated plantain on the nose. Taste is wickedly spiced, with a faint salinity and dry heat to the finish.

LA MAUNY

Driving east from Fort-de-France, an enormous Hollywood-style sign on the hillside announces your approach to the island's southernmost distillery: Trois Rivieres. Sadly, the sign is just as artificial as the region of Los Angeles that the real Hollywood sign designates. Trois Rivières is still there, but the distillery stopped producing in 2002. The still was uprooted, along with all the casks of maturing spirit, and transported 10 minutes further down the road to La Mauny. The purchase of Trois Rivières by La Mauny, in 2001, means that La Mauny is, along with the Duquense brand, the second-biggest *rhum* producer in Martinique. But with its aircraft hangar of a still house, lined with five large column stills, it sure does feel like the biggest.

La Mauny was founded in 1891 and named after "Count Mauny" Joseph Ferdinand Poulain, a counsellor of the Martinique Court of Appeal, who bought the land around Rivière Pilote in the 18th century. The Laurent family were the first to run an estate on this site, as far back as the 17th century. During the Martinique sugar crisis of the 1880s, the mill was sold to the Codé family, who in 1891 installed the island's first pot still and began making rhum. The distillery and refinery passed to the Bellonnie brothers in 1923, who were experienced rum and sugar merchants from Fort-de France. They undertook a process of modernization that included the installation of a modern column still. Theodore Bellonnie allied with the Bourdillon family upon his brother's death in 1969, forming the BBS group (Bellonnie, Bourdillon & Successors). Jean-Pierre Bourdillon arrange the relocation of the distillery 100 metres (330 ft) up the road, and re-developed the plantation fields which were at the time too rugged for mechanical harvesting. He also acquired equipment

from a mothballed operation in nearby Acajou, which increased the distillery's throughput.

In 1994, La Mauny acquired the Trois Rivières distillery from Martini & Rossi. As part of the deal they also got the Duquesne rum brand which was then, and remains today, one of the top-selling brands on the island. The new millennium saw a bunch of buyouts and mergers, which left La Mauny in the hands of La Martiniquaise, who already had their hands on Saint James and Depaz. Between all those brands the company commanded over 60% of the Martinique rum market. The authorities deemed it a monopoly and La Martiniquaise were forced to sell La Mauny distillery to the Chervillon Group.

The first indication of scale at La Mauny is the enormous crane grabber that clutches great clawfulls of cane and sends it on its way to the roller mills. La Mauny has 295 hectares (730 acres) of cane-growing land, which accounts for around 30% of their requirements. The mill is a sophisticated system, whereby water is added to extract optimal levels of sugar, but the exact amount of water is constantly adjusted by a computer that measures the Brix of the juice after crushing. Consistent sweetness of juice means a consistent fermentation, which is necessary here since La Mauny use six different yeast strains. Once the juice arrives at one of the 27 fermentation vats (each of them with a capacity of 57,000 litres/15,000 US gallons), the correct yeast culture is added depending on whether it's La Mauny, Trois Rivières, and Duquense-branded rum that

BELOW Every drop of rum produced at La Mauny is made from sugarcane that has been handled by this terrifying machine (far left and middle left). Once pressed, the burnt husks of cane generate steam for the still house (middle right and far right), but the mills themselves are diesel-powered.

ABOVE Trois Rivières is one of the better-known Martinican export brands, even though the distillery closed 15 years ago.

is being made. Three of the fermenters serve as "mother tanks", which run on a semi-continuous fermentation, periodically sharing one-third of their contents with a fresh tank of cane juice before being topped up with more juice itself. The process is something akin to a solera ageing system (see page 55), though of course unrelated to maturation, guaranteeing consistency between tanks and relieving the distillery staff of the need to add fresh yeast in all 27 tanks.

Next is the still house, with its five separate column stills. Three are reserved for La Mauny, and one each for Trois Rivières and Duquense. Master distiller Henry Vicrobeck has the job of managing these beasts, which are affectionately named after cars – one known as the "F1"; another is the "2CV"; and so on – and between them can produce up to 3 million litres (6.3 million US gallons) of alcohol a year. In practice they make around half of that. Most of the 5,000 casks here are ex-bourbon, but there are plenty of French ones too, that are used for Trois Rivières and La Mauny expressions. All casks are filled with white rum at a strength of 60–65% ABV. As I wander through the barrel house I notice sherry casks too, and Cognac, Port and Muscatel barrels.

CUVÉE DE L'OCEAN (42% ABV)
UN-AGED MARTINIQUE RHUM AGRICOLE AOC

Vegetal, with crisp citrus, some salinity. Banana bread and seaweed too. Delicate on the palate, with gentle zippy citrus. Still slightly saline, with black pepper and pineapple.

ROUGE (45% ABV)
UN-AGED MARTINIQUE RHUM AGRICOLE AOC

Hot rubber, grapefruit, cereal and plantain. Warmer on return: hot and funky. There's carpet, green (bell) pepper and citrus rinds. Much less vegetal.

SIGNATURE (40% ABV)
AGED MARTINIQUE RHUM AGRICOLE AOC

Red fruits, diesel, ginger, grape sherbet. Ginger beer, long white pepper and some pot-still characteristics. Tastes like Cognac.

LE NOUVEAU DE MONDE (40% ABV)
AGED MARTINIQUE RHUM AGRICOLE AOC

Chocolate-coated strawberries, coffee butter and generally big fruitiness. Some aroma of old cigars and apricot fudge. Palate yields grippy alcohol and toasted oak. Remains bright and not too cloying.

TROIS RIVIÈRES VINTAGE 2000 (42% ABV)
AGED MARTINIQUE RHUM AGRICOLE AOC

Light florals, iris and honey, leading to summer fruits, vanilla and soft fudge.

TROIS RIVIÈRES TRIPLE MILLÉSIME (42% ABV)
EXTRA-AGED MARTINIQUE RHUM AGRICOLE AOC

Orange flower, raisin, butter and orange cream. Taste is intensely citric – orange cordial, oak and vanilla. There's a slight acidity to it.

TROIS RIVIÈRES 12-YEAR-OLD (42% ABV)
EXTRA-AGED MARTINIQUE RHUM AGRICOLE AOC

Woody and taut. Boozy trifle, marzipan, almost sherried, shortbread, caramel and marmalade. Long and concentrated through the finish. Hours of fun.

LE SIMON

Le Simon is the only distillery in Martinique that is not readily accessible to the public, and the only one that does not produce rum under the distillery's own name. In distillery circles, it is something of a ghostwriter, but performs the important role of surrogate parent and guardian to two of the most cherished names in Martinique *rhum agricole* (as well as some other, lesser-known labels): Clément and Habitation Saint-Étienne (HSE). It is surprising to learn that these brands are not distilled in their original locations, although both Clément and HSE are transported home for ageing, blending and bottling. The history of both brands, as well as Le Simon itself, is extensive, and to better appreciate it, it's worth telling the tale in concert. So here it is, a tale of three distilleries:

Le Simon was built in 1862 by Emile Bougenot, a young engineer, who arrived from France on behalf of the J.F. Cail engineering firm. Bougenot is responsible for a number of architectural beauties on the island,

but his greatest successes were with sugar. Bougenot managed nine seperate refineries in his time, had shares in over a dozen, as well as outright ownership of Le Galion: the last operating sugar mill in Martinique today. For the first 70 years of its life, Le Simon was a fully operational sugar refinery that made *rhum industriel* as a sideline. Cane was supplied by five nearby habitations: Fontaines, La Digue, Palmistres, Union-Roy and Petit France, totalling 1,000 hectares (2,470 acres) of land between them.

During the same period, Dr Homére Clément was also getting into the sugar business. Clément was a radical socialist politician, who served in the French National Assembly as deputy of Martinique from 1902-1906. He was popular, in as much as a politician can be, and was considered by many the uncrowned king of Martinique. In 1883 Clément bought a sugar mill in the Acajou region, not far from Le Simon.

That same year, another sugar mill, near St. Stephen, in the central-north of the island, was sold to Amedé Aubery. The mill had been originally founded in 1862 (the same year as Le Simon) and the new owner renamed it Habitation Saint-Étienne.

While the mills at Le Simon and Saint-Étienne were still quite new, Clément's mill had been in operation since 1770, and was in desperate need of modernization. Clément added a distillery, and enjoyed some success marketing *rhum industriel* under various brand names, though none that used his own name. In time, the distillery and mill was passed on to Homére Clément's son, Charles, who was responsible for marketing the family's first *rhum agricole*. Charles was also faced with the challenge of rebuilding the distillery in 1938 after it was destroyed by fire. Charles Clément went on to become president of the union of *rhum agricole* distillers, helping to establish the criteria for the Martinique AOC.

Around the same time that Habitation Clément was burning, Le Simon distillery began making *rhum agricole* too. Likewise, production of *rhum agricole* at Habitation Saint-Etienne began in the 1930s, and during the slump of the 1950s HSE became the top-selling brand on the island. It was also the backdrop to Patrick Chamoiseau's "Seven Dreams of Elmira", which poetically frames the tradition and legacy of Saint-Étienne:

"The shadows of the machines shimmered with all the souls who had worked there before: the one's who'd kept the books in the plantation grocery; the one's who'd cut the eternities of sugarcane; the one's who'd worn out hand-trucks carrying it; who'd tamed the brilliance of the forge; who'd made the steam boiler rumble; who'd kept the hydraulic mill running under the fury of the canals; the master-distillers who orchestrated the spirit of our rum in the chaudfroid of the coils. All those people!"

In 1971 Le Simon was bought by a Groupement d'Intérêt Economique (GIE) headed up by Yves Hayot, and from thence forth it produced both *rhum agricole*

RIGHT At Le Simon, there are blending vats big enough to make your mouth water.

BELOW The Clément range covers a rainbow of colours and all manner of flavours (except rainbow flavour).

CLÉMENT BLANC (50% ABV)
UN-AGED MARTINIQUE RHUM AGRICOLE AOC

Burnt clutch and soft gooey bananas. Aroma is not intense and alcohol is ever present. Prickly on the palate with green pineapple, green pepper, warm hay and papaya.

CLÉMENT VO (40% ABV)
AGED MARTINIQUE RHUM AGRICOLE AOC

Peaches and apricots, orange soda, dried coconut chips and melon. More robust on the palate, with dried mango and a touch of soft tobacco. Orange through the finish.

CLÉMENT XO (42% ABV)
AGED MARTINIQUE RHUM AGRICOLE AOC

Soft shavings of cacao, burnt caramel and toasted hazelnut. Subtle on the nose. The palate is peppered and sustained. Drifts into spiced sugar and bitter chocolate.

CLÉMENT 10-YEAR-OLD (42% ABV)
EXTRA-AGED MARTINIQUE RHUM AGRICOLE AOC

Punchy esters and a slight acetone note. Gives way to plum pudding, almond frangipani and banana candy. Taste is hot and sticky: pineapple chutney, sultana (golden raisin) and burnt milk. Fresh apricot and apricot kernels on the finish.

CUVÉE HOMÉRE CLÉMENT (44% ABV)
EXTRA-AGED MARTINIQUE RHUM AGRICOLE AOC

Apricot with tobacco, almond, vanilla ice cream and just a gentle lick of orange. The taste is like hot Dr Pepper, vanilla candy, cherry cola, dentine gum and tobacco.

HSE ISLAY CASK (44% ABV)
AGED MARTINIQUE RHUM AGRICOLE AOC

Unmistakably Islay. Smoky notes are tamed by tropical fruits (pineapple, banana) and seasoned with black pepper. The taste is typically peaty, but the smoke is almost sour before sweet wood drifts through. It's balanced, but more whisky than *rhum*.

ABOVE Modern racking systems such as these make it relatively easy to move casks in and out of warehouse space.

and *rhum industriel*, the former distilled from molasses imported from Guadeloupe. This was a testing time for Martinique *rhum*, which forced the closure of countless distilleries and the consolidation of others. In 1986 Yves Hayot rescued Habitation Clément and moved production to Le Simon two years later. The business was subsequently sold to Yves's brother, Bernard, and in 2005, Habitation Clément was converted in to an all singing and dancing museum of rum history.

A tour of the old distillery, immaculate grounds, palm groves, and colonial house is narrated by a multi-lingual audio guide. There's a museum that regularly showcases the works of local artists, and the tasting room and boutique is all glossy white surfaces and clean lines. Some of the most sought-after rums in the Caribbean have been, and still are, bottled under the Clément name, and the brand has been instrumental in establishing the super-premium section of the *rhum agricole* category.

Habitation Saint-Étienne was retired in 1988, and production of Saint-Étienne rums moved to La Favorite (see pages 136–37) for a few years. In 1994, the brand and original column still were bought by Yves and José Hayot, and fermentation and distillation (including the still itself) were moved to Le Simon, thus completing a merger of distilleries 130 years in the making.

HSE rum is today distilled at Le Simon, then transported north to the original distillery in St. Stephen, where it is cut with water from the River Lézarde before bottling. The *rhum* is available in an impressive array of marques these days, from the standard white offering through to extra-aged expressions and liquids finished in single malt (including Islay), sherry and Sauterne casks.

Le Simon is the most technologically advanced distillery on Martinique. The distillery doesn't own a plantation, so cane is sourced from various farms across the south of the island. After pressing it is fermented using a Belgian baker's yeast that takes 24–36 hours to turn the sweet sugarcane juice (*vesou*) into boozy cane wine. The plant has four columns: one brought over from Habitation Clément, used to produce (you guessed it) Clément; and the original still from St. Stephen that is used to make HSE. There are another two column stills that are used to make other products for the domestic market.

NEISSON

Neisson is the smallest distillery on Martinique, accounting for less than 2% of the island's output. But if history tells us anything, it should be never to underestimate the French when they arrive in ambitious, compact packages. Nelson's *rhum blanc* is the most popular white *rhum* on the island. You can sense a certain loyalty to this place, which has remained in continuous operation since 1931 – even through World War II – and is today, along with La Favorite (see pages 136–37) one of only two remaining family-run distilleries on Martinique.

The Neisson family first started farming sugarcane on Martinique in 1922. The location Hildevert-Pamphille Neisson picked was the small town of Le Carbet, about 15 km (9 miles) north along the western coast from Fort-de-France. Distillation was introduced in 1931, and the distillery was later handed over to Hildevert's sons: Adrien and Jean. Jean trained in Paris as a chemical engineer and took over the running of the distillery when Adrien died in 1971. When Jean Neisson died, there was no male heir to take on the mantle. The responsibility fell to his grandson Grégory Vernant. At only 15 years old, Grégory was quite clued up on the technicalities of making *rhum*, but he was too young to be drinking, let alone running a distillery by himself. The solution, which rescued the distillery, was for Claudine Vernant Neisson (Grégory's mother and Jean's daughter) to step in. A trained hospital physician, Claudine took over as master distiller while Grégory finished his studies. Thirty years on, and this mother and son duo are still running the distillery today.

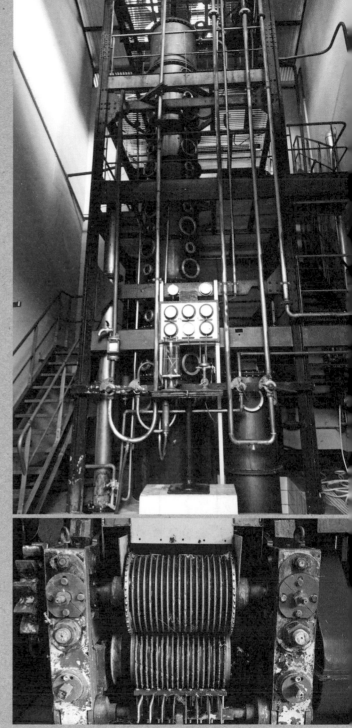

THIS PAGE The copper column at Neisson features portholes which make it look like a giant copper octopus tentacle (above); the roller mill at Neisson – it's best not to get too close to these (bottom).

BLANC (50% ABV)
UN-AGED MARTINIQUE RHUM AGRICOLE AOC

On the nose it's wildly fruity, with tinned pear, candied fruits and the typical banana notes. Try harder and you'll also find lime juice and golden syrup. The palate is drier than anticipated, but the heat is kept in check nicely, with soft flutters through the finish.

RHUM (52.5% ABV)
UN-AGED MARTINIQUE RHUM AGRICOLE AOC

Big waxy banana skin on the nose, with hints of fruity bubblegum and model glue. The taste is sweeter than the 50%, but with fuel enough to heat your guts up.

SPECIAL RESERVE (42% ABV)
AGED MARTINIQUE RHUM AGRICOLE AOC

Fruit caramel, fruit cake. Tobacco, dark chocolate and gently herbaceous on the palate. Lively but not without depth.

EXTRA VIEUX (45% ABV)
AGED MARTINIQUE RHUM AGRICOLE AOC

Tobacco and fruit leather on the nose, relaxing into vanilla and caramel. Grippy yet somehow zippy on the palate. Finish is like sour butterscotch and white wine.

Neisson use a proprietary yeast strain to make their *rhum*. This came about after the distillery undertook a study on the biodiversity of yeasts naturally present in their parcels of sugarcane.

Partnering with SOFRLAB, a company that is deeply invested in the technical aspects of yeast genetics and fermentation characteristics, they assessed over a three-year period how cane terroir influences yeast biodiversity.

An initial sample of 200 yeast cultures was narrowed down to six, which were then tested through fermentation and assessed for their efficiency and for the organoleptic properties of the resulting ferment and *rhum*. Two yeast cultures were finally selected, and

for the first time in a long while, a Martinique distiller was using native yeasts to make *rhum*.

The yeast has a lower rate of efficiency than the distiller's yeasts typical of the other producers, so this draws out fermentation for up to five days. The result is a wine of around 4.5%, but it's the complex array of flavours that set it apart from the rest. Over this sustained period, oxygen has further opportunity to react with the alcohol as it is produced and this, along with the unique array of congeners generated by Neisson's proprietary yeast, results in the formation of new aldehydes and esters – the building blocks of fruity flavours.

Neisson's Savalle still was installed in 1952 and is the only one on the island made entirely from copper. The tower is painstakingly deconstructed, cleaned, and put back together again once a year, during the wet season.

All Neisson *rhum vieux* are matured for a minimum of four years (a whole year over the legal requirement). Around 70% of the barrel stock are ex-bourbon casks, the remainder being 350-litre (93-US gallon) French oak casks, some of them new, and some of them previously used by the Cognac industry. The warehousing at Neisson also holds half a dozen circa 1,000-litre (264-US gallon) oval-shaped blending vats for mixing mature spirit before bottling.

Neisson bottle five different *rhum blanc* at four different strengths (50%, 52.5%, 55%, and 70% ABV) but this is more than just a case of choosing how drunk you wish to get. Through a combination of cane variety and terroir, Neisson have created a range of white *rhums* that highlight the potential variation in flavour that these agricultural details can impact. The standard 50% and 55%, for example, are made from five varieties of cane, sourced from Saint-Pierre and Carbet. The 52.5% uses only Thieubert Carbet Blue cane grown adjacent to the distillery. The L'esprit is made from the same Blue cane and Crystal cane varieties, and the still is managed slightly differently resulting in an un-cut 70% ABV spirit – the highest strength of French *rhum agricole* you can find.

Bottling at 70% has caused a few eyebrows to become raised, and not only from those who are drinking the stuff. High-strength *agricole* appears to go against the grain of French *rhum* tradition. I applaud Neisson for their boldness in this matter, and for their continued efforts in furthering the category through their explorations.

SAINT JAMES

It's difficult to miss the Saint James distillery. Dropped like a military aid parcel in the middle of Sainte-Marie, an otherwise pretty little seaside town on Martinique's north-east Atlantic coast. It's no wonder this distillery feels so incongruous to the town's low-slung shacks and beachside snack bars. Saint James moved to Saint-Marie following the decimation of the original plantation during the Mount Pelée eruption of 1902. Survival instinct is in the staves and bolts of all of Martinique's distilleries, but no other can claim the dogged determination of Saint James. It's Martinique's biggest *rhum* distillery, with the largest stock of mature *rhum* in the French Antilles and the capacity to fill the equivalent of 3.5 million 70-cl (25-oz) bottles a year.

It was in 1765 that one Révérend Père Edmond Lefébure (the learned alchemist and Supérieur of the Convent of Brothers of Charity) set up a sugar mill and distillery in Saint Pierre (see pages 133–134). Being a man of the cloth, it wouldn't have been unforeseen that Lefébure chose "Saint Jacques" as the name, but it was later changed to Saint James to adopt a more English-sounding name that would attract foreign trade from the colonies in New England.

The plantation changed hands and in 1882, shortly after the pot stills had been replaced with columns, the brand was trademarked by Paulin Lambert. Lambert was a Marseille-based importer of Saint James (among other brands) and purchased the business in 1890. Lambert also attempted (but failed) to patent Saint James's square bottle shape, which was intended to catch the eye, but also to make transportation of the product safer. A few years later, other brands like Johnnie Walker and Cointreau would make the square bottle iconic, but by my reckoning it was Saint James that first innovated in the field. The distillery on Martinique was obviously doing well by this point, as one traveller in 1890 noted that there were huge letters indicating "Plantations Saint-James" on the hills that overlooked what was at that time the *rhum* capital of the world: Saint Pierre.

All trace of that sign, and the distillery itself, were lost during during the devastating eruption of Mount Pelée. For some three decades following the disaster, Saint James's *rhums* were produced across a range of other distilleries that Lambert acquired with the insurance payout. In 1929 a new, dedicated distillery was built, but it wasn't until 1974 that production

TOP Martinique's biggest distillery is just like the Saint James bottle: square-shaped and full of *rhum*.

ABOVE When you're filling as many casks as Saint James do, an on-site cooper is an essential component.

moved permanently to the newly renovated site in Sainte-Marie.

The early 1900s was the era in which product marketing was established, and Lambert was one of the first individuals in the spirits business to understand the value of it. Moving forward, Lambert's son, Pierre, and nephew, Ernest, took over the running of the distillery in 1947. At that time Saint James were bottling 2 million litres (4.2 million US gallons) of *rhum* a year, which sounds impressive, but it was soon to be their undoing. Over-production and a slump in demand meant that the value of *rhum* plummeted and Saint James filed for bankruptcy in 1958.

Some 10 years later, the brand was bought by its French importer Picon (famous for their "Bière" aperitif), who were in turn bought by Cointreau in 2003. Today the business is run by the La Matiniquaise group, who also own Depaz and Dillon brands.

The last 40 years of Saint James have been marked by the presence of Mr Jean Claude Benoît, who has managed the operation since the early 1980s. During his time he has successfully preserved the artisanal practices of the operation even through significant expansion. More than that, Benoît has been a key player in the crusade for quality Martinique *rhum*, and in the development of the Martinique AOC in the 1990s.

Today, the Saint James estate includes 120 hectares (300 acres) of cane-growing land and supports a network of 50-or-so smallholders who grow cane on their behalf. Inside the distillery there are six stainless-steel column stills, capable of processing one ton of cane per minute during the harvesting season. That's a lot of juice, and in order to meet the demand, there are four individual banks of roller mills, and a combined fermentation capacity of 1 million litres (2.1 million US gallons) spread across 24 vats. Fermentation takes 36 hours.

The range of *rhum* produced at the distillery is staggering, and it starts with five *rhum blanc* expressions. There are numerous aged *rhums* too, many with double-digit maturation periods assigned to them. In fact, there are few distilleries in the Caribbean that can match the range of marketed expressions that Saint James currency output.

In addition to the *rhum* distilled in the single-column stills, a pot still, resembling the one depicted on the label, is used to make small amounts of a bottle known as Coeur de Chauffe ("Heart Heating"). This still, which is illustrated on the label of the bottle, was once wood-fired, but is now powered by steam. Distilled from fresh cane juice, this *rhum* is difficult to get hold of from anywhere except the distillery, and is bottled at 60% ABV. It's the only pot-distilled *rhum agricole* made on Martinique, but because it's made in a pot and is distilled below the required 65% ABV threshold, it cannot be classified as AOC Martinique Rhum Agricole.

As if all this *rhum* wasn't a good enough reason to visit Saint James already, the distillery also operates two museums. One contains a rich trove of artefacts and literature relating to the brand; the other spectacularly brings the history of distillation to life. It's probably the best museum of distillation in the world. Next-door to the museum is a small workshop. When I visited, there was a cooper hard at work repairing barrels and converting old barrels into pieces of furniture and authentic Martinican drums. Imaging my surprise when he stopped work and demonstrated the drum to me, hammering away at the skin of the thing with the palms of his hands and tips of his fingers. I've never seen a drum made from a *rhum* barrel before, and even though he played only for a minute, that sound will remain with me for some time.

IMPERIAL BLANC (40% ABV)
UN-AGED MARTINIQUE RHUM AGRICOLE AOC

Wholesome nearly-ripe banana, burnt plantain. Balanced and relatively soft on the palate with heat holding the mid-palate and the finish sticking with yellow tropical fruits.

COEUR DE CHAUFFE (45% ABV)
UN-AGED POT-STILL CANE JUICE RHUM

Aroma is forest-like, with spearmint, eucalyptus and tree coming through. Hot and spicy but fruit hangs in there too.

FLEUR DE CANNE BLANC (50% ABV)
UN-AGED MARTINIQUE RHUM AGRICOLE AOC

Wet sidewalks, lime rind and banana ice cream. Really hot on the palate, with big funky tropical notes accompanied by hot white pepper, (bell) pepper and general alcohol.

BLANC (55% ABV)
UN-AGED MARTINIQUE RHUM AGRICOLE AOC

Big and fruity on the nose, but with a soft sweetness on the palate. Exceptionally restrained for a 55% rum.

VIEUX 3-YEAR-OLD (42% ABV)
AGED MARTINIQUE RHUM AGRICOLE AOC

A tropical breeze! Coconut, raw pineapple and some spicy barrel influence. Coffee and cold tea on repeat visits. On the palate it's hot and a little bitter. Relatively straightforward in taste: heavy on the wood, oily and full.

2000 MILLÉSEME 8-YEAR-OLD (43% ABV)
AGED MARTINIQUE RHUM AGRICOLE AOC

Polished wood and varnish. Preserved stone fruits and cherry candy. Big wood hit on the palate, cherry and almond, then pine oil.

12-YEAR-OLD (42% ABV)
EXTRA-AGED BLANC MARTINIQUE RHUM AGRICOLE AOC

Banana pancakes, frangipani and dates. Wood is kept in check by big *agricole* element. Peppered heat plays ringmaster to soft tropical fruits and spiced cask characteristics. A good balance.

15-YEAR-OLD (43% ABV)
EXTRA-AGED BLANC MARTINIQUE RHUM AGRICOLE AOC

Fruit is more suppressed at first, getting brittle toffee and soft sugar. Then banana skins creep in. It's almost humid, and alive. Thick and complex on the palate, where fruit is green and soft or dark and rotten. The cask is well-integrated and drifts between panela sugar and gentle nutmeg and mace.

J. BALLY 12-YEAR-OLD (45% ABV)
EXTRA-AGED BLANC MARTINIQUE RHUM AGRICOLE AOC

Dry, but elegant. Maybe a touch flat, but Hot, with purpose and poise. A well-integrated spirit. Marmalade, cherry blossom, vanilla, mandarin peel, bitter orange and lime. Some tobacco and wood on the finish, which slowly evolves into juicy blackcurrants.

PUERTO RICO

Puerto Rico, aka "la Isla del Encanto" ("The Isle of Enchantment") has, perhaps beyond all other Caribbean islands, enjoyed the greatest successes in its capitalization of the romance of rum. It has had some advantages in this arena, of course: Puerto Rico is an overseas department of the US, and therefore bound by laws and to some extent the culture of the motherland – for better or worse. This makes San Juan, the island's capital, and particularly Old San Juan, a top tourism hotspot for millions of Americans, who appreciate the safety net that federal law casts under them, but also yearn for something exotic and non-American. The casual holidaymaker can expect the uninhibited nightlife of Old San Juan, sweltering heat "where men sweat 24-hours a day" (to borrow a quote from Hunter S. Thompson's *Rum Diary*, set in San Juan) and bottomless bottles of rum, which, all in all, fits the bill quite nicely.

The first sugar plantations on Puerto Rico date back to the 16th century, and were known locally as *ingenios* or *trapiches*. In 1523, Genovese native Tomás de Castellón established the first sugar mill in San Germán, naming it San Juan de las Palmas. In the 1540s more mills were founded along the banks of navigable rivers near San Juan. As with most of the Caribbean's Spanish colonies, sugar was a contributor to the island's economy, though stifled by shortsighted trade restrictions. That's nothing that a couple of hundred years of history couldn't resolve, however. The agrarian reforms of 1776 and the Spanish crown's Real Cédula (Royal Decree of Graces) of 1815 stimulated the growth in the industry. By the middle of the 19th century, there were 789 sugar plantations on the island. Puerto Rico had become a fully fledged sugar isle.

Cane began a slow decline from then, struggling to compete with European sugar beet and struck from the land to make way for coffee. Distilling was very much active, however, with the island producing 145,000 litres (3,850 US gallons) in 1899. Distillation was mostly conducted at an artisanal level, especially in the Arecibo region, where the famous Roses, García y Co. was bottling their *Ron de la Casa de Roses* as early as 1868. Other haciendas like San Francisco and San Gabriel, produced molasses rum in small alembic pot stills.

In the early 20th century, as the rest of the Caribbean sugar industry faltered, Puerto Rico's newfound status as a territory of the US transformed it into the American candy store. Cane harvests temporarily increased and capital investment from the US paid for newer and bigger sugar factories – 40 mills processed 100,000 hectares (250,000 acres) of sugarcane in 1930. There were negative sides to being American too. No sooner had the Jones Act been signed, in 1917, making Puerto Rico an official US territory, Puerto Ricans were given the chance to vote on whether or not to introduce prohibition. Incredibly, they voted "yes", and the bill was passed immediately. Being a colonial island, it was much harder to enforce the ban of liquor sale and production than on the mainland, however, so the illicit production of alcohol no doubt occurred. But for many Puerto Ricans, prohibition was a chance to embrace the newfound sense of US patriotism.

One distillery that didn't do too badly out of the situation was The Puerto Rico Distilling Co., which was a merger of various smaller operations incorporated in 1911. At the time it was still a subsidiary of the giant Canadian liquor firm Joseph E. Seagram and Sons Ltd., and during prohibition, the distillery started making industrial alcohols, as well as over 250 different brands of "bay rum" – an extremely popular type of herbal lotion made from among other things, bay leaves.

Prohibition was lifted in 1933 and sugar production resumed steadily, reaching its zenith in 1952, when Puerto Rico was second only to Cuba in the Caribbean. Rum production positively exploded, increasing from 1.2 million litres (320,000 US gallons) in 1934 to 32 million litres (8.5 million US gallons) in 1935! The following year Bacardi opened their first distillery on the island, further spiraling the figures. In 1936 Puerto Rico had 17 distilleries in total and was biggest rum producer in the world. Also launching at that time was Ron Candado, a joint venture with Florida Cane Products, Inc., which spawned a new corporation, Ron Rico, whose flagship product was the Ronrico rum, a brand that enjoyed considerable success in the US.

Sugar declined steadily thereafter, succumbing to competition from Brazil and India, and at the turn of the millennium, operations ceased at the last mills

still functioning on the island: Roig in Yabucoa and Coloso, which had operated for nearly 100 years in the municipality of Aguada. Today, four operational distilleries remain on the island.

San Juan is the most highly developed city in the Caribbean: a melting pot of Spanish, Taino, African and American influences, more recently joined by an influx of Chinese and Lebanese immigrants. The modern, industrial part of San Juan with its fast-food chains and electronics stores could just as easily be a part of mainland America, but in the Old Town we find a thriving Latino culture, beautiful architecture, and plenty of tourists and locals enjoying the vibrant nightlife.

But rum here is by no means reserved only for the tourists. Puerto Ricans drink rum with an almost frenzied dedication, and it's a well-known fact that when the island is under threat from hurricanes, the first task is to head to the store and buy rum and mixers. Only once a stock of rum is assured should you head home and secure your property. And if you're Puerto Rican, you'll almost certainly be buying Destilería Serrallés's Don Q, which was launched in 1865. Puerto Ricans are loyal to the Serrallés family, and in spite of Bacardi's 50-hectare (126-acre) distillery, with its 200,000 annual visitors, Don Q still commands around 80% of the native rum market – there's little room here for foreign brands.

Special mention must go to the Fernández family, who, in the early 19th century established the island's oldest rum brand at their Santa Ana plantation in Bayamon. As far back as 1804, they were making a type of quasi-rum from fermented sugar and honey, which was allegedly aged in European oak barrels. In 1827, the Fernández family ordered 127 slaves to build an enormous stone tower/windmill on their plantation that would be used for crushing cane, which remains

in place today. Pedro Fernando Fernández took charge from 1880, and using a column still, launched a very popular rum that became known as "Ron del Barrilito" (translating as "rum from the little barrel"). The original distillery has since closed, but Fernando's grand-son (also called Fernando) continues to market the Ron del Barrilito brand. Perhaps the most interesting part of the Fernández story, is the so-called "freedom barrel". This single barrel of rum was laid down in 1942, and was put aside with orders that it should only be opened when Puerto Rico becomes a free and independent nation. If that ever happens, the cask will be taken to the town square in the centre of Bayamón and its contents will be offered free to all those who wish to drink from it.

BACARDI

There are a number of distilleries in this book that produce multiple rum brands, but only one that produces the same rum across multiple international locations. Bacardi currently operates three distilleries, the main one in Puerto Rico, plus one in Mexico and India. There are none in Cuba – a statement that might seem odd for a company that proudly promotes its Cuban heritage. The reasons for this are complex, and entire books have been dedicated to the subject. I'll attempt to sum it up in a couple of pages:

Bacardi is the story of how a Spanish immigrant to Cuba established the basic principles of a new style of rum, one that was lighter and more refined than those that came before it. It's also the story of how his descendants transformed Bacardi into the world's best known rum brand and the largest family-run spirits firm in the world, standing up against the tyranny of Spanish rule and the rule of Cuba's own home-grown dictators in the process. This is a story of courage and, occasionally, controversy, as an ever-expanding dynasty (500 members at last count) tries to balance conflicting interests of family, business, politics and patriotism.

Don Facundo Bacardí Massó was born in the port town of Sitges, just south of Barcelona, Spain. It was in the 1830s that a 15-year-old Facundo (along with his brothers Magín, Juan and José) emigrated to Santiago de Cuba on Cuba's eastern coast. Catalonians were recognized as hard workers (the Bacardí family were trained stonemasons) and the brothers set up a grocer's store called El Palo Gordo ("The Big Stick") in the busy town. It was a success, and some years later, in 1843, Facundo had saved 6,000 Cuban gold pesos (equivalent to ten thousand dollars) and broke away from the family business, opening his own store. Things did not go as planned, however – an earthquake in 1852, followed by a cholera epidemic brought Santiago to its knees. Facundo was now married to wife Amalia and had four children – Emilio, Facundo Junior, Juan and Maria – but the family was forced to return to Spain for a time.

When Bacardí returned to Santiago, new opportunities presented themselves. Sugar production had been on the rise in Cuba since the Haitian revolution, and by the

1830s the island was outpacing all the British colonies combined. Rum exports from Cuba had remained quite low though the early 19th century, but there was no shortage of molasses lying around. The only problem was, the Spaniard didn't know how to make rum.

Enter José Léon Boutellier: a French resident of Santiago and a tenant in the house of Amalia Bacardí's godmother. Boutellier ran a small distillery in Santiago, which also operated as a confectioner. The pair teamed up, forming Bacardí, Boutellier & Compania, selling their rums through a shop owned by one of Facundo's brothers. Over time, the business grew from a backroom operation, and in 1862, they bought their first distillery. It's this date that is commonly accepted as the founding of the Bacardi brand.

There are various factors that can be attributed to the success of the early Bacardí/Boutellier rum. The two entrepreneurs experimented extensively with yeast, isolating a strain that produced a fast-acting, low-ester wine. They also explored charcoal filtering as a means of both clarifying their liquid and polishing its flavour. Charcoal filtering is commonplace these days, but this was the first known example of a such a process in the rum world. Their distillery in Santiago also used one of the earliest column stills in the Western Hemisphere, and it's with this piece of kit that the duo happened across their winning formula: a blend of low-strength *aguardiente* and high-strength *redistillaro*. The Bacardi recipe is still based on the same blending principles – and so is virtually every other rum in Latin America today.

Bacardí and Boutellier also recognised the importance of branding their product. This was becoming a more common practice among blenders in the late 19th century, who bought in their product from distilleries and mixed it to a proprietary recipe or formula. It was highly unusual for a distillery to market and brand its own products, however, and Bacardi were one of the pioneers of this approach.

After Boutellier's retirement, Don Facundo passed the business on to his sons in 1877 and died some 10 years later. Emilio Bacardí took on the role of president, and it was under his leadership, and later that of his brother-in-law, Enrique Schueg, that Bacardi would become a Cuban household brand. Facundo Jr. became the company's first *Maestro de ron* (Master Blender) a

position that he held for over 30 years. He was the company's most valuable asset, and perhaps the greatest living distiller of his era.

Despite the growing popularity of their rum, the turn of the 20th century was also a turbulent period for the Bacardí family. The Cuban independence movement was in full swing and Bacardís were passionate adversaries of Spanish colonial rule. Emilio Bacardí collected donations for the rebel army that were active in the Cuban hinterland, and also served as one of its city-based contacts for secret communications. His son Emilito even became actively involved in combat by joining the rebels and fighting under the command of the popular rebel leader Antonio Maceo. The Spanish were not oblivious to the Bacardí's stance on independence. Aware of this, the family took the decision to exile many of the female Bacardís to Kingston, in Jamaica. On one fateful occasion, a militia marched up to the door of Emilio's house and forced a gun into his hands, ordering him to fight for the Spanish crown. Emilio threw the gun on the ground and refused, landing himself a spell in jail. That stretch was extended when he refused to publicly support the Spanish government. He spent three years in a Cuban jail, and was later jailed in Spain too.

After the signing of the Treaty of Paris in 1898, which ceded Cuba, Puerto Rico, Guam and the Philippines to the US, the political and economic situation in free Cuba stabilized significantly. As vocal advocates of the liberation, Bacardi were in a position to grow their business, which got big quickly thanks to new trading opportunities with the US.

Historically, Bacardi had dealt only in rum up until this time, but the rising status of the family meant that the Bacardi business and their political interests soon began to stretch far beyond a generation of rum distillers. Emilio was appointed Mayor of Santiago by the American

military governor of Santiago during the Spanish-American war and, among other things, negotiated the arrival of electricity in the town. The Bacardí family were also involved in various charitable endeavours around Santiago, including the handing out of cash every year on February 4 to commemorate the founding of the company. Bacardi diversified into brewing too, establishing the Hatuey brand (named after the fierce Taino chief who repelled Spanish attempts at colonizing Cuba) which, during prohibition and the Wall Street crash, helped to bankroll the wider Bacardi interests.

From the perspective of rum, the post-war era was a period of enormous international expansion for Bacardi, starting with a bottling plant in Spain in 1910, then one in New York in 1915 (which subsequently closed during prohibition). Next on the list was an upgraded distillery in Santiago, which opened in 1922 and was capable of processing 75,000 litres (20,000 US gallons) of molasses a day.

Emilio Bacardí died later that year, age 78. The next era of Bacardi expansion was overseen by Enrique Schueg, and then his son-in-law, José "Pepín" Bosch. A rising star in the rapidly growing family, Bosch was the son-in-law of Enrique Schueg, and had spent time serving as Cuba's finance minister. Bosch was an intimidating and controversial individual, but it's thanks to his relentless determination that the ship was successfully steered through the turbulent waters of the mid-20th century.

The family's first international distillery opened in 1931, in Mexico City. The site that was chosen was on *Calle de Cerdos* ("The Street of Pigs"). A rum distillery may have seemed out of place in a city positively swimming in agave-based spirits, but Bacardi's new home was directly opposite the Coca Cola factory – the most enduring of all of Bacardi's love affairs. It wasn't long before the locals began referring to Calle de Cerdos as "Avenida de Cuba Libre" ("The Avenue of Cuba Libre").

Just four years after the opening of the Mexican operation, Bosch and Schueg began touring sites in Old San Juan, Puerto Rico. An old factory was chosen as the site of the company's second international distillery, and it commenced production in 1936.

In 1956 a new distillery was built in the state of Puebla, around 100 km (60 miles) south-east of Mexico City. This region had been supplying sugarcane to the distillery in Mexico City since the 1930s, and relocating production to the same area made significant savings in transportation costs. The move ended up saving more than just money, however: it probably rescued the entire Mexican operation as, on July 28, 1957, an earthquake with a magnitude of 7.9 – the worst Mexico City had ever seen – levelled some of the old distillery buildings, taking thousands of barrels of nascent rum stocks with it. The distillery in Puebla continued fermentation and distillation operations while a new ageing and blending facility was constructed on the outskirts of the capital. But there were bigger disasters yet to come…

Like most Cubans, Bacardi were, at first, strong supporters of Castro's revolutionary movement. Fidel promised democracy and an end to the iron-fisted era of former dictator Fulgencio Batista – a chance to reclaim the sentiment of the original Cuban War of Independence, perhaps. Pepín Bosch personally donated money to Castro's cause, and as a leading Cuban businessman, even accompanied him to Washington D.C. on a media trip in 1959. The relationship deteriorated quickly following

Castro's victory, after his politics rapidly shifted left and the revolutionary authorities began seizing private property. Bacardí were a proud Cuban family, and one that was deeply embedded in the fabric of Cuban culture. The seizure of their businesses, along with the betrayal that came with it, cut deeper than Castro could possibly have known.

For a time, some members of the family remained in Cuba, involving themselves in underground anti-Castro organizations. Others convinced themselves that this was not the start of a communist regime and that everything would return to normal soon. Pepín Bosch was not so ignorant to the reality of the situation. Furious at the betrayal, he relocated the company headquarters to the Bahamas.

The loss of Cuba could have gnawed away at the Bacardís like an infection. Instead, it sparked an almost dangerous level of tenacity that drove the company forward. Bosch became consumed by a determination to see Fidel Castro removed from power, an obsession that allied him to the CIA and, some would say, the Mafia. Thomas Gjelten writes in his *Bacardí and the long fight for Cuba* (2008), "Bosch was willing to spend large sums on the anti-Castro cause, and on occasion [it] took him to the edge of illegal activity."

From a business perspective, exile from Cuba did wonders for Bacardi. It diverted attention away from brewing, forcing Bacardi to focus on expanding its rum business. It also helped that similarly exiled Cubans, now residing in the US, were hungry for a taste of home. The 1960s and 1970s saw the Bacardi empire grow by 12% a year, punctuated by new distilleries opening in Puerto Rico in 1958, then Brazil (1961), and the Bahamas (1965). Next came a distillery in Canada, followed by new facilities in Martinique, Panama and Spain. It remains today one of the most rapid phases of growth ever witnessed in a spirits company.

The latter part of the 20th century was a period of continued growth for Bacardi, and by 1980, Bacardi was the biggest spirits brand in the US, and the biggest rum brand in the world. Today, the distillery in Puebla, Mexico outputs 5 million cases of Bacardi rum a year. That, however, is not a lot, when compared to the quantities

OPPOSITE Although many processes at Casa Bacardí are automated, lab work must be done by hand. These tiny fermentation samples will be multiplied up to the distillery's 20 x 50,000-litre (13,000-US gallon) fermentation vessels.

CARTA BLANCA (40% ABV)
AGED WHITE RUM

Trademark mushroom fungal, rotting wood and dank forest. Just a touch of Roquefort cheese, pencil shavings and a slight dairy quality. Good weight on the palate – more earthy fungal and soft sweetness brings a funky nuttiness. Finish sweetens up into sesame and popcorn.

CARTA OCHO (40% ABV)
AGED RUM

Sandalwood, dried mango, vanilla butter, and chocolate orange. Good depth and body to the mouthfeel; it really clings to the palate but retains that lightness. Sweet, peach nectar, mace and pimento. Softly smooth, little in the way of bitterness.

SPECIAL RESERVE (43% ABV)
EXTRA-AGED RUM

Tobacco syrup, dried cherries, marzipan, oloroso and Nutella. Juicy cherry bubblegum too. Spicy tobacco on the palate, with clean passion fruit juice. Light and gently sweet through the finish.

manufactured at the company's San Juan distillery, which produces 12 million 9-litre (2.4-US gallon) cases of rum a year. Bacardi have also retained a third distillery, in India, which produces just under 1 million cases of rum for the local market.

True to the Spanish style that they helped establish, Bacardi use only column stills to make their rums. There are five of them in each of the three distilleries, tasked with making two different types of spirit – *redistilaro*, a 95% ABV near-neutral spirit that utilizes all five columns; and a juicier *aguardiente* that is made using only one of the columns and comes off at around 80% ABV. Both spirits are matured and charcoal-filtered separately before being blended together according to the specific flavour profile of each expression. Spirits enter the barrel anywhere from 55–80% ABV based on the specific extractives the master blender is after. The *aguardiente* also undergoes charcoal-filtration prior to maturation. This intervention aims to remove some of the brighter distillery characteristics that can evolve into overly pungent fruity notes during maturation. For the *redistilaro*, fermentation is a 24-hour process at 32°C (90°F), and slightly longer for the *mosto* that is intended for making *aguardiente*.

When volumes are this high, large chunks of profit are at stake, so everything must be critiqued to the most exacting standards. Molasses arrives from Mexico, Brazil, Costa Rica and Fiji, and samples are constantly being analyzed; for the alcohol yield they will provide but also for the potential organoleptic qualities it will provide in the *aguardiente*. The decades-old Bacardi yeast strain is handled like a precious artefact – which I suppose it is. Stocks of this yeast are locked in a temperature-controlled vault, and regularly destroyed and replenished to avoid mutation. In the lab, a team of white-coated men and women use medical-grade photo-analytical equipment to measure yeast cell counts – a process that was once done using a microscope and a hand-clicker.

After that earthquake in Mexico, Bacardi adjusted their barrel-racking strategy so as to stack casks on their ends (rather than on their sides) to better combat the threat of future earthquakes. Bacardi also claim that this method slightly lowers the effects of oxidation in their ageing process.

The rums in Bacardi's warehouses are typically matured for 1–14 years and the barrels (which are all ex-bourbon) may be refilled up to four times in a lifespan.

LEFT The bat symbol is said to have derived from the family of bats that lived in the rafters of the original distillery.

The emptying and filling room is done in an automated fashion that is reminiscent of a milking parlour, where one set of hoses sucks the liquid out and another immediately fills the empty cask back up.

Mexico bottles its own product, but in Puerto Rico the rum is shipped to the relevant market for bottling: Malaga, in Spain; Jacksonville in Florida; or Brazil. Each tanker holds 50 storage containers of rum – approximately 2.5 million bottles of rum per shipment.

The most famous of the Bacardi expressions is Carta Blanca – which is a blend of rums at least one-year-old that has been charcoal-filtered to remove colour. Besides Carta Oro (gold) and Black, other, older expressions, are beginning to materialize, such as Bacardi Carta Ocho 8 Años and the fantastic Casa Bacardi Special Reserve (10–16-years-old), which you can buy straight from the barrel if you visit the San Juan distillery.

CLUB CARIBE

Club Caribe is one of the newest distilleries in the Caribbean. It opened in 2012 at a cost of $40 million (£32 million) on the site of a former pharmaceutical plant. If that sounds a bit bleak to you, it's worth mentioning that the distillery is located in the mountain town of Cidra, which enjoys some of the most *buena* of vistas on the island.

Club Caribe LLC is in fact an arm of Florida Caribbean Distillers, who own a further two distilleries in Florida; one at Lake Alfred, and the other at Auburndale. The distilleries work in tandem, wherein molasses from the southern states of the US, is fermented and distilled in Florida, then transported at 80% ABV to the Club Caribe distillery in Cidra, where it is distilled for a final time. The effort of shifting rum around the place is rewarded by tax breaks, as the finished spirit is considered a product of Puerto Rico, not Florida. Under the Federal Rum Excise Tax Refunds program, the government of Puerto Rico receives a refund of

$13.25 (£10.50) per gallon from the $13.50 (£10.90) excise that is imposed per gallon of rum sold in the US.

The fermentation (which takes place in Florida) is done with molasses at 23° Brix using distiller's yeast. A quick fermentation produces a wine of 8–10% ABV. This is then processed through the distillery's five-column set up, each with 25–72 plates, resulting in a rum of 95% ABV. It's not all tall columns and plates here, however – Club Caribe also houses one of the largest pot stills in the Caribbean, reminiscent of the type of alembic still used in Cognac production. In the future, this pot still will produce heavy-bodied marques of rum from molasses fermented on-site.

It's early days for this new distillery, but at a projected 45.5 million litres (12 million US gallons) a year, you can expect to be tasting rum from here fairly soon – most likely without a Club Caribe label on the bottle. Being a wholesale powerhouse is one thing, but more important to me is the inclusion of a pot still, proving that the best means of diversification in a modern rum distillery is achieved by looking back, at the origins of rum in the Caribbean.

CRUZ

Cruz is a newcomer to the Puerto Rico scene, having been built in 2009. It's not the easiest place to get to. Dropped in the centre of the cool mountains in the middle of the island, it's right near the town of Juyuya – named after the Taíno tribal leader, Hayuya, it's a sleepy place, renowned for its skilled wood carvers. The Cruz

SILVER (40% ABV)
UN-AGED RUM

Very light on aroma, with a touch of coconut sugar, lime oil, brioche and whipped cream. Taste is also light, with a slight buttery note floating on top of some gentle, neutral spice.

distillery is small – one of the smallest in the Caribbean –
and reminiscent of the countless new craft distilleries that
have popped up across the US and Europe in recent times.

Cruz produce the PitoRico rum, which sounds
innocuous enough, but when I spoke to some locals
about PitoRico it was met with some nervousness. It
turns out that PitoRico is a play on the word *pitorro*,
which is the Puerto Rican term for moonshine. Since
prohibition times, clandestine *pitorro* or *cañita* production
has been going on in Puerto Rico's secluded mountain
towns, and this new brand hopes to leverage some sales
from the tradition, but in a wholly legal fashion.

The distillery bottles two white rums: PitoRico 106,
which is designed to be a true representation of the
(stronger) *pitorro* style rums; and PitoRico Elite, a softer
formula that is more reminiscent of a typical un-aged
white rum from the Spanish-speaking islands.

SERRALLÉS

The Serrallés distillery is in the south of Puerto Rico,
in a city called Ponce. The "Pearl of the South" as it is
known, is second in size only to San Juan, and one of the
most beautiful towns in Puerto Rico. It's named after
Juan Ponce de Leon, a Spanish Conquistador hell-bent
on discovering the mythical "fountain of youth" back in
the 16th century. The inevitable irony of such a pursuit
is that you die trying, but years later, in 1682, Ponce's
great-grandson founded the city of Ponce, so you could
say that Juan has in some ways been immortalized.

The geography of the Ponce region is perfect for
growing cane, as the south facing slopes of Puerto Rico's
central mountains slip down towards the ocean; rain,
sunlight, drainage and soil are all favourable to farmers in
this region. This is why Ponce was once the centre of the
Puerto Rican sugar industry. Sebastian Serrallés knew

this when he travelled to the island from Catalonia, Spain
in the 1810s. He bought a small plot of land known as
the Hacienda Teresa to grow cane on. Some time later,
he returned to Spain, and left the business in the hands of
his son, Juan Serrallés, who founded Hacienda Mercedita
in 1861 and in 1865 imported a stout five-tray column
still from France that was used to convert molasses into
delicious rum.

Serrallés bottled under various brand names for
the local market until prohibition closed the plant in
1919. Following prohibition, a burgeoning market and
established reputation of the family meant that Serrallés
had a solid platform from which to launch their Don
Q rum brand in 1934, named for Don Quixote, the
chivalrous protagonist from the classic Spanish novel
by the same name. The following year they opened
Distileria Serrallés, Inc.

Over time, Don Q became the biggest rum brand on
the island. Today it's not exaggeration to say that *ron* in
Puerto Rico means Don Q. Around three-quarters of
all the rum consumed in Puerto Rico has a picture of
Don Quixote on the label – an impressive feat when one
considers that Puerto Rico has served as the surrogate
home of Bacardí since 1936.

As the Serrallés empire grew, it earned the family
the freedom to acquire the assets of other (failing)
producers, such as Puerto Rico Distillers, Inc. That
particular acquisition also landed them with Seagram's
manufacturing facilities in the towns of Camuy and
Arecibo, as well as local rum brands like Palo Viejo, Ron
Llave and Granado. Oh, and the licence to manufacture
Captain Morgan. This broad range of products meant
that Serrallés had something to offer for every budget,
cementing the company's popularity in society.

The distillery is now looked after by the sixth
generation of the Serrallés family, in the shape of Roberto
Serrallés. Roberto has a PhD in environmental sciences,
which in my mind is a sensible academic route to go down
if you're a 21st-century heir to a distilling dynasty. The
list of cutting-edge environmental features at Serrallés is
extensive. It includes such things as aerobic and anaerobic
digesters that generate biogas for producing steam; steam-
powered generators that produce electricity for the plant
and warehousing with solar-panelled roofing. This might
be the most environmentally sustainable distillery in the
region, but by Roberto's own admission, "you can't make
a fully sustainable distillery". A futile pursuit then, but
he's not giving up. The next step in the Serrallés plan

CRISTAL (40% ABV)
AGED WHITE RUM

Crisp and steely, with lemon quickly drifting into a slight iodine note. Taste is bright and vivid with citrus peels and a light buttery note that draws a slight linger.

AÑEJO (40% ABV)
AGED RUM

Flinty and mineral rich, chocolate-coated banana. Dry and tactile on the palate, silky toffee sauce, burnt milk, vanilla and Bellini. Finish is soft yet tactile as the rum gently slips away. A benchmark añejo.

GRAN AÑEJO (40%)
EXTRA-AGED RUM

There's a good hit of that trademark column-still mushroom note here, which over time turns to blue cheese. Restrained on the wood side of things, with just a touch of whipped cream to couple with dried apricot. Palate is like a caramel-dipped mushroom, with bitter dark chocolate, finishing in gentle vegetal funk.

2005 SIGNATURE SINGLE BARREL (40% ABV)
EXTRA-AGED RUM

Crème caramel, butterscotch sauce. Juicy and full, and exceptionally well-rounded. All the tastes of an old maturation cellar. The linger is solid and surprisingly complex given how "safe" the alcohol content is.

is to grow their own sugarcane. Until 20 years ago, the molasses used to make Don Q came from the Central Mercedita sugar mill and Snow White Sugar American Sugar Company next to the distillery. Both mills have since closed, so molasses is now mainly sourced from Guatemala and Brazil. This arrangement works fine for rum making, but the variable mineral and ash contents of the molasses means that processing waste waters can be tricky – recycling the effluent of what is already another industry's effluent is no mean feat! This is set to change (again) as the Serrallés family are plotting to rejuvenate the Puerto Rican sugar industry by cultivating up to 6,050 hectares (15,000 acres) of cane-growing land and opening a refinery to process it. No sugar will be made at this refinery, only cane syrup, which will soon make up 70% of the distillery's needs, with the rest coming from imported molasses. Besides the control over the base material that this approach offers, it also grants Serrallés greater control over what happens to the leftovers of that material once it has been turned into rum.

Looking at the lineup of Don Q rums, there is something for all tastes. Don Q Cristal is aged for 12 months prior to filtering for clarity. Don Q Añejo is a blend of 3–8-year-old rums, and the excellent Gran Añejo is a mix of 6–12-year-old rums. From the top shelf, there's Gran Reserva de la Familia – a blend of rums at least 20-years-old. More recently, the distillery has released a range of 10-year old single-cask rums.

ST. LUCIA

St. Lucia was first settled in the 1550s by a 330-strong force of French men led by the infamous privateer, François Le Clerc. Better-known by his nickname "Jambe de Bois" in French, "Pie de Palo" in Spanish, and as "Peg Leg" to the English, Le Clerc was the first known pirate of the modern age to sport a wooden leg – an inevitable consequence of his eagerness to be the first man to board an enemy ship – and thanks to a decade or so of brutal raids across Cuba, Panama, Hispaniola and Puerto Rico, he did a damn fine job of perpetuating the timber-limbed pirate cliché that we all know and love today. Trailblazer as he might have been, Le Clerc got into the pirating game too soon to have ever laid eyes on a bottle of rum.

The first attempt at colonization of St. Lucia occurred in 1605 when an unfortunate band of English settlers, who were heading to Guyana on the good ship *Olive Branch*, landed on St. Lucia after having been blown off course. Sixty-seven colonists waded ashore, where they purchased land and huts from the extremely hospitable Caribs. After a month, the party had been reduced to only 19 – the rumour being that that the others were boiled alive – and the survivors promptly fled the island in a dugout canoe.

On a clear day, St. Lucia is visible from the former British colony St. Vincent in the south, and Martinique in the north, an overseas region of France. It's not surprising then, that St. Lucia was a hotly contested chunk of land. After the French took ownership in 1674, the next century or so saw the island switch ownership between the British and French over a dozen times. Somehow, throughout all this political upheaval, sugar plantations were established, and in 1770 the island made almost 1 million litres (265,000 US gallons) of rum. It was 1803 when the British finally took permanent possession (formally recognized in 1814), while the French had their hands full failing to manage a slave rebellion in Sainte-Domingue. More than 200 years later, the noticeably French variety of *patois* spoken here, along with a great number of place names, are a lasting legacy of French occupation. Indeed, St. Lucia's one rum distillery pays homage to the island's French roots by distilling a little *rhum agricole* each season.

RIGHT Why exactly there is fake parrot in the still room of the St. Lucia Distillery I do not know. But there is one.

That small plot of sugarcane accounts for most of the sugar grown on the island today, and even the tradition of St. Lucian farmers travelling to Martinique to cut cane came to an end in the 1970s. At the dawn of the 20th century, there were three remaining distilleries in St. Lucia: Marquis Estate, producing Marquis rum; Troumassée Estate, producing Troumassée rum; and Cul-de-sac Estate, which was making a cane juice rum. The Marquis Estate stopped making rum in the 1920s and Troumassée burnt to the ground in 1931, which left only two rum producers on the island: Cul-de-sac and the sugar refinery at Vieux Fort, which opened in 1920. The following year, the Barnard family established their sugar refinery at Dennery, which along with Cul-de-sac, would be the only two to survive the 1960s, which saw the island shift its attentions to bananas. Long yellow fruit now makes up almost one-quarter of St. Lucia's economy.

The St. Lucian appetite for cane spirits has remained undiminished, however. St. Lucia is second only to Grenada in the battle for "who in the Americas can drink the most". The local favourites are Crystal and Bounty, which are both column-still rums; the former is filtered to remove colour and the latter has some caramel added to add colour… go figure. The more premium offerings tend to follow the Barbadian style, whereby column-still rums are spruced up with a touch of pot-still potency. Over 90% of the rum drunk in St. Lucia is St. Lucian in origin, and the most popular,

THE SPIRIT OF ST. LUCIA

local tipple is aged rum mixed with coconut water. Local spiced rums are also very popular, to the point where most family homes have a bottle stashed away in the medicine cupboard (or bedside table). Outside of the home, it can be picked up from one of the roadside sellers or "hole in the wall" bars, which mix a proprietary formula of honey, cane juice, sugar and spices to combat various ailments. These concoctions are constructed with a base of "Denros Strong Rum" (which is sold at 80% ABV) and can contain any or all of the usual spices, and sometimes more exotic ingredients like (whole) snakes and centipedes. For the more entrepreneurial types, it's possible to visit the St. Lucia Distillery and hand over $1,100 (£890) for an entire blue-coloured 200-litre (52-US gallon) barrel of the stuff – quite a bargain at only $6 (£4.80) per litre!

ST. LUCIA DISTILLERS

The rum distilleries of the British Windward islands (Dominica, St. Vincent, Grenada and St. Lucia) mostly only service their domestic markets. St. Lucia is a big exception to that rule, however, as in the past 20 years, St. Lucia Distillers have performed an incredible feat of premiumization. It started by taking back their home turf, which in the 1990s was dominated by imported Mount Gay and Cockspur, both of which were seen as being of a higher quality than the native Bounty brand. Next they focused on the premium export market, with popular releases of Chairman's Reserve and super premium Admiral Rodney, the latter being an "ego project" to show just how good St. Lucian rum could be. Numerous further releases have occurred since then, elevating the status of the local hooch, while also drip-feeding quality new releases into the hands of top international bartenders. It's certainly not been easy. There have been scandals, sieges, fires and flames to contend with, but St. Lucia Distillers now represents the best example of what Caribbean rum can be, when the market is correctly identified and the rum sufficiently nurtured.

The Barnard family first founded their Dennery distillery on the east coast of the island in 1932. Forty years later, having made a name for themselves producing strong white rum, the Barnards entered into a joint venture with Geest (a Dutch banana company)

THIS PAGE The tiny high-wine retort at St. Lucia Distillers, which is connected both to a low wine retort and the John Dore pot still (top); barrels provide much of the character of Chairman's Reserve (bottom left); where would we be without cane cutters like Ako (bottom right)?

LEFT 200-litre (53-US gallon) casks of Denros Strong Rum are sold by the barrel at 80% ABV.

and moved their operations to the current location in the Roseau Valley.

There's virtually no cane on St. Lucia so to speak (although see below) so all the molasses used here is sourced from Guyana or the Dominican Republic, and arrives by a boat that pumps the syrup off-shore, up a 2-km (1.25-mile) pipeline that runs parallel to the Roseau River. The distillery has enough storage space to hold up to 2,500 tons (2,750 US tons) of molasses, which when needed is routed to the fermenters via a machine that automatically adds water to the syrup, adjusting the mixture to 20° Brix. Two types of yeast are used, and for the sake of distinguishing them from each other we'll call them "Yeast A" and "Yeast B". Yeast A is used only for the distillery's "High Strength" white rum, and is a workhorse designed to leverage every drop of alcoholic potential from the molasses. "Yeast B" has a bit more about it; it's slightly slower-working, and produces a fruitier wine.

The fermentation process is semi-continuous, meaning that a yeast propagation system is used, which quickly builds up the cell-count in 300- and 1,000-gallon (360- and 1,200-US gallon) tanks, and then sends the yeast-rich fluid to one of two 5,000 gallon (6,000-US gallon) steel "mother tanks", which in turn distribute the liquid into concrete fermenters along with fresh molasses. The entire fermentation takes approximately 36 hours, at a constant temperature of 32°C (90°F).

Blending is the name of the game here, and in reflection of this, the St. Lucia Distillery has a neat collection of stills. There are both pot stills and columns stills, small and large, each producing there own weight, strength and intensity of rum. The first is a two-column still, which can be used to produce five different types of rum based on how the plates are set in the second column. Then there are three copper pot stills, the oldest of which is a John Dore still that was installed in the mid-1990s. It's a mere 100 gallons (120 US gallons) in size and has two connecting retorts, resulting in a middle cut of just 30 litres (8 US gallons) of 88% ABV high-ester rum. The second of the John Dore stills (installed in early 2003) performs the same task, but it's six-times the size. The third and final still is a copper pot, manufactured by the Vendome company in the US in the late 1990s. This still has a short rectifying column on top, and the added ability to recycle condensed rum back around for additional reflux. It produces a slightly lighter rum than the John Dore instruments, which forms a key component of the Chariman's Reserve blends.

Right now, the distillery is pumping out some rather delicious bottlings. Chairman's Reserve, which is no slouch itself, has been augmented by a "Forgotten Casks" release, aged for a total of 9 years; these casks were genuinely forgotten about so I'm told, so, presumably, in limited supply, since it's implausible for St. Lucia Distillers to continue losing casks! One set of casks that certainly won't be forgotten about is the collection of plastic-wrapped barrels that I spotted on my tour. They are part of an ongoing experiment to reduce the angel's share, and I was fortunate enough to taste the results of some of these experiments, which proved very interesting indeed. Another ongoing experiment is the production of sugarcane juice rum, made in the *agricole* style, the results of which make up around 10% of the 2014 and 2015 releases of the 1931 bottling.

All that's left to mention is the "fire and flames" I hinted at earlier. In the early hours of May 2 2007, armed men wearing masks stormed the distillery and immobilized the security staff. They then moved to the offices and tore open filing cabinets, spreading their contents across the floor, dousing the papers in – you guessed it – rum, and setting it alight. The fire grew, and ultimately wiped out the entire administrative section of the distillery, and most of the blending house. Fortunately, most of the production areas were saved from the blaze. Following an investigation, the fire was deemed to be an act of sabotage, purposely started to destroy evidence of fraudulent goings-on at the distillery.

CHAIRMAN'S RESERVE (40% ABV)
AGED BLENDED RUM

Apricot, toffee, vanilla fudge and milky coffee. Delicate notes of almond and dried mango. Silky and slick with caramel on the palate. Dryness creeps into the finish. Nicely balanced.

CHAIRMAN'S RESERVE FORGOTTEN CASKS
AGED BLENDED RUM

Darker fruits, with plum jam, Christmas cake, tobacco and dried cherries. The taste is sweet and juicy at first; the spice locks in the flavour, which is bitter chocolate, passion fruit jam and peach nectar. Delicious.

ADMIRAL RODNEY (40% ABV) EXTRA-AGED RUM

Dried fruits, cacao nibs and old oak. Light and dark do battle, with intense vanilla and creamy fruits. Kept delicate and floral by the gentle weight of the spirit. Finish is bitter bark, pipe weed and barrel bung.

1931 – 2011 RELEASE (43% ABV)
EXTRA-AGED BLENDED RUM

Grape juice, tobacco, incense and rose, almond croissant. Taste is very concentrated. Vanilla, grape juice and more almond.

1931 – 2012 RELEASE (43% ABV)
EXTRA-AGED BLENDED RUM

Much more delicate: soft caramel, coffee liqueur, brown butter. Coffee cake, date syrup, walnut bread and clotted cream.

1931 – 2013 RELEASE (43% ABV)
EXTRA-AGED BLENDED RUM

Treacle tart, burnt vanilla, red stone fruit, brown sugar and tobacco. Sweetly soft, unctuous and creamy. Nuance is lost slightly, but it's enormously indulgent. A guilty pleasure.

1931 – 2014 RELEASE (43% ABV)
EXTRA-AGED BLENDED RUM

Brittle chocolate, blackberry crumble. Dessert trolley. A river of chocolate with tobacco floating down it. Lengthy and weighty, but not cloying. Finish flits between sweet and dry.

1931 – 2015 RELEASE (46% ABV)
EXTRA-AGED BLENDED RUM

Pungent and bright – pot pourri and honeysuckle. Then there's honey, jasmine and apricot. The extra 3% ABV is noticeable in a good way, cutting through sweetness and elevating florals. Tobacco turns a shade of pink through the long linger.

The distillery was forced to adopt rudimentary blending techniques, and even borrowed lab equipment from one of the local schools. It was two years before production was fully back on track, but in the words of Marketing Director, Michael Speakman, "the incident set the company back by five." I have a feeling that this setback may turn out to be the making of this little distillery.

Quite recently, the company was purchased by the Bernard Hayot Group, who are the same firm that own J.M (see pages 135–36) and Clément (see pages 140–43) on Martinique, and if those two distilleries are anything to go by, we can expect to see marvellous things from St. Lucia. What doesn't kill you makes you stronger, and St. Lucia Distillers are looking mighty fine to me.

RIGHT Blending column and pot-still rums is a sure bet when it comes to producing characterful spirit. Both of these products are made in that fashion at St. Lucia Distillers, though Elements 8 is a privately owned brand.

ST. VINCENT & THE GRENADINES

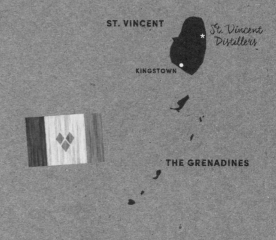

The conquest of St. Vincent eluded the British for far longer than they anticipated. Their first attempt to capture it from the French took place in 1627, but it wouldn't be for another 170 years until the island enjoyed some degree of security. This was partly due to wars with the French and Spanish, but more so with the fierce indigenous population of "Yellow Caribs", who, according to legend, provided refuge for African slaves fleeing from Barbados, Grenada, St. Lucia and even survivors of shipwrecks, from as far back as the 1630s. While most of the region brazenly profiteered from slavery, St. Vincent quietly became a safe-haven for fleeing African men and women.

The protracted siege didn't end until 1797, when General Abercromby secured possession of the island for the British and successfully exiled most of the "Black Caribs" – which were most likely former slaves of at least some African descent – to the nearby island of Balliceaux, and then eventually on to Roatán, off the coast of Honduras. Little love was lost between the British and remaining Carib population, however. In 1806, Fort Charlotte was constructed on the outskirts of Kingstown; peculiar in that the cannons point inland rather than out towards the ocean. Even today, the native Garinagu as they are now known, consider St. Vincent their spiritual home, taking regular pilgrimages there from all over Latin America. Some towns in the north of the island, like Sandy Bay, have a majority population of Garginagu. In short, St. Vincent is one of the best links historians have to the ancient history of the Caribbean region.

This slow colonization of St. Vincent meant that sugar came late to the island. This was quickly remedied however, and for the greater part of the early 19th century, St. Vincent was the leading sugar producer in the Windward Islands. Over 70% of the slave population worked on sugar plantations, and the island also had one of the highest ratios of sugar to slaves – a reliable gauge of draconian working conditions. The landscape is still scattered with the stone shells of former windmills, especially on the Windward (eastern) coast, each of them a shrine to a lost sugar mill and its associated distillery. About halfway up the west coast of the island is the Black Point Tunnel. This 110-metre (360-ft) long tunnel was drilled to enable the easier transport of sugar from the mills of Grand Sable Estate to the wharf at Byreau. It was constructed in 1815 using slave labour, and was a marvel of engineering for its time – these days it's a popular recreational spot for families.

No sugar is grown commercially on any part of St. Vincent and the Grenadines today. The industry died out in the early 20th century, replaced by bananas, arrowroot (for which it is the leading global producer), and on to tourism. The houses and shops on this island seem brighter than most: salmon pink, lime green and electric pink. A good deal of the tourism revenue also comes from the cluster of 30-or-so islands south of St. Vincent, known as the Grenadines. Islands like Mustique and Bequia have captured quite a celebrity following in recent years, and the hope is that the main island of the group will benefit by association. The recent completion of the island's second airport gives us some clues as to just how serious they are about this.

LEFT Although not well known, the cellars at St. Vincent Distillers are turning out some delicious rums these days.

ST. VINCENT DISTILLERS

St. Vincent Distillers is a relatively new distillery, having been built on the site of a former sugar mill that closed in 1985. That mill, known as the Mount Bentnick Estate, was first built in 1925, but the slow demise of the sugar industry on the island put an end to it. The mill was salvaged by the St. Vincent government in 1963 and renamed St. Vincent Distillers, then sold to the current private owners in 1996.

Since the island has no sugar refinery and no commercially grown sugarcane today, St. Vincent Distillers ship their molasses in from Guyana, which arrives into port at the capital, Kingstown, before being piped onto a truck and transported an hour north, along the winding coastal road, to Georgetown. The distillery has its own water supply from the Georgetown River, which is used for diluting the molasses and for bottling. Distillation is in a double column still, which produces a 95% ABV spirit. Some of the old equipment is still lying around the distillery – the boiler room, for example, is like a "ghosts of boilers past" exhibition, featuring

ABOVE LEFT Best not to even flick a light switch when there's an open bottle of this stuff around.

ABOVE RIGHT Smart, clean, professional. If St. Vincent Distiller's can follow the lead of St. Lucia, we'll be hearing more about them in the years to come.

a diesel boiler from the 1960s, as well as the original wood-burning engine from 1925.

St. Vincent is perhaps not the first, or even the 21st, place that springs to mind when one thinks of award-winning rum, but perhaps it should be. The "Captain Bligh XO" brand, won both World's Best Golden Rum and World's Best Rum at the World Drink Awards in 2014. The rum is named after Captain William Bligh, who so famously fell fowl to mutiny aboard the *HMS Bounty*, and who, some years later successfully transported breadfruit trees from Tahiti to Jamaica via St. Vincent.

More recently, in 2016, their "Sunset Very Strong Rum" won the World's Best Overproof Rum award. If there was an award for "World's Most Overproof Rum" it might win that one too – it's bottled at the incredible strength of 84.5% ABV. To the best of my knowledge, this is the strongest commercially produced rum you can buy, and right on the cusp of the 85% ABV limit that is agreed upon by most of the countries of the world as the legal limit. Of course you'll never (legally) get a bottle of the stuff out of St. Vincent anyway, as airlines will not let you travel with it.

You might wonder how one is supposed to drink a spirit bottled at such a brutal strength. This rum is borderline masochistic – it's impractical, silly and really rather dangerous. Well, it turns out the locals drink this stuff neat. No ice. Just down the hatch with a prayer.

SPARROW'S 5-YEAR-OLD (40% ABV)
AGED RUM

Some alcohol on the nose, butterscotch, cinnamon doughnut. Coffee and cigarette too. Light on the palate, like diluted banana custard. Vanilla cream there as well. Finish is gently peppered and sweet in the finish. Pleasant.

CAPTAIN BLIGH XO (40% ABV) (FORMERLY SUNSET) AGED RUM

Sweet dessert qualities, tiramisu, butterscotch and nutmeg. Palate is light, gently sweet and slightly greasy. Lightness makes it highly quaffable and the balance of sweet elements makes it desirable.

VERY STRONG RUM (84.5%)
OVERPROOF RUM

Very light and lively on the nose, but with suspiciously low amounts of alcohol. Quite neutral in flavour, with a hint of vegetation and ripe plum. Big on the palate and drys the tongue on contact – nay strips it. Surprisingly fruity, however, with big juicy stone fruits and a linger of baked courgette (zucchini).

TRINIDAD & TOBAGO

TOBAGO

PORT OF SPAIN ✻ *Angostura*

TRINIDAD

On the journey from the airport to the centre of the capital, Port of Spain, visitors are left with little doubt as to the significant role that rum plays in modern Trini culture. Advertising boards and bunting for local rum brands, like White Oak, Royal Oak and Forres Park don the fronts of village bars, and off-licences. And as the highway slowly penetrates Trinidad's capital, numerous Coca-Cola billboards flash by as well as the Coca-Cola bottling plant. A short while later you pass the House of Angostura, a site dedicated to the production and celebration of Trinidad's one and only rum maker.

Trinidad was the first Caribbean island that Columbus arrived at on his third voyage, on July 31 1498. He sailed through the Serpent's Mouth (the narrow stretch of water that separates Venezuela from Trinidad) and ordered drums to be sounded to attract the attention of the native Caribs of the island. Things didn't go as planned, and Columbus's fleet of six ships were intimidated by the locals and promptly fled. Columbus named the island "Trinidad" after – what else from a Catholic explorer – the holy trinity. Further exploration was hampered by the light trade winds and the equatorial current that naturally carried ships northward. The island's official conquest didn't occur until 1530, when Antonio Sedeño was made the first governor of Trinidad.

Over the next two centuries, Trinidad remained under Spanish rule but became a melting pot for seamen of Dutch, French and British origin, and was popular with smugglers dealing in tobacco, sugarcane and European goods. Growth was, for the most part, slower than other Caribbean islands, on account of the aforementioned light winds, which made trade routes laborious and trading vessels easy targets for pirates and corsairs. In 1797 British forces successfully captured the island from the Spanish, precipitating a steady influx of settlers from Great Britain and slaves from Africa. Sugarcane became the dominant economic activity on the island in the early 19th century, and after the abolition of slavery, the British attracted new labourers from India and the Far East to work the fields. This rich ethnic diversity brought about a culture of impassioned and fiercely patriotic people.

And man do they know how to party. It happens here on a nightly basis, but Trinidad is never better expressed than at carnival time where Port of Spain's urban landscape is transformed into a living, breathing, sea of colour and celebration. The noise of the steel pan rhythm and the calling of the crowd is the perfect countermeasure to the soothing sensation of a headful

LEFT It doesn't matter where you go in the British Caribbean, you simply cannot escape from rum and cricket.

of rum. A night of "liming" ("hanging out", in local speak) in Port of Spain is not always without peril however. The rum bars are fun, sexually-charged spaces and the streets are never short of some *roti* (stuffed Indian flat breads) or fried chicken from "the world's busiest KFC". But the rum and cokes arrive in plastic cups and some of the bars are, quite literally, secured behind metal bars. The locals hardly seem to notice, but these are unwelcome reminders of the possibility of violent crime and muggings that has come about through the rise of gang culture in downtown Port of Spain.

Just as treacherous as downtown Port of Spain, is the Forres Park brand of rum. After working my way through half a bottle with a pair of friendly locals, they told me that it's known colloquially as "f★★k or fight" rum. It was at that point – with slightly blurred vision – I studied the label, only to discover it is bottled at a gut-wrenching 75% ABV. Approach with caution.

ANGOSTURA

The Angostura distillery on the outskirts of Port of Spain is big… big enough to need its own roads and a small fleet of buggies to traverse the 8-hectare (20-acre) estate. In fact, this is the largest rum distillery by volume of any of the Caribbean islands, excluding Bacardí in San Juan. Of course the Angostura rum brand alone is not so big to warrant such a mighty refinery, and turns out Angostura rums account for only 3% of total production. Most of the branded product made here is local stuff, like White Oak, Royal Oak and Forres Park. Most of it never leaves Trinidad. The distillery also produces significant quantities of bulk wholesale rum for independent bottlers and blenders, both big and small. On top of that, there is the rum that's used as a base for producing what is surely this distillery's best-known product: Angostura Bitters. The world's best known bitters brand shifts the equivalent of 3.5 million 20-cl (7-oz) bottles a year, and all of it is made here.

The story of this distillery is the story of the Angostura Bitters, which begins with Dr Johann Siegert, a German-born doctor, chief medial officer for Simón Bolívar, and veteran of the Battle of Waterloo in 1815. He moved to the town of Angostura, Venezuela, in 1820, and began manufacturing medicinal tinctures using various barks, roots, spices and other tropical ingredients, to which he gave the name "Aromatic Bitters". The bitters were

THIS PAGE It's nice of Angostura to colour-code their column stills for us: from left to right we have the stripping column, hydroselector, rectifier and a final column for good measure (top); barrel ends are stacked like pancakes in the cooperage (above).

THIS PAGE Defects in casks that lead to leakages are marked with chalk by the cellar master and are then sent to the the cooperage for repair. This generally involves the careful removal and replacement of a damaged stave.

originally used to treat stomach ailments, then later to flavour food. In time, they were were exported, landing in Trinidad in the 1830s and England shortly thereafter. In time, Siegert's son's joined the business: first Carlos D. Siegert, and then Alfredo C. Siegert, following the death of their father. By the 1850s, the bitters were appearing in cocktails. In 1874 Mark Twain penned a letter to his wife, requesting that she stock the bathroom (of all places) with "Scotch Whisky, a lemon, some crushed sugar, and a bottle of Angostura Bitters."

In the 1870s, revolutionary fever swept Venezuela and the atmosphere became erratic. The Siegert brothers took the decision to relocate the business to Trinidad and their younger brother Luis B. C. Siegert joined their enterprise. In 1879, they built their first distillery on George Street in Port of Spain.

Just after the Angostura distillery was built, a man named Joseph Gregorio Fernandes arrived in Port of Spain by way of Maderia. Along with his father, he established a wine shop on Henry Street. Years later, the younger Fernandes got into the rum-blending game, and when the Government Rum Bond was burnt down in 1932, he acquired rum that had been put into casks in 1919. That same rum was later released as a 13-year-old bottling marked "1919" and the family later bought the Forres Park Sugar Estate, which came complete with a distillery.

Back on George Street, the bitters business was in the third and fourth generation of Siegert ownership, headed up by Alfredo G. Siegert (the son of Alfredo C.) and his son Robert W. Siegert, who was a trained chemist. In 1937, Robert established a chemical control and research laboratory, which set the stage for Trinidad Distillers Ltd., and the family's first dedicated rum distillery. It was in that same year that Thomas Gatcliffe joined the firm. As one of Trinidad's most celebrated businessmen, Gatcliffe chaired no less than 11 blue-chip companies in his time, and went on to become the first non-Siegert to head up the Angostura business. Gatcliffe steered the company through the latter part of the 20th century, negotiating the purchase of Fernandes Distillers Ltd. (and the Forres Park Rum brand) in 1973, thanks to a strategic partnership with Bacardí (who at one time owned 45% of Angostura). The following year, an ultra-modern rum distillery was opened in Laventille, on the outskirts of Port of Spain, and this was followed by the release of Old Oak rum. Gatcliffe was also involved in the establishment of the West Indian Rum and Spirits Producers Association (WIRSPA) and served as the organization's chairman in the early 1980s.

Trinidad Distillers is today headed up by John Georges, a chemical engineer who joined the company in 1982. His approach is one of engineering rum

5-YEAR-OLD (40% ABV) AGED RUM

Greasy wood, vanilla and coconut. Honeyed and creamy on the palate, starting with toffee and gentle fruity notes, then drifting into wood spices and tannin.

SINGLE BARREL (40% ABV) AGED RUM

Pungent and dirty on the nose. Cacao, compost and dark spices brooding. Big vanilla, milk chocolate and bitter espresso on the taste. It's quite sweet and chilli/chile-spiced cacao dominates through the finish.

1919 (40% ABV) AGED RUM

Light on the nose, but with plenty of bourbon characteristics and the usual vanilla-scented culprits: coconut, milk chocolate, caramel and vanilla. Sweetness on the palate, which is more maple syrup then toffee, soft forest fruits, settling into baking spices through the finish.

1824 (40% ABV) EXTRA-AGED RUM

There is more cask concentration here, which compresses fruit into tobacco, and those vanilla elements into rich caramel sauce and slick honey. Taste is reflective of this, with a sweetness that delivers on the promises of the nose. Pleasant as that is, it is also somewhat one-dimensional.

ABOVE The 1824 is matured for a minumum of 12 years in charred ex-bourbon American oak casks.

through a scientific approach to its manufacture. This distillery remains one of the most high-tech operations in the Caribbean, where every section of the operation is scrutinized to the minutest detail – they even manufacture their own spirit caramel. The rum they make remains some of the most highly celebrated around. Everything here is molasses-based, and since the early 2000s (around the time that the Caroni distillery closed), it's been sourced outside of Trinidad. Fermentation takes 48–72 hours.

The original distillery had both a Savalle still and a pot, but these were done away with in the 1970s, replaced by no less than seven column stills, which, handily, are colour-coded (but in the cryptic words of John Georges, "only four of them really count"). As some of the biggest columns in the business, they are visible over rooftops from many blocks away. Perhaps it's the fact that Trinidad bases its economy largely on oil these days, or maybe it's the close proximity to Latin America, but Angostura is one distillery that bucks the trend as far as English-speaking islands go – you won't find any pot stills here.

The first column takes the molasses wine from 5% up to around 80% ABV, resulting in a relatively characterful spirit that contains 300-500 parts per million (ppm) of congeners. Some of this spirit will be set aside for maturation and blended later down the line. The rest of the spirit is distilled a further three times; once through a rectifier, once through a hydroselector, and then once more through a final column still. The purpose of all this fine-tuning is to nurture a spirit that is light, but not plundered of all its character.

As with before, these rums are sent for maturation and then, according to each recipe, are blended with the mature rums from the first distillation to form finished products.

Barrels are all of the ex-bourbon variety and there are around 70,000 of them in total. That's in excess of 12 million litres (3.1 million US gallons) of maturing rum at any given time – one of the largest holding stocks of rum anywhere in the world.

U.S. VIRGIN ISLANDS

ST. THOMAS
CHARLOTTE AMALIE
ST. JOHN

Cruzan
ST. CROIX

The western section of the Virgin Island archipelago is officially recognized as an insular area of the United States. There are something like 50 islands in the group, which is situated just 60 km (37 miles) off the eastern coast of Puerto Rico. St. Thomas and St. John are the biggest islands in the cluster, but another 60 km (37 miles) south, all on its own, is St. Croix – the largest of all the Virgin Islands. Considering their diminutive form, it's surprising to learn that the Virgin Islands were once among the most hotly contested prizes in all of the Caribbean. Sitting at the crossroads between the Old and New Worlds, no less than seven different nations have have planted flags on their fertile shores, starting – of course – with Spain. Next came England and Holland, who jointly inhabited St. Croix during the 1620s.

When the Spanish attempted to recapture the island, by launching an assault from neighbouring Puerto Rico, the French seized the opportunity and quickly moved in, liberating St. Croix from the Spanish and establishing it as a French colony, which lasted until 1733. Under the direction of the French-chartered Compagnie des Îles de l'Amérique, St. Croix was briefly sold to the Knights of Malta, in 1651. The Maltese Caribbean colonization effort was short-lived however, as the island was sold back to the French company just four years later. Meanwhile, the Kingdom of Denmark successfully established a settlement on St. Thomas in 1672, and St. John a few years later. It's thought that the Danes first brought sugarcane to the islands, although most of the plantations were owned by wealthy British planters. In 1685, the Danes signed a treaty with the Dutch that allowed the Brandenburg American Company to establish a slave-trading post on St. Thomas. Under Dutch rule, the island became a hangout for pirates, which helped establish a powerful merchant economy.

But it was sugar and slavery that drove the economy through the 18th and 19th centuries. The Danish Virgin Islands were one of the biggest beneficiaries of the American Revolution, as St. Croix and St. Thomas had long been important stepping stones between the Caribbean rum and sugar trade and the North American colonies. This tradition continued, as they operated as tactical smuggling routes during the period leading up to and during the Revolutionary War. George Washington himself supplied St. Croix rum to his troops at the military camp Valley Forge. What kind of rum was it? Pot-still certainly, and probably not dissimilar to the Barbados-style that was popular in America at the time.

During the 19th century, rum production remained strong, so strong in fact that molasses was imported into St. Croix and St. Thomas from Puerto Rico. But by the time the US purchased the Virgin Islands for $25 million in 1917 ($325 million or £262 million today), the islands were exporting around 380,000 litres (100,000 US

LEFT Pepino Mangravite's vivid illustration of family life in St. Thomas reminds us that rum-making was still a household activity in the mid-20th century.

ABOVE The USVI has always been dedicated to alcohol consumption. The capital city Charlotte Amalie was known as Taphus in the 17th century, which is the Danish for "beer hall".

gallons) of rum a year – one-tenth of the volume from a century before. That soon changed, though. By the 1930s the US was importing 1.5 million litres (400,000 US gallons) of rum a year from the Virgin Islands, which shot up to 6.4 million litres (1.7 million US gallons) in 1943, during World War II. But that's nothing compared to the eye-watering heights of present-day production figures. Thanks to Diageo's USVI rum distillery, which has made rum for the Captain Morgan brand since 2008, St. Croix produces more rum per square kilometre of land than any other island in the world.

The USVIs have garnered no shortage of negative press in recent years, on account of the huge cash subsidies handed to Diageo from Washington. Totalling an estimated $2.7 billion (£2.2 billion) over 30 years, the subsidies include: a new $165-million (£133-million) distillery, support payments to keep prices low for molasses, subsidies on advertising and income tax, exemption from property taxes, and 47.5% of all tax revenue collected on Captain Morgan rum. By some estimates, Diageo's net cost to produce Captain Morgan rum is zero.

A similar situation occurs in Puerto Rico, which, while stimulating growth in international rum brands like Captain Morgan and Bacardi, also destabilizes the rum market, by undercutting smaller producers across the Caribbean region.

CRUZAN

The island of St. Croix has a permanent population of only 50,000 people, yet it manages to get through over 1 million litres (265,000 US gallons) of rum a year – roughly 20 bottles per person!

Of course, a large chunk of this consumption comes from tourists, but if you've ever visited the US Virgin Islands, you will no doubt have noticed that practically all of the rum drunk on St. Croix comes from the Cruzan distillery.

Cruzan has its origins in a sugar mill established on St. Croix during the 1750s. Being a mill, it was also a rum distillery too, fed with the leftover molasses from the sugar-refining process. There were over 100 similar mills on this island at one time, and the rum they produced was known as "Cruzan" Rum, which comes from the word "Crucian" – meaning a resident of St. Croix.

In 1910, while the island was still under Danish rule, the estate comprised 100 hectares (250 acres) of land and an old pot-still factory. It was sold to Malcolm Skeoch, who rebooted rum-making on the estate and changed the name to "Estate Diamond". Being an overseas American territory, the distillery was forced to close when US prohibition took effect in 1920. After prohibition was repealed 13 years later, Estate Diamond re-launched as "Cruzan Rum" – the only surviving rum in the USVI and an *aide-memoire* to the plantation era.

During the 1950s, the company changed its name to St. Croix Sugar Industries Inc., and in 1953, the Cruzan Rum trademark was registered and the pot stills removed. Ten years later, the name was changed again to Cruzan Rum Distillery, which was around the time that the Nelthropp family (an old dynasty of St. Croix distillers) purchased shares in the company. The Nelthropp family have continued to manage the operation, which between 1993 and 2008, has experienced a pass-the-parcel scenario, having been acquired by Todhunter International, then Angostura, V & S Spirits, Pernod-Ricard, Beam Inc. and now Suntory.

The rum pedigree on St. Croix has its roots in English and Dutch planters, which means a liberal use of pot stills. But the gravitational draw of nearby Puerto Rico – and the Spanish style – has left its mark in the form of the continuous still. But this isn't exactly a Spanish-style rum either (the Spanish have not been here since the 17th century), as unlike Havana Club or Bacardí, this is not a delicate blend of *aguardiente* and *redistillaro*, but a simple five-column-still distillate added to cask. It's quick and mercilessly efficient, and the result is a very pure spirit. If anything, Cruzan is a modern American rum.

No sugar is grown on the island these days, so the molasses is shipped in from Guatemala, Nicaragua and the Dominican Republic. Once in port, it's loaded into tanker trucks and driven to the distillery. Eight to ten of these trucks arrive at Cruzan every day, and the underground molasses storage tanks hold 6.8 million litres (1.5 million US gallons). The molasses is pasteurized by briefly being heated to 115°C (239°F). When needed, it is mixed with water to 16° Brix and then transferred to one of nine fermentation tanks inside the blue building, which each hold 115,000 litres (30,000 US gallons). Fermentation uses a standard

distiller's yeast and takes 24–36 hours, and compressed air is bubbled through the mixture, which has the effect of lifting carbon dioxide up to the surface of the liquid, thus improving the fermentation efficiency.

The distillation column at Cruzan is housed at the second-tallest building on the island – the first is the airport's air traffic control tower, which is less than a kilometre away and can be seen quite easily from the still house. Cruzan's tower has five columns, starting with a stripping column, then a "purification" column, a "clarification" column, and finally, two rectifying columns. The spirit comes off the still at 94.5% ABV – so as near as damn it to pure and neutral.

Maturation is conducted across a number of warehouses, holding a total of 23,000 casks. It's in the blending that the first piece of true artistry comes into play, as the neutral canvas sucks up oak characteristics. The standout product is the Single Barrel, which is not exactly from a single barrel, but a blend of 5- and 12-year-old rums that have been blended and re-casked in new American oak (then bottled from that "single barrel") – unsurprisingly, it both looks and tastes a lot like bourbon whiskey. I've said it already, this is American rum.

LEFT The old Reef Bay sugar-refinery, on the south coast of the island of St. John, was added to the US National Register of Historic Places in 1981.

CENTRAL AND SOUTH AMERICA

GUATEMALA

GUATEMALA CITY

Guatemala is the cradle of Mayan culture, and home to the largest indigenous population of any country in the Western hemisphere. It's not a big country, but the topography here is dramatic and the weather prone to changing quite violently. It has had its share of natural disasters over the years, from volcanic eruptions to floods, earthquakes and hurricanes. Nearly two-thirds of the country is perched over a mile above sea level, where cool, humid conditions are perfect for growing bananas (the main export crop) and top-quality coffee. Guatemala has some of the highest and most active volcanos in the world (take it from someone who has climbed one of them), which seasons the surrounding valleys with black fertile soil. It is here, where the country borders the Pacific, along the vast, sunny, coastal planes with their mixture of clay and volcanic soils, that we find the sugarcane.

As with all of nations of Central America, the history of rum and sugar in Guatemala is not so long as that of the islands of the Caribbean. Guatemala, for one, is certainly making up for lost time. Sugarcane plantations in this country have grown by 3% every year for the past 10 years, to the point where smallholders are slowly being pushed out. Companies like La Unión, which owns Guatemala's third-largest sugar mill, approach sugar agriculture like a military operation, seizing new patches of land and literally setting up base. During the harvesting season (January–May), they employ up to 5,000 *cortadores de caña* (cane cutters), who live in army-style barracks with dormitories, clinics, dining rooms and exercise areas. The walls of these places are plastered with pieces of motivational propaganda, reminding the workers of how appreciative they should be of their employment. A typical *cortador* is paid $2.65 (£2.10) an hour and expected to cut 10 tons (11 US tons) of cane in a single day. Even though Guatemala is posited as the most economically developed country in Central America, the chasm between the rich and poor is also the widest in the region.

In the 2014 harvest, Guatemala exported 2 million tons (2.2 million US tons) of sugar – more than the sugar exports of El Salvador, Nicaragua, Honduras, Costa Rica and Panama combined. Guatemala now ranks as the world's fourth-largest sugar exporter, after Brazil, Thailand and Australia. Sugar today represents 14.4% of Guatemala's

RIGHT All products labelled as rum in Guatemala must be made from the fermentation of sugarcane syrup by yeast derived from pineapple.

FAR RIGHT Guatemala has a total of 33 volcanoes, which is good news for soil fertility but bad news if you live there.

total exports, 27.1% of its agricultural exports and 3% of its gross domestic product.

As far as rum is concerned, Guatemala does have certain regulations that form the basis of a Geographical Indication. It's as loose as GIs come mind you: the rules state that rum must be made from cane juice syrup, and it also makes a distinction between the "solera" (see page 55) system as well as the use of special casks (refill sherry, port, Cognac, wine casks etc.) and that the casks must be filled with spirit cut to 60% ABV. What they don't regulate is how age statements can be used. Neither do they cover added flavourings (wine, grape must, sugar) or colouring. What does this mean for the consumer? Well, it means you shouldn't place too much trust in the age statement on a bottle of Guatemalan rum. Nor should you be under the illusion that all of the flavour in a bottle of Guatemalan rum is derived only from the fermentation, distillation and maturation of sugarcane-based materials. It won't be.

The most common mode of transportation in Guatemala is the *camioneta*, or "chicken bus." These refurbished, colourfully painted buses follow a designated route and can accommodate up to 30 people. They're often crowded with passengers and sometimes chickens, hence the name. But travelling 50 km (30 miles) "as the crow flies" can take up to four hours as the bus leisurely winds up or down the endless hills. If someone else is paying (as they were in my case) it's far better to travel by helicopter. In this manner you not only get an uninterrupted view of the scenery, but also an appreciation of the climactic shift between the high-altitude towns and the low-altitude cane plantations.

INDUSTRIAS LICORERAS DE GUATEMALA

There are technically four distilleries in Guatemala, but three of them (Pantaleon, Palo Gordo, and Magdalena) are large-scale industrial refineries with ethanol plants bolted on to the side. They produce only industrial alcohol and molasses-based *aguardiente* intended for local consumption. These spirits are not classifiable as rum under the Guatemalan GI, which leaves us with just one rum distillery: Industrias Licoreras de Guatemala (ILG). ILG is the biggest of the four, and it too is an ethanol plant, but this plant also wins lots of awards for its rum.

The distillery was founded by the Botran brothers: Venancio, Andrés, Felipe, Jesús and Alejandro, who between 1911 and 1923 emigrated to Guatemala from Burgos in Spain. They set up Locorera Quetzalteca in 1939, named for the mountain-top town of Quetzaltenango. This town is where Botran and Zacapa rums are still matured today, and at 2,300 metres (7,500 ft) above the sea level, it is far cooler than the coastal areas where all the cane is grown. This cooler climate naturally slows the maturation process, reducing the angel's share and extending the spirit's interaction with oxygen. This, along with so-called "solera" ageing systems (see page 55) is the reference marker for the Guatemalan style. But I'm getting ahead of myself…

To be labeled rum in Guatemala the spirit must be distilled from fermented virgin sugarcane honey, a dark, concentrated, syrup made from freshly squeezed sugarcane juice. This honey is made by filtering fresh sugarcane juice and then boiling off the water until the syrup contains about 72% sugar. Only sugarcane grown in Guatemala is used to make this virgin sugarcane honey since it would be impossible to transport cane cut in another country to a Guatemalan sugar mill.

Lorena Vasquez is the pint-sized master blender for Zacapa, and Guatemala's answer to Peggy Mitchell (that joke is applicable to Brits only and hopefully lost on Lorena herself). Lorena is actually a Nicaraguan national, who came to Guatemala after finishing her studies in pharmaceutical chemistry and nutrition. She joined ILG as a member of the quality-control department, before graduating to master blender.

Both Zacapa and Botran rums are made using what ILG call a "Sistema Solera", which is borrowed from the Spanish sherry-ageing process. The approach here is far more convoluted – to the point where you wonder if it's intended to be that way – but I will try to explain it.

For Zacapa, there are four types of cask used to make the rum: ex-bourbon; re-charred ex-bourbon; oloroso sherry; and Pedro Ximenez sherry. The rum is effectively a blend of these four cask types, with a measure of older stocks of rum added in afterwards. The older stocks comprise rums held back from the previous blend (which itself contained older stocks) so you can see there's a strand of continuity that passes through every bottle. This means it's possible that some small percentage of the rum in the bottle is 23 years old, but if you want my opinion, I would say that this rum is a blend of 6–7 year old spirits or thereabouts. To that

BOTRAN SOLERA 1983 (40% ABV)
EXTRA-AGED RUM

Lots of dessert flavours in the aroma of this rum: crème brûlée, crisp shortbread, rum-and-raisin fudge and barrel-aged maple syrup. The taste confirms it, though – there's less sweetness here than Ron Zacapa, but there's enough to carry those sweet aromatics through. The linger dissipates slowly, leaving with it a strange sweet/savoury edge.

RON ZACAPA SOLERA 23 (40% ABV)
AGED RUM

The nose displays plenty of soft, dried fruits along with a slightly fungal, tobacco note. There's alcohol there too, suggesting a lightness to the spirit. Taste is sweet and winey, with chilli (chile) jam, sweet sherry, and unctuous liqueur qualities. Finish is spiced and long.

RON ZACAPA RISERVA LIMITADA 2013 (45% ABV) EXTRA-AGED RUM

Quite light in aroma: a smudge of caramel popcorn, a drop of lime peel oil and and some subtle fungal notes. More forthright in taste, as a generous dash of sugar and that higher strength draws upon dates and semi-dried grapes. It's somewhat one-dimensional, however, leaving a sticky residue that's more like a (heavily) fortified port wine than a rum.

RON ZACAPA SOLERA XO (40% ABV)
EXTRA-AGED RUM

Aroma presents more red fruits than the "23", particularly fresh raspberry and strawberry, which replaces much of those dried grape charactersisics of its younger sibling. On the palate it's concentrated and juicy, sweet and rather more-ish! There's not a great deal of wood flavour, however. Taste dries through the finish.

ABOVE Every bottle of Ron Zacapa wears a "petate" band – a traditional Mayan craft woven from palm.

end, the bottle used to proudly declare "23 annos", but it was misleading to say the least and since 2011 it says only "23". Zacapa XO is effectively the same rum, with the addition of some 4–6 year old ex-Cognac cask-aged rum mixed in to the final blend – I prefer it because it's not as sweet as the "23".

Botran is a similar set up (because it happens in the same place) – the point of difference being the use of port casks in place of PX. The two expressions to look out for are "Reserva" (a blend of rums between 5–14 years old) and the "Solera 1893" (a blend of rums between 5–18 years old). Unlike Zacapa, you can also buy Botran as a white rum, which – in adherence with Guatemalan law – is also aged and then filtered through charcoal to remove the colour.

One thing that I must commend both Botran and Zacapa for, is their commitment to driving the super-premium end of the category. The problem lies in the distinction between super-premium by price and super-premium by quality. Certainly the packaging of these brands suggests luxury and top-drawer liquid, but is this a case of perceived value over real value? One might argue that it doesn't matter – value is value and perception is everything – but if the industry doesn't tread carefully, it may find itself on a trajectory similar to that of vodka, where true value is misplaced in favour of marketing spin and modified liquids.

GUYANA

With its enormous Essequibo River, which at its mouth is 32 km (20 miles) across, to the Guiana Shield (a 1.6-billion-year-old mountainous mass of sandstone) and a landmass of which up to 75% is covered by rainforest, Guyana is a nation of super-sizes. The country's capital, Georgetown, is not so big in size, but it makes up for it in terms of noise. Thanks to a Dutch occupation in the 17th century, the city boasts a giant sea wall that places most of Georgetown below sea level and some of it on lands reclaimed from the Atlantic Ocean. The town is laced with a network of hardworking canals and kokers (sluice gates) that were once filled with horse-drawn barges spilling sugarcane into the Demerara River. The poet Mark McWatt described the rainforests of his home nation as "the central spider in our web of dreams, that weaves the net of Eldorado, that launches the drunken boat."

And this is a dream that's easy to get tangled up in, in part because these days you don't need to leave Georgetown to find boats, spiders or indeed, the El Dorado. Guyana gained its independence from Britain 50 years ago, which is not so long that it doesn't still feel colonial in its mentality. It's the sound of busy engineering firms and street vendors (selling cut-up chunks of pineapple) that fill the air, but even their noise is drowned out by the blaring procession of music carts that weave through the madness. Guyana is a South American nation, but a long history of British occupation has left Georgetown feeling more like Kingston than it does Caracas. The Guyanese wouldn't have it any other way.

Thanks to the country's proximity to the equator, there are two cane harvests a year in Guyana, which is one reason why the area has seen such success in the sugar trade. Guyana supplies molasses to around half of all the rum-makers in the Caribbean. The other reason is the mineral-rich silt deposits offered up by the Demerara, especially around the area where it meets the ocean. Those minerals are imparted into the cane and also transmit through to the molasses and, in turn, orchestrate flavour into the rum.

As with all the rum-producing regions of the Caribbean, the story so far, where both rum and sugar are concerned, has been one of consolidation. At the turn of the 19th century, there were around 300 rum distilleries in Guyana, mostly located around the Demerara river (one of the world's best know sugarcane-growing regions) and mostly making molasses rums as appendices to sugar mills. In 1849 there were 180 estates in Guyana and by the turn of the 20th century the number had shrunk to 64. Jump forward to 1952 and there are just two rum companies remaining: Guyana Distillers Ltd. and Diamond Liquors Ltd., who were operating a total of nine distilleries between them. In 1971, the number of distilleries had fallen to just three: Diamond, Uitvlugt and Enmore.

Such was the popularity of Guyanese rum that the preservation of distillation equipment and the amalgamation of operations was crucial to keep up with demand. Each British blend was formulated to a specific recipe, and abandoning the equipment required to make it would be sacrificial to the foreign business. As the number of estates decreased, these remaining distilleries got much bigger.

BELOW LEFT Dedicated rum bars are a rarity in Guyana, but you won't find any bars that don't stock rum.

BELOW RIGHT Like the stills at DDL, St. George's Cathedral in Georgetown was built from the local greenheart wood.

GEORGETOWN
Diamond
Distillery

In 1966 Guyana gained its independence from Britain and prime minister and future president Forbes Burnham focused on gaining control over foreign companies, which drove most of Guyana's economy. In the 1970s, the government began buying shares in the remaining distilleries, forming the state-owned holding company known as the Guyana Liquor Corporation. Then, in 1983, the distilleries merged under one holding company, known as Demerara Distillers Limited (DDL). By the mid-1990s, the government had divested all of its shares and DDL became independent for the first time. This was followed by the closure of Enmore (circa 1993) and Uitvlugt (2000) leaving just the monolithic Diamond distillery, on the east bank of the Demerara. And so it was that 300 years' worth of collected baggage, combined knowledge, distilling artefacts, brands and expressions were crammed under one roof. The entire distilling history of one nation, all in one place.

Notwithstanding the "bush rum" producers that hide-out in villages here and there, colouring their rums with aromatic barks and woods, Diamond is the only remaining distillery in Guyana today. The frontman for this operation is Dr Yesu Persaud, who, at 97-years-old is one of Guyana's most successful and dearly loved businessmen. Local legend states that Persaud was born on the Diamond Estate, and if Diamond is a temple to the nation's long history of rum (and it surely is) Persaud has to be its curator, originator and religious minister.

There may only be one distillery, but it's a big range of rum that gets made there, and some big flavours to go with it. Demerara rums, whether bottled by DDL or otherwise, have garnered recognition for their concentrated, sometimes bordering on liqueur-level, sweetness. Expect honeyed sweetness and rich oak notes as a consistent theme among old Guyanese rums.

Rum-drinking in Guyana is a pastime best practiced with "cutters". These salty morsels of food, which are generally fried, can take the form of fish, chicken or cassava. The fat and salt from the cutter does a nice job of "cutting" through the sweetness and alcohol of the rum itself. The various rum bars that populate the eastern coast of Guyana are, more often than not, graded by locals not on the rums that they stock (the offering rarely deviates from the standard fare) but from the quality of the cutters that the rum is served with. Either way, they're easy to spot, sponsored advertising supplied by El Dorado rum is picketed along the street like DDL have branched out into the real estate business.

ABOVE Coded casks indicate which still made the rum: VSG (Versailles), PM (Port Mourant) and SV (Savalle).

DIAMOND DISTILLERY

On a good day, the Diamond distillery can go through 220 tons (242 US tons) of molasses. The molasses is diluted at a ratio of 4:1 with water, which takes it to around 18-21° Brix. Yeast cultures are grown in small propagators, before being added into any one of the fermenters. Some of the fermentation vessels are open-top, others are closed. For the latter, the carbon dioxide produced during the process is collected and piped 9 metres (30 ft) across the adjacent highway, to the Pepsi bottling plant where it's used to carbonate the soft drinks. Now, with a yeast cell count of 150 million per millilitre, the process takes just 24–32 hours. Next it's on to distillation, and what is surely the most eccentric still house on the planet.

To describe DDL as a single distillery would be somewhat misleading. It is multiple distilleries that happen to be squeezed under the same roof. The distilling apparatus and technical practices pay noble homage to the history of rum in Guyana, and it's thanks to this that over two dozen styles of rum can be produced across 14 individual pieces of distillation apparatus. These range from a small copper pot stills to a steel multi-column tower that can output up to 60,000 litres (15,850 US gallons) of 96% alcohol in a single day. Guyana is historically known as "the land of many waters", but going on the potential output of its one and only distillery, "the land of many rums" would be just as fitting a moniker.

There are only three known examples of wooden pot stills in the world and all of them are at the Diamond distillery in Guyana. There's only one known example of a wooden Coffey still, and that lives at Diamond too.

These historic artefacts, despite being worthy museum pieces, are very much in day-to-day use, however. "They leak, the maintenance is expensive, and the spirit recovery is diminished," DDL's master distiller, Shaun Caleb, tells me. But apparently it's all worth it. The unique spirit that they create is a crucial component of the El Dorado blends and perhaps impossible to produce using modern kit. Not content with just using the equipment, Shaun is digging deeper into the principles behind wooden distillation equipment, "Now we're trying to elevate beyond the craft. To understand how the stills work on a scientific level, so that we can develop new styles of rum that have never been seen before."

From a visual standpoint, the wooden pots take on the forms of a giant barrels. They're constructed from staves, but through years of use they have become gnarly, as a hardened skin of distillery residue clings to their surfaces like barnacles to the hull of a ship. The "head" and lyne arm of all three stills is made from hammered copper. One of the pots works by itself, with a single metal retort. It was taken from the old Versailles Estate which was founded in the 1890s. Like all the stills at DDL, the rum is coded, and in this case it's VSG rum that the pot still makes, which is classed a a medium to heavy pot-still rum that comes off the still at around 84% ABV. The other two wooden pots are linked (performing a double distillation) and according to the historians at the distillery they date back to the founding of the Port Mourant Estate, in 1732. If that's true, it's quite possible that they are the oldest working pot stills in the world. Distillation takes approximately 18 hours for a complete run, with only 8 hours of that time spent collecting the heart of the spirit. PM (Port Mourant) is also a medium-bodied rum.

Opposite the wooden pots, on the far wall of the still house, is the real showstopper – the Edward Henry Porter wooden Coffey still. Looking like two giant "Jenga" towers, linked by pipes, the structure of the still is entirely wood but the internal components are copper. It dates back to the 1880s, when it once made rum at the Enmore Estate. These days, it produces three expressions of "sweet" rum designated as "EHP", which is named after Edward Henry Potter, the founder of the Enmore Estate. As with the other wooden items, the still is constructed from green heartwood, a local oak variety that is known for its hardiness.

It's difficult to get your head around why someone would be compelled to build a wooden still. The risk of fire alone should be a good enough deterrent. But in the past it was more common than one might imagine. Guyana is a country that has an abundance of wood, even St George's Cathedral, in Georgetown – one of the largest wooden structures in the world – is built entirely out of wood. "Building stills from wood was not unorthodox at the time," Shaun tells me, "it's only extraordinary that they have survived so long."

With all these wooden wonders, it's easy to overlook some of the other treasures housed within Diamond's cache. There are two French Savalle stills, which were obtained from the 18th century Uitvlugt Estate, on the west coast of Demerara County. They consist of multi-linked columns, so can be tailored to produce an assortment of rum styles, from medium-bodied right through to nearly neutral. There are also a total of three Coffey stills, two of them date from the 1950s and they are used to make rums with light floral notes, distilled between 91–94% ABV. Next is the Tri-Canada still, which is not currently in use but was once used to make high-strength neutral spirit. Last but by no means least, is a steel John Dore pot still that is linked to two copper retorts. This still produces DHE (Demerara High Ester) rum – a crucial contributor of heavy fruity character to all of the El Dorado expressions as well as other brands, like Lamb's Navy Rum.

As you might expect, with all these unique distillates floating around, the four enormous warehouses at the Diamond Distillery are a complex arrangement of maturing stocks that total approximately 3 million litres (660,000 US gallons). Freshly made rums are matured separately and blended together, to the formula prescribed by each individual expression.

Diamond is an important distillery. For the history of its equipment, for the diversity of rum styles it makes, and for its size. It is without doubt the most incredible distilling operation in the world. Of any spirit category. Over half of the blended rums in this book contain wholesale Demerara rum from Diamond, and some, like Wood's, Pyrat and OVD, are composed entirely of Guyanese spirit made here.

From the perspective of DDL, however, there is only one: El Dorado. Owned and exported by Demerara

OPPOSITE The rum flavour of Guyana is diverse, but best summarized as "dark" – dark sugar, with hard-working grease, rubber and char. Georgetown is packed with automobile workshops, so perhaps there's a connection there?

QUALITY
IS
JOB #1

RESTRICTED AREA

EL DORADO 3-YEAR-OLD (40% ABV)
AGED WHITE BLENDED RUM

Vanilla cheesecake, coconut, white chocolate and mace. More coconut on the palate. Gentle and sweet.

EL DORADO 5-YEAR-OLD (40% ABV)
AGED BLENDED RUM

Brown butter, hemp, old rope and mineral notes. Maritime notes on the palate, with seaweed and BBQ sardines. It caramelizes into butterscotch, vanilla and sweet, dried fruits.

EL DORADO 12-YEAR-OLD (40% ABV)
EXTRA-AGED BLENDED RUM

Fried banana caramel, juicy bubble gum and concentrated pineapple. Custard tart and cream pie, too. Sweet and concentrated on the palate. The sweetness cuts some of the complexity in favour of clarity and linger. It's aromatic spices along with dried tropical fruits that win over.

EL DORADO 15-YEAR-OLD (40% ABV)
EXTRA-AGED BLENDED RUM

Penny toffee and banana pancake. Less complex, but powerfully complete as an expression of aged Demerara. Fruity rubber and cane syrup. Some liquorice (licorice) and more bung cloth smells. Massive sweetness on the palate. Almost gritty, full and syrup-like. Alcohol cuts through slightly, but grenadine and toffee sauce linger.

DELUXE SILVER (40% ABV)
AGED WHITE BLENDED RUM

Greener, with coconut, slightly minty, sponge cake, pistachio butter, cardamom and eucalyptus. Coconut milk, creamy, vanilla and soft white chocolate, too. Slightly more character than the El Dorado 3-year-old.

"ICBU" SINGLE BARREL (40% ABV) AGED RUM

Dried dark fruits, red wine cork, cacao, peppermint and fruit juice. It's darker on the palate, with brooding cacao, wood spice and chocolate fudge. Silky smooth with subtle sweetness. A peppery tingle announces itself through the finish.

"EHP" SINGLE BARREL (40% ABV) AGED RUM

Fruit-and-nut chocolate, butterscotch, fleshy ripe peach or plum. There's sweetness too, as well as plump tobacco. More concentrated on the palate; good integration of spice and sweetness. Finish is longer, continuing with dark fruit and bitter barks.

"PM" SINGLE BARREL (40% ABV)
AGED POT-STILL RUM

Buttery banana pancakes, burnt plantain, greasy industrial rubber and cut-grass flavours. Big and round on the palate, more skidding tyre, oiled leather, greasy wood sap and spice.

Distillers Limited, El Dorado rums are renowned for their concentrated sweetness, with the 15-year-old expression in particular being somewhat of a sugar-bomb. DDL have continued to rebuff claims of heavy sugaring of their rums, stating that only caramel is added after blending. For what it's worth, I find it improbable that a blended rum can exhibit such a degree of residual sweetness through maturation alone – even accounting for the mystical effects of the world's only wooden stills. Having sampled PM and EHP 15-year-old rums directly from the cask during my time at the distillery, I can also attest to their balanced (but not overwhelming) sweetness.

RIGHT The launch of El Dorado in the 1990s marked the beginning of rum's slow premiumization.

NICARAGUA

Nicaragua is the largest country in the Central American isthmus but it's also the poorest. Earthquakes, hurricanes, flooding and landslides – you name it, and Nicaragua has seen and felt it. Political upheaval and civil war have left their mark too, making Nicaragua the second poorest rum-producing country in the world after Haiti, and the average Nicaraguan is over 10 times poorer than the average American.

Since the mid-19th century, coffee has been by far the nation's biggest export, and like most of Central America, sugar was introduced late to Nicaragua. The first mill was erected in the 1880s, in San Antonio on the Pacific coast, and by the end of the century the sugar industry was a major contributor to the country's modest economy.

At the turn of the 20th century, the Nicaraguan coffee trade was entirely controlled by foreign interests and a small domestic elite. The economy came to resemble a "banana republic", and when coupled with the potential for enormous fluctuations in the coffee market, Nicaragua found itself in a precarious position. In reflection of this, Nicaragua attempted to diversify its agriculture in the 20th century and sugarcane performed a major role in this process. Unlike Cuba, Peru or Puerto Rico, the sugar industry has been kept out of the hands of American companies. It was, and is, owned by Nicaraguan nationals. After World War II, further sugar factories were established, all of them in the north-west of the country, near the Pacific coast, which tends to be excused from the worst of the natural disasters. Since 2005, sugar and rum exports from Nicaragua have more than doubled. Harvesting takes place from November to May each year, and sugarcane currently occupies an area of 660 square kilometres (255 square miles).

In recent years the sugar (and rum) in Nicaragua has come under scrutiny because of serious outbreaks of Chronic Kidney Disease (CKD), which appears to have been already present in the region for two decades. While not limited to Nicaragua (Guatemala, El Salvador and Costa Rica have all seen considerable rise in cases of the disease) it is at its most serious here, and especially among sugarcane workers.

Evidence suggests that the prevalence of the disease among the cane harvesters is a result of heat and dehydration during the *zafra* (harvest) period, and possibly exposure to harmful pesticides. CKD is now the second-biggest killer of men in Nicaragua. In the western plains around the sugar town of La Isla – which means "The Island" – so many lives have been lost to CKD that the locals have taken to calling the town "La Isla de las Viudas" – "The Island of the Widows". News of this reached American bartenders in 2015, provoking some to take action and publicly post images online of them disposing of their stocks of Flor de Caña rum.

Poor working conditions on plantations is not a new thing; poverty has blighted the sugar industry in the Americas consistently over its 500-year history. But while the penury at the centre of the industry is easy to conceal behind a bag of white granules or in manufactured products, the emergence of super-premium rums from some of the biggest offenders may prove to be a tipping point. Unlike candy, a product

RIGHT Nicaragua is big – so big, that you could fit the entire island of Puerto Rico into Lake Nicaragua, the country's largest body of water.

that commands a high price point opens itself to a degree of scrutiny, and as bartenders and consumers become curious around matters relating to provenance and sustainability, the glossy veneer that price and packaging provides will quickly melt away.

FLOR DE CAÑA

Ingenio San Antonio is the oldest and the largest of Nicaragua's four sugar mills. It's owned by Nicaragua Sugar Estates Ltd. (NSEL), which is itself owned by the Pellas Group, who are entering their fifth generation of involvement in the Nicaraguan agricultural industries and are among the most powerful families in the country. Today this factory processes half of Nicaragua's total annual crop.

Compañia Locorera de Nicaragua (CLN) is the distilling arm of the San Antonio operation, which traces its origins back to 1937 when it started producing *aguardiente* for the locals and industrial ethanol for export (though the two were probably indistinguishable from one another). These days they also make the multi-award-winning Flor de Caña rum. This strange marriage of ethanol plant and super-premium rum is certainly not unique to Nicaragua; in fact it's a consistent theme among most of the Latin American rum producers.

Flor de Caña, meaning "Cane Flower", blossomed into existence after an extensive distillery upgrade that took place in 1996. This led to CLN being the first distillery in the world to be awarded ISO-9001 certification, for quality standards. For such a poverty stricken country, CLN is quite the modern distillery and not short of some energy saving innovations.

Molasses arrives by tanker from the Ingenio San Antonio sugar mill, and is then cut with water to the correct sweetness before fermentation. During the 36 hour fermentation, excess carbon-dioxide from the fermentation tanks is routed through pipes and collected, before being sold on to the Coca-Cola bottling plant. The distillery features a five-column still set up, which is powered by steam generated through the burning of *bagasse* from the San Antonio mill.

One major point of difference between CLN and most other producers is that each of their expressions is distilled to a different specification (using a different combination of columns). This means that both

7-YEAR-OLD (40% ABV) AGED RUM

Rounded and woody on the nose, with soft nougat, toffee sauce, and white chocolate. The taste features solid wood structure, which gives this rum grip and intensity. While there's little in the way of cane character, it's still one of the best tasting 7-year-old rums on the market.

12-YEAR-OLD (40% ABV)
EXTRA-AGED RUM

The aroma is surprisingly light: grassy, woodsy, and leather, drifting into juniper territory… almost. Taste is equally obscure, with dried mint and ash combining to make a curiously fungal-tasting rum. The linger delivers some citric and softer wood characteristics.

18-YEAR-OLD (40% ABV)
EXTRA-AGED RUM

Despite being fully fledged, this rum retains youthful qualities. There's fresh cream, citrus peels, and a touch of rose water to match the pumpkin pie, and dried stone fruits. The taste is creamy and brimming with oak character, but not overpowering. Finish is long and sultry.

during distillation, and during the cask-filling stage, it's already known to the master blender Pedro Uriarte which bottle the newly-made white rum will end up in. There's little in the way of confusing blending systems going on here, either. There is, however, some confusion when it comes to the age of these rums. Each expression is designated by a number (7, 12, 18, 22) but these numbers are not age statements, or at least not anymore after the word "annos" was dropped from the label a few years ago.

Flor de Caña describe their process as "slow ageing", which sounds beyond the realms of physics to me, but what I think they're getting at is that there's no "cheating" involved. Certainly they can be commended for their restrained use of sugar, and on the whole these are tasty Spanish-style rums.

RIGHT Flor de Caña rums are entirely column-distilled, which means almost all of the flavour comes from the barrel. Fortunately, the cellar masters Compañia Locker de Nicaragua seem to know what they are doing, as Flor de Caña 7 is a cracking rum for the price.

PANAMA

E ver since Panama was first colonized in the early 16th century, this thin strip of land that holds the Americas together has relied on one major advantage – its geography. Exploitation of this advantage began soon after the Spanish arrived, when the conquistadors used Panama to transport gold and silver from Peru to Spain. As the New World frontiers met for the first time, this gateway between the Pacific and Atlantic oceans happily profited from the international trade that passed through its shores.

Now commodity prices rise and fall, but geography does not shift. By the mid-17th century, Panama City was the most highly populated and wealthiest city in the western hemisphere. That's why, in 1671, Captain Henry Morgan (of Captain Morgan fame – see page 191) besieged the city with a force of 1,200 cut-throats, deserters, criminals, runaway slaves and traitorous Spanish. Despite being massively outnumbered, the Spanish garrison fled, and Panama City burned for two straight weeks. It was one of the most implausible military victories ever fought, and along with the rum that carries his name, it cemented Henry Morgan's place in history for all time.

Agriculture simply didn't feature in Panama until the turn of the 20th century. The country's first sugar mill (Varela Hermanos – see right) opened in 1908, just after the formation of the Republic of Panama, and just prior to the completion of the Panama Canal in 1914. The Great Depression of the 1930s shrank international trade, causing unemployment and the establishment of subsistence farming. History repeated itself following World War II, and this paved the way for more industrial farming practices. In the 21st century, sugar is Panama's second most valuable crop after bananas, though nowadays the country generates as much export revenue from rum as it does sugar.

We find the cane fields in Panama's southern peninsula, crossing state lines between Herrera, Cocle, and southern Veraguas. The region is a geographical carbon-copy of some of the best cane-growing islands of the Caribbean, with its nutrient-rich, volcanic soil, which is sufficiently watered by a network of mountain streams, percolating their way down into the valleys.

There are three active distilleries in Panama today. There are also other liquids that claim Panamanian origin, such as Melecon and La Cruz, which are bottled by that the most Panamanian-sounding of producers: The Caribbean Spirits Company. Among the "real" distilleries we find Cichisa, which produced the Carta Vieja brand, described to me once as "The stuff the drunks drink", along with the more respectable Las Cabras (see below) and Varela Hermanos distilleries (see right).

LAS CABRAS

The Las Cabras distillery is less the story of a distillery, and more the story of a man. That man is Franciso Jose "Don Pancho" Fernandez Perez – The Godfather of Latin American rum.

Don Pancho is a Cuban national who was trained by the Cuban Ron Maestro, Don Ramon Fernandez Corales. He worked as the master blender (before the title existed) for Havana Club for some 35 years and was the Director of the Cuban Beverage Industry in the mid-1970s, assisting in training master blenders in distilleries around the world. He's also a trained

LEFT A central spine of mountains and hills forms Panama's continental divide. It's south of these mountains, where all of the sugarcane is grown.

biochemist and microbiologist, and now moving into his sixth decade of rum making he is considered by many as the greatest living distiller of classic Cuba-style rum.

It was in the mid-1990s that Don Pancho moved to Panama, originally enlisted as the master blender for Varela Hermanos (see right). During his time there, he came across an old sugar mill in the Las Cabras region, just south east of Pesé, among Herrera's dense ocean of sugarcane. The mill had been established in the early-1900s but fell into neglect. Amazingly, the copper column still remained in place, bearing a plaque with the words "American Copper & Brass Works". Originally built in Cincinnati, Ohio, in 1922, this four-column still has now been lovingly restored back to production capability and is today used to make all the Las Cabras rums.

In the early days of La Cabras, Don Pancho was making un-aged *aguardiente*, which eventually developed into a release of Carta Blanca bottlings and then on to a healthy cache of aged stocks. From that point, he became a bit of a "Yoda" figure. Budding distillers and brand-owners would travel to Panama to visit Don Pancho, who would educate in matters of rum and assist in liquid development.

Among the brands that he continues to produce for, are Cana Brava (for the New York-based "The 86 Co") and Selvarey rum, who are based in Los Angeles. Don Pancho also developed the early bottlings of Ron de Jeremy (named after the renowned adult movie actor who is almost as legendary as Don Pancho himself). Ron de Jeremy is now a blend of other Caribbean rums.

The distillery uses proprietary yeast, extracted from pineapples, and developed by – who else – but Don Pancho himself. Molasses is sourced from one of the local mills. After distillation, the spirit is 92–94% ABV, and this is cut down to mid-70s for ageing in ex-bourbon casks filled at 75% alcohol by volume.

More recently Don Pancho has released a range of his own rums that bare the Don Pancho name. Known as "Origines", these rums are designed to replicate the old Cuban style that was familiar to Don Pancho as a young man. They are available in 8-, 18- and 30-year-old expressions, though it's not entirely clear to me where the oldest member of this line-up was distilled, as it certainly pre-dates the renovation of Las Cabras.

CAÑA BRAVA 3-YEAR-OLD (40% ABV)
AGED WHITE RUM

Nose begins dry, with a hint of cocoa powder, a touch of matcha tea, and dried apple. Taste has some body to it, with barrel character pairing nicely with greener elements. Finish is slightly medicinal, with lime and ground ginger.

CAÑA BRAVA RESERVA (40% ABV) AGED RUM

Chocolate is full-frontal, accompanied by a White Russian cocktail, pear (poached in red wine), and richer wood notes. Texture is thicker, and the taste is more polished, with coffee, date, and pistachio coming through. Finish is dry, so not at all cloying, lingering with tobacco.

ORIGENES RESERVA ESPECIAL DON PANCHO 18-YEAR-OLD
EXTRA-AGED RUM

The nose on this rum is Cuban in style – tobacco leaf, blackcurrant leaf, apple pie and nutty wood notes. Taste moves away from fruit and into deep resin notes of wood spice and cigar. Finish is vanilla and bitter cake mix.

VARELA HERMANOS

The town of Pesé, in Herrera, is an island surrounded by a sea of sugarcane. Crowds flock to Pesé once a year, to watch a reenactment of the crucifixion of Christ. But pilgrimages to Pesé are also made on account of it being home to the nation's favourite drink – Seco Herrerano. Produced by Varela Hermanos, this company has a somewhat legendary history in the area. Firstly, for the construction of Ingenio San Isidro, in 1908, which was the Republic's first sugar mill. But also because the mill's founder, Don José Varela Blanco, also established the town of Pesé itself.

Don José had nine children, and in 1936 his oldest sons, José Manuel, Plinio and Julio, asked their father if they could build a distillery and make spirits from sugarcane juice. Don José agreed, and the following year an extension to the refinery was built, and the family began making their first cane juice spirit. The company was renamed Varela Hermanos (Varela Brothers) after Don José's death, and built a modern distillery on the

AÑEJO (40% ABV) AGED RUM

A green-smelling rum, with cut pine, gentle herbals, and a cool, almost cucumber-like, freshness to it. The taste is pleasant, beginning as a simple nutty little number before developing the aforementioned herbal note into something minty, sappy and slightly spiced.

AÑEJO 12 AÑOS (40% ABV)
EXTRA-AGED RUM

There is undoubtedly some portion of old rum in this bottle as the aroma is all dusty books, old tea chests, and blackberry jam your grandmother made half a century ago. The taste is much lighter than that ancient smell suggests, however, with washed-out dried fruits and diluted golden (light corn) syrup making things seem altogether a little bit thin. Linger revises some of that fruit found on the nose, but now it's rotten and actually far more interesting!

AÑEJO XV AÑOS – TAWNY PORT CASK FINISH (40% ABV) EXTRA-AGED RUM

The influence of port is immediately apparent on the nose, which has aromas of strawberry yogurt, plum jam and dried figs. The taste is bright and slightly sweet, but with depth and complexity that flits between old cellar, ancient wood and sweet berry compote.

site of the old one in 1976, named "Distillería Don José". Varela Hermanos has now passed into the third generation of family ownership.

In Panama, Varela Hermanos is still most famous for its "Seco Herrerano", which is basically the national drink, accounting for almost 90% of the Panamanian spirits consumed on home soil. Seco is made from a wash of fermented sugarcane juice, which is distilled to near neutral and flavoured with mystery ingredients, and sweetened before bottling at 35% ABV. The spirit is generally mixed with fruit juice or coke, but also with milk, when it is known as "seco con vaca" (rather you than me). Seco Herrarano is exported all over the world, but outside of Panama this distillery is far better known for Ron Abuelo (meaning "Grandfather's Rum") and Cortez (named after the infamous conquistador, Ramon Cortez), which are both legally classifiable as rums.

The harvest season in Panama runs from January to May, during which time Varela Hermanos employ 500 individuals who cut a total of 50,000 tons (55,000 US tons) of sugarcane across an estate of 800 hectares (2,000 acres). Cortez rums are made from molasses, whereas Ron Abuelo uses cane honey as its starting point, but both products undergo the same rum-making process. The base material is fermented using a proprietary yeast strain before being sent for distillation where the spirit passes thorough an analyzing (beer-stripping) column, then a rectifying column, followed by the hydroselection column, and finishing neatly with the demethylizing column. The resulting distillate is (unsurprisingly) all-but neutral in quality.

The rums are matured in ex-bourbon casks, and bottled in 7-, 12- and 15-year-old (XV) expressions, where the latter are available in tawny port, Cognac, and oloroso cask flavoured finishes. With evaporative losses at around 10% per year in Panama, you can expect a cask of rum to have misplaced three-quarters of its original contents after 15 years' maturation. That is of course if you're willing to believe the stated minimum age of the rum. If, like me, you're sceptical, Abuelo also bottle a non-age statement entry-level option known simply as "Anejo" – ignorance is bliss.

VENEZUELA

Sugar was once Venezuela's chief export, but the discovery of oil in 1922 meant that by the 1960s, this country that borders Guyana to the east and has the Caribbean to its north, was one of the wealthiest nations in the world. How times have changed. Despite having the largest proven oil reserve in the world, an almost complete dependance on oil coupled with a drop in global oil prices, has decimated the economy here. The socialist government's response is to print more money, and the Venezuelan bolívar has subsequently devalued. At the start of 2013, $1 would have bought you around 20 Venezuelan bolívar. At the start of 2016, the same $1 would buy you over 1,000 Venezuelan bolívar. Planning a trip to Venezuela? Better take a spare suitcase with you, as the highest denomination banknote in Venezuela is 100 bolívar (roughly 40 p/50 cents). In the past, an unstable Venezuelan economy has been to the benefit of local rum industries, as locals switch to rum and *aguardiente* over imported products. Just 25 years ago, Venezuela was the biggest importer of Johnnie Walker Black Label in the world, but now that nobody can afford imported whisky, native spirits are on the up. But the current crisis has sent the cost of energy soaring, and is so severe that it has a knock-on effect that percolates down through virtually all industries.

The Santa Teressa distillery temporarily stopped production of their popular Rhum Orange liqueur early in 2014, because of a shortage of glass bottles after Chávez ordered a seizure of US-owned glass-making plants in 2010. Imported goods that distilleries rely on are scarce too, with everything from cardboard boxes to ink and bottle closures being rationed. But the Venezuelan rum industry faces a far worse threat still – a lack of raw material. In 2014 Santa Teresa distillery suspended distillation for two months due to a shortage of sugarcane from the Aragua valley. This fertile valley once produced 1 million tons (1.1 million US tons) of cane a year and provided Venezuela with as much as two-thirds of its annual sugar requirements. But the land seizures of 2007 instigated by Chávez as a means of diversifying into vegetable and corn crops, means that Venezuela now imports most of its sugar,

and the Aragua Valley grows less than 20% of the sugar it did a decade ago. Couple that with the prohibitively high cost of fertilizers and rising price controls on sugar, and you're left with very little incentive to grow cane in the current climate. Many sugar mills have simply shut up shop in 2016, and fields have sat unharvested.

It's testament to the quality of the rum made in this country that Venezuela's rum industry continues to survive amidst the political and economic upheaval. Some ten years ago, the country's rum makers launched a campaign for the designation of origin "Rum of Venezuela". Now all Venezuelan rum must be aged for a minimum of two years – which, along with Cuba, is longest minimum ageing of any rum-producing country.

Venezuelan rum style is difficult to put a finger on. Like neighbouring Guyana, sugar and distillation has a longer history here than in most of Central and South America. Venezuelans have shown a reluctance to let go of the pot still entirely, choosing instead to blend with column distillates, and throw in a hefty whack of barrel influence to boot. There's heavy sugaring, "solera" systems, old stills, new stills, and a good measure of history too. In many ways Venezuela is representative of the entire rum category – worts and all.

LEFT Economic unrest masks the beauty of this country. At almost 1,000-metres (3,300-ft) tall, Angel Falls in southeast Venezuela is the highest uninterrupted waterfall in the world.

DESTILERIAS UNIDAS

Destilerias Unidas S.A. (DUSA) is probably best known for the Diplomático rum brand, although this Venezuelan distillery also produces the Cacicque and Pampero brands on behalf of spirits giant Diageo. Being of Latin American origin, you might expect these rums to be fashioned from high-strength column-still spirits, light, pure and almost completely characterless. And you would be wrong. It's unusual to find one pot still in a Spanish-speaking distillery, let alone two, plus a range of column stills and a one-of-a kind "batch still" that looks like it was pilfered from a steam locomotive. Were it not for DDL in neighbouring Guyana, DUSA would stand a good chance as being the most versatile and quirky rum distillery across South and Central America. But while this facility specializes in rum, it also processes cereals and rice for the production of local white spirits, and even has a seperate gin distillery – and it's those additional elements that make this one of the most capable distilleries in the western hemisphere.

DUSA was established in 1959 and known at the time as LUSA (Licoreas Unidas S.A.). It was formed from an amalgamation of various previously existing Venezuelan distillery operations, but with Seagram's as the main shareholder, which at that time was one of the biggest spirits companies in the world. The location that was chosen was in the plains northeast of the Andes mountains, outside the town of La Miel and just over 1,000 km (620 miles) north of the equator. Seagram's main interest was in the production of the Cacique rum brand, which is still produced at DUSA under a contractual agreement with Diageo. The distillery was sold in 2002, entering a new era of 100% Venezuelan ownership for the first time in its history. The first dictum of the Ballesteros family was to launch the premium Diplomatico rum brand into the international market.

Set over 12 hectares (30 acres), this is one of the largest distilleries in South America. The distillery makes rum from both molasses and cane honey, the latter being used for the heavy rum recipes. There are 18 epic steel fermentation tanks here, each of them like an enormous baked bean can. The distillery's proprietary yeast is first propagated through a series of tanks before being mixed with 100,000 litres (26,500 US gallons) of diluted molasses (or cane honey) at 18° Brix. The fermentation then takes 24–28 hours to complete for molasses rums and up to 48 hours for

cane syrup rum, which allows enough time for additional esterification.

The distillation process is complex here, resulting in numerous different marques (or weights of rum). Most rums begin their journey through a single copper column "stripping" still with six plates. Light rums (molasses-based) are drawn off at around 55% ABV and sent to on to a pair of stainless-steel column stills, producing a spirit of over 96% ABV. Those destined to become heavy rums are stripped to just 45% then undergo an altogether different ordeal, where they are sent to one of two copper pot stills, each with two linked retorts. The retorts are loaded with low and high wines from the previous distillation run, and spirit is drawn off the still at about 81% ABV – still possessing much of the fermentation character that will carry through to the blend. The distillery also makes a "semi-heavy" rum, which is molasses-based, and undergoes a second distillation in a 40,000-litre (10,500-US gallon) copper cylinder. This piece is quite unique, appearing to be little more than a very large boiler, but producing distillates of over 90% ABV. Sometimes, the stripping still is removed out of the equation, and the fermented *mosto* is sent directly to the column, batch, or pot still, for immediate distillation, resutling in yet another range of differently weighted rums.

The resulting spirits are all matured separately in one of the 20-or-so warehouses on the site, containing around 400,000 barrels of rum. Most of the casks are ex-bourbon, but there are sherry butts there too and experiments with further wine casks. Most of the Diplomatico expressions are a blend of light, heavy and semi-heavy rums, but the 'Vintage' is a mix of only "batch-still" and pot-still rum, while the Ambassador is 100% pot-still.

Diplomatico's super-premium expressions are among the sweetest rums available to buy. I have mixed feelings about this. While sweetness is part of this particular style of rum – and Diplomatico are quite honest about the sweetening of their rums – this is not something that is mentioned on the bottle and probably not something that most people who buy the rum are wise to either.

If sweet rums do it for you, you'll probably like Diplomatic Reserva Exclusiva, which is sweetened with the same degree of enthusiasm that you might

RIGHT The equipment at DUSA is impressive. The angle of the lyne arms connecting the stills to the retorts (below) has led some to compare it to the Loch Ness Monster!

DIPLOMÁTICO PLANAS (47% ABV)
AGED WHITE RUM

Dried blackcurrant, light herbals and coconut water. Taste is surprisingly soft – gently fragrant and rich with spice.

DIPLOMÁTICO MANTUANO (40% ABV)
AGED BLENDED RUM

Light and bright with treacle, almond and refried beans. Reasonably dry on the palate. Hot and creamy, with just a fleeting suggestion of dried fruits.

DIPLOMÁTICO VINTAGE 2001 (43% ABV)
EXTRA-AGED BLENDED RUM

Dried peach skins, juicy plums and fried banana. Sweet, which accentuates leathery soft fruits, apricot brandy and Battenberg cake. Spice does its best to creep in through the finish but sugar beats it back.

DIPLOMÁTICO AMBASSADOR (40% ABV)
EXTRA-AGED POT-STILL RUM

Heady blackcurrant, blackberry and pipe tobacco. Cacao and coffee are present too. A great balance of aroma. Autumn fruit cordial, fruit nectar and some tropical fruits, but it's ripe berries that steal the show. Sweet.

PAMPERO AÑEJO ESPECIAL (40% ABV)
EXTRA-AGED BLENDED RUM

Aroma starts (and continues) with hard toffee and banoffee pie topped with aerosol cream. Quite a one-dimensional rum. Palate is silky to the touch, sweet and glossy. Buttered popcorn and caramel take away the finish.

PAMPERO ANNIVERSARIO (40% ABV)
EXTRA-AGED BLENDED RUM

Potato peelings and big oxidized sherry notes. Then comes the darkness: molasses, Garibaldi biscuits (cookies) and dank cellars. But always that savoury potato edge.

encounter from an overweight French pâtissière – better get your dentist on speed dial...

Cacique is still the highest volume rum product made here, and competes only with Santa Teresa for the nation's top spot. Today, the brand is owned by Diageo and produced by DUSA under contractual agreement. DUSA also makes the "heavy rum" component of another brand, Pampero, which is blended with other column-still spirits to make finished rums. The Pampero range offers something slightly different, where the aroma is highly suggestive of saccharine things, but in the taste we discover it has been toned back. The brand was founded in 1938 by a the Margaritan fisherman Alejandro Hernandez. The packaging seems to suggest a kind of wild-west or cowboy theme, and indeed the seal bears an icon of a horse and cowboy, taken from the Argentinian "Pampas" plains. Special mention must got to Pampero Anniversario, which is dark as hell and comes in a squat little cannonball of a bottle slipped into a tan-coloured suede pouch – perfect for long days on horseback roaming the Los Llanos.

SANTA TERESA

The Santa Teresa distillery is located about an hour south west of Caracas in the state of Aragua. It's run by the fifth generation of the Vollmer family, whose history stretches back to its founder, Gustavo Julio Vollmer y Rivas, the son of German-born Gustav Julius Vollmer and Francisca Ribas, a cousin of Simón Bolívar – "El Liberator". Santa Teresa was Venezuela's first registered distillery, and the fourth business of any kind to be registered there. It was within the walls of the Santa Teresa plantation that Bolívar ratified the abolition of slavery in 1818.

But in the early 2000s, this distillery was suffering from crushing debt and at great risk of bankruptcy. Fortunately a young Alberto Vollmer intervened and restructured the entire business, stripping away redundant product lines and cutting costs. The turnaround has been dramatic and Santa Teresa is today recognized as one of the great names in Latin American rum.

Vollmer is some what of a socialist progressive. He has appeared on television with Hugo Chávez and is the brains behind Project Alcatraz – a social scheme that gets troubled youths into playing rugby as a means of getting them off the street and into productive society. The project came about in 2004 after a gang member was caught violently beating a member of the Santa Teresa security staff who had been marked for death. Vollmer gave him an option: work for 3 months unpaid, or let the police deal with you. The youth chose work, which he enjoyed, and which attracted the attention of other disadvantaged youngsters in the area. Soon, Vollmer was employing dozens of gang members from rival factions.

CLARO (40% ABV) AGED WHITE RUM

Pungent on the nose. Pickled walnut and fermented vegetables dissipate into sweeter realms: lemon bon bon and cocoa. There's also a suggestion (as with the colour) of soft caramel. Texture is solid on the mid-palate, with a lick of nutmeg and bubblegum that plays nicely with a lingering memory of oak.

AÑEJO (40% ABV) AGED RUM

More nutmeg, as with the Claro, which this time pairs with a creaminess that hints at pumpkin pie. To accompany that, there's ground ginger, cinnamon, and fenugreek at work here too. On the palate, the integration is less precise than the Claro.

LINAJE (40% ABV) AGED RUM

Begins in s similar vein to the Añejo. Whipped cream, vanilla fudge and more of that pervasive nutmeg warmth. In time, a treacle aroma appears, then disappears, replaced by anise and alcohol heat. Taste is sweet and full, taking on some soft tobacco characteristics, honey and supple wood. A longer linger with pleasant butter and cocoa bitterness.

1796 (40% ABV) EXTRA-AGED BLENDED RUM

A different beast entirely. Sweaty sultana (golden raisin), tobacco pipe and brass polish. There's depth that can only be awarded by time, but there is an elegant lightness to it. A full texture on the palate, but not too sweet: more tobacco, melting brown sugar and butter, some florals – jasmine-scented shortbread. The finish is slightly orangey, and there's more dried fruits to boot.

RIGHT 1796 bears almost no resemblance to the rest of the Santa Teresa pack, and if you ask me, that's more to do with the use of pot stills than it is complex maturation systems.

Rugby was introduced as a means of instilling discipline and venting anger. Alcatraz is now recognized by the World Bank and has been the subject of a Harvard University paper.

The distillery has operated column stills since 1905 at which point there was still a sugar refinery on site. Sugar production was relocated in the 1950s, however, (and remains under control of another Vollmer family member) and the column was upgraded in the 1940s and then again in 1979. It's a four-column system capable of producing 80,000 litres (21,000 US gallons) a day, that produces two marques of alcohol: a 75% ABV heavy rum from just the first column; and a 95% light rum from all four columns. Both rums follow from a lightning-fast 14-hour continuous fermentation process that is achievable through the use of yeast propagators and the slow feed-in of molasses. The spirits are cut to 60% and matured separately for a minimum of two years. Santa Teresa have 18 warehouses, holding a total of 100,000 casks of rum.

The core expression of the brand are Santa Teresa "Claro" and "Gran Reserva", aged for 2–3 years and 2–5 years respectively. The distillery has recently launched an extra-añejo rum under the name "Linaje" (lineage) which is matured for 4–14 years in American oak barrels.

In 1988 Santa Teresa reinstated a pot still. It's a modern example, steam-jacketed, and 1,800 litres (475 US gallons) in size. It's used to produce rum for Santa Teresa's flagship "1796" bottling – the product of a special "solera warehouse" that features 540 Limousin oak barrels that have not been emptied since 1992 when the system was instated. The rum for bottling is drawn from only one section of the warehouse, but the barrels in this section are never emptied beyond half-full. Those barrels are in-turn topped up from another section of casks, and so on. Barrels from the last section are topped up with a blend of 4–34 year old rums from a mixture of light, heavy and pot-still aged stocks.

BLENDERS AND BOTTLERS

Without the blenders of this world, it's quite likely that all of us would all still be driving along worn distillery paths, returning with a jerry can full of white rum hanging from each arm. From the 19th century onwards, the blenders formed the missing link between wholesale product and marketable brand, transforming rum from industrial oddity to trustworthy liquor. Although the greater part of this book is concerned with the famed rum distilleries of the New World, these places would never have evolved into what they are today were it not for the hard graft of the blenders.

Virtually all of the distilleries in this book conduct some sort of in-house blending (different ages of rum, or different distillation marques), but the rums in this section are concerned with blended spirits from multiple distilleries and multiple countries of origin. Rum has always been an international spirit, and blending is a celebration of that. Blended rums are some of the oldest-surviving and best-selling spirit brands in the world. A good blend is a mark of dependence; a familiar friend in a sea of obscurity.

Also deserving of our attentions are the independent bottlers. On the face of it, it's strange that a distillery wouldn't wish to bottle rum under their own label. But some operations specialize in selling rum to third parties, and others are just happy to sell rum by any means possible – be it by the bottle, barrel or shipping container. In some instances, a distillery might have gone silent (closed down) in which case there is nobody or no brand to bottle the product. But where there are casks left lying around, it stands to reason that somebody will be happy to pay for them. Independent bottling of rum is not as commonplace yet as it is with whisky, but there is a growing market for it. And as we shall see in the pages that follow, some of the best rums on the planet are sold this way.

BANKS

Banks is named after Sir Joseph Banks, the explorer and botanist who sailed alongside Captain Cook, and who backed a certain William Bligh as the governor of New South Wales – an appointment that ultimately led to the Rum Rebellion of 1808. Banks wasn't a rum blender, or distiller, but it's certain that he would have enjoyed a tot or two during his time at sea.

The brand was founded in 2010 by Arnaud de Trabuc and R. John Pellaton, and is blended by E&A Scheer (see pages 192–93) in Amsterdam. Trabuc and Pellaton have certainly got their money's worth out of the Dutch blending powerhouse: the core expression contains spirit from Jamaica, Trinidad, Guyana and Barbados, as well as Batavia Arrack from Java – a type of Indonesian cane spirit that is traditionally used in the punches of old.

Taking liquids from such a broad range of sources could quite easily result in a complete mess, but this is top-drawer sipping spirit, and a liquid that flags up all sorts of opportunities as a mixing spirit. Don't be fooled by the numbers on the bottle: these are not age statements but a reference to the number of islands and territories that feature in the bottle. In Banks 5, there are chewy pot-still esters, just as there are vegetal *agricole* notes. Banks 7 ups the ante even further, with the addition of rums sourced from Panama and Guatemala. The Central American influence cuts through some of that youthful bad temper and carries with it a range of confected qualities.

BANKS "5" ISLAND (43% ABV)
AGED WHITE BLENDED RUM

Banana, treacle, airfix glue, toffee sauce and a touch of leather. Taste is lithe, juicy and pithy. Earthy and fresh through the finish.

BANKS "7" GOLDEN AGE (43% ABV)
AGED BLENDED RUM

Buttery vanilla fudge, banana bread and chocolate milkshake. Mace and pimento cake on the palate, bitter banana peels and fruitcake.

CAPTAIN MORGAN

The Captain Morgan brand was launched by Seagram's in 1944 and now sells over 10 million 9-litre (2.4-US gallon) cases of rum a year, which makes it the second biggest international rum brand after Bacardi. The story of this brand is an interesting one, in respect of the big business approach to production, as well as the tale of Sir Henry Morgan himself, who was once a real person. Every bottle of Captain Morgan has a grinning illustration of the "The Captain" on the label, but few people are aware that the real life "Captain" was one of the most ruthless and unprincipled villains of his age, with a lifetime of deeds far darker than the colour of his namesake rum.

Morgan was born in south Wales in 1635, the son of a relatively wealthy farmer. He had no inclination to follow in his father's muddy footsteps however, so instead followed the lead of his uncles, who were both distinguished military men. Some accounts suggest that Morgan was captured and shipped off to the Caribbean as a white indentured servant, which was arguably an even worse existence than that of the black African slave, who were considered more valuable. Other accounts state that he willingly joined the Royal Navy as a junior officer. Either way, that's where he ended up, and at the age of 19, he found himself in the Caribbean fighting alongside Admiral Penn when the English captured Jamaica from the Spanish in 1655.

Morgan settled in Jamaica for around five years, during which time he became hardened by the cruelty of existence in the nascent colony. At some point Morgan was recruited by a pirate crew, which turned out to be a profession that he was rather good at. After a few years, Morgan and a few of his new associates pooled their resources and bought a ship, and Morgan was nominated as Captain.

Pirating was a little like the Mafia in those days, and the head of the organization was the Dutchman Edward Mansvelt. He controlled hundreds of pirate ships, and made Morgan the "vice-admiral" of his fleet. These two plundered many Spanish colonies in the years that followed, setting up island bases off the South American coast, but always returning to Jamaica to divide up the booty.

As Morgan's success and notoriety grew, so too did the size of the fleet he commanded, which at times totalled up to 37 ships. As grand as that may sound, the brutality of encounters with the Captain garnered him a

St HEN MORGAN

ABOVE Henry Morgan was made a baronet in 1674 by King Charles II – quite a change in the pirate's fortunes considering that the King had ordered his arrest two years earlier.

reputation as one of the most barbarous individuals of the time. During sieges, he used nuns and priests as human shields, correctly predicting that the Spanish would be too pious to fire arrows at holy men and women. After successfully taking the fort town of Portobello on Panama's coast, Morgan personally knocked on doors, forcing the town's residents to provide information that would lead to the discovery of hidden gold caches. Those who resisted were tortured in various cruel and creative ways: men were strung up by their testicles while their wives were raped. Others had burning twigs tied between their fingers, or were stretched by their thumbs and toes until something gave way.

Morgan's most legendary feat occurred in 1671, during the sacking of Panama. At that time, Panama was the second-largest city in the new world, and a key New Spain trading route for Spanish conquistadors, as well as being home to a thriving mercantile community. Morgan knew this, and in January of that year landed at San Lorenzo with an "army" of 1,200 men. They marched overland to Panama City, and despite the larger numbers and fortifications of the Spanish defenders, they were terrified of Morgan and abandoned their defences. The city burned for four straight weeks.

The sacking of Panama stands today as one of the most extraordinary military campaigns ever fought.

After Panama, Henry Morgan returned to a Jamaica much changed from the one he had left. In the Treaty of Madrid, signed in 1670, England had agreed to suppress piracy in return for Spanish recognition of its sovereignty in Jamaica. In 1672, Morgan was transported back to England to be tried for piracy, but he was received more as a romantic hero than as a vicious criminal. Relations with Spain deteriorated once again, and in 1674, he was made a baronet. Later that year, he returned to Jamaica as Lieutenant Governor Sir Henry Morgan, even serving as acting governor from 1680 to 1682. He died in 1688 – rich, respectable, morbidly obese and an enduring contradiction to the adage that crime does not pay.

You might be wondering by this point why anybody would feel compelled to base a rum brand around this man. But it has to be said that Morgan's crooked past has done little to damage the success of the brand. In the eyes of many people, high-strength alcohol has always walked a fine line between social lubricant and moral contaminant. Perhaps "the Captain" represents that better than most. Still, it's quite amusing that Diageo, which has been the brand owner since 2001, currently use the tagline "Live like the Captain" to promote

the brand. But I suppose it's an improvement over the altogether more sinister-sounding "Everybody's Got a Little Captain in Them!", which was retired in 2014.

The production specifics of Captain Morgan are vague to say the least. We know that Jamaica's Clarendon distillery (see pages 126–26) produces a lot of rum for the international version of the blend, and that Diageo's Virgin Island operation does the same for the US version. It's possible that the story ends there, but there are rumours that wholesale rum shipments occasionally arrive at these distilleries too, so who's to say that Diageo aren't blending in other rums?

E&A SCHEER

If you fancy yourself as a bit of a rum blender, you're going to need more than just a finely-tuned palate and a love of cane spirits to build a brand. A good list of distillery contacts, warehouse space, logistical expertise and some skills in commercial negotiation are all essential. Not to mention bottling and packaging equipment and storage for all this stuff. You cannot simply walk up to the door of a few Caribbean distilleries and expect to walk out with your own blended bottle. And that's just what you need to get you started. What about when certain rums run out? How do you go about adapting the blend?

The long and short of this is that you can't do it on your own, and the truth is that very few blenders do. Help is at hand however, in the form of the Amsterdam-based rum broker and blender E&A Scheer.

Even though you'll struggle to find their name on any bottle of rum, this book would be incomplete without a mention of this blending powerhouse. They are one of the most important gears in the global rum engine and for the superstitious readers among you, this is the rum world's "man behind the curtain". Indeed, E&A Scheer would prefer to remain unknown, as their business is in the supply and building of other people's brands, not their own. And they supply a lot of brands. Exactly how many is a bit of a mystery, but I think it's fair to assume that the majority of the blended rums out there pass through the doors of E&A Scheer.

In fact, some would say that this company is so deeply entrenched in the rum category, that establishing a blended rum brand of any worth without their assistance would likely prove a cripplingly difficult endeavour – if not impossible.

The "E" and "A" of the company name are the initials of Evert and Anthonie Scheer, Dutch brothers who formed a trading company in the Amsterdam in the middle of the 18th century. Originally intended as a general purpose trading company, by the 19th century, the company had sensibly narrowed its focus to the trading and blending of rums and Batavia Arrack (an Indonesian cane-based spirit). They were doing well enough at that to propel their company forward in the rum business for the next 250 years.

These days, E&A Scheer employ 18 people from their Amsterdam-based offices, and buy rum from 20 different countries. As individual batches of rum arrive in Amsterdam, they're nosed and blended down into a couple of dozen "intermediate" blends and stored in neutral containers so that no further maturation can occur. These blends are described with names known only to the blenders and form the building blocks of the multitude of finished products that E&A Scheer produce. From 200 litres (53 US gallons) to 25,000 litres (6,600 US gallons), E&A Scheer will tailor your blend to your specific tastes, budget and regional preferences.

E&A Scheer also owns the Main Rum Company, located in Liverpool in the UK. The Amsterdam office focuses on younger rums and blending; the Main Rum Company focuses on older, vintage rums, some of which are still in cask and therefore still maturing.

ELEMENTS 8

Elements 8 is a British independent rum blender who source all of their liquids from the St. Lucia Distillers Ltd. The brand was launched in 2006 by Carl Stephenson and Andreas Redlefsen, who both previously worked for J. Wray & Nephew. They partnered with the late Lauri Barnard of St. Lucia Distillers to produce a blend that celebrates eight suggested factors of rum flavour influence: terroir, cane, fermentation, distillation, ageing, blending, filtration and water.

The product has a noticeably dry characteristic, which made it great for mixing with, and by 2008 it had become the go-to premium speed-rail rum for many of the top London bars. Just like Pyrat (see pages 203–04), here was a rum to challenge the clichéd convention of Caribbean rum, through preaching about process and provenance. The product was also packaged in an unusual, box-shaped bottle. Ten years on, and it feels as though Elements 8 has lost some of that initial momentum. The packaging has been refreshed, and while the glassware is a little more sensible than the previous long, boxy bottle, the labelling still leaves a little to be desired in this author's opinion. The liquid on the other hand gives little cause for complaint. That's not surprising given the provenance of the juice, but this is carefully balanced stuff that succeeds at highlighting the various elements of rum-making.

FINE AGED VENDOME (40% ABV)
AGED BLENDED RUM

Pot-still rum gives depth here, from the light heights of orange esters and violet flowers, down to dried apricot, deeper, baking spices and vanilla-flavoured coffee. Milky and well-structured on the palate. Light battles dark, as florals are overrun by fruit-and-nut chocolate and wood resin.

GOSLINGS

Bermuda is not the kind of island that gets stumbled upon by accident. That is, unless you happen to be the Spanish navigator Juan de Bermúdez, who was probably the first human to ever lay eyes on the archipelago, in 1503. This cluster of islands has a total area of just 53.5 square kilometres (21 square miles), but is over 1,000 km (620 miles) from the nearest sensible-sized chunk of land on the east coast of North Carolina. It's also around 1,500 km (930 miles) north of the Caribbean, placing it well above the Tropic of Cancer where it enjoys warm summers and mild winters on account of the warm Gulf Stream currents that emanate from the Caribbean. There's little in the way of arable land on Bermuda, so when coupled with its mild climate, it's altogether a pretty poor place for growing sugarcane. And it's for that reason there's absolutely no history of rum distillation on the island.

Indeed, were it not for William and James Gosling, it's likely that Bermuda would be known only for its long surf-shorts and mysterious triangle. The year was 1806, when the father and son duo set sail from Gravesend in Kent, England. They spent three desperate months attempting to cross the Atlantic, on a voyage bound for Virginia carrying a cargo of wine and spirits worth £10,000 (£1.2 million or $1.5 million today). Tired, dejected and probably quite wet (though not without a stiff drink to raise the spirits), they headed for the nearest port, which was St George's in Bermuda. Any port in a storm, so the saying goes, but St George's must have appeared an especially favourable place, because they scrapped all plans of completing their charter, bought a shop, and William invited his second son, Ambrose, to the island to help them out.

James and Ambrose's grocer's shop was originally on the King's Parade in the island's capital, Hamilton. They traded in all kinds of goods, from textiles to coffee, rice, sugar and of course, rum. As was common for the time, a grocer would produce a proprietary blend of rum, brandy or sherry, from stocks that arrived through the port. The locals would turn up to the store with an empty container and fill it straight from the barrel. Few spirits (and least of all rum) were bottled in glass in the 19th century, since it was too costly to manufacture and ship the bottles. Champagne was one drink for which glass bottling was a pre-requisite, however (due to the requirement of fizz) and as these bottles became more

numerous, many spirit- and liqueur-makers opted to recycle the bottles as packaging for their own premium range of liquids. Getting a supply of empty Champagne bottles was quite easy for the Goslings, thanks to the many officers in the nearby Royal Navy Dockyards, who had a healthy appetite for good French wine.

In the 1860s, the business passed into the hands of Ambrose Gosling's three sons, William, Edmund and Charles, and the name of the company changed to Gosling Brothers. The family marketed their first rum, which was known simply as "Old Rum". Over 150 years later, Old Rum is still available in dark Champagne-style bottles with a thick black wax seal on top.

That wax has a lot to answer for, as it's thanks to that gloopy black seal, which speaks of tarred decks and greased chains, that Gosling Brothers rum was soon referred to as the "Black Seal" rum. It became the most popular brand on the island, to the point where it was said that to be a true Bermudian, a man needed only to do three things: "attend Trinity Church, read the Royal Gazette and buy his rum at Goslings." In the 1960s, the Black Seal became officially part of their branding, when their labels changed to include an image of a black seal juggling a barrel of rum.

It's certain that the constant presence of the Bermuda Garrison (which existed primarily to defend Bermuda's Royal Navy Dockyard) contributed to the success of the rum brand. Military personnel, and particularly those at sea, are known to enjoy a tot of rum, and Goslings served as a taste of the island to servicemen both on the island and back in Britain. The Navy even erected a ginger beer bottling plant on the island so that they had something to mix the rum with.

Gosling Brothers Ltd. is still a family enterprise, currently run by the seventh generation of the Gosling family: Malcolm Gosling Jr., (the great-great-great-grandson of Ambrose Gosling); his sister, Nancy Gosling, who is the CEO; and his cousin, the Right Worshipful Charles Gosling, who is the current mayor of Hamilton.

Goslings Black Seal is a blend of rums from Trinidad, Guyana, Barbados and Jamaica. The distillate arrives at 9 Dundonald St. in Hamilton in stainless-steel tanks, where it is aged and blended according to an old family recipe that quite likely calls for a large measure of caramel colouring to give the rum that rich, inky appearance. The portion destined for the local market stays behind. The rest goes back in the tanks and journeys by sea to Port Elizabeth, New Jersey, and thence by rail to Bardstown, Kentucky, where it is diluted, bottled and cased for shipment around the world.

GOSLINGS BLACK SEAL (40% ABV)
BLACK RUM

Hot fumes of muscovado sugar, tempered by pineapple and tamarind. There's a touch of freshly cut red apple. Overall, it smells intensely sweet. Taste is burnt meringue, butterscotch and banana. Finish is bitter and light, with lingering molasses flavours.

GOSLINGS 151 (75.5% ABV)
NAVY STRENGTH BLACK RUM

Delicious licks of pecan pie, and toffee sauce on the nose. Alcohol arrives with a cool kick of anise. Taste is like a bomb going off – any sense of subtlety has well and truly disappeared – as hot pineapple, black pepper and shiny plastic fruits kick in. The finish is better described as an "aftermath" as you attempt to pick up the pieces of what was once your mouth.

JOHN WATLING'S

While it is widely acknowledged that Columbus's favoured island – or the one he believed most likely to contain gold – was Hispaniola, the first *terra firma* the navigator sighted after 29 days at sea was in fact the Bahamas. The present day archipelago is made up of over 700 individual islands and islets, so as to which one specifically Columbus landed on October 12 1492 is a matter of great debate (though it seems generally accepted that it was the island of San Salvador). Once on shore, he encountered the Lucayan people, a branch of the Arawakan-speaking Taínos, and true to form he enslaved the "sweet and gentle" people, swiftly transporting his cargo onward, to Cuba and Hispaniola.

For over a century, the islands were ignored by the Spanish who deemed them too small to be of any use, and they remained uninhabited until the mid-1600s. But their secluded position and close proximity to wealthy colonies like Sainte-Domingue and Santo Domingo, soon made the Bahamas an ideal hideout for buccaneers and pirates. Meanwhile, a newly established British colony of Charles Town on the island of New Providence, became the target of Spanish corsair raids, culminating in its complete destruction by fire in 1684. It was rebuilt, and given a new name: Nassau.

Nassau didn't fare much better than its predecessor, however, suffering sustained attacks from the combined Franco-Spanish fleet between 1703 and 1706. With the city all-but deserted, pirates quickly took up

BELOW Bottling at Watling – big or small, fast or slow, I always find bottling lines mesmerizing.

some occasions up to eight men "swang off" the same post in Nassau. The recapture of Nassau marked the beginning of the end of the Golden Era of Piracy.

Back to the modern era, and Bacardi opened a distillery here in 1965, but it closed in 2009, leaving a big rum-shaped hole on the islands. Now that's a big hole to fill, but in 2013 it was — to some extent at least — plugged, by the John Watling's distillery, located in the historic Buena Vista Estate in Downtown Nassau.

The use of the word "distillery" is a touch misleading in this case because it is in fact not a distillery at all, but a blending house. John Watling's is named after one of the Bahamas' most notorious privateers of the 17th century. John (or sometimes George) Watling served under Captain Bartholomew Sharp, plundering the east coast of Central America, unsettling Spanish colonial interests through systematic raids along Panama and Honduras and befriending Mosquito Indians (who take their name from the word *miskito*, a reference to their mixed Indian and African blood) even to the point of taking one, who he named "Will", under his wing in a Lone Ranger/Tonto sort of scenario.

Watling and Sharp took down dozens of Spanish ships in their time, amassing a small fortune. When the crew mutinied against Sharp, Watling became the new leader, known by many as the "Pious Pirate" since he observed the Sabbath and forbade gambling. Later on, Watling established his headquarters on San Salvador in the Bahamas, where it was rumoured that he buried a considerable cache of treasure.

Thanks to his famed escapades in the area, the island was nicknamed John Watling's after him. And now, more recently, Watling has a distillery to add to that.

occupancy. And so it was that the "Republic of Pirates" was formed, which, at the height of its power had over 1,000 pirate members, all living in a quasi-democracy under the jurisdiction of their magistrate, Edward Teach (aka Blackbeard). Besides Blackbeard, the "Republic" was dominated by two more famous pirates who were bitter rivals: Benjamin Hornigold and Henry Jennings. Hornigold was Teach's mentor, along with "Black" Sam Bellamy and Stede Bonnet. Jennings was mentor to Charles Vane, "Calico" Jack Rackham, Anne Bonny and Mary Read.

Nassau was the Port Royal for the next generation of pirates, but unlike the Jamaican town, this place was entirely operated by criminals, former sailors, indentured servants and runaway slaves. These were tumultuous times in the Caribbean, but among all the anarchy, Nassau offered freedom for everyone; men and women of colour could be equal citizens, and leaders were chosen or deposed by a vote.

But as their numbers swelled, establishing a fighting force strong enough to take on Royal Navy frigates, the situation as far as the Navy was concerned had become too unstable. In 1718, just five years after the establishment of the Republic, the Navy conducted a strategic eradication of all the pirates in the region, and as many as 600 pirates were killed or captured by British forces in that year. The assault was so efficient that on

AMBER RUM (40% ABV) AGED BLENDED RUM

Aroma plays it safe with vanilla and oak lactones, supplemented by toasted pecan and plum jam. The taste is soft and a little play-it-safe, where butterscotch mousse plays nicely with coconut cream and flaked almonds. Finish is gentle and clean, with cream and caramel.

LAMB'S

Rum blenders plied their trade at an early age in the 19th century. In 1849, Alfred Lamb was just 22-years-old when he set up as a wine merchant and spirits blender. He did have a leg up in to the business, mind you, thanks to his father, William Lamb, who was a respected wine and spirit importer in London. It would be rum with which the Lamb name would become eternally synonymous, though, and Alfred allegedly used a mixed bag of rums from 18 different Caribbean territories, including Barbados, Guyana, Jamaica and Trinidad, to formulate his first Navy blend.

The story continues that Lamb used to store his rums in vaults that sat beneath the River Thames. The cool, cellar environment wasn't subject to seasonal fluctuations in temperature or large fluctuations from day to night, and this is reckoned to be one of the secrets behind the unexpectedly smooth taste of his rum. The only problem with the tale is that Lamb's offices were on Great Tower Street, which is located at least 100 metres (330 ft) from the banks of the Thames and thus was unlikely to have cellars stretching so far.

Alfred was joined by his son, Charles H. Lamb, in 1875 when Charles was just 16, and the company later became known as Alfred Lamb & Sons. Charles blended rum right through his father's death, in 1895, and right up until he retired in the 1920s. On May 11 1941, Alfred Lamb & Son were bombed out of their London premises on Great Tower Street during the Blitz. On the same evening, another rum merchants, E. H. Keeling & Son, who were famous for bottling "Old Demerara Rum", also lost their premises to an air strike. Portal, Dingwall & Norris (yet another rum merchant) took pity on both Lamb and Keeling and allowed them to share their premises at 40 Eastcheap, which was just a block up the road. Five years later, the three companies merged to form United Rum Merchants.

The brand was tossed about during various mergers and acquisitions during the 1980s, and finally ended up in the hands of Corby Spirits in Canada, who still own it today and license the brand to Pernod Ricard UK. Canada and the UK also happen to be the brand's two biggest markets, where it has more or less established itself as the *de facto* Navy Rum offering. In the UK

RIGHT Above all else, blending requires an understanding of how barrels work and how best to utilize them.

especially, there's hardly a pub that doesn't have a dusty hexagonal bottle of Lamb's permanently stuck to a back bar shelf. Lamb's continued to bottle some of their rum at true Navy Strength (57%) right up until the 1970s, and decanters of these have become highly collectable. If you hunt around internet auction sites, you might also encounter 100% Demerara examples too.

The standard "Genuine Navy Rum" blend is today bottled at 40% ABV and still comprises rums from various Caribbean islands. All of the rums used are matured for a minimum of one year, which comes as quite a shock, given the dark colour of the liquid. But like so many of its seafaring brethren, Lamb's brazenly practises the time-honoured tradition of blackening overproof rum into something that looks as though it has been stashed in a oak barrel since before the Navy rum ration was abolished.

If you've a desire for a sweeter style of Lamb in your life, the core expression has more recently been joined by "Lamb's Spiced" (not to be confused with Spiced Lamb – a dish on an Indian restaurant menu) and "Lamb's Spiced Cherry Rum". I wouldn't bother with either.

LEMON HART

Lemon Hart was a Cornish-born man (just like yours truly) of Jewish descent. In 1720, Hart's grandfather, Abraham, arrived in the town of Penzance – a market town with a harbour, and the most westerly town in England. Abraham established himself there as a goldsmith. Things went well for the family, who over the next 50 years, diversified their interests into shipping and the importation of Jamaican rum, becoming one of the most successful family-run businesses in the region. The business passed on to the next generation in the form of Lazarus Hart (Abraham's son) who, through a combination of bad luck and stupidity, managed to sink an expensive ship and rile up the local Customs house, to the point where he was forced to sell the business. Fortunately, things picked back up again, and when he finally died in 1803, he left the floundering business to his only son, Lemon.

151 (75.5% ABV)
AGED BLENDED OVERPROOF RUM

Considering only a small proportion of this liquid isn't alcohol, there's surprising character to the nose. Fruit cake soaked in booze, cinder toffee, and telltale Demerara raisins, and molasses. Alcohol dominates the taste, which is like a mouth full of hot fruit… lingering for some time.

A strange name, perhaps, although "Lemon" is a historic surname in Cornwall. When life gave him lemons, Lemon chose to make money, developing a sideline of ship brokering and ownership in Penzance and accelerating the wine and spirit trade right up to the next level.

The "Lemon Hart" trading company was established in 1804, and in the same year, he began bottling rum under that name too. It wasn't too long before Hart's growing empire became the official supplier of rum to the Royal Navy, and by the time Lemon died in 1845, the company had relocated to the Isle of Dogs in London and were supplying the Royal Navy with 455,000 litres (120,000 US gallons) of rum annually – equivalent to nearly 10% of Jamaica's total export volume for that year.

The brand became incredibly popular in the 1950s, partly thanks to a viral advertising campaign that was illustrated by Ronald Searle. The adverts depicted a slender gentleman dressed in a lemon-coloured suit, knocking back rum in various implausible situations. The tagline was "Have a Good Rum for your Money".

These days Lemon Hart is available in three expressions: Original 1804, Blackpool Spiced Rum, and Lemon Hart 151. All of them are made and mixed at the Diamond Distillery in Guyana (see pages 175–78). The most famous of the three is the 151, which has for a long time been a popular overproof go-to for Tiki enthusiasts.

MATUSALEM

Matusalem enjoyed some success in the early 21st century, at around the time that I first started tending bar. Playing off its Cuban roots, it was seen as a valid

LEFT Looks like a nice day for drinking rum on the beach in a bright yellow suit, wouldn't you say?

challenger to Bacardi in a similar way as Havana Club was. It turned out that the brand had more in common with the former, however, as Matusalem is yet another Cuban rum dynasty that fled the island during Castro's Revolution. Indeed, Matusalem was founded in Santiago de Cuba by the Camps Hermanos (the Camps brothers) just 10 years after Bacardi, in 1872. The trio of brothers had some experience working with sherry and Cognac back in Spain, and they applied the principles of solera ageing to their Ron Matusalem Extra Viejo. The name "Matusalem" is the Spanish word for "Methuselah", the Old Testament patriarch who was said to have lived for more than 900 years.

By the middle of the 20th century, Matusalem was in fierce competition with Bacardi, and the two brands regularly employed aggressive sales tactics to undercut one another. Matusalem would have been far better off spending their time establishing overseas operations (like Bacardi) which might have saved them from becoming the revolutionary collateral damage that they did.

These days the product is still made in Santiago, only this Santiago is in the Dominican Republic. The brand are not overly forthcoming when it comes to details; certainly they don't own a distillery in the Dominican Republic, and it seems questionable that they are filling their own casks, so it's for that reason that I have categorized them as a blender.

MEZAN

Mezan touts itself as "the untouched rum" — that is to say, it has had absolutely no sugar or colouring added to it. As such, some members of the range are surprisingly straw-coloured in their appearance, which just goes to show the quantity of caramel that gets added to many of the world's favourite rums. For me, this is a very refreshing approach to rum marketing, and a welcome antidote to heavily doctored liquids

PLATINO (40% ABV) UNAGED RUM

Cream soda and butter candies dominate the nose of this rum, which is a little confusing for a un-aged spirit. There's an unnatural sweetness on the palate that carries butterscotch and toffee apple right through to the finish. Strange.

CLASICO (40% ABV) AGED RUM

Picks up where the Platino left off, with penny toffee and a vanilla-scented bubble bath. Densely textured on the palate, in a kind of toffee-flavoured gravy way. Almost liqueur levels of sweetness, which hampers the level of complexity that might be there. Difficult to know if there's a rum hiding under all the exaggerated barrel character.

GUYANA 2005 (40% ABV)
EXTA-AGED BLENDED RUM

On the nose, it has trademark Guyanese darkness with engine oil, nutty caramel and brown sugar. Taste brings forth some fruit (tropical and citrus), aloe oil, green chilli (chile) and more of that light oak sweetness.

XO JAMAICA (40% ABV) AGED BLENDED RUM

Pale banana colour belies the pungency of this rum, which is all at once lemon rind, barbecued pineapple and new oak. Taste is lighter than expected, with salty citric notes that pair well with re-fill wood and a lick of Jamaican funk. Finish is black pepper and pineapple.

PANAMA 2006 (40% ABV) EXTRA-AGED RUM

The aroma is as one might expect from a 10-year-old Panamanian rum: gooey caramels, the slightest suggestions of fruit (dried apricots and fig) and some oak muscle to structure the whole thing. Taste is highly reflective of this, though (of course) dry, which leaves a residue of nutmeg, pimento and mace.

emerging from some producers. My only regret is that the rums in the Mezan range are cut to 40% ABV prior to bottling, it feels like a lost opportunity to raise the bar a little and package at a higher strength.

Currently there are four rums in the range: two Jamaican, one of which is a blend and the other sourced from an early Worthy Park distillate from 2005; a bottling of a 1996 Caroni from Trinidad; and a Panama bottling from 2006.

PLANTATION

If you want to see one of the most diverse rum cellars in the world, you're better off in France than the Caribbean. Nobody knows wood like the French, and in Cognac they have been nurturing the relationship between oak and spirit for some 400 years through their use of fine French oak, but also in the arcane practice of élevage (see page 54). Sadly, Cognac is a spirit category that has struggled to evolve with the times, and its outdated marketing and bureaucracy have made for a rather standardized range of products in the market. One man set on changing this is Alexandre Gabriel, frontman of Maison Ferrand, one of the most progressive Cognac houses in the region. Ferrand are not only interested in innovating grape spirits, Alexandre has also spent the last 20 years nurturing a growing rum business that goes by the name of Plantation.

Alexandre bought the struggling Maison Ferrand Cognac house in 1989, when he was just 23. He built the business by travelling from bar to bar, sleeping on sofas, and simultaneously training for 10 years as a cellar master. While the business was still in its infancy, he sold some Cognac to a Jamaican distillery who later defaulted on payment. In return – and in keeping with trade arrangements from a few centuries ago – Alexandre accepted payment in rum. This was to be the catalyst for Alexandre's fascination with the rum category and the establishment of his rum business, starting with the launch, in France, of the Kaniché brand.

Alexandre didn't want to just source and bottle rum, however – he wanted to place his own mark on the spirit, a signature that would amplify the base characteristics of the liquid and celebrate the distillery and the island in which it was born. So, using a bit of that Cognac know-how he began conducting additional 1–3 year maturation cycles in Cognac casks on all the rums he bought.

5-YEAR-OLD (40% ABV) AGED BLENDED RUM

A great arrangement of classic Bourbon cask aromas: there's caramel and coconut, but also soft leather, banana split and a ripple of vanilla ice cream. Sweetness on the palate carries the aromas well, as milky latte and *beurre noisette* carry a gently spiced finish.

ORIGINAL DARK (40% ABV) BLACK RUM

Chewy esters and brooding depth give this rum a kind of burnt pineapple and new carpet aromatic. There's a dark fudgey note there too, liquorice (licorice) and soft brown sugar. Gentle sweetness carries gloopy molasses notes, pineapple chunks, pimento and nutmeg. Finish lingers with cinder toffee and macaroon.

MULTI-ISLAND BLEND (44% ABV) AGED BLENDED RUM

A fruit salad of a rum: muscat grapes, vanilla seeds, dried cherry, papaya and soft mango fill the nose. The taste is soft, sweet and well-balanced, as great wafts of fermenting fruit and sticky wood line the palate.

BARBADOS, FINISHED IN MACKMYRA WHISKY CASK (55% ABV) AGED BLENDED RUM

Initial dried fruit and toasted cereals ease into subtle tropical fruit notes. Things then take a herbaceous turn, with mint sauce and dried papaya. Taste is spiced and slightly smokey: brined fish, samphire, nectarine and black pepper.

REUNION CASK SAMPLE 12-YEAR-OLD (66% ABV) AGED CANE JUICE RUM

Coffee cake, walnut and polished, soft leather. Candy floss (cotton candy), pine, and cigar bung. Mineral and clean, green pepper and spiced peppermint. Incredible structure and awesome balance between fresh cane and old oak character.

Kaniché found some success (and it is still available today as a 100% Barbadian blend), but Alexandre's curiosity was piqued, as he discovered new rums from islands and distilleries that had previously been under the radar. By the early 2000s, Plantation had released dozens of expressions from as many countries, and established themselves across Europe as one of rum's greatest independent bottlers.

In accordance with the practices of Champagne production, Plantation add a dosage to their rum, which is another way of saying "they sweeten it". But this isn't just any old sugar. It's a blend of white rum and sugar syrup that has been aged in Cognac casks for 10–12 years. More than a sweetener, Plantation's dosage is a delicious fingerprint that's smeared all over the contents of every single expression they produce. Disciples of the anti-sugaring campaign (see pages 56–57) have criticized Plantation in the past for its sugaring policy, but the fact that the brand is transparent about sweetening, and that the sweetening itself is in keeping with the traditional wine- and Cognac-making practices of France, as well as the fact that the rums taste excellent… well, that makes it difficult to contest.

Plantation have 14 expressions in their core range, which includes three expressions geared towards mixed drinks: 3-Stars, a white mixing rum; Original Dark, a black rum; and Plantation Overproof, an aged overproof rum. The "Signature Blends" is a range that's better suited to sipping or light mixing and include Plantation 5-year-old, a benchmark aged blend; 20th Anniversary, a curiously coconut-y blend of 12–20-year-old Barbados rums; and a pair of extra-aged rums. From there, you have a bunch of vintage rums, which are effectively the single malts of the range – each from a specific distillery and produced in a specific year. Lastly, there's the "Single Cask" range, which change annually and feature rums from a dozen different distilleries, finished in ex-wine casks and individually bottled and numbered from – that's right – a single cask.

A tour of Alexandre's warehouses reveals even more experiments that are currently underway. Thanks to a partnership with Mackmyra, the Swedish whisky distillery, Plantation are maturing rums in 50-litre (13-US gallon) ex-whisky casks. Plantation are exploring alternative wood types for their casks too, such as chestnut and acacia. Ever the innovator, Alexandre has plans afoot to place a warehouse on a barge floating on the River Seine, just to see how the gentle rocking of the boat will affect the ongoing maturation process.

THIS PAGE The great thing about Plantation, is that it's almost possible to explore the entire breadth of the rum category without straying from their impressive array of expressions.

PUSSER'S

When the last Navy rum ration was dispensed at "6 bells to the forenoon" (11am) on July 31 1970, it marked the end of 315 years of Royal Navy tradition. The remaining stocks of Navy rum were sold at auction and they quickly spread far and wide among bars and private collections, disappeareing like spilled rum through cracks on the deck of a ship. The vast majority of this rum was drunk before the turn of the millennium, but it is still possible to find rare flagons of the stuff floating around auction houses, as well as smaller packagings, like the rather pricey "Black Tot: The Last Consignment" bottling that's sold by Speciality Drinks in the UK – yours for a mere £650 ($800) a bottle.

If your budget doesn't stretch that far, there is an alternative. In 1979, nearly a decade after the Royal Navy abandoned the custom of the daily tot of rum, Charles Tobias, an entrepreneurial sailor-type based in the British Virgin Islands, founded Pusser's Rum after obtaining the rights to the blending information for the naval rum ration along with the licence to use the Royal Navy flag on his packaging. The terms of the deal also stipulated that Pusser's donate a proportion of annual profits to the Royal Navy Sailor's fund (also know as the "Tot Fund"). And they still do. In 2015 alone they handed over £25,000 ($31,000), which will be used for a whole range of projects that support the active and ex-servicemen and women of the Royal Navy.

Back to the rum: the name Pusser's comes from a corruption of the word "purser", which was the former title of the the ship's store man – the man upon whose shoulders it fell to ensure that sufficient quantities of rum were stocked aboard the ship and that it was of suitable quality. And by "quality", I mean strength, and this was determined by conducting a proof test with gunpowder (see page 25).

Pusser's rum is aged rum comprising "predominantly pot-still rum". Guyanese rum certainly features heavily (it contains some spirit from the Port Mourant still at DDL – see pages 175–78) and so too does rum from the Angostura distillery in Trinidad (see pages 165–67). Some of the expressions also contain rum from Barbados, too.

The blending and bottling of these rums all takes place on the British Virgin Islands, which also happens

(see page 25). / see pages 175–78 / see pages 165–67

RIGHT An iconic bottle, with some rope, naturally. Funnily enough, Pusser's 15-year-old rum does taste rope-y.

ORIGINAL ADMIRALTY RUM (40% ABV)
BLACK RUM

Lime peel, sticky dates, orange sherbet and just a hint of banana milkshake. Mellow and creamy on the palate, switching from cream soda and ginger through to leather and liquorice (licorice).

GUNPOWDER STRENGTH (54.5% ABV)
NAVY-STRENGTH RUM

Restrained, yet potent on the nose – like licks of a hot, sulphurous flame. After a while, solvent notes permeate to the surface, along with hot metal, soggy wood and engine grease. On the palate, there is hard-working steel, burnt treacle and a numbness that conceals the possible taste of blood.

PUSSER'S 15-YEAR-OLD (40% ABV)
EXTRA-AGED BLENDED RUM

Hot deck paint, resin, waxed rope. Old wood spices eventually overcome the more robust elements of the aroma, revealing sweaty sultana (golden raisin), banana loaf and powdered tobacco. Sweet and full on the palate, with bitter fruit and leather giving way to fleshy plums and dried apricot. Linger is burnt garlic, bitter caramel and sweet fruits.

to be the home of the Pusser's Pub and the Painkiller cocktail (see pages 238–39).

The bottle strength of this rum has been fiddled with a few times over the years. When Pusser's iconic "blue label" rum was first launched in 1980, it was bottled at the original Navy strength of 54.5% ABV. At one time in Germany, it was even possible to pick up a rare "green label" Pusser's that was bottled at 75% ABV! But in 2012, the brand quietly dropped the alcohol percentage of its "blue label" down to 40% while simultaneously launching Pusser's "Gunpowder Strength", which, in spite of being a fantastic name, is seemingly the same 54.5% "blue label" rum you would have bought as standard a few years back. Apparently the reason for lowering the alcohol content was so that the brand could supply British Naval bases, which are forbidden from holding spirits that are above 40% ABV. It's probably the best excuse for watering down rum that I've come across.

PYRAT

Whether it's pronounced *pye-rat* or *pi-rat* (nobody is sure) Pyrat is worthy of some recognition as one of the first blenders (along with Plantation) to elevate rum to the realms of "super-premium". But there's a funny thing about the "super-premium" designation – the fact that it's awarded only on the basis of price, not quality. I'm not saying that Pyrat is a terrible rum, but it is certainly divisive. When I first started bartending it, Pyrat's "Pistol" expression was a bit of a cult hero, partly because it was packaged in a lean "pistol" shaped bottle, which was, and still is, atypical to the category's traditional "clothing". Innovative as it perhaps once was, the rum world has moved on, and these days Pyrat is not shown the same degree of affection it once was. Why? Well, the fact that "Pistol" is no longer available, hasn't done it any favours, but the main reason is because of the way it tastes. There really is only one readily available expression of Pyrat available today – XO – and either it's the colour of the label and the orange ribbon working some serious subliminal magic, or these rums have a strangely pervasive tangerine aroma.

The official home of Pyrat is the tiny island Anguila, named for the French word for "eel" on account of its long and slippery shape. The rum was originally blended on the island from a mix of "nine pot-still rums", but these days there's little information about Pyrat's current

ABOVE Orange, inside and out. You can do this yourself with a bottle of Grand Marnier and the rum of your choosing.

production process available to the common man. I did some delving and it seems that the Anguila connection is in danger of becoming a rather difficult claim to sustain for the Pyrat brand. In 2010, The Anguila Rum Company, who make Pyrat, were bought by Patrón Spirits, who are based in Nevada and best known for their hugely successful Tequila brand by the same name. Since then, the rum has been blended at the Diamond distillery in Guyana, and made from a blend of high-ester Demerara rum and "other Caribbean rums". Whether these rums are all matured in Guyana too remains a mystery, but they are certainly bottled there – on a private bottling line, no less – which does bode the question, where exactly does Anguila fit into the story today? And while we're in the mood for questioning things: why is there a cartoon picture of a Buddha on the bottle? This is the sort of information that a brand website might normally provide, but at the time of writing, Pyrat's has been under maintenance for an extended period.

Equally mysterious is the story of this rum, which is about as tenuous a tale as any I have come across. It starts with C.J. Planter, a travelling seaman, who, in the early

1800s, abandoned ship and fell in love with an Anguilan girl. She turned out to be the illegitimate daughter of a local plantation owner and the local witch. Planter moved in with the family, and shortly afterwards, the mill and house burned to the ground, killing the girl's father. Planter took over the running of the estate, and in order to woo his future wife, decided to make her a rum. Enlisting the help of her witch-mother they created the Pyrat rum blend, which soon became the talk of the island because it was rumoured to be imbued with mystical powers.

The name is simply an alternative spelling of the word "pirate", but I could find no historical evidence of a rum ever existing under this name. As for the omnipresent orange aroma, there have been rumours that some of the casks used to mature the spirit were previously used to mature orange liqueurs (such as Grand Marnier), which would certainly explain a lot. In some respects, practising this kind of thing is no different to using a sherry or port cask, but one does have to question when wine or liqueur casks stop being a "seasoning" and start becoming an added flavouring. In the case of Pyrat, I do wonder if the balance is slightly lost, but if you're a fan of orange in your alcohol you need look no further.

SMITH & CROSS

Unlike most of the surviving blends that based themselves out of London's Docklands, Smith & Cross is a 100% Jamaican rum, as opposed to Demerara rum. The brand has roots that go back as far as 1788, when the company owned blending warehouses and a sugar refinery at 203 Thames Street, not far from the Old Billingsgate market. The blend is cut to Navy Strength (57% ABV) and comprises a mixture of rums sourced from the legendary Hampden Estate (see pages 126–27) in Jamaica's Trelawny parish. Known for its high-ester

rums, untamed Hampden can destroy the palates of the uninitiated. Fortunately, Smith & Cross has learned some manners – a six-month-old Wedderburn-style high-ester number paired with an 18–36-month-old medium-bodied Plummer-style rum – and what we're left with is a fantastic Jamaican mixing spirit, perfect for all kinds of funk-driven Tiki concoctions.

THE DUPPY SHARE

One of the biggest new releases of recent years, The Duppy Share has won over both bartenders and consumers with its cute packaging and strong liquid provenance. The brand is the brainchild of George From and Jess Swinfen, and plays off the concept of the angel's share by instead assigning the millions of gallons of evaporative losses that the Caribbean rum industry produces every year to the "duppies" – it's what they call ghosts in Jamaica.

The rum is a blend of 3-year-old Jamaican pot-still rum sourced from Worthy Park, and 5-year-old Barbados column-still rum sourced from the Foursquare distillery. Both rums are matured in ex-bourbon barrels prior to blending.

RIGHT Fabulous packaging and quality liquid – The Duppy Share is everything you can want in a blended rum.

LEFT The transformation of liquid in a wooden cask is one of the great wonders of the edible world.

haven for pirates, second only to Port Royal in Jamaica as a criminal trading outpost, raiding launchpad, and as a centre for recruitment for the likes of Captain Henry Morgan (see pages 191–92). The gold and loot that flowed through Tortuga was sufficient enough that in the 1660s, the French used Tortuga as the capital of their Sainte-Domingue colony (present-day Haiti).

Tortuga is not a big island (it's about the same size as Marie-Galante), but the green hills in the south known as the "Low Land" were suitable for growing cane, and it's here where the port was located, too. Did the French make rum there? Certainly. But there's little in the way of a surviving record.

Enter the Cayman Islands and the Tortuga Rum Company, which was founded in 1984 by Robert Hamaty and his wife Carlene, an air-hostess. The pair launched Tortuga rum as a novelty item for the growing tourism industry on the island. It is made from a blend of Jamaican pot-still and Barbados rums. It was the launch of Tortuga Rum Cake (a fourth-generation recipe don't y'know…) a few years later that truly changed the business and changed the focus to one of rum-flavoured cake. The company now bakes a range of long-shelflife flavoured cakes on Cayman, Jamaica Barbados and the Bahamas, and exports to all corners of the world.

In 2015 Tortuga's 5-year-old and 12-year-old rums began to be distributed in the US. I can already attest to the popularity of this blended rum among American travellers in Cayman, who return ladened like pack-horses with duty-free cartons of Cayman Island rum.

TORTUGA

Tortuga are a Cayman-based rum blender, named after the legendary isle of Tortuga which contrary to popular belief is not the island of Tortola (one of the British Virgin Islands) but actually a small island off the north coast of Haiti. The bulbous countours of Tortuga were first sighted by Europeans on December 6 1492, when Christopher Columbus saw what looked to be a giant turtle ("tortuga" in Spanish) emerging out of the morning mist.

During the early 17th century, the island was contested on multiple occasions between the Spanish, French and English, and it was probably this constant sense of insecurity that attracted the attentions of pirates and buccaneers. The island became a legendary safe

5-YEAR-OLD (40% ABV) AGED BLENDED RUM

There's a nice melting butter aroma on this rum, cooled by menthol and green banana. Taste is quite light, but a gentle nudge of pot-still character carries things along. Finish is short, leaving a sensation of prickly oak and vanilla.

12-YEAR-OLD (40% ABV)
EXTRA-AGED BLENDED RUM

Toasted chestnut, vanilla fudge and cacao nibs, which makes way for a lighter fennel seed and anise. Taste is not as concentrated as you might hope, with a herbaceous twang that couples well with old wood. Not bad.

VELIER

Velier are an independent Italian spirits importer, which happen to specialize in bottling top-quality rum. In a world where whiskies are labeled as "cask strength" or "barrel proof" and even gin is getting the high-strength treatment, rum has lagged behind somewhat. Velier are leading the charge that will change this, through their "Habitation Velier" range, and through other exclusive releases. This is the bleeding edge of rum innovation, and I believe that it is through "pure pot-still" and natural strength rums such as those in the Velier range, that we shall see the rum category mature with dignity over the coming years.

Velier's head-honcho, Luca Gargano, is an unstoppable force who, over the years, has had unprecedented access to rums from some of the great distilleries of old, not to mention new brands from lesser-known operations. Take Caroni for example: a Trinidadian distillery that went silent in 2002, from which Luca acquired casks, bottled them, and pumped life back into a lost brand for an audience of eager rum lovers across the globe. Luca's close relationship wth Yesu Persaud of DDL in Guyana granted him, for some years, exclusive access to some of their oldest and best stocks from the legendary Diamond Distillery (see pages 175–78). Then there's Velier's work in Haiti, bottling spirits from some of the hardest-to-get-to distilleries on the planet, and ennobling a Haitian craft for spirits that few people would ever have otherwise noticed. Velier's relationship with the Bielle distillery (see pages 104–05) on Marie-Galante has created a partnership that's unheard of between importer and producer, whereby Velier have installed a pot still and now share the pressing equipment in order to make their "Rhum Rhum" brand.

It's no exaggeration whatsoever to suggest that Luca Gargano is the most innovative character in the rum industry today. The products in the Velier range demand a high price tag, but they do so for a very good reason. The Velier liquids are exclusively top-drawer. These are not people who mess about with generic flavours and "safe" blends. They are designed to stand out. They do stand out, in both flavour and in the quality of the packaging – which is among the best clothing you're every likely to see on a bottle of rum. My only real complaint is that the rum all sells out so quickly!

CARONI 12 (50% ABV) EXTRA-AGED RUM

Rough rope, hemp, plum pie and beef stew. Date and almond muffin. Sweet on the palate too, with strong pepper, and a vicious lick of stewed fruits and capsaicin. Sweetness lingers as heat slowly drifts away. The aftertaste is raisins and caramel sauce.

CARONI 17 (55% ABV) EXTRA-AGED RUM

Dusty sandal wood, oat cake and cigar box. Sparkly texture and nice level of concentration. Antequated and refined, like Armagnac. Poised with dry spices, but the extra alcohol drys things out, leaving just a hint of sweetness through the finish.

FOURSQUARE 2013 (64% ABV)
AGED BLENDED RUM

Soft and nutty, brown tweed and walking boots. More ethereal vanilla notes creep through afterwards and soft cocoa underlies it. Delicately spiced on the palate. White chocolate, white pepper and sandalwood finish.

FORSYTHS WP 502 (57% ABV)
AGED POT-STILL RUM

Vegetal funk, grilled aubergine (eggplant), buttered mushroom and bruised plum. Diesel, too. Taste is softer than expected – dry and weighty. Burnt autumn vegetables and the bastard child of a banana and a crayon through to the finish.

HAMPDEN 2010 (68.5% ABV)
AGED POT-STILL RUM

Absurd. Cat vomit quickly replaced by waxy banana, milky coffee and candy. There's a greasy mineral note, like new engine oil, which becomes strawberry and sweet cherry. Dry, and sour cherry candy-like, with alcohol stripping the palate of any moisture. Concentrated fruit juice fills the very lengthy finish.

WOOD'S

There are plenty of Black Rum options out there for those with aspirations of joining the Navy or becoming a pirate. All of them rely heavily on the authenticity of their heritage in order to sell their product, and each have their own take on how to approach this subject. Wood's do it the right way, by bottling their rum at 57% ABV, which is the old measure for 100% Imperial proof. In fact, Wood's have been bottling their Demerara rum at this strength for 130 years, during which time it is alleged that the recipe has remained faithful to the original formula too. It seems that the only thing that has changed at all is the packaging.

In fact, the Wood's bottle underwent a significant and much needed redesign in 2016. Prior to this, it was packaged in what is quite literally the cheapest spirit bottle you can buy, complete with flimsy aluminium cap, and jaded label slapped on the front. Not so anymore. The new bottle is a sturdy-looking affair (better suited for rough seas) with a proper cork stopper, and a new cleaned-up label that subtly celebrates the themes of the old bottle while allowing the typography to sing a little louder. It is sure to appeal to the hipster set, at land and at sea. It appeals to me.

The redesign had been on the to-do list for some time of course, as the Scottish family-run firm William Grant & Sons bought the brand from Seagram's back in 2002. They also snapped up O.V.D. Rum and Vat 19 in the process – the latter being a rum of Trinidadian origin, and the number-one selling aged rum in Northern Ireland at the time. The newly formed tag-

team of Wood's and O.V.D (both of them Demerara rums) gave William Grant & Sons a good chunk of the Scottish rum market at the time, which, when coupled with spiced rums, shifts about as many cases in Scotland annually as the entire malt whisky category put together.

The Wood's brand was founded in the Albert Docks in Liverpool, England in 1887. Like many of the companies that got into rum blending, the Wood's Trading Company traded whatever they could to make a quick buck: spying some barrels of Demerara rum on the docks one day, the company saw and opportunity and branched out into rum blending. Lucky they did, since all traces of the original Wood's Trading Company have been lost… only the surviving rum brand serves as testimony of them ever having existed!

The rum is a blend of three stills at the Diamond distillery: two of them are four-column Savalle stills originating from the Uitvlugt distillery (see pages 174–75), which closed in 2000 and the other being the Versailles wooden pot still (see page 176). The rums are matured separately in Guyana then shipped to the UK for bottling. Once the rum lands on British soil, William Grant & Sons perform a marrying process, in refill American oak barrels. The rum is rested in these casks for an average of three years (in addition to the maturation the spirit has already undergone in Guyana), but the barrels they use are deliberately very old and exhausted of wood character. The reasoning behind this is that so much character is deemed to come from the Versailles still spirit that it's necessary to further strip out some of the volatile notes through the continued oxidation and evaporation of the spirit.

LEFT Authenticity without the cliché – the new label for Wood's Navy rum is a masterclass in product packaging.

XM

The XM rum brand is a blend of Guyanese rums. Nothing new there then, except with XM there is one notable point of difference: it's owned by a Guyanese company. Banks DIH (not to be confused with Banks rum) was founded in the 1840s by Jose Gomes D'Aguiar. The DIH in the company name comes from the abbreviation of Demerara Ice House. The company has its roots in rum blending and liquor stores, but it quickly became involved in other areas of trade and commerce. As the company expanded and bought the Demerara Ice House (DIH) which was at the time used to hold the enormous glaciers that were shipped down to Guyana by Canadian schooner – handy if you wanted some ice in your rum.

These days, Banks trade across multiple platforms, with shares in banks and shipping companies to their name, as well as the Banks Brewery on Barbados. Demerara Distillers stand as one of Banks DIH's main competitors, but that doesn't stop them from purchasing rum from them, which they bottle under the XM brand.

The packaging of XM – with its liberal use of airbrushing and raised gold typography – ought to be enough to put people off the brand. The liquid inside is textbook Guyanese, however, and altogether rather difficult to distinguish from the El Dorado range. There's a liberal helping of nutty dessert-like qualities and that present sweet density.

RIGHT I am not a fan of the XM labels, but it's easily forgiven when you get a taste of the rum inside – sweet, forbidden, and altogether rather satisfying.

7-YEAR-OLD (40% ABV)
AGED BLENDED RUM

Danish pastry, toffee and pecan. Wood notes are honeyed and sticky. Initial sweetness is warming, carrying juicy stone fruits and Garibaldi biscuits (cookies) along a light mid-palate. Sugar also masks a molasses bitterness that rises up towards the finish of the rum.

PART FOUR
RUM COCKTAILS

MAI TAI

55 ML/2 FL. OZ. WRAY & NEPHEW 17-YEAR-OLD SUBSTITUTE BLEND
(see below and on page 214) **OR USE EXTRA-AGED POT-STILL RUM**
25 ML/1 FL. OZ. LIME JUICE • 10 ML/2 TEASPOONS PIERRE FERRAND
DRY ORANGE CURAÇAO • 10 ML/2 TEASPOONS ROCK CANDY SYRUP
10 ML/2 TEASPOONS ORGEAT

Wray & Nephew 17-year-old substitute blends (mix in equal parts):
For a fruity and spicy Mai Tai: Banks 5-Year-Old and Plantation Original Dark
For a full-bodied, vegetal Mai Tai: El Dorado 15-Year-Old and Saint James Rhum Vieux
For an aromatic and waxy Mai Tai: Depaz Hors d'age 2002 Vintage and Doorly's 12-Year-Old

You can swizzle this drink straight in the glass if you prefer, but the proper way is to shake it. Add the
ingredients to a cocktail shaker along with 200 g (7 oz.) of crushed ice. If your ice is a little wet, it's
worth putting it through a salad spinner to dry it out first as this will limit the dilution of the finished
drink. Shake well, then pour the entire contents of the shaker into a large rocks glass. Use the spent lime
shell to garnish the top, and add a sprig of mint to decorate.
Tama'a maita'i!

While it's certain that Mai Tai is one of the great pinups of the Tiki anthology, regrettably this is perhaps the least tropical-tasting drink of this family of tropical-tasting drinks. No pineapple juice, no passionfruit, no grenadine and no coconut – it's enough to make an overproof rum float spontaneously extinguish! In fact, the original version of this drink created by Tiki legend Trader Vic is little more than a Rum-based Margarita or Sidecar with the addition of almond-flavoured syrup. It's the simplicity that makes the drink such a genius concoction and second only to the Daiquiri in rum cocktail fame.

This legendary drink was created by Vic Bergeron in 1944 at the original Soakham branch of Trader Vic's. Bergeron was making drinks for two Tahitian friends, Easham and Carrie Guild, when he combined Wray & Nephew 17 with "fresh lime, some orange curaçao from Holland, a dash of Rock Candy Syrup, and a dollop of French Orgeat, for its subtle almond flavor." This was mixed with "a generous amount of shaved ice and vigorous shaking by hand". The story goes that Carrie

Guild took a sip and according to Vic commented "Maita'i Roa A'e", which means "out of this world" or "very good" in Tahitian.

The drink spread throughout Vic's franchised restaurants, and across the US, gobbling up supplies of Wray & Nephew 17 in the process. When stocks of the rum had been depleted, he switched to Wray & Nephew 15, until that began to dry up too. Vic took the decision to stretch out what remming rum he had by mixing it with Red Heart (which at the time was a Jamaican blend) and Coruba (a Black Rum from Jamaica). By the mid-1950s, Wray & Nephew had been dropped all together, and Vic had turned to a mixture of Jamaican rums combined with *rhum agricole* from Martinique.

Order a Mai Tai these days, and it's usually pot luck as to what you will receive. Some recipes call for bitters, while others use pineapple juice, and more often than not, you'll get an overproof rum float in there too. The original version is by far the best – the only issue being that the legendary Wray & Nephew 17-year-old is no

Victor Bergeron, the founder of Trader Vic's in the original
Trader Vic's bar in Oakland, California.

easier to come by now than it was in the 1950s. So just replace it, right? Not so easy. This high-ester pot-still number was the key element that elevated the Mai Tai from the flat and flabby into the sun-drenched realms of Polynesia. There are only a handful of Wray & Nephew 17 bottles still in existence, and most of them are unopened.

I have been lucky enough to taste it in its natural form (thanks Jake Burger), and what a rum it is: with aromas of hot rubber, puffed cereals, tar and freshly greased engine parts. The taste is green peppercorn, bitter artichoke, bitter almond and beef fat. Trader Vic described it as "surprisingly golden in colour, but with a rich and pungent flavour particular to the Jamaican blends". It is/was a highly stylized spirit, and there are few available rums today that come close to imitating its unique flavour profile, which means that making an authentic tasting Mai Tai in the modern era is no mean feat.

Fortunately for you, I have taken some time to formulate a few blending options that come close to my tasting notes of the original, and they are listed on the previous page. As for the rest of the ingredients, they shouldn't prove too difficult to track down. Rock candy syrup is a supersaturated sugar syrup (or gomme) made by heating two parts sugar with one part water, and allowing to reduce in a pan for five minutes. Once it cools, it should be as viscous as honey.

Try experimenting with different types of sugar (Demerara or light muscovado) for a richer-tasting finished drink. Alternatively, Trader Vic's sell their own branded version of the product..

MOJITO

12 FRESH MINT LEAVES • 50 ML/1⅓ FL. OZ. HAVANA CLUB 3-YEAR-OLD
20 ML/1 FL. OZ. LIME JUICE • 10 ML/2 TEASPOONS SUGAR SYRUP (see page 214)
SODA

Judging by the number of bad Mojitos I've been served in my time, this is not an easy drink to balance. The mistake that many bartenders make, is muddling/crushing whole wedges of lime into the drink. This is a poor tactic, because limes vary dramatically in the amount of juice they offer up, and unless the sugar is balanced accordingly, you'll be landed with something that's insipidly sweet or far too sour. The peel on the lime is better avoided too – it's quite a potent flavour that tends to mask the cool aromatics of the mint.

Take a chunky highball and throw the mint leaves in there. Please don't "slap" them as is the ritual of some cocktail makers – in doing so you're merely aromatizing your hands. Gently bruise the mint leaves using a muddler (a rolling pin works fine, too). It's essential that you're gentle – if you crush the leaves you'll release bitter-tasting chlorophyll into the drink. Douse the leaves in the rum and give a good stir, then add the lime juice and sugar syrup. Throw a scoop of crushed ice in there (you can use cubed, but crushed ice will give a far better appearance) and give the mixture a good "churn" with a long spoon. Pile more ice on top, give it another stir, then fill any space with soda. Stir again, add more ice (if needed) then garnish with a lime wedge and a fresh sprig of mint. Drink with a straw.

There aren't many drinks that speak to rum so much as the Mojito. It's packaged Cuban mojo; the perfect antidote to the heady spice of a fine Cuba cigar. A liquid embodiment of all that is sprightly, fresh and spirited.

The earliest reference to the Mojito was in Sloppy Joe's Havana Bar, which were giving away a souvenir cocktail pamphlet in 1931 with the recipe. Those of you who are well-read when it comes to cocktail history will be aware that the pamphlet actually listed two versions of the drink: one under "Bacardí Cocktails"; and another under "Gordon's Gin Cocktails". The latter, of course, uses a base of gin in place of rum, and the former is based on Bacardí, which is essentially the same drink we make today (though it won't be with Bacardí if you're drinking it in Havana). The dual versions were again offered up in the legendary El Floridita's cocktail book, published in 1939, which offered a Mojito Criollo

#1 (with rum) and Mojito Criollo #2 (with gin). These twin faces of the Mojito have led some bar historians to suggest that the original cocktail was actually based on an American drink called the "Southside".

The timings do indeed make this a possibility, because the earliest story to mention the Southside comes from the Southside Sportsmen's Club in Long Island, during the 1890s. Fizzes were very much on-trend back then, and through the actions of some adventurous bartender, mint leaves appeared in a Gin Fizz one day, and thus the Southside was born.

If it sounds simple, that's because it is. So simple in fact, that the mixture of lime, water, booze and mint has in fact been going on for far longer than than either the Southside or the Mojito. The earliest known example of this is really an early form of Navy Grog, which was named El Draque, after the Spanish nickname for the

British privateer Francis Drake. Made from *aguardiente de caña*, lime, sugar and mint, this fiery mix would likely have been closer to a Ti Punch (see pages 226–27) than a Mojito, but clearly cut from the same cloth. Whether Drake actually drank one of these things is questionable, since he lived in the late-16th century, a time when cane spirits were difficult to come across outside Brazil. Plus, it seems an incredible coincidence that one of the greatest explorers of his time was also the world's first mixologist. But if indeed he did have a hand to play in the drink's conception, El Draque has a fair claim to being the world's oldest cocktail.

However it was invented, the drink became very popular among the Cuban peasantry in the early 1800s, some 90 years before the Southside or the Daiquiri (see pages 224–25) – another drink it is claimed to spawn from – were invented. It was also in the second quarter of the 19th century that El Draque turns up (as the "Draquecito") in *El Colera en la Habana*, a story by Cuban poet/novelist Ramón de Palma.

The etymology of the Mojito is not entirely clear. It could come from the Spanish word *mojadito* (meaning "a little wet"), or it might have evolved from a recipe for "Mojo" – a lime- and mint-based salsa.

Blanche Z. De Baralt's *Cuban Cookery: Gastronomic Secrets of the Tropics, with an Appendix on Cuban Drinks*

(1931) included a recipe for "Rum Cocktail (Cuban Mojo)" and directions to make what is quite clearly a Mojito.

If La Floridita is the cradle of the Daiquiri, it's Old Havana's La Bodeguita Del Medio where the Mojito rests its head (Hemingway was once known to pen words to the same effect). This modest little boozer was a latecomer to the Havana bar scene when farmer Angel Martinez opened it on Calle Empedrado in 1942. The bar soon established a reputation among the locals for its unassuming style and was visited by luminaries including Hemingway and Pablo Neruda. These days it's characterized by decades' worth of handwritten messages on the walls, and the fact that the bartenders here mechanically churn out up to a dozen Mojitos a minute. If that kind of product volume doesn't flash warning signs at you, let me make it crystal clear for you: if it's a great drink you're after, La Bodeguita del Medio is better avoided.

As is the unfortunate norm with cocktails and the bars that originate them, a thriving tourism trade has done away with any suggestion of quality that may (or may not) have once existed here. Pre-packaged lime juice, mint stalks and overzealous measures of Havana Club 3-Year-Old are the themes that populate my all-too-hazy memories of the experience.

The bar at Havana's legendary yet understated La Bodeguita Del Medio – the birthplace of the Mojito.

CUBA LIBRE

50 ML/1²/₃ FL. OZ. AGED WHITE RUM
120 ML/4 FL. OZ. COCA-COLA
HALF A LIME

In accordance with the version of this drink in Charles H. Baker's *Gentleman's Companion* (1939), I'm a strong advocate of a quick lime muddle as the first step of construction. Squeeze the lime juice into a separate vessel, and drop the spent shell into a highball glass. Squash it to remove the oils, then add cubed ice, rum, lime juice and coke. Give it a good stir, and add more ice or coke if desired.

Substitute the aged white rum for a white overproof rum (such as Bacardi 151) and the drink becomes a "Cuban Missile Crisis"!

Sometimes the simplest drinks are the best. In fact, more often than not the simplest drinks are the best. This is certainly true of the Cuba Libre, which comprises only two ingredients plus a very necessary garnish. Some would argue this isn't a cocktail at all, but a spirit and mixer. But those folks fail to recognize the genius of Coca-Cola as a bittersweet ingredient and the complexity of its composition.

A quick scan over the key flavours of Coca-Cola: lemon, orange, lime, cinnamon, nutmeg, neroli, lavender and coriander/cilantro; shows a set of ingredients that match nicely with rum as stand-alone modifiers. Indeed, most of them have coupled historically with rum in punches and other cocktails. What all this means is that the affinity between rum and coke is a favourable accident – there is something at work here that blends these flavours into something unnaturally tasty.

So where did it come from? Well, the Cuba Libre ("Free Cuba") is named of course for the Cuban War of Independence, which was fought from 1895–98. We can be sure that this drink didn't exist in Cuba prior to this, because Coca-Cola wasn't available there until after the war, and not bottled for export until 1899. The

year of the birth of the Cuba Libre cocktail is cited as 1900, and in an unprecedented turn of events, this was sworn under a legal affidavit by a man named Fausto Rodriguez in 1960. Rodriguez was a messenger with the US Army Signal Corps who claimed to have walked to a Havana bar in 1900 and bore witness to an officer by the name of Captain Russell, ordering a Bacardi and Coca-Cola on ice with a wedge of lime. More soldiers arrived and a second round was ordered, to which the bartenders suggested a toast of ¡Por Cuba Libre! to celebrate of the newly liberated Cuba.

It later transpired that Rodriguez was on the Bacardi payroll and that the affidavit only came to light as a result of a full-age advertisement in *Life* magazine taken out by Bacardi in 1966. For what it's worth, I suspect the story has some truth to it. But as for the brand, well, that's anyone's guess.

Whatever the origins, the drink travelled north, into the US, and quickly became popular among the Cola-guzzling southerners. By 1920 there were 1,000 Coca-Cola bottling plants (compared to two in 1900) and rum was the go-to adulterator. This practice was sustained during Prohibition, as Caribbean rum was

The Andrews Sisters pose for a portrait around
1944 in New York City.

one of the few spirits that found its way across US border. The Cuba Libre became the most dependable beverage, especially during wartime, when sugar and other sodas were rationed. During World War II, coke was distributed among soldiers, so there was always a plentiful supply to mix with the steady influx of rum.

The drink's celebrity status was confirmed once and for all in 1945 with the popular calypso hit "Rum and Coca-Cola" by the Andrews Sisters. As a trio of sisters from Minnesota, the Andrews had to put on faux–Caribbean accents in order to hit the correct calypso vibe. The melody had been previously published as the work of Trinidadian calypso composer Lionel Belasco

on a song titled "L'Année Passée," which was in turn based on a folk song from Martinique. The lyrics to "Rum and Coca-Cola" were provided by Rupert Grant, another calypso musician from Trinidad who went by the stage name Lord Invader, and it was he who adjusted the song to reference the off-duty activities of American soldiers.

The song was a massive hit among the locals, despite the allusion to prostitution, the glorification of drinking and free advertising for Coca-Cola. Perhaps it was the transformative nature of the song, with its weird lyrics and kooky accents. Maybe it was just the fact that rum and coke is a fantastic drink.

Since the Yankee come to Trinidad
They got the young girls all goin' mad
Young girls say they treat 'em nice
Make Trinidad like paradise

Drinkin' rum and Coca-Cola
Go down Point Koo-mah-nah
Both mother and daughter
Workin' for the Yankee dollar

DARK AND STORMY

120 ML/2 FL. OZ. LUSCOMBE ORGANIC "HOT" GINGER BEER
50 ML/1²⁄₃ FL. OZ. GOSLINGS BLACK SEAL RUM
WEDGE OF LIME

Build the drink into a highball glass filled with plenty of ice.
Unlike most cocktails, it's nice to take a backwards approach and add the rum to the glass
last, along with a squashed wedge of lime. This means you get the full effect of the "storm"
as the light and heavy liquids fight to remain separate. Some people add a dash of Angostura
Bitters and a sprig of mint, moving the cocktail more in the direction of a Moscow Mule, but
if your ginger beer is good enough, there really is no need for further distractions.

There are only a handful of cocktails on the planet that are legally trademarked, and for reasons unknown, all but one of them (the Sazerac) is based on rum. No prizes for guessing that the Bacardi Cocktail (a Daiquiri with grenadine) is one of them; less obvious is the Painkiller (see pages 238–39) and less desirable is the Hand Grenade (a sweet punch served in nasty little green plastic "hand grenades" from late-night bars in New Orleans), and then there's the rather appealing Dark 'n' Stormy.

Yes sir, this drink – which is made using Gosling's Black Seal rum, ginger beer and, occasionally, lime juice – has been under the stewardship of Gosling Brothers in Bermuda since it first manifested itself around the time of World War I. The flavour pairing has more distant origins (which we'll come on to) and of course you're free to call a dark rum and ginger whatever you like, but if you're using the name Dark 'n' Stormy) (or Dark & Stormy) on a cocktail menu or even in a book, you are legally obliged to use Gosling's in the recipe.

This is no great hardship, as Black Seal is a benchmark blend featuring high-ester Jamaican rum and sweet-lingering Guyanese, topped off with a good slug of spirit caramel for added effect (for more on Gosling's, see pages 194–95). Gosling's first trademarked the drink in the late 1970s, and since then, Bermuda has become the unofficial home of the drink. Its spiritual home is of course, at sea, which makes Bermuda as good a choice as any since it's nearly 1,000 km (620 miles) from the nearest landmass.

By the late 19th century, the spice trade on some Caribbean islands, like Grenada, had surpassed that of sugar. Merchant sailors, who plied their trade between the sticky ports of the Caribbean and the British Isles, would regularly transport shipments of rum alongside their spices. These spices appealed to blenders, who used them to flavour their rums, but they were also used to make sodas and medicinal tonics too. Ginger beer really was the flavour of Victorian Britain, and just like tea, it was a celebration of the British Empire's conquests abroad. The British Royal Navy took a keen interest in the stuff and began provisioning ginger beer on board their ships. Perhaps it was an attempt to curb alcoholism among the ship's crew, or to help with sea sickness, or maybe it even served as a heartening taste of home – either way it was popular enough that between 1860 and 1920 the Royal Navy Dockyard on Ireland Island (in Bermuda) even had its own ginger beer bottling plant. And even though there's no documented evidence to prove it, I don't think it's too much of a stretch to suggest that one or two sailors dipped a toe into the water and experimented with mixing their rum ration with ginger beer.

Back in London, the city was awash with ginger beer, with street vendors on every corner peddling their own unique recipes. One of them, William John Barritt, came to Bermuda from England and in 1874 opened a dry goods shop on the corner of Front and King Streets in Hamilton, Bermuda. This is where the Bermuda's now-famous Barritt's Ginger Beer first started. Even today, after five generations, it's still going strong.

Gosling's themselves have dabbled in ginger beer called "Gosling's Stormy Ginger Beer", which is touted as "the only ginger beer created strictly to make Dark 'n' Stormy cocktails". It's alright stuff, but finer specimens can be found if you hunt around.

My preference lies with the bottle-fermented kind, such as the one made by Luscombe, a soft drinks company based in Devon, England. This location is well-suited to the task because Devon, after all, is the birthplace of the word "rumbullion" (see page 19). More important than that is the flavour of the product, which is outstanding. It comes in two different temperatures: "cool" and "hot". I prefer the "hot", which induces a sufficient volume of sweat to have you believe you're sailing in very warm waters. With its densely concentrated, almost chewy, texture, this disturbingly opaque beer is more than a match for the richness of Gosling's Black Seal.

As for the name "Dark 'n' Stormy", well that was likely chosen on account of the drink's brooding appearance when mixed. Dark clouds of alcohol and spice engulf each other in an altogether discomforting fashion. But the term "Dark and Stormy" may in itself have been borrowed from *Paul Clifford*, a successful novel of 1830 by Edward Bulwer-Lytton. The novel's opening paragraph begins, "It was a dark and stormy night; the rain fell in torrents", and is often invoked as the archetypal example of melodramatic prose in fiction writing.

"It was a dark and stormy night; the rain fell in torrents"

Paul Clifford (1830) by Edward Bulwer-Lytton

DAIQUIRI

60 ML/2 FL. OZ. BACARDI CARTA BLANCA • 15 ML/½ FL. OZ. FRESH LIME JUICE
10 ML/2 TEASPOONS SUGAR SYRUP (see page 214)

Add all the ingredients to a cocktail shaker and shake vigorously with cubed ice for at
least 30 seconds. Strain into a frozen coupe glass. Don't garnish it – there's no point – the
drink will be gone before you (or your guests) even notice it's there.

During the course of the Spanish-American War in 1898, thousands of acres of Cuban sugar plantations passed into American ownership. US control over mining also expanded, and this resulted in a huge influx of expatriated American workers to Cuba in the latter years of the 19th century. Jennings Cox was one such man, an American mining engineer who in 1896 worked for the Spanish-American Iron Company, near the village of Daiquirí (correctly pronounced dai-ki-REE), close to Santiago de Cuba. Conditions in the Sierra Maestra region of Cuba was tough (yellow fever was highly prevalent) and the workers were compensated (in part) with tobacco and Bacardi Carta Blanca rum rations.

The story goes that Cox was entertaining some friends with cocktails one evening when he ran out of gin. Not wishing to end the party early, he called upon a bottle of Barardi rum, serving it mixed with sugar, "lemons" and water, and pouring it into a tall glass filled with ice. The recipe for this "Daiquiri" was recorded by Mr. Cox on a handwritten sheet of paper. There are some obvious discrepancies between Cox's original formula and the standard accepted Daiquiri of today. Most notable is that the drink was served long, but with the simultaneous rise of the Martini in the early 20th century, the drink seems to have shifted allegiances to the coupe glass. Cox's version also calls for lemon juice instead of lime, but there's a little more to this than meets the eye. Limes were far more common in Cuba than lemons at that time (they still are) and were known to Cubans as limón, so it's quite likely that what Cox was really referring to was a lime after all. While the above creation story seems the most credible, there are many others that place American military officers and even Don Facundo Bacardí Masso at the crime scene (who presumably appeared as a ghostly aspiration since he died in 1886). All of this, of course, is slightly fatuous, as, if you'll allow me to quote myself in *The Curious Bartender: The Artistry & Alchemy of Creating the Perfect Cocktail* (2013):

"It doesn't take a mining engineer to work out that a drink as simple as this probably pre-dates Jennings Cox, albeit under different titles. Surely many a rum punch has existed containing only rum, lime, sugar and water? – and you only need to look at the Brazilian Caipirinha to see a cousin of the Daiquiri, comprising much the same ingredients all served over ice."

The Daiquiri is not a forgiving cocktail when it comes to subtle changes in its formula, and one of the things that really rattles me when it comes to the Daiquiri, is when it is confused with a Sour. Now, the sour family of cocktails are a simple bunch: four parts spirit, two parts citrus, one part sugar – you can't go wrong really. A proper Daiquiri cannot be made like this though, as the light, Cuban-style rum is easily overshadowed by all that sweet and sour. This cocktail is about discretion and finesse, and to balance it correctly, you need a higher ratio of rum: eight parts rum, one part lime, and just over one part sugar (depending on how sweet your sugar syrup is). With this formula, the drink is less opaque, and seems to glow with a soft turquoise luminance. It tastes far better too, as those soft *aguardiente* notes are gently sweetened, penetrating through fleshy citrus with grace. Also, the subtle sourness means you can skull three of them in quick succession and not experience that puffy mouth feeling that comes from one too many sweet and sour cocktails.

TI PUNCH

50 ML/1²/₃ FL. OZ. BIELLE PREMIUM BLANC

(any *rhum agricole* will do but this is one of my favourites)

SMALL WEDGE OF LIME

1 SMALL TEASPOON BROWN SUGAR

Add the lime to a small rocks glass and gently squash with the back of a spoon. Next add the rum and the sugar. Give everything a good stir until all the sugar has dissolved. If you prefer, you can make a sugar syrup (see page 214) and forgo all of the stirring, but the French tend to opt for granulated sugar, which draws out more of the lime oils.

The Ti Punch (pronounced tee-pawnch) is a drink that hails from the French islands of the West Indies, and is synonymous with the drinking of the local *rhum agricole*. This "little punch" as it translates to is, in many ways, more than a mixed drink or a cocktail. For many, it's the final stage in the making of the rum, as if the liquid in the bottle was never intended to be served "as-is", but to be seasoned with a squeeze of lime, carefully sweetened with a spoon of sugar, then stirred, sipped and enjoyed.

It's customary not to use ice in a Ti Punch which, when coupled with the typically high strength of *rhum agricole*, makes for a fiery little drink that's packed full of flavour. It's for this reason that folks probably decided to make them nice and compact. Some, indeed, can be laughably small – barely a mouthful. My friend Patricia, who lives in Pointe-à-Pitre, Guadeloupe, would make Ti Punches in tiny blue glasses hardly bigger than an egg cup. The drink would be consumed within a couple of minutes, and then she would return to the ritual of muddling the tiny lime slice and slowly dissolving the sugar into the rum. And it is perhaps this ritual of squashing, spooning, pouring and stirring, that makes it such an evocative drink to enjoy. Pound

for pound it's one of the most arduous drinks to put together, but much like a shot of espresso, the reward is certainly worthy it.

If you go into a bar in the French Caribbean and order a Ti Punch, more often than not they will serve you an entire bottle of rum, lime wedges, sugar and an empty glass, then invite you to mix your own. This means you can get your hands dirty and easily tweak the proportions to your own preferred levels of strength, sourness and sweetness. It also means things can quickly escalate, as half a bottle of 50% liquor vanishes in a matter of minutes. In these circumstances, the bartender will gauge how much of the bottle has gone and charge you accordingly. By that point you're happy to go along with anything.

Making a Ti Punch is as easy as it gets, and a great backup plan for when you run out of ice. The golden rule is that you must use *rhum agricole*, but as far as the other parts go it's your choice as to whether you use lemon or lime, and white sugar or brown. My preference lies with the latter in both cases. If you prefer, you can use a vieux (aged) rum, but I think this drink is better suited to the feral aromatics of *agricole blanc*.

PLANTER'S PUNCH

400 G/14 OZ. DARJEELING TEA

120 G/4¼ OZ. DEMERARA SUGAR

3 G/¹⁄₁₆ OZ. SALT

150 ML/5 FL. OZ. LIME JUICE

50 ML/1²⁄₃ FL. OZ. GRAPEFRUIT JUICE

300 ML/10 FL. OZ. AGED POT-STILL RUM

(makes 1 litre/34 fl. oz.)

Start by brewing the tea (nice and strong) and while it cools, dissolve the sugar and salt into it. Juice your citrus fruits, strain out the pulp, and mix it with the rum. Once the tea has cooled, mix everything together, pop it in a bottle, and leave in the fridge until needed (it will keep for up to two weeks). Simply pour over ice cubes to serve.

Punches pre-date cocktails by at least 200 years and form the basis of the sour and fizz cocktail families. Some punches are quite specific in their recipes, while others are a touch more conceptual; Planter's Punch certainly falls into the latter category. It's been known as "Jamaican Rum Punch" in *The Savoy Cocktail Book* and referred to as "Creole Punch" by the British novelist Alec Waugh, and it probably started its life as a mixture of pot-still rum, citrus, sugar and water. Nowadays it's not uncommon to find folk adding liqueurs, grenadine, orange juice or passion fruit to a Planter's Punch. On this one occasion I would advocate a *carte-blanche* approach to your punch-making. So long as you stick by the classic ratio of "two of sour, one of sweet, three of strong (rum) and four of weak," you pretty much can't go wrong.

You'll know if it's worked, because you'll experience an irrepressible desire to go back for a second or third glass. This is the whole point of punch – a convivial drink that would look absurd if served in a large glass, but positively tragic if offered only once and in a small quantity. Of course, the effect might not be instantaneous, as writer Patrick Chamoiseau reminds us: "a rum punch takes a good six hours to penetrate the soul. Six hours, between the midday punch that wards off the sun's madness and the push before your evening soup, the commander of your dreams."

In the past, punches were made with a type of sugar known as "loaf sugar", which was named for the fact that you bought it in tall loaves that look a bit like missile warheads. The shape was on account of the earthenware moulds into which the molten sugar was poured for setting. Loaf sugar was graded for quality, with white stuff (not dissimilar to our modern-day table sugar) reserved only for the well-off. Most folks could only afford a loaf that sat somewhere in the realms of light muscovado or Demerara sugar, which was no bad thing as far as the punch bowl was concerned, because these sugars offered up flavour as well as sweetness.

As for the rum itself, this is not the occasion to shy away from flavour. Punch and rum co-existed in an age of British pot-still liquid stink. A slight "grottiness" to your punch therefore only heightens the authenticity of the beverage.

PIÑA COLADA

25 ML/1 FL. OZ. DON Q CRISTAL WHITE
25 ML/1 FL. OZ. BACARDI 8-YEAR-OLD
50 ML/1⅔ FL. OZ. PRESSURE-COOKED COCONUT MILK
(can be substituted for the regular stuff)
60 ML/2 FL. OZ. PRESSED PINEAPPLE JUICE
10 ML/2 TEASPOONS LIME JUICE
0.5 G/PINCH OF SALT

Add all the ingredients to a blender along with 100 g/3½ oz. of ice (per serving). Blitz
it for a good 30 seconds, or until it's silky smooth and lump-free. Serve immediately in a
hurricane glass (you know the one, it's like an elongated wine glass with a short stem) with a
straw, and garnish with a wedge of pineapple and a fresh cherry.

If it were possible to bottle the concentrated flavour of a holiday by the beach, it would probably taste something like a Piña Colada. Little wonder that sunscreen manufacturers borrow the classic combination of pineapple and coconut to aromatize their products. Hell, the Piña Colada even looks like a holiday, and a lazy one at that – quietly content as it wallows in its cool and gloopy state, all ludicrous in its bulging proportions and ostentatious garnishing. If Piña Colada were a vehicle, it would be a carnival float. If it were a person, it would lounge by the pool in a skin-tight, leopard-print swimming thong to match its day-glow tan and moustache. There are only two types of people in the world: those who love a Piña Colada, and those who don't admit to loving them. You see, it's ok to be a holiday drink, so long as you treat it with some respect – the golden rule being that you shouldn't drink Piña Colada on a weekly, or even monthly basis. This is for the same reasons that it's impractical to take a vacation every week – you'll put on weight, won't be able to hold down a job and your friends will laugh at you.

No, the Piña Colada is far more a dessert that happens to contain alcohol than a mixed drink; a guilty pleasure when nobody is looking. After all, a single glass can often contain the same amount of calories as a cheeseburger, only without the associated stigma of ordering a second burger. Indeed, given the right conditions, a decent Piña Colada can slip down with surprising ease, with the rum passing by almost completely undetected. It's a WMD in disguise, but not just from an alcohol standpoint. If you put away three or four of them quickly, you may find your hands trembling from the hyperglycemia. Next comes the "crash" and that's followed up by a side serving of Type 2 Diabetes.

I jest, of course. For many people the Piña Colada is the definitive cocktail – one that best represents the glitzy vulgarity of 1980s Tom Cruise bartending. Nostalgia like that is a difficult sentiment to shatter, no matter how impractical the drink may be.

The good news is that it's laughably easy to make, and requires only three ingredients (rum, coconut milk and pineapple juice), along with ice and a blender. Of course, if you have access to a "slushy" machine, all the better. That's how they make them these days at Barrachina, in San Juan, Puerto Rico, where the drink was purportedly invented. Hordes of tourists rock up to this joint every day, and the staff rapidly churn out the cocktail at the peculiarly exacting price of $7.81 (£6.30) a piece. The drink's inventor – Ramón Portas Mingot – created it at Barrachina in 1963, although that recipe also included condensed milk. Like most drinks, the claim is contested, by another Ramón as it happens: Ramón Marrero. He was allegedly working at San Juan's Caribe Hilton in 1954 when he created the drink. One thing that both gentlemen can agree on is that the inventor was called Ramón.

The creation of the drink was only made possible thanks to the arrival of the Coco López brand of coconut cream, launched in Puerto Rico in 1948. The Piña Colada is now the national drink of Puerto Rico and is celebrated on National Piña Colada day, on July 10.

The classic Piña Colada formula calls for light rum, pineapple juice and cream of coconut. It's too sweet and too light on the rum to my tastes, so I suggest using a combination of light and dark rums, and cutting back on the pineapple slightly.

For bonus points, you can "pimp your piña" by popping the sealed can of coconut milk in a pressure cooker set to maximum temperature for an hour or so. This kickstarts Maillard (browning) reactions, as the sugars and enzymes go to work on each other, which results in a toasted, biscuity, almost buttery, coconut milk that makes the normal stuff seem bland. Don't skimp on the pineapple juice, make sure you buy the best stuff you can find and sweeten according to your taste, which for me means barely sweetening at all.

HURRICANE

GRENADINE

500 G/17½ OZ. CASTER/SUPERFINE SUGAR • 500 ML/17½ FL. OZ. WATER
200 G/7 OZ. POMEGRANATE SEEDS • 200 G/7 OZ. RASPBERRIES
2 G/½ TEASPOON SALT

(makes approx 1 kg/34 fl. oz.)

Add all the ingredients to a plastic zip-lock bag and pop it into a pot of hot water set at 50°C/122°F (or alternately use a *sous vide* water bath). Keep a constant temperature of around 50°C/122°F for 4 hours, then carefully strain the ingredients through a mesh sieve/strainer. If you're planning on storing your grenadine (in the fridge) for more than a week, it's worth adding 100 ml/3½ fl. oz. of vodka to the finished syrup as this doubles its shelf life.

60 ML/2 FL. OZ. AGED BLENDED RUM
25 ML/1 FL. OZ. FRESH ORANGE JUICE
15 ML/½ FL. OZ. FRESH LIME JUICE
25 ML/1 FL. OZ. PASSIONFRUIT SYRUP

(store-bought stuff tends to be quite good)

10 ML/2 TEASPOONS GRENADINE

Add all the ingredients to a cocktail shaker filled with ice. Shake for 10 seconds, then strain into a rocks glass (or Hurricane glass) filled with ice. Garnish with a pineapple leaf.

The Hurricane is probably the biggest and silliest member of the entire Tiki family. But it's an important drink, as it lends its name to glassware which goes by the same name, which is also used to serve drinks like the Piña Colada and Zombie.

The unlikely home of this drink is Pat O'Brien's Irish bar in New Orleans's French Quarter. New Orleans is probably home to more classic cocktails than any other city in the world, with the possible exception of New York and London. Present day New Orleans is a curious mixture of colonial French dining rooms, wood-panelled grand hotels, sticky-floored karaoke joints and all-night dive bars. The infamous Bourbon Street is at the centre of all this: a long and grotty strip of neon debauchery, masking the greatest bars in the history of the American cocktail.

But some of these bars are greater than others. In the case of Pat O'Brien's, we have as abstract an interpretation of the Irish bar concept as you're likely to find.

The bar allegedly started as a speakeasy with the not-at-all-suspect sounding name of "Mr. O'Brien's Club Tipperary". The password to gain entry was "storm's brewin". After Prohibition, Pat explored various ways to rid himself of all the low-quality rum that had been smuggled into New Orleans during the 1920s. The story goes that Mr. O'Brien mixed a few ingredients together (rum, lime, orange and passionfruit) and marketed it to sailors by serving it in a glass that was the same shape as a hurricane lamp.

The popularity of the drink grew, and with it so too did the bar. Pat O'Brien's now occupies an old colonial property just off Bourbon Street, but the merriment spills into a paved rear courtyard with its flaming fountains and garish green lighting. The tacky lights will do little to detract your attention from your drink however – as is so often the case with bars whose drinks become more famous than they are, it's the direst possible interpretation of the drink that you're presented with.

A Pat O'Brien's Hurricane is one of the great wonders of the modern world; the colour of glacé/candied cherry and the size of a small leg. Don't order one unless you have an empty stomach, because it's positively rammed full of sugar and artificial flavours. Most people don't have the stamina or the inclination to finish one – if you have any sense of self-worth, I would implore you not to. The Hurricane is widely recognized as a strong drink, and while the New Orleans original may contain a lot of alcohol, in this instance it is completely overshadowed by fruit juice and syrups. A Pat O'Brien's Hurricane is a regrettable meal in a glass; like a dozen melted popsicles fortified with bad rum. But Pat O'Brien's has made a serious business off the back of flogging these things, both in the bar, as well as in powdered sachets of "Pat O'Brien's Hurricane mix" – perfect for reliving the abomination in the comfort of your own home. Pat O'Brien's even bottle their own rum (so you don't need to waste a decent brand in the drink). It really is rare to see a bar capitalize so completely on the association of a single drink.

For my version of the Hurricane, I've kept things simple and made the drink a little shorter, so it's more like a long Daiquiri modified with passionfruit and pomegranate. The drink is traditionally prepared with a blend of aged and un-aged rums, but if you're careful about selecting the right rum in the first instance, I think you can get by just fine with only one. You can substitute the homemade grenadine for a store-bought option, but it's really worth going to the effort making your own grenadine, as the commercially available options are awful.

EL PRESIDENTE

50 ML/1⅔ FL. OZ. AGED BLENDED RUM

35 ML/1¼ FL. OZ. DOLIN BLANC VERMOUTH DE CHAMBÉRY

5 ML/1 TEASPOON PIERRE FERRAND DRY ORANGE CURAÇAO

Stir the ingredients together over cubed ice,
then strain into a chilled coupe glass.

An altogether under-recognized and under-ordered cocktail, El Presidente is a lost treasure from the golden age of the Cuban Club de Cantineros. It was invented in Havana at some point during American Prohibition and probably named for Gerado Machado – a man who would score a B+ on the Latin American dictator brutality scale – who served as president from 1925 to 1933. Many historians point to Eddie Woelke, an American bartender at the Jockey Club in Havana for the creation of both the El Presidente and the Mary Pickford cocktail (rum, pineapple, maraschino and grenadine).

The drink later became the house serve at Club El Chico in New York's Greenwich village, which was run by Spanish immigrant Benito Collada. Following prohibition, El Chico had its own brand of Cuban rum bottled for use in the drink. In 1949, *Esquire's Handbook for Hosts* commented: "The vanguard of Manhattan cognoscenti has discovered what regulars of El Chico in the Village have known for many a moon: the El Presidente cocktail is elixir for jaded gullets."

For many, El Presidente is rum's answer to a Manhattan or Rob Roy cocktail (whisky, vermouth and bitters) but once you get to know the drink intimately, you come to realize that it sits in a family of cocktails all of its own. There are no bitters for a start, instead we have orange curaçao and occasionally grenadine as modifiers. But the fact that both of these ingredients are quite sweet, and the fact that rum and vermouth are both prone to wander into sweetness too, means that El Presidente is a drink that's prone to differ enormously depending on who's got their hands on the barspoon.

The 1935 *La Floridita Cocktail Book* lists the drink simply as equal parts Bacardi Oro (gold), and Vermouth Chambéry, with a teaspoon of orange curaçao. It's stirred over ice and garnished with a cherry and orange zest. The important distinction here is the use of blanc vermouth de Chambéry, which is a colourless, sweet vermouth style, that's more herb-centric and less spicy than Italian rosso vermouth. It was originally commercialized by Chambéry producer Dolin, who have an Appellation d' Origine Contrôlée (AOC) designation on the style.

Later versions of the drink increased the quantity of curaçao and threw in some grenadine, which might have been an effort to combat the less sweet "dry" vermouths that became popular in the mid-20th century.

It just so happens that the original recipe (very nearly) got it right, so assuming you can get your hands on a blanc vermouth, you needn't worry about the grenadine at all. For my tastes, I do prefer to drop the ratio of vermouth ever-so-slightly, however.

PAINKILLER

50 ML/1²/₃ FL. OZ. PUSSER'S RUM

50 ML /1²/₃ FL. OZ. PRESSED PINEAPPLE JUICE

25 ML/1 FL. OZ. CREAMED COCONUT

10 ML/2 TEASPOONS FRESH ORANGE JUICE

5 ML/1 TEASPOON SUGAR SYRUP (see page 214)

Add all the ingredients to a cocktail shaker and shake with cubed ice.
Next, dump the ice and shake the cocktail again (with no ice) – this has the
effect of "fluffing" the drink up a bit, lightening the texture. The same can
also be achieved with a handheld milk frother, or even a blender. Pour into a
highball glass and garnish with a dusting of ground cinnamon and nutmeg.

Just like the Dark 'n' Stormy (see pages 221–23), the Painkiller is one of a select breed of cocktails that has been awarded a trademark. The trademark belongs to Pusser's (more about them on pages 202–03), who will send the Feds round to your house if you even dream of using a different rum brand to make your "killer" part of this cocktail. On paper the drink is not a world away from a Piña Colada. But unlike the Piña Colada, it's built rather than blended, and topped off with a dusting of cinnamon and nutmeg as a garnish. It's these slight deviations from the Piña Colada, along with the richness of the rum required, that transforms a leisurely ride on a pleasure boat into a perilous journey though treacherous waters.

At times, I have wondered if the inventor of the Painkiller misplaced a comma in the drink's name, because "Pain, Killer" would be a more fitting description. Once, during a notably masochistic session of Painkiller consumption, with some Australians in a beach bar in Cane Garden Bay on the British Virgin Islands, which has for better or worse designated itself as the holy keeper of the Painkiller – I returned to my lodgings in high spirits. Little did I know that the alcohol content was considerably higher than I had expected, so high in fact that I was bedridden for the better part of the whole of the following day. That was the "pain" part. The "killer" blow happened when I found myself back in the same bar the same day ordering another Painkiller.

The problem, as with all the world's most dangerous drinks, is the apparent ease at which these things slide down. It is a trait of the Tiki movement for sure, but the Painkiller is the grand master. For many people, a great cocktail is one that successfully conceals the alcohol. I wholly disagree with this; good integration of alcohol into a drink can focus flavour and lengthen finish, balance sweetness, and serve as a welcome reminder to slow down. But if we were to grade cocktails on their ability to conceal booze, the Painkiller would be up there with the best of them.

My version of this drink is shorter than the classic, taking it further away from Piña Colada territory and more into the realms of Treacle (see pages 240–41). You will find that the subtle heat from the alcohol is a welcome addition, and that the concentrated flavour of pineapple interplays nicely with the spices. If you prefer to make the classic version, I advise a ratio of 2:1:1:1 in favour of the pineapple juice. Whatever you do, be sure to use the best-quality pineapple juice that you can get your hands on.

TREACLE

50 ML/1²/₃ FL. OZ. AGED POT-STILL RUM

20 ML/²/₃ FL. OZ. APPLE JUICE (from concentrate)

10 ML/2 TEASPOONS SUGAR SYRUP (see page 214)

2 DASHES OF ANGOSTURA BITTERS

Add all the ingredients to a rocks glass with a large scoop of cubed ice. Stir for a minute,
then garnish with a small twist of lemon.

The naming of food and drink is a culinary art form in its own right, and one that is best observed in bar culture. With food, a name is seldom more than descriptive, but with cocktails, a name has the opportunity to be truly evocative. Take "Treacle" for example: you might have never had one before, yet the name paints a vivid picture of something that is sweet, viscous and perhaps a little fruity. And that's exactly what a Treacle is.

The drink was invented by late, great British bartending legend Dick Bradsell, who was almost single-handedly responsible for the revival of cocktail culture in London during the late 1980s. Like most of Dick's drinks, Treacle is unpretentious and easy to put together. It's based on an Old Fashioned (Bourbon, sugar and bitters) but – given that this is a rum book –

the whisky is replaced with pot-still rum, and a splash of apple juice is added to pep the whole thing up.

Dick was adamant that the drink should only be made with cheap (brown) apple juice, not the expensive pressed variety. And it's true that substituting one for the other does result in an entirely different kind of cocktail; both are tasty, but the cheap juice offers a glossier texture and a closer resemblance to treacle.

As for the rum, you're going to want something dense and funky to ride that apple wave. Jamaican is the obvious choice, but Demerara works equally well if it's genuine treacle flavour that you're after. Feeling experimental? Why not blend the two together? You can also experiment with switching up the sugar: for a darker variety, or for maple syrup, or honey.

SPICED RUMS

If there's one gaping omission from this book that will go unnoticed by some, it's that I have neglected to mention spiced or flavoured rums throughout the rum tour and tasting notes. Over half of the distilleries featured in this book produce a flavoured rum of one kind or another, and most of the blenders do too. In the UK, spiced/flavoured rum is the fastest growing category of rum style and in the past 10 years spiced rums have more than quadrupled in volume, and now constitute almost one-third of all the rum consumed in the British Isles! So why leave it out?

Well, for starters, they're not true rums. Spiced rums are flavoured and sweetened products that happen to be based on sugarcane, and most of them taste awful. Some, such as Morgan's Spiced, are not even legally classifiable as rum, because it falls under the minimum ABV requirement of 37.5% (study a bottle of Morgan Spiced and you'll notice that it never claims to be rum).

So instead of wasting pages of tasting notes that attempt to describe "vanilla" in all sorts of colourful language, I'm giving you, dear reader, a few recipes to make your own.

STEPHENSON'S SPICED

800 ML/27 FL. OZ. AGED BLENDED RUM
150 ML/5 FL. OZ. EXTRA-AGED POT-STILL RUM
10 G/⅓ FL. OZ. FRESH THYME LEAVES • 5 G/⅛ OZ. CRUSHED ALLSPICE BERRIES
5 G /⅛ OZ. CRUSHED BLACK PEPPERCORNS • 2 G /1/16 OZ. MACE BLADES
1 G/1/32 OZ. GRATED NUTMEG • 1 SMALL CINNAMON STICK • 3 STAR ANISE BLADES
2 G/1/16 OZ. SALT • 50 ML/1⅔ FL. OZ. PEDRO XIMENEZ SHERRY
50 G/1⅔ OZ. SUGAR

Add the rums and the spices and seasonings to a Kilner/Mason jar and allow to macerate for two weeks. Strain through muslin/cheesecloth, then sweeten the spirit with sherry and sugar to taste.

This is my recipe, but in theory you can use whatever spices you like, and if you don't like some of the ones that I've listed, by all means substitute them. One spice I would avoid using at all costs, however, is vanilla. This is the most common ingredient you'll encounter in the spiced rum world, because it does an okay job of simulating age in an un-aged rum base (which is what most spiced rum companies use). We have no need for a cover-up job, as it'll be good quality, aged rum that we're using in the first place. Adding vanilla will only serve to muddy the natural maturation distinction.

What we're looking to do with our spices is enhance the natural flavours of the rum and amplify the natural wood spices that you might encounter in a spirit aged in European oak casks. So think along the lines of clove, pimento, nutmeg, mace, ginger, cinnamon, pink peppercorn, cocoa and cardamom.

One approach to making spiced rum is to macerate each ingredient separately and then blend the infusions to the flavour that you desire. The only problem is, you might end up wasting some of your infusions if you only use a little.

PEPPERED PINEAPPLE

500 G/18 OZ. WHITE CANE JUICE RUM
(preferably 55% ABV or higher)
400 G/14 OZ. PINEAPPLE
(cut into chunks – skin and leaves included)
10 G/⅓ OZ. PINK PEPPERCORNS
5G/⅛ OZ. GREEN CARDAMOM PODS
400 ML/14 FL. OZ. AGED POT-STILL RUM
SUGAR (optional)

Mix the white rum with the pineapple chunks and spices and allow to sit for two weeks. Carefully pour off the rum (which will float), strain the liquid through muslin/cheesecloth, then mix with the pot-still rum to finish.

The best flavoured rum on the market right now is without doubt Plantation Pineapple (see pages 200–01). It is a tribute to the esteemed Reverend Stiggins whose favourite drink was the "pineapple rum" in *The Pickwick Papers* by Charles Dickens. According to booze historian David Wondrich, Dickens's cellar was also known to keep a stock of "fine old pine-apple rum".

The production process of Plantation's rum is complex, as different parts of the pineapple are distilled or macerated with Plantation rums, before being separately aged and blended together to form the finished product. The effort is worth it though and evident in the authentic, not-too-sweet but not-too-dry, green pineapple taste coupled with actual rum flavour.

My Peppered Pineapple is far easier to put together, and still produces results that are better than most spiced rums. The sweetness of the finished product will vary depending on how ripe your pineapple is, so feel free to add some sugar once you're done.

PIMENTO DRAM

500 ML/17 FL. OZ. OVERPROOF JAMAICAN RUM
100 G/7 OZ. CRUSHED (or blended) **PIMENTO BERRIES**
1 SMALL CINNAMON STICK
15 G /⅛ OZ. WHOLE MACE BLADES
500 ML/17 FL. OZ. AGED POT-STILL RUM
600 G/21 OZ. CASTER/SUPERFINE SUGAR
300 ML/10½ FL. OZ. WATER

Add the spices and overproof rum to a kilner jar and allow to infuse for a couple of weeks. The high-strength spirit acts as a better solvent than a lower-strength spirit, so extracts flavour more effectively. Strain the spices out and mix the infusion with the the pot-still rum. In a pan, gently head the sugar and water until the sugar dissolves. Mix the syrup with your spice infusion and bottle.

Pimento dram is a traditional liqueur in Jamaica, which is made using the trademark flavour of pimento/allspice berries. Ten years ago, this stuff was hard to find outside of Jamaica, but there are a couple of off-the-shelf options available these days (St. Elizabeth and Bitter, Truth, for example), which can be put to good use in a whole variety of cocktails such as sours and swizzles.

In effect this is a much sweeter, single-spice version of spiced rum. I've added cinnamon and mace to mine too, which are not supposed to be detectable in the flavour of liqueur, but rather bolster some of the more subtle facets of the allspice zing.

FALERNUM

400 ML/14 FL. OZ. WHITE BLENDED RUM
30 G/1 OZ. CHOPPED APRICOTS
10 G/⅓ OZ. KAFFIR LIME LEAVES
5 G/⅛ OZ. CHOPPED LEMONGRASS
3 G/¹⁄₁₆ OZ. GROUND GINGER
2 G/¹⁄₁₆ OZ. CLOVES
300 G/10½ OZ. SUGAR
400 ML/14 FL. OZ. WATER
5 G/⅛ OZ. CITRIC ACID
5 G /⅛ OZ. SALT
3 G/¹⁄₁₆ OZ. ASCORBIC ACID

Add the fruit and spices to the rum and allow to infuse
in a Kilner/Mason jar for at least a week. Strain, then mix
the other ingredients in until the sugar has dissolved.

You're not a Tiki bar unless you have a good stock of
falernum – it's called for in all manner of Tiki drinks.
The ingredient seems to have originated in Barbados
where it is based on a mixture of rum, ginger, almond,
cloves, and most important of all, lime. As for when it was
invented, nobody seems to have a conclusive answer. One
of the earliest written references comes from an 1892
edition of Victorian magazine *All Year Round*, which talks
of "a curious liqueur composed of rum and lime juice."

Taylor's Velvet Falernum is the best-known brand
of falernum, and was developed by John D. Taylor
in Bridgetown, Barbados. These days it's made at the
Foursquare distillery (see pages 68–71).

My recipe calls for lime leaves and lemongrass in
place of the fruit, as the flavour is more aromatic and
more consistent. I add a touch of citric and ascorbic acid
to emulate the subtle acidity of a classic falernum. The
apricots are unconventional, but they add some almond
aroma and also give the liquid some body and colour.

RUM AND RAISIN ICE-CREAM

100 G/3½ OZ. EGG YOLKS • 5 G/⅛ OZ. SOYA LECITHIN (for creaminess)
75 G/2⅔ OZ. SUGAR • 150 ML/5 FL. OZ. AGED POT-STILL RUM
75 ML/2.5 FL. OZ. PEDRO XIMENEZ WINE • 40 G/1½ OZ. MILK POWDER
300 ML/10 FL. OZ. WHOLE MILK • 50 ML/1⅔ FL. OZ. DOUBLE/HEAVY CREAM

Add each ingredient to a stainless-steel food mixer on a medium speed in the order listed
above, leaving the first three to mix on their own at high-speed for a couple of minutes.
Once everything is in there and mixed to a smooth batter, add sufficient liquid nitrogen to
freeze the ice cream into a solid, creamy mass. In the unlikely event that you don't have any
liquid nitrogen handy, this recipe can be made in a household ice-cream maker.

Imagine my surprise when I discovered — after creating a rum and sultana/golden raisin flavoured cocktail — that there was once a place called the Sultanate of Rûm. Bearing absolutely no connection to rum the drink (or dried grapes for that matter), the Sultanate of Rûm was a Muslim state that existed between Turkey and Persia during the Middle Ages. Now, with that brief history lesson behind us, let's get on with discovering more about this boozy dessert.

One of my favourite childhood treats was rum and raisin ice-cream — in fact it's probably where I first encountered the taste of rum. That sensation of the raisins popping in your mouth, while the sweet and silky rum flavoured ice-cream cools your palate. It seems like an obvious pairing of flavours, and when you consider the intense, heady, bordering-on-boozy sweetness of dried fruit, it's no great wonder that spirits pair so well with it. And with the possible exception of brandy, there's no better example than rum, where oak and spice reformulate the DNA of the fruit, amplifying and embellishing the natural flavours.

Dried fruit and alcohol has a much longer history than ice-cream, as folks have been using wine to preserve fruits since Ancient Egyptian times. Later, these preserved fruits were used as ingredients in baking, to make steamed puddings, fruit cakes, flans, and that queen of British desserts — trifle.

In the context of ice-cream, rum and raisins first encountered each other in Italy, where the combination is often referred to as "Málaga". This name comes from the specific variety of Málaga raisins that are used in the preparation, which are made from Muscat and Alexandria grape varieties — both known for their high natural sugar content. The Sicilians were the first ones to create Málaga gelato, which was originally made with sweet wine instead of rum. The raisins were soaked overnight and mixed into vanilla gelato, providing a sweet burst of alcohol in every bite. The trend caught on, and in the 1980s, Häagen-Dazs introduced a rum and raisin ice cream to the US market.

My ice-cream recipe doesn't use raisins as such, but instead calls for Pedro Ximenez wine. This dessert wine is like bottled concentrated sultana (golden raisin) flavour. It's technically a sherry, matured in oak casks in Spain — some of which are used to mature rums. The wine takes on a thick, glossy lustre, and it positively turbo-charges the flavour of my ice cream. The rest of the ingredients are quite standard. I chose to use a combination of Jamaican pot-still and Demerara rums, which nudges that high-ester flavour right to the forefront of the dessert.

You can make this drink using an ice-cream maker, but for best results, I recommend using dry-ice or liquid nitrogen — both of which are surprisingly easy to track down these days.

GLOSSARY OF DISTILLERIES

This appendix recognizes the big and small brands that didn't quite make the final cut, and it will hopefully give you an introduction into the depth and breadth of rum-making going on around the world today. Do bear in mind that this list is by no means exhaustive.

ARGENTINA

PABLO IBARRECHE
Located in Tucumán, the sugarcane-growing region of northern Argentina, this copper column distillery produces a white rum from a long (one-week) fermentation of molasses. The rum made here is branded as "Isla Ñ" and also includes a gold rum matured in French oak casks.

AUSTRALIA

BEENLEIGH
This longstanding distillery is based on an old mill established by English farmers John Davy and Francis Gooding, near Brisbane, Queensland, in the 1880s. They produce rum in a similar fashion to bourbon whiskey, by first stripping fermented molasses in a wash column, then increasing its strength in an old copper pot still that's aptly named "Old Copper". Beenleigh bottle a non-age statement rum, a 5-year-old, and a no-age statement rum.

BUNDABERG
The iconic Queensland distillery often referred to as "Bundy" started life as a sugar mill before the Bundaberg Distilling Company began operations in 1888. The bottles feature a polar bear on the label, which was thought to imply the warming qualities of the rum. These days it's owned by Diageo and produces numerous expressions including "Red", "Master Distiller's Collection" and some flavoured options.

HOOCHERY
The Hoochery Distillery claims to make the only rum produced in Western Australia. It's a farm distillery, in Kununurra, which produces about 50,000 bottles of Ord River rum a year. The products are made from local cane, then fermented, distilled and bottled on-site. As the distillery's proprietor, Raymond (Spike) Dessert III, says, "there are no gimmicks and no fancy label, just bloody good dinky-di Kimberley Spirit to enjoy around the table!"

MT. UNCLE
As the name suggests, this distillery is high up, right in the Cairns highlands and about 600 metres (2,000 ft) above sea level. The cane for their rum expressions is sourced locally, and its syrup is used to make their 37% ABV "Platinum Cane Spirit". Mt. Uncle also produce "Iridium Gold Rum" which is matured for four years in oak casks.

BELIZE

CUELLO
This Belizean distillery was founded by Ignacio Cuello in the 1950s. It's still family-operated and produces the top-selling domestic rum in Belize. Exports are slowly finding their way into the US.

TRAVELLERS LIQUORS LTD.
With its origins in a bar in Belize City, Travellers became a rum blender, and then distillery in the 1960s. After 50-or-so years, it's still operated by the Perdomo family, who bottle under the "Belizean Rum" brand name among others.

BRAZIL

ORONOCO
A rum distilled by cachaça makers Vicente and Roberto Bastos Ribeiro. Oronoco gets 10/10 for its packaging, which is bound in leather and embossed with a map of Brazil. The rum is based on fermented cane juice, triple-distilled in copper columns, then blended with un-aged Venezuelan rum, before being finished in Brazilian Amendoim wood casks. It's filtered to remove colour before bottling.

CUBA

TECNOAZUCAR

This rum powerhouse was founded by Heriberto Duquesne in the 1960s, and is located in the central region of Cuba at Villa Clara. The distillery produces rum for a whole range of Cuban brands, most notably Ron Mulata, and Ron Vigia, the former being a rum that is beginning to gather pace internationally.

FIJI

SOUTH PACIFIC DISTILLERIES

Based on the island of Lautoka, this distillery produces spirit for the Fiji Rum Co., who bottle "Bounty Rum" as well as supplying rums to various independent bottlers including Duncan Taylor, Hunter Laing and Cadenhead. The rums are based on molasses derived from the manufacture of Fijian sugar.

INDIA

MOHAN MEAKIN

Based in Uttar Pradesh, this Indian producer makes the cult brand "Old Monk". The product has been around since the 1950s and has grown organically to become one of the top three best-selling rum brands in the world (though it's rarely seen outside of India). The ever-popular "Dark" expression is blended from a selection of rums, all of which are (allegedly) aged for a minimum of eight years.

UNITED SPIRITS

Producer of the world's biggest selling rum brand – Mc Dowell's No.1 Celebration – which was first introduced in 1991. Like Old Monk, it's not exported, and little is known about the production specifics. But at around 18-million 9-litre (2.4-US gallon) cases a year, they sure do sell a lot of it.

JAPAN

NINE LEAVES

Based in the Shiga Prefecture of Japan (just east of Kyoto), in my opinion Nine Leaves produce the better

ABOVE Ryoma rum is one of the few aged rums produced in Japan. It doesn't come cheap.

of the two currently available Japanese rums. The base is Japanese muscovado sugar, and spirit is distilled in copper pots made by Forsyths in Scotland. They currently bottle four expressions: "Clear"; "Almost Spring", which is matured for six months in Cabernet Sauvignon casks; and two "Angel's Half" releases, which are each matured in American or French oak for six months.

KIKSUI

This Japanese distillery produces rum from sugarcane grown on the island of Shikoku, which they age in oak barrels for seven years and bottle under the "Ryoma" label. The result is a light, vegetal rum, that smells of Marmite and tar. It's quite expensive.

MAURITIUS

CHARAMEL
Producer of a great range of *agricole* rums made from cane grown on their own estate. Charamel use both a copper column and pair of copper pots to make two distinct distillates for their range of expressions. The products feel quite Cognac-esque in their styling and naming convention. The Single Barrel 2008 is a belter.

GRAYS & CO.
This company started out as an investment firm that bought the amusingly named "OK Distillery" in the 1930s. The company diversified into the importation of spirits and pharmaceuticals, and the OK Distillery was changed to Gran's Refinery in the 1980s. They produce rum under the New Grove brand, which crosses off a broad section of rum styles with just half a dozen bottles. Featuring both molasses and cane juice bases, there's everything from un-aged *agricole*, to a 25-year-old "solera" expression packaged in a crystal decanter.

MEDINE
The Medine Sugar Factory and Distillery has been in continuous operation since 1926 and it forms one half of the partnership that comprises Penny Blue Rum (the other half being Berry Bros. & Rudd).

OXENHAM
Edward Clark Oxenham founded his wine import business in 1932, and in the 1980s, the company branched out into spirits. They now produce and bottle Fregate Rum which is column-distilled from molasses.

RHUMERIE DES MASCAREIGNES
This distillery was built in 2006 as part of a huge renovation project on the 150-year-old Château de Labourdonnais. The distillery uses a column still to produce pure two labels of *agricole* rum: Rhumeur and La Bourdonnais.

ST. AUBIN
A Mauritius-based distillery producing rums in the *agricole* fashion (from sugarcane juice). Alongside *blanc* and *vieux* expressions, St. Aubin also bottle various flavoured rums. You can spot St. Aubin from a mile off thanks to its squat, square-shaped bottle.

RÉUNION

ISAUTIER
Réunion's oldest distillery was founded in 1845 and has remained in the hands of the Isautier family ever since. In 2011, the distillery moved from its original location to a modern production plant. The distillery makes both *traditionnel* and *agricole* rums, as well as *vieux* expressions matured in French oak.

RIVIÈRE DU MÂT
Like the other two Réunion distilleries, Rivière du Mât produce rum molasses and cane juice rums from Réunion cane. This distillery seems to specialize in older rums, such as their "Agricole Reserve 6-year-old" and vintage rums from 2004 and beyond.

SAVANNA
A producer of both cane juice and *agricole* rums, Savanna was founded in 1948. My pick of their range is their 5-year-old "Grand Arôme" which is molasses-based and finished in port barrels.

PERÚ

CARTAVIO
Founded in 1929, Cartavio have been knocking out some decent bottles under their own brand and as wholesale rums to third parties. The distillery features a stainless-steel column still and copper pot, and their cellars house American, French and Slovenian oak casks.

PARAGUAY

HOGERZEIL
Located just outside of Asunción in the middle of Paraguay's cane fields, this distillery produces both molasses rum and a pot-still *rhum agricole* bottled under the "Jules Verne" label. There's no added sugar or caramel here, and to top it all off, their cane is certified organic!

PAPAGAYO
This Paraguayan distillery was founded in 1993 by Eduardo Felippo and a co-operative for local sugarcane smallholders. It has since expanded to incorporate some 1,000 families. The rum made here is based

on molasses, available in "White" and "Golden" expressions, and produced in a pot-still juice. It's bottled at 37.5% for the UK market and certified organic and Fair Trade.

PHILIPPINES

TANDUAY
The Tanduay Distillery is located in Manila, and has been going strong since 1854. They produce what is currently the third best-selling rum brand in the world – Tanduay (although you'll probably never see it outside of the Philippines). Despite these rums being a blend of industrial alcohol, sugar and other flavours, they taste better than you might expect, with the Superior (aged for 12 years, so we're told) full to the brim with all the characteristics that you might expect to find in a 12-year-old rum.

THE NETHERLANDS

ZUIDAM
The Zuidam family have been distilling spirits in the Dutch village of Baarle-Nassau for 40 years, and along with he production of genever, gin and whisky, they also produce "the first rum distilled in mainland Europe" under the Flying Dutchman brand name. It's distilled for a molasses base, in copper pot stills, and matured for 12 months (No. 1) or 36 months (No. 3) – the latter seeing some time in oloroso and PX casks, too.

SOUTH AFRICA

MAINSTAY
The legendary South African "Cane" was first released in 1954. Initially, it was sold in local shebeens. From the 1960s, a growing number of consumers in KwaZulu-Natal and Gauteng, started taking to cane spirits, and Mainstay soon became the top-selling brand in the country. It's five-column distilled and basically tastes like vodka.

TAHITI

MANA'O
Translating to "thought" or "desire" this Tahitian rum is made in the *agricole* style, from cane grown on the island of Taha'a. The cane is pressed and fermented, then sent by schooner to Paea, where it's distilled in a copper pot by the liquor firm Avatea. Mana'o is currently only bottled as a white 50% ABV rum.

TRINIDAD

CARONI
A Trinidad distillery that was founded in 1923 and closed by Angostura (who at the time held 49% of the company's shares) in 2002. The distillery, like Angostura, used column stills to make its rum, but was renowned for a much heavier style of rum. There are still plenty of Caroni bottlings being released by the likes of Velier and Rum Nation.

USA

CANON BEACH
An Oregon-based distillery that uses cane syrup as the base material for its Dorymen's Rum, their un-aged expression, and molasses for its Donlon Shanks Amber rum. Both are distilled on a custom-made Vendome rectifier.

HALEAKALA DISTILLERS
Located on the slopes of Haleakala volcano, Maui, this distillery was founded in 2003 by Jim Sargent and is the first Hawaiian distillery since the 1970s. They make Maui Gold rum, but it's difficult to get hold of outside of Hawaii.

JOURNEYMAN
Based in Three Oaks, Michigan, this distillery specializes in whiskey, but also produces Road's End Rum, which is made from organic molasses and matured in Featherbone Bourbon barrels for 12 months.

LOST SPIRITS

A California-based distillery and bottler specializing in "flash-ageing", which uses photocatalytic light to break down wood polymers and dramatically speed up the maturation process (so they say). Called Tessa, the reactor can mimic a maturation of up to 20 years in just 6–8 days. Lost Spirits currently bottle a 68% Navy Rum, and "Cuban Inspired" aged overproof.

LOUISIANA SPIRITS

Bayou branded rums are pot-distilled from unrefined Louisiana cane sugar and molasses. There's a silver (un-aged) option, or Bayou Select, which is aged in American oak casks. They also produce a satsuma-flavoured rum.

PRICHARD'S

Prichard's was founded by Phil Prichard in 1997, which makes it one of the first of the new wave of rum and whisky distilleries in the US. Based out of an old school building in Kelso, Tennessee, Prichard's produce "Fine Rum", which is matured for at least three years in American oak casks and "Private Stock" which bears no age statement but is aged in 15-gallon casks for – I would imagine – about 10 years.

PRIVATEER

The Privateer distillery makes Privateer Rum in two expressions: "Silver Dry" and "True American Rum". Both are based on a six-day fermentation of molasses and brown sugar with the former being un-aged and the latter aged in whisky and brandy casks.

RATIONAL SPIRITS

Like Lost Spirits, with whom Rational have a working partnership with, this Charlestown-based distillery is from the progressive camp of new distilleries. They currently bottle two rums: "Cuban Inspired Rum", that – in a very non-Cuban manner – is distilled in a potstill; and "Santeria", which is a Jamaican-inspired rum that uses lab-grown bacteria to simulate the effects of a dunder pit (see page 48).

RICHLAND DISTILLING COMPANY

Made in Richland, Georgia, Richland Rum produce Single Estate Old Georgia Rum, which is based on cane syrup partly derived from the Vennebroeck Estate. The fermented syrup is distilled in a 1,000-litre (53-US gallon) pot still, then matured for around three years in American oak casks before bottling.

SKIP ROCK DISTILLERS

Based in Snohomish, Washington, Skip Rock produce the Belle Rose rum brand, which is made from Louisiana turbinado cane sugar. Belle Rose Light Rum is aged in vintage white wine barrels, Amber Rum spends time in ex-bourbon casks, while the Double Barrel Rum starts in bourbon barrels and finishes in French oak red wine barrels.

ST. GEORGE

The craftiest of California's craft distilleries makes two *agricole* rums from sugarcane grown in the Imperial Valley of Southern California. The first is an intensely grassy un-aged expression; the second has been matured for four years in French oak.

WIGGLY BRIDGE

This Maine-based distillery uses a homemade copper pot still that's just 60 gallons in size. The barrels they use are small too – hence the name Small Barrel Rum – and they also bottle a white rum.

WICKED DOLPHIN

Founded in 2012, in Cape Coral, Wicked Dolphin use 100% Florida-grown sugarcane to produce their copper pot still rums. The spirit is then matured in ex-bourbon casks for a minimum of one year.

UK

MATUGGA

A Cambridgeshire distillery making rum from African molasses in a 200-litre (53-US gallon) pot still. Matugga "Golden Rum" is matured for an undisclosed period in English oak casks and bottled at 42% ABV.

SPIRIT MASTERS

Cambridge-based distillers of Glorious Revolution! Rum which launched in 2014. The products made from fermented molasses are sourced from Africa and the Americas, and distilled on what must be one of the smallest commercially operated copper pot stills out there.

GLOSSARY

Añejo A Spanish term used to mean "aged" or "old", indicating that the spirit has spent time in an oak cask.

Angel's Share A portion of maturing spirit that is lost due to evaporation from the cask.

Blackstrap (molasses) The black viscous left-overs from sugar refining; the base material for most of the big rum brands.

Bourbon cask 180–200-litre (48–53-US gallon) charred American oak cask.

Brix A measurement of sweetness in molasses or cane juice/syrup. A liquid of 30° Brix will consist of three parts sugar to seven parts other materials.

Butt Large 500-litre (132-US gallon) cask traditionally used for storing sherry.

Caramel Non-sweet colour additive used to add the effect of longer maturation and for colour consistency. Not permitted in bourbon and straight whiskey.

Charring Non-penetrative and aggressive flame burning of the internal surface of a cask to liberate flavourful compounds and aid with spirit interaction; barrels may be charred to various degrees.

Chill Filtering Controversial finishing process used for some whiskies wherein the liquid is cooled to below 0°C (32°F) and filtered to remove flavourless residual haze that can be unsightly. Critics believe the process also removes body and flavour.

Cooper Maker and mender of barrels for the wine and spirits industry.

Ester A chemical compound formed by the interaction of an acid and an alcohol. Typically smells fruity and floral.

Ethanol Ethyl alcohol, the main type of alcohol present in fermented and distilled beverages.

First-fill A barrel that is being filled for the first time with malt whisky/Irish whiskey, but has typically already been filled with bourbon or sherry - so actually it is a second fill!

Finishing The practice of taking a mature spirit (generally aged previously in an ex-bourbon cask) and ageing it for an additional short period of time in another type of cask. The period of finishing can be anywhere from six months to many years, and it's usually sherry, wine and ex-brandy casks that are used.

Mothballed A distillery that has ceased production, but not been decommissioned (i.e. its equipment remains in place).

Oxidation (in reference to maturation) the process of converting alcohol into aldehydes and acids in the cask, which leads to ester formation.

Pot Still A traditional distillation kettle used to concentrate fermented products into a spirit. Typically pot stills are heated by gas, steam, or direct fire (wood, coal).

Solera From the Spanish word meaning "ground" or "earth". This is a system of cask maturation whereby casks are filled in tiers from top to bottom with the lower tiers being filled from the upper. Spirit is only removed from the bottom tier, hence the name "solera". Each tier is never completely emptied, meaning that some small amount of rum will remain in the system throughout the lifespan of the system, aiding in consistency and sort of doing the job of a blender.

Stave Shaped piece of wood used to construct a cask.

Toasting A process of heating the inside surface of a barrel/cask through radiant or convective heat (rather than direct flames as is the case with "charring").

Vesou fresh sugarcane juice.

Vieux A French term meaning "old" that is used to signify a rum that has been matured for a period of time.

Viejo A Spanish term meaning "old" that is used to signify a rum that has been matured for a period of time.

Vin (in reference to *rhum agricole*) Fermented cane juice.

Vinasse (in reference to *rhum agricole*) the waste water left over from the distillation of *vesou* (cane wine).

Virgin (in maturation) a new cask that has not held any liquid

Worm tub Traditional manner of converting alcohol vapour into liquid. A "worm" is a coiled pipe that sits in a "tub" of cool water. As the vapour passes through the coil, it condenses into new-make spirit. Worm tubs typically give a heavier, more sulphurous spirit.

INDEX

ACKNOWLEDGMENTS

To my family: Laura, Dexter, Robin, Mum, Linda & Rod.

The extended family: Tom & Mona, Craig & Emma, Barrie & Amie, Daryl & Hannah and Jake (thanks for the WN17).

To my rum-mates all over the world: Mike Aikman, Jimmy Barrat, Jacob Briars, Dave Broom, Ian Burrell, Ryan Chetiyawardana, Arnaud Chevalier, Paolo Figueiredo, James Fowler, Simon Ford, Matt Hastings, Peter Holland, Stu McCluskey, Jason Scott, Thomas Soldberg, Tom Walker and Claire & Dan Warner.

To Darren Rook, my one and only travelling buddy who joined me on the no-seatbelt tour of Haiti and who is probably the sole reason that I am not still there.

To those who helped orchestrate or fit in with the various impossibly complex elements of the rum tour: Aurelie Bapte, Daniel Baudin, Shaun Caleb, Gordon Clark, Matt Dakers, Henry Damoiseau, Dan Dove, Benjamin Jones, Alexandre Gabriel, John Georges, Jon Lister, Michael Callwood, Calbert Apollo Francis, José Class, Enrique Comas, Jenny Gardener, Karen Garnik, Yenia Gomez, Phillipa Greaves, Alexander Kong, Pascal Lambert, Ian McLaren, Paul McFadyen Margaret Monplaisir, Alexx Mouzouris, Nestor Ortega, Darrio Prescod, Lynn Valerie Romain, Stephen Rutherford, Michel Sajous, Meimi Sanchez, Chris Seale, Richard Seale, Roberto Serrallés,

Don Shillingford, Allen Smith, Miguel Smith, Michael Speakman, Joy Spence, Jordan Telford, Lorena Vasquez, Fritz & Itsel Vaval, Henry Vickrobeck, Jassil Villanueva, Leanne Ware and Simon & Larry Warren.

To all of the hosts that put me up along the way, and in most cases shared a glass of rum or two: Gilles and his old bottle of Dillon, Patricia & Gabriel drinking Ti punch, Sylvain & Marie Anne sleeping in hammocks, Val & Nico on their wonderful boat, Warren & Tracey and their jungle retreat, Tereen, Larry & Terrel in fantastic Grenada, Hannes & Sara for a whirlwind three days in Barbados, Martha for organising everything, Karyn, Cyril for the coconuts, Luis & Amber, Akeem, Lorenzo, and last but not least, Sergio.

Thanks also to Simon & Lori Crompton for a great night out on Grand Cayman. I owe you both a drink.

Other kind and hospitable folk I met along the way: Kenrick, Gideon, Delon… and many, many more whose names escape my memory but of whom the memories do not.

Finally, to the amazing production team at RPS and beyond: Nathan (glutton for punishment), Geoff, Julia, Leslie, Cindy, David, Christina and Trish. And to Addie, Lei and Sari.

Five down… that's gone quickly.

PICTURE CREDITS

MEXICO

GUATEMALA

HONDURAS

NICARAGUA

COSTA RICA

PACIFIC OCEAN